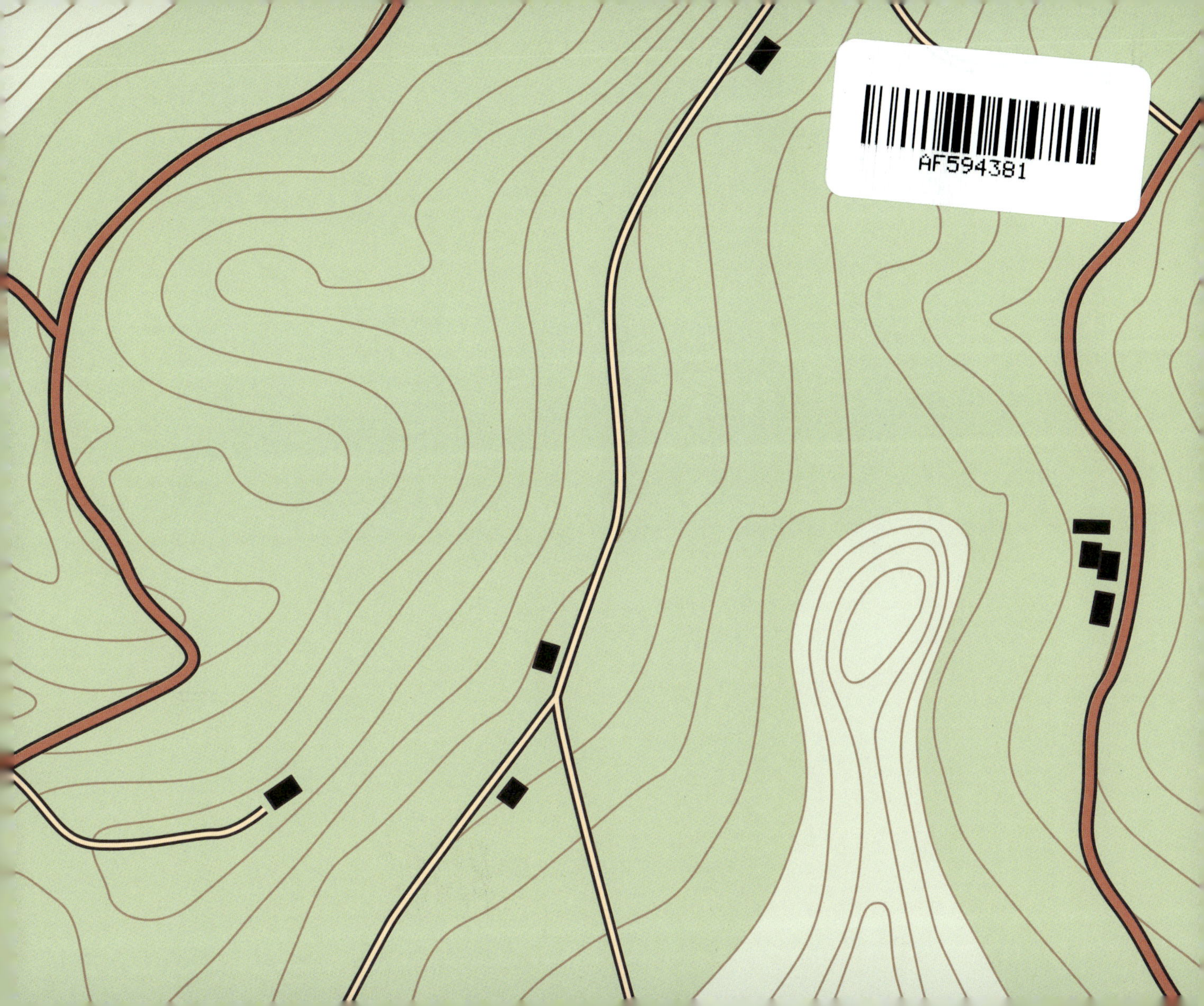

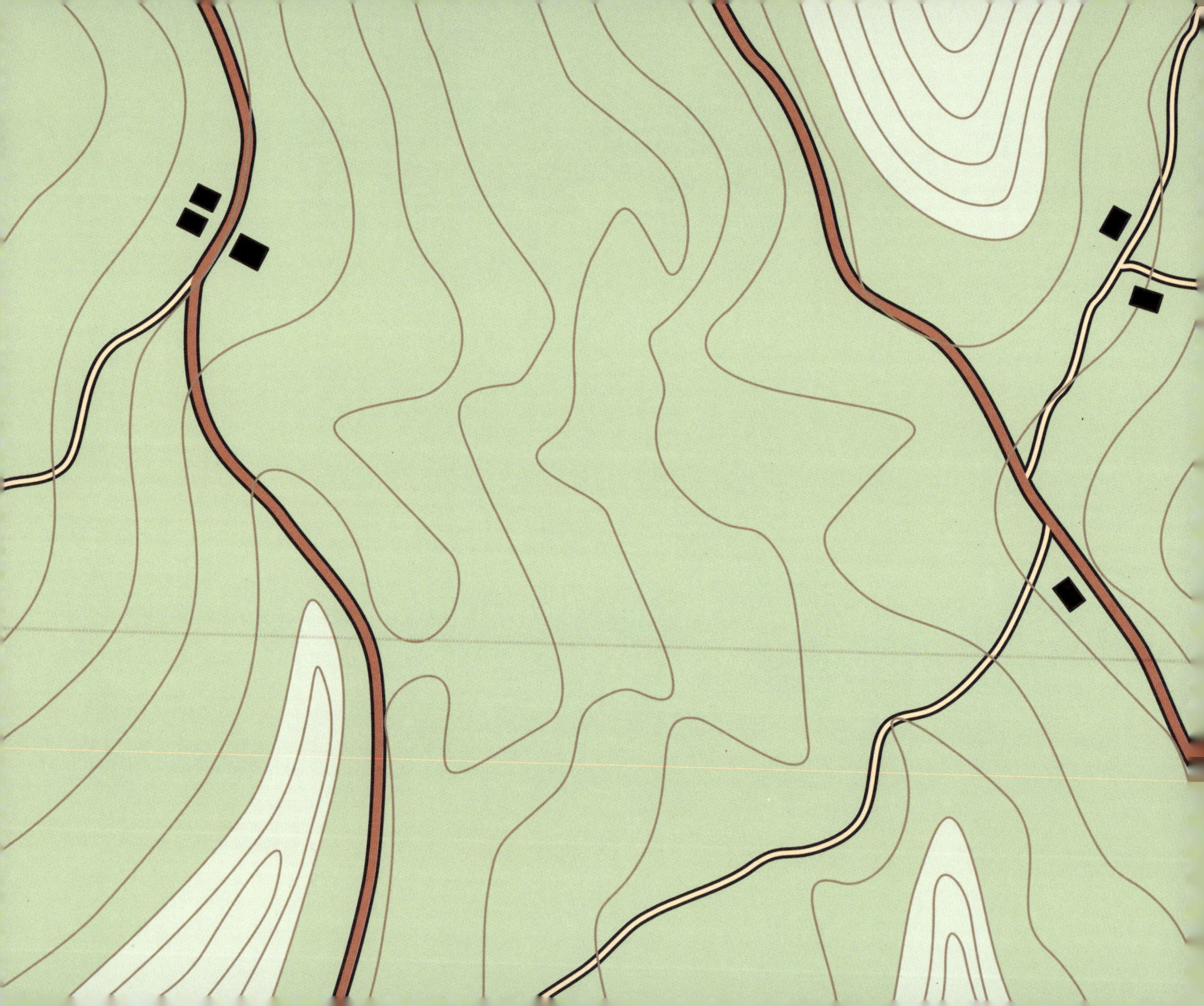

SSSR

SOVIET SIGNS AND STREET RELICS

JASON GUILBEAU

FUEL

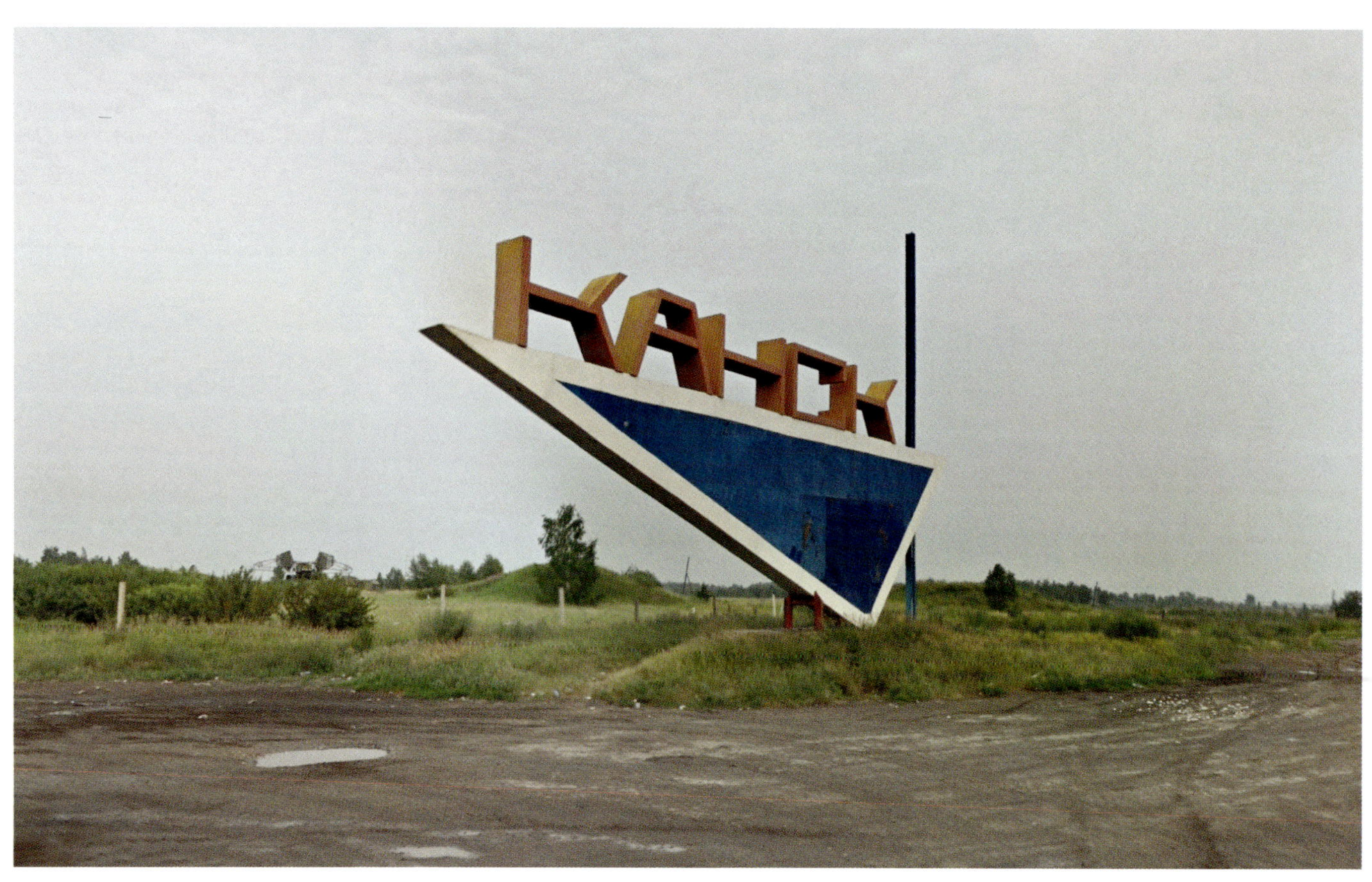

 KANSK, RUSSIA

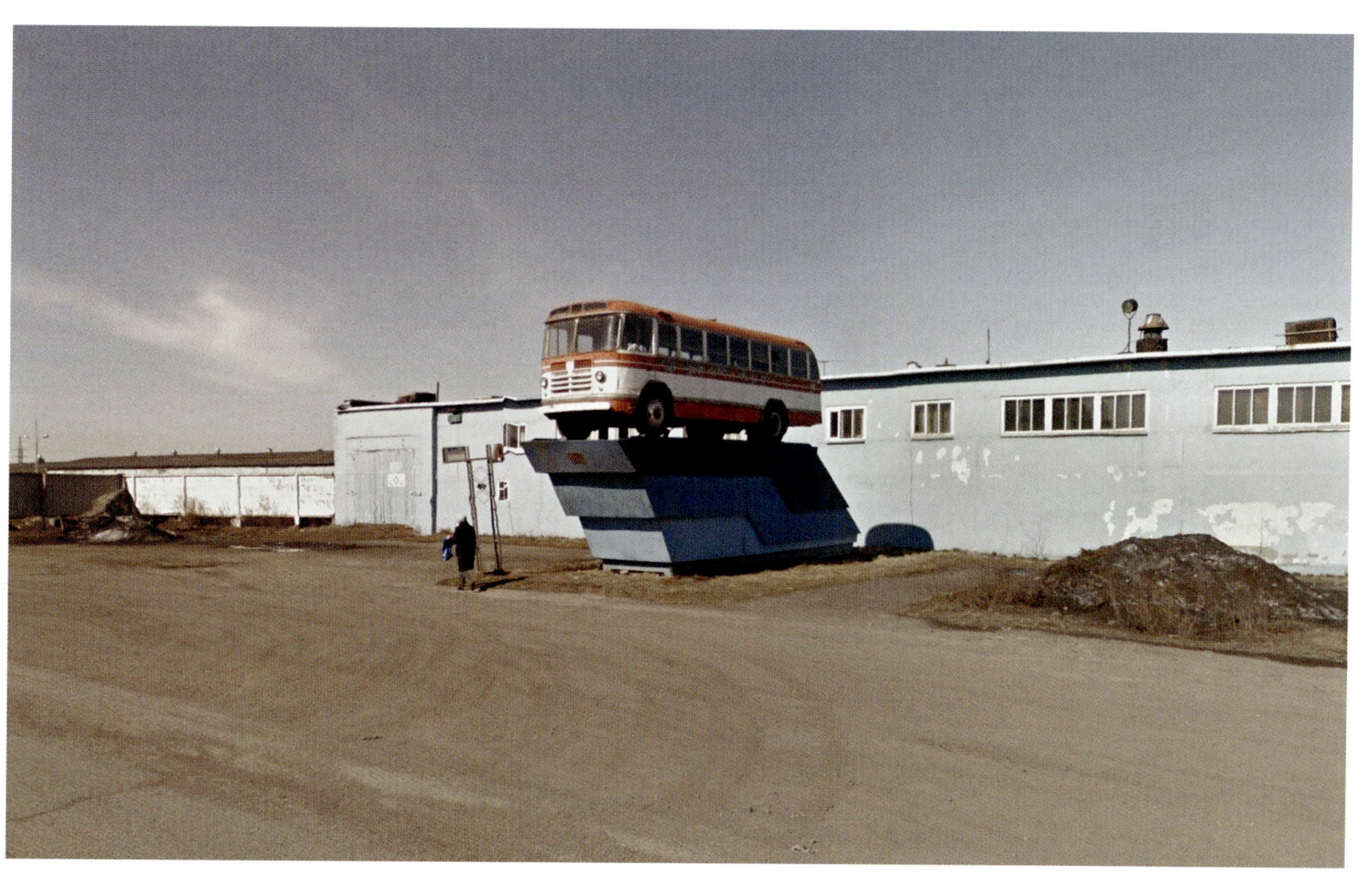

VORKUTA, RUSSIA

SIGNPOSTING AN EMPIRE

CLEM CECIL

Relics of the Soviet past have the power to transport us through time and space. Those featured in this book lie far off the beaten track, in places it is unlikely we will ever visit. Each one is a minor monument to a Soviet vision of the future, the foundations of which crumbled away some thirty years ago. As Russia grows nostalgic for this period, it becomes increasingly difficult to ascertain the meaning of these objects: are they an uncomfortable reminder of abandoned hopes, or rarely glimpsed phantoms haunting remote parts of the landscape? As in the final scene of *Planet of the Apes* (1968), when the astronaut George Taylor (played by Charlton Heston) is enraged to find the Statue of Liberty half-buried in the sand while his companion Nova (played by Linda Harrison) is oblivious to its significance, so it is for us looking at these mysterious remnants.

The tradition of state-sanctioned political street art dates back to the early days of the Soviet Union. In the initial celebrations marking the communist revolution, the streets of Moscow were lined with hoardings and fencing painted with brightly coloured motifs, embodying the energy and forward momentum of the new regime. Processions were held in Moscow's Red Square as well as in the main squares of the country's newly socialist cities. Huge props were carried by hand or balanced on floats: they depicted tractors, trains and other emblems of industrial prowess, as well as caricatures of bloated Western capitalist businessmen. Such was the visual language of the revolution – a piece of public theatre, in which the symbols being celebrated were carefully controlled. And it established the blueprint for the sculpture and signage – effective ways of communicating to a predominantly peasant population – produced throughout the whole of the Soviet empire.

Mikhail Yampolsky writes: 'It is well known that Lenin's plan for monumental propaganda emphasized mass production. Of course, this was accompanied by unprecedented iconoclasm, the destruction of old monuments. The point was to replace some monuments with others quickly, as if the emptiness created by the broken idols possessed some sort of destructive force that had to be subdued.'*

The broken idols included religious iconography, churches and statues of the tsars. These had to be replaced, and fast. The 'struggle' for the dominance of Soviet symbology continued throughout the communist period: even under Gorbachev in the 1980s, churches were still being demolished in the Russian countryside.

Beside their practical value, street signs provided an opportunity to promote Soviet ideals and victories, including, later on, during the Second World War (known throughout the Soviet Union as the Great Patriotic War). These minor monuments, pieces of street art and insignia performed as a kind of supporting infantry to the major monuments, such as Mother Russia situated on the outskirts of Volgograd (formerly Stalingrad). Mass production meant that communist symbols could be spread across the new territories of the ever expanding Soviet empire, from the Baltic states to the Central Asian republics, and on to the Far East.

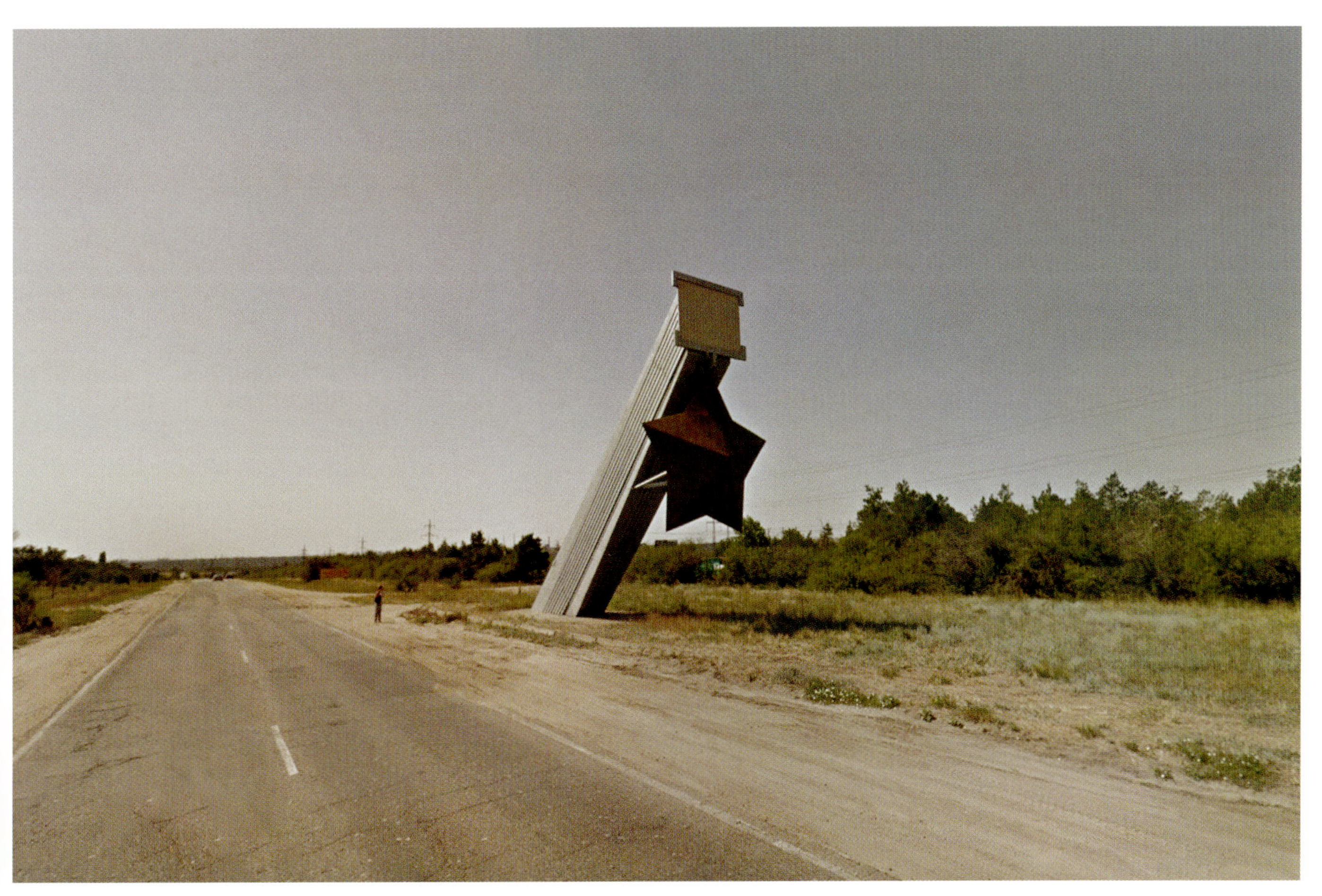

VOLGOGRAD, RUSSIA

Life for the pioneers of the first Soviet republic was peripatetic. Young couples were offered jobs the length and breadth of the country, far from their homes. The idea of permanent roots was discouraged, the primary task being to serve the state and its vision of communism. And while that vision remained stable, people's lives were destabilised in its service. Indeed, whole populations were uprooted and relocated (as in, for example, the case of the newly created Jewish 'autonomous' region of which Birobidzhan was the main city). The road system assumed huge significance as an entire nation perpetually travelled towards (and never arrived at) a bright future. Like bystanders cheering on marathon runners, roadside propaganda was there to work as a morale booster in the exhausting collective endeavour.

Monuments in the shape of tractors, steam trains, trucks, cars and aeroplanes (later to be joined by space rockets) helpfully reminded citizens that, in their efforts to reach new peoples and places, the Soviet authorities had conquered movement in its many forms.

Agriculture was celebrated using the motif of the sheaf on individual monuments, place-name decoration and *kolkhozy* – vast collective farms created in the 1920s by amalgamating peasant smallholdings. The artists' inventiveness can be seen in the sheer variety of sheaf designs. Collectivisation was aggressively enforced and the propaganda machine was utilised across every available medium – from graphic art and film, to sculpture and poetry, and of course street signs. A number of the signs in this book appear to be for collective farms, and they still exude a sense of false jollity and artificial promise (pages 88-89, the wonderfully poetic Poultry Farm of Army No.62, imaginatively surrounded by plaster casts of chickens in cages).

Commissioned by local authorities, the desire of the regime to signpost all parts of its empire corresponded with the desire to keep everyone employed, including artists. Using limited materials and a prescribed vocabulary of symbols, the anonymous creators of these works strove for originality. Although the result of their work was propaganda, the imaginativeness and dynamism they exhibit echoes down the decades (as does their wit – behold the giant watermelon on page 111 revealing a juicy red centre).

'It is quite possible that the greatest achievement of Soviet culture was the maximal suppression of chronological time and the creation of the illusion of stability and stasis indispensable for the functioning of the masses,' writes Yampolsky. Monuments in the form of space rockets and MIG fighter planes, frozen in mid-air, achieve precisely this. Even the incorruptible eternal flame is complicit in this deceit (my favourite on page 45). This deception is bolstered by the uncertainty as to when these objects were created – time slips and stumbles in Russia. While a gigantic five-pointed Soviet star is being commissioned, the regime is crumbling. The construction of some of these relics is more recent than we might assume: a number of them appear to be from the *perestroika* era, the propaganda machine still churning out its products, oblivious, perhaps wilfully so, to the imminent collapse of the state.

After the fall of communism, images of statues being toppled proliferated in the media, becoming as iconic as the monuments themselves. Lenins were reduced to rubble, communist heraldry was everywhere stripped out. But as we can see from these photographs, the remnants – the flotsam and jetsam of the Soviet era – are still sloshing around the former empire. The removal, remodelling or otherwise neutralising of the major monuments has rendered the lesser ones inert. They appear without agency, as if the electric current of communist ideology no longer runs through them.

Jason Guilbeau has travelled through the former Soviet Union virtually, using Google Street View to capture these images. Stripping them of their practical use by removing navigational markers, he presents his own vision of the Soviet shadow that continues to be cast over modern Russia. Outside Zernograd an elegant hammer and sickle stands by the roadside (pages 42-43); in Dnipropetrovsk Oblast a skeletal tractor sits on a cast-iron platform (page 31); in Primorsko-Akhtarsk a jet fighter is anchored to the ground by its exhaust plume (page 48). Perhaps these objects persist because of their invisibility. Nobody sees them any more. Tides of towns, villages and factories have washed around and against these relics. They are the last physical remnants of the Soviet Union, obsolete survivors, captured by an omniscient technology that is continually deleting and replenishing itself. The focus of the new times has been transferred to the self, rather than the collective: a girl gazes at her phone against the background of a gaily painted Yakovlev fighter plane in Novosibirsk (page 70).

Around the static Soviet relics, scenes of everyday Russian life are captured by the all-seeing eye of Google Street View. The town sign for Kotovsk is used as a makeshift climbing frame by two children (page 113). In Alexeyevka a conversation takes place between traffic police and the driver of a car with tinted windows and alloy wheels (page 177). In Volodymyrskyi Raion a stork looks out from its nest on top of a concrete sign while juggernauts thunder past below (pages 28-29). By a bus stop in Shatki a man wearing a T-shirt sits on top of an armoured personnel carrier (page 172). Is he waiting for the next bus, or orders from his commander?

Some monuments play hide-and-seek behind encroaching trees (like the tank on page 148), while others have become abstracts of abstracts - symbols devoid of symbolism - such as the angled piece of rusting metal by the side of the road in Dobrich (page 154). Others have already disappeared completely. They are victims of progress, now only existing on these pages, the loss of their physical presence made apparent by the constant updating of views to reflect the current landscape.

Google Street View cameras are typically set at 7 or 8 feet high. This is particularly fitting for the objects Guilbeau pursues, which were created to rise above eye level, like towering Shock Workers of Communist Labour who stride across the country in seven-league boots.

These lonely markers defined the ideology and territory of an enormous empire. Their fundamental message was that space and time had been conquered. The state that originally commissioned them could not have predicted that within a few generations of its inception, the entire edifice of Soviet Russia was to collapse, divesting them of their meaning, or that within a few years of that downfall an American technological company would be micro-mapping every inch of their country.

* *Soviet Hieroglyphics: Visual Culture in Late Twentieth-Century Russia.*
Edited by Nancy Condee, Indiana University Press 1995.
Essay by Mikhail Yampolsky: 'In the Shadow of Monuments - Notes on Iconoclasm and Time' translated by John Kachur, pp. 93-112.

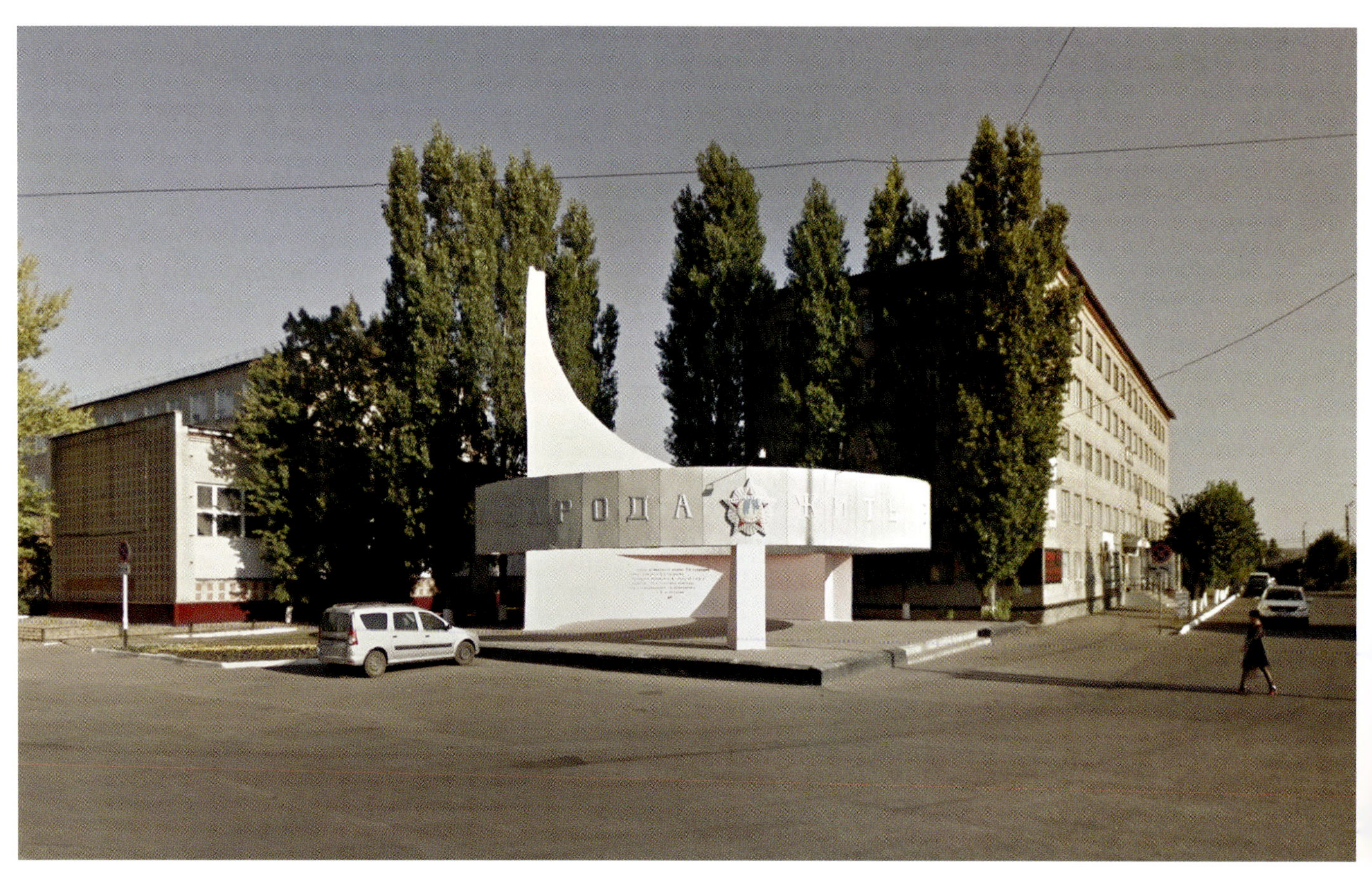
РОДА

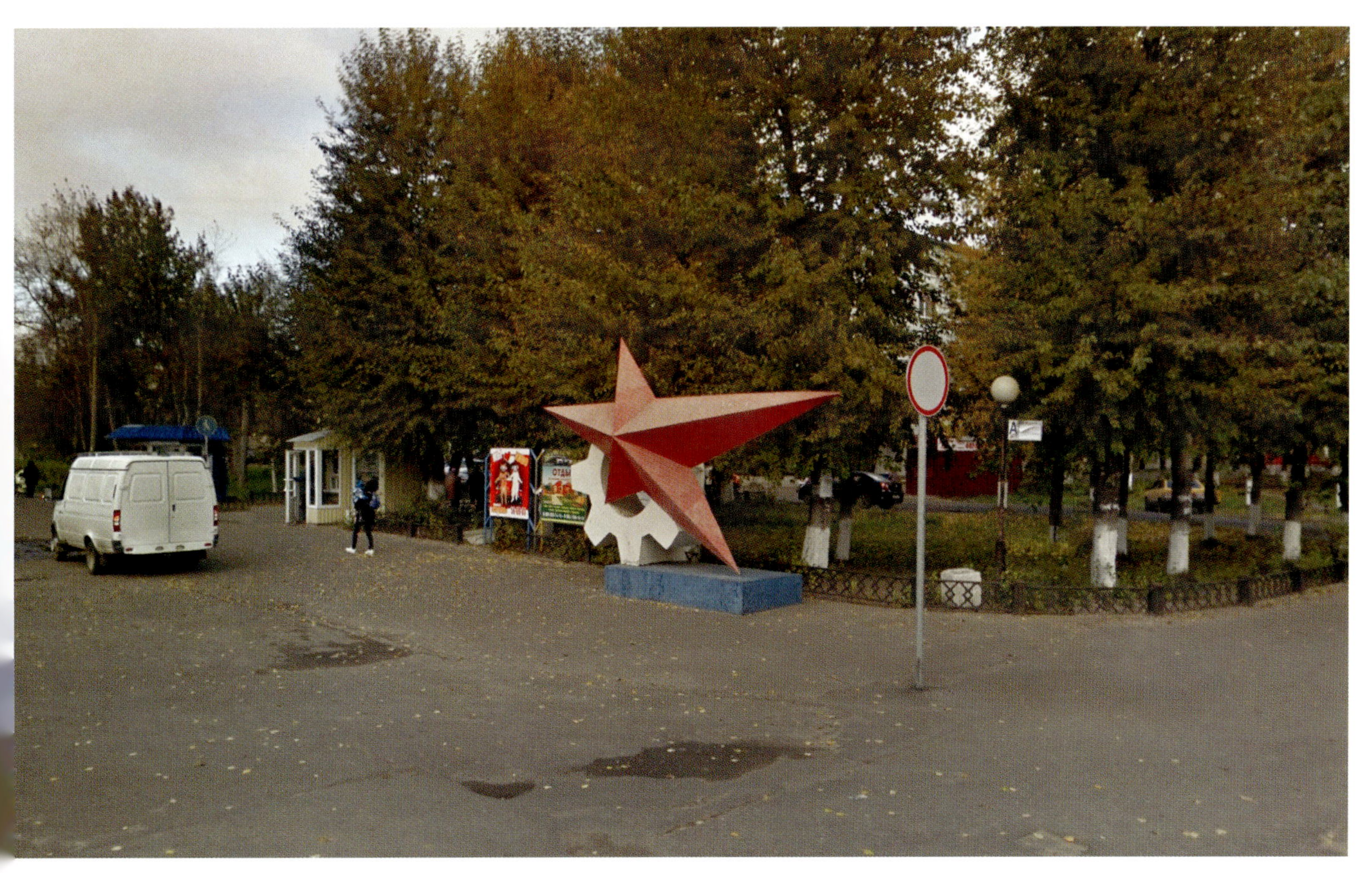

SEVERODVINSK, RUSSIA

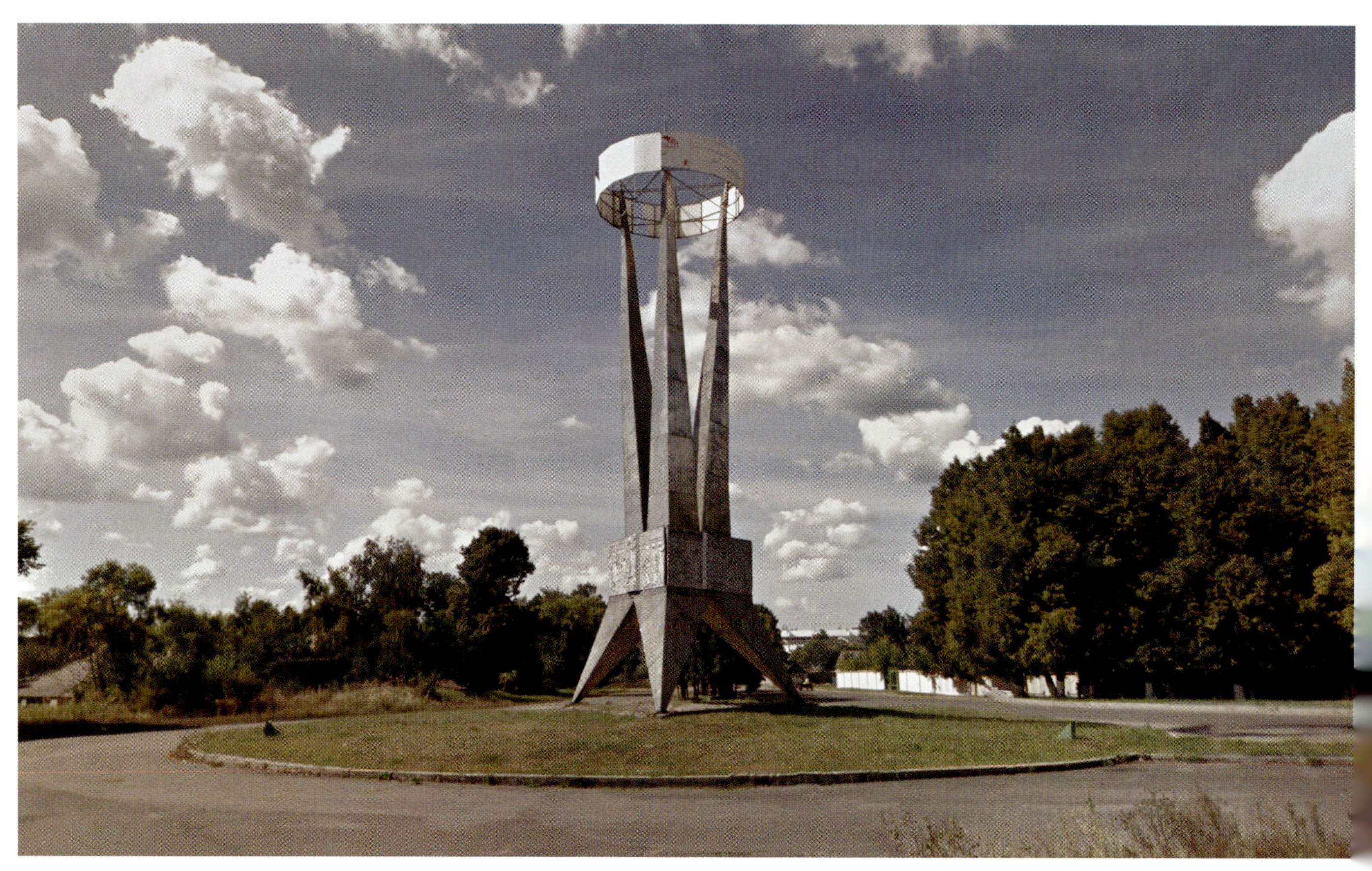

 DYATKOVO, RUSSIA

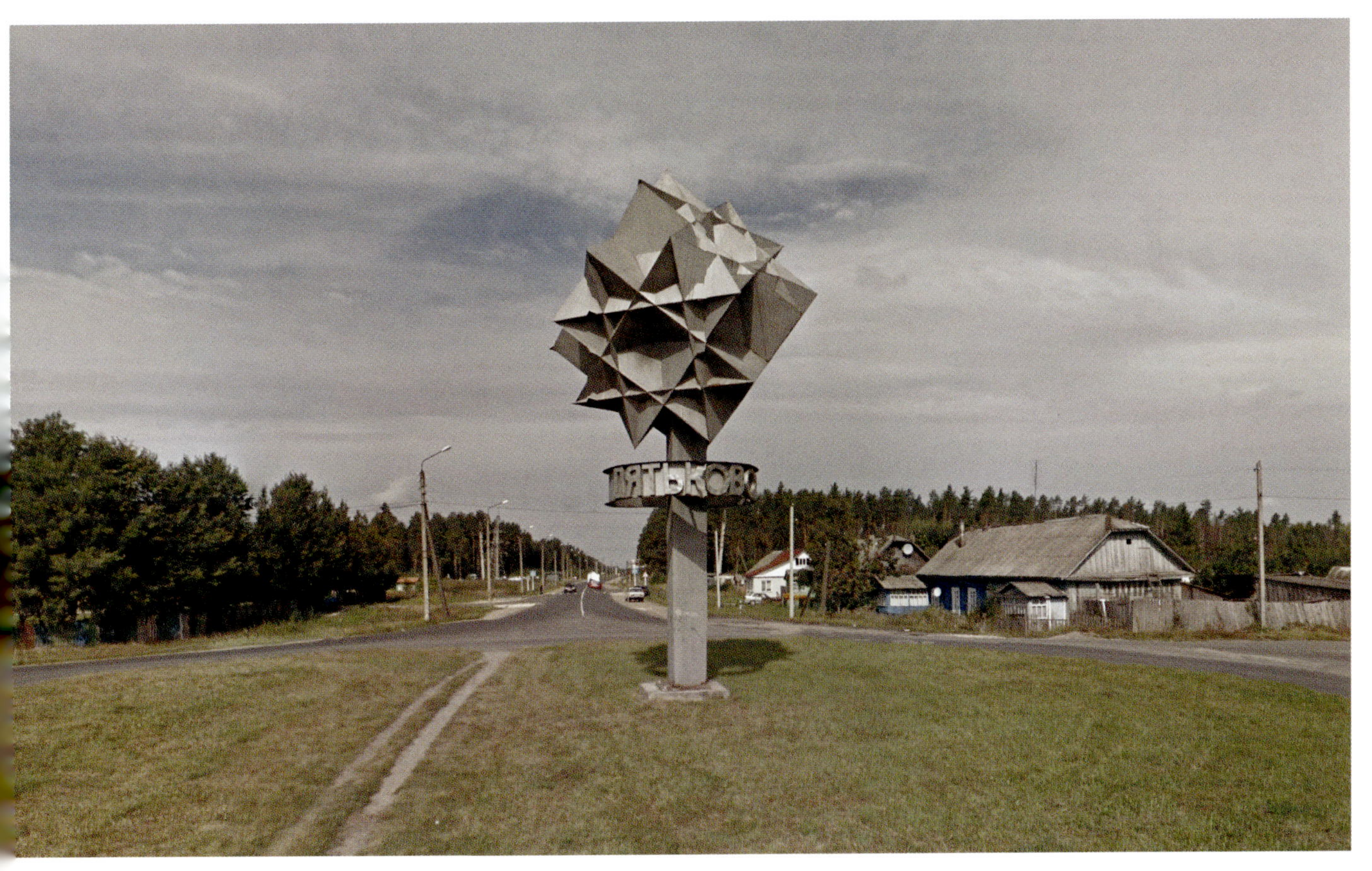

DYATKOVO, RUSSIA

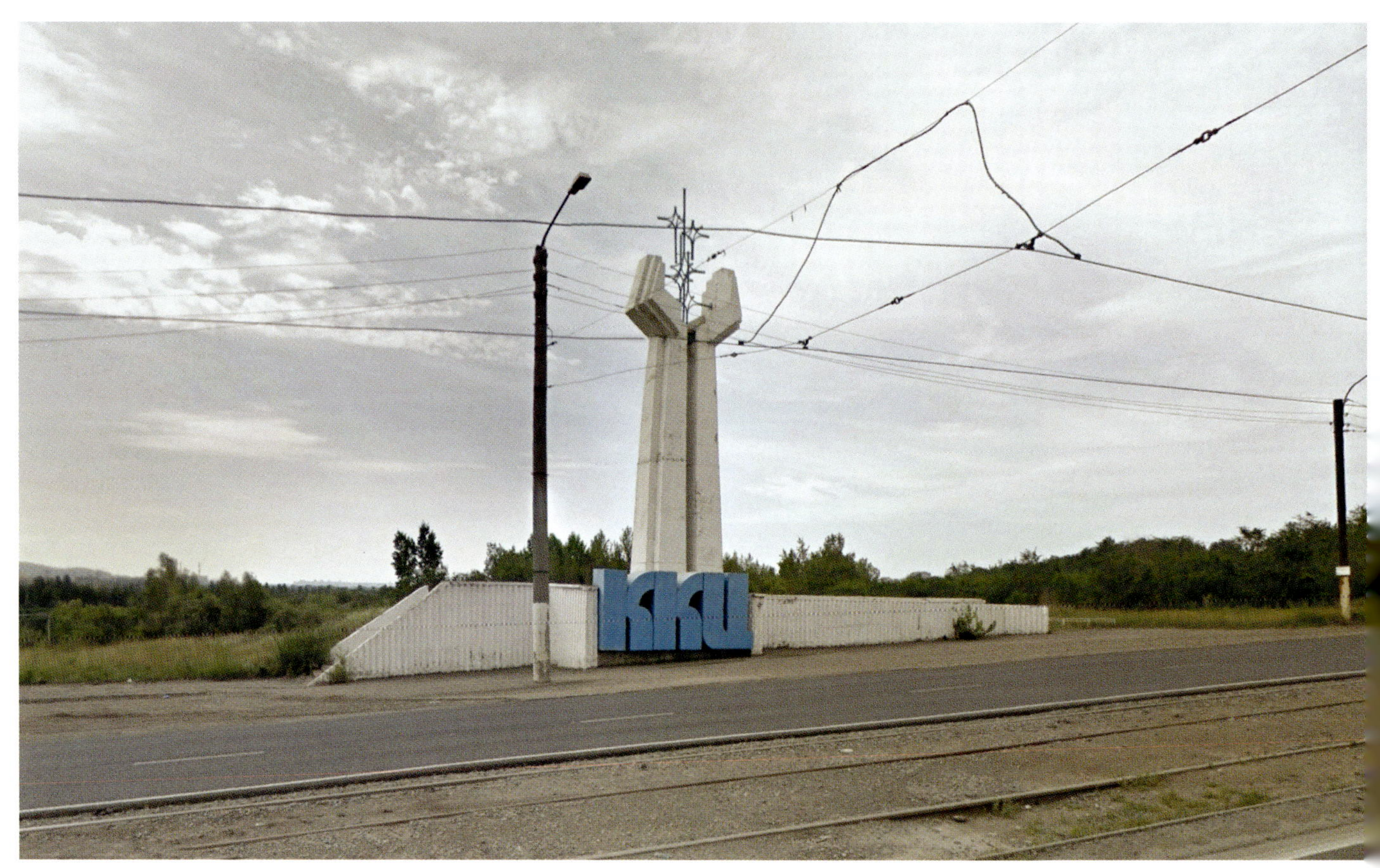

MAGNITOGORSK, RUSSIA

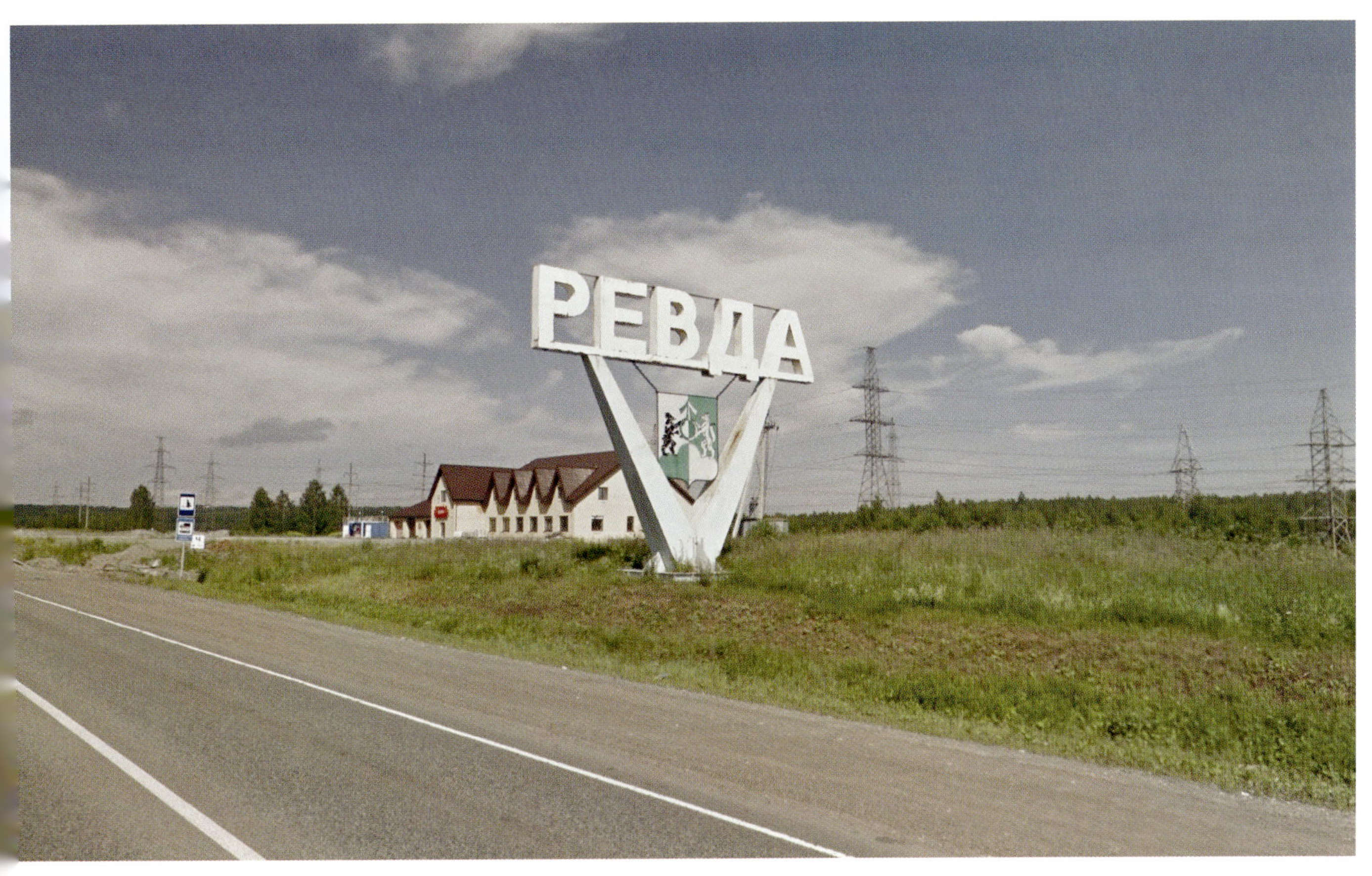

REVDA, RUSSIA

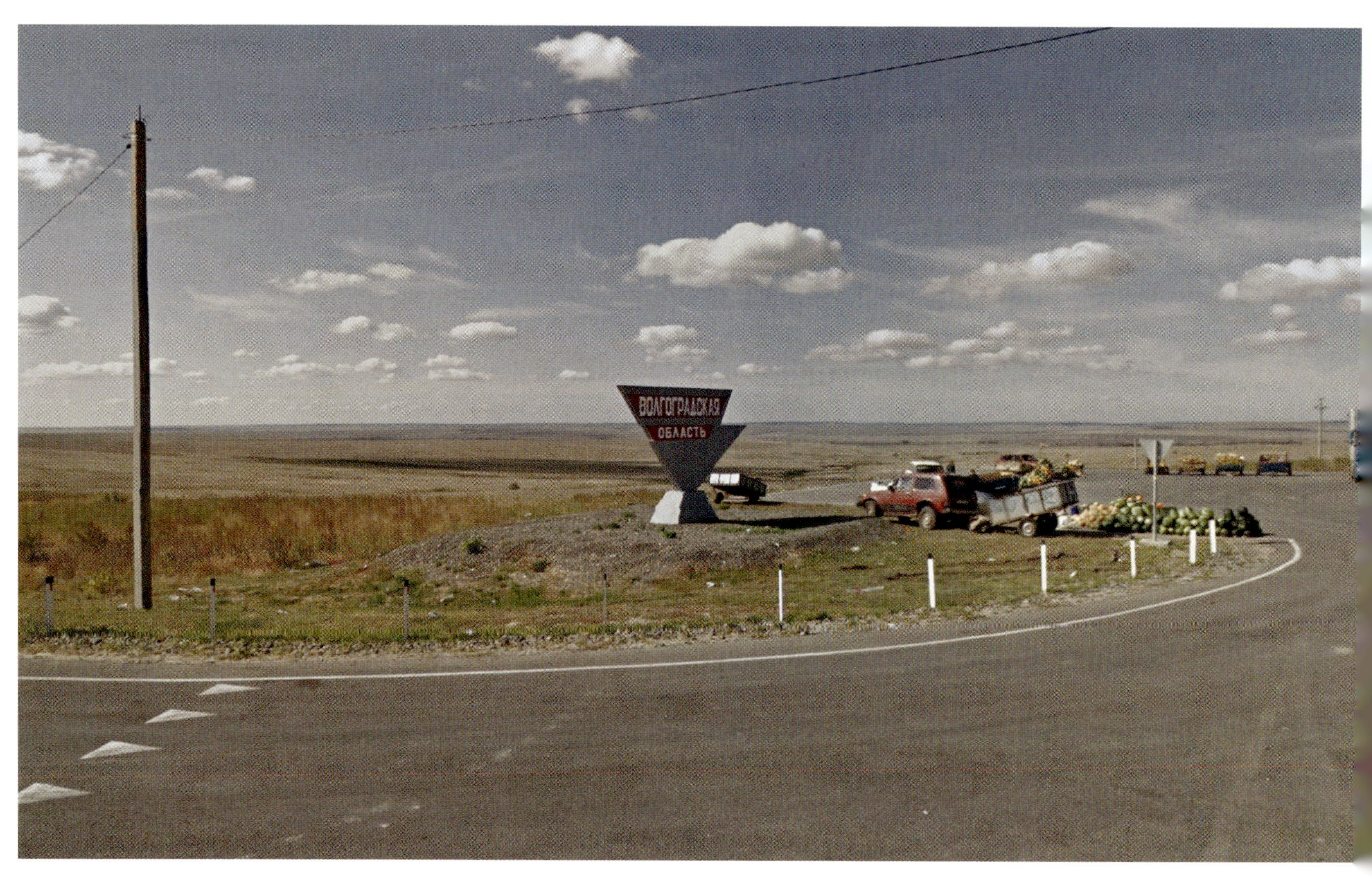

 VOLGOGRAD OBLAST, RUSSIA

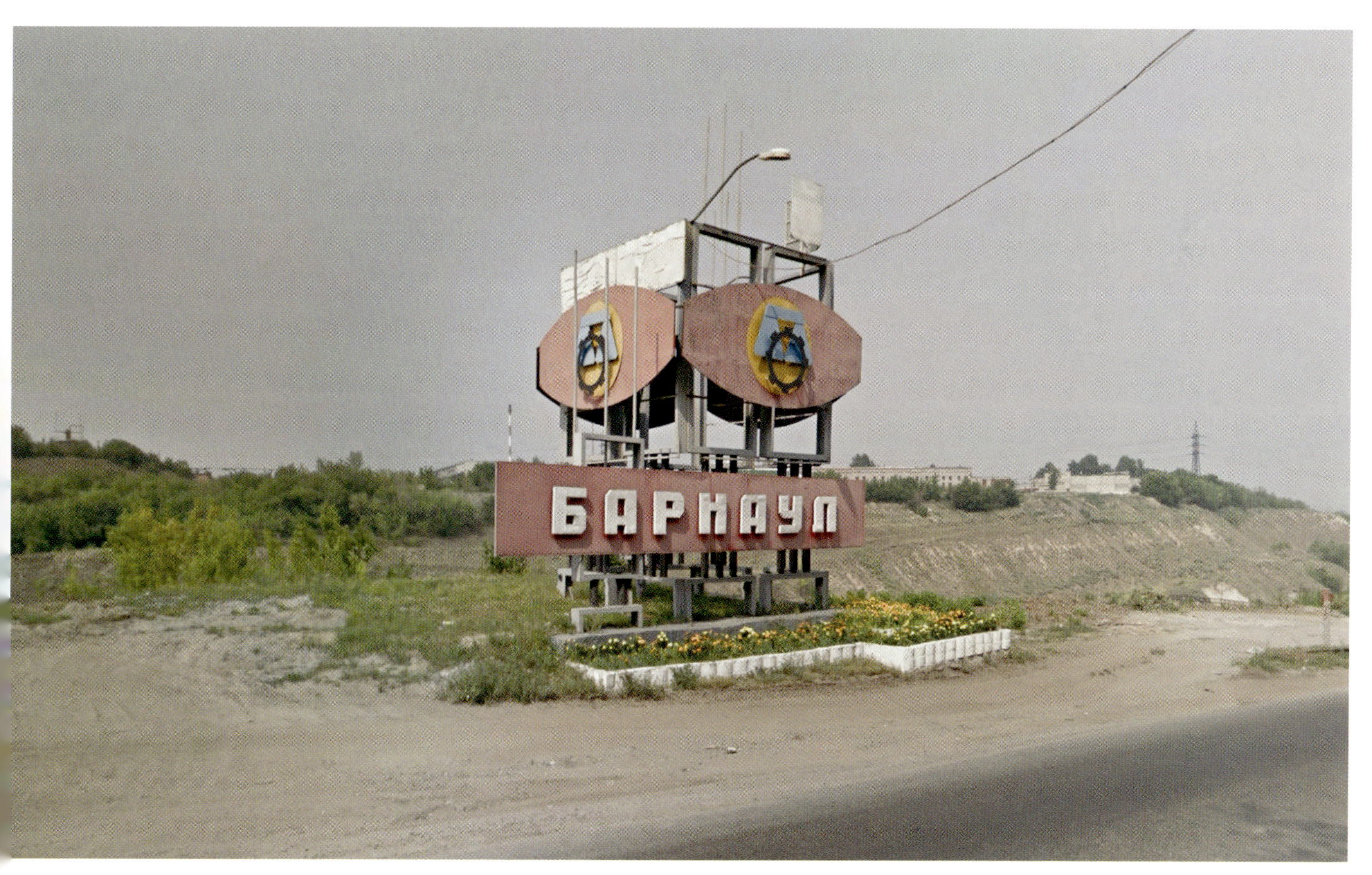

BARNAUL, RUSSIA

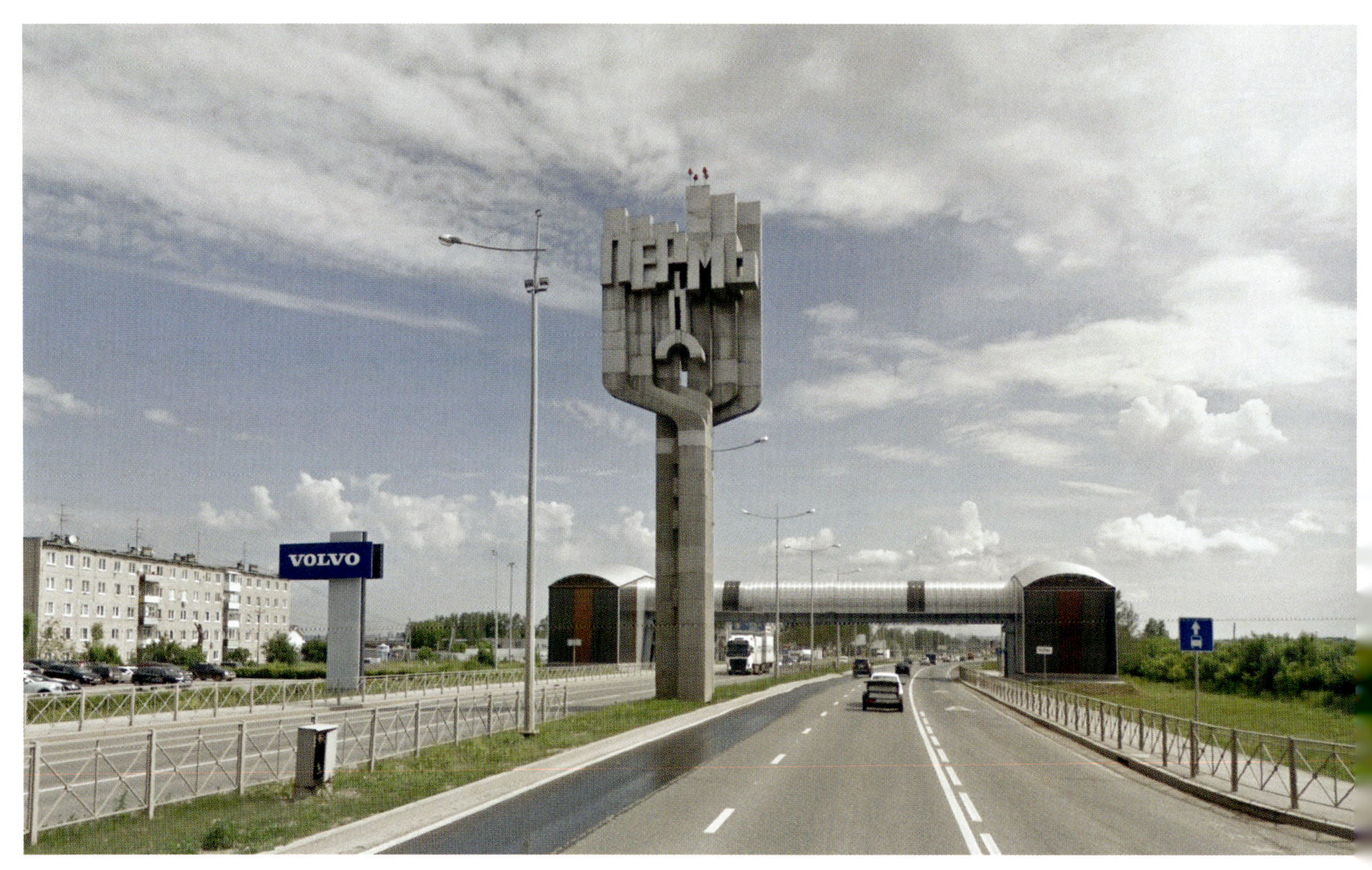
VOLVO

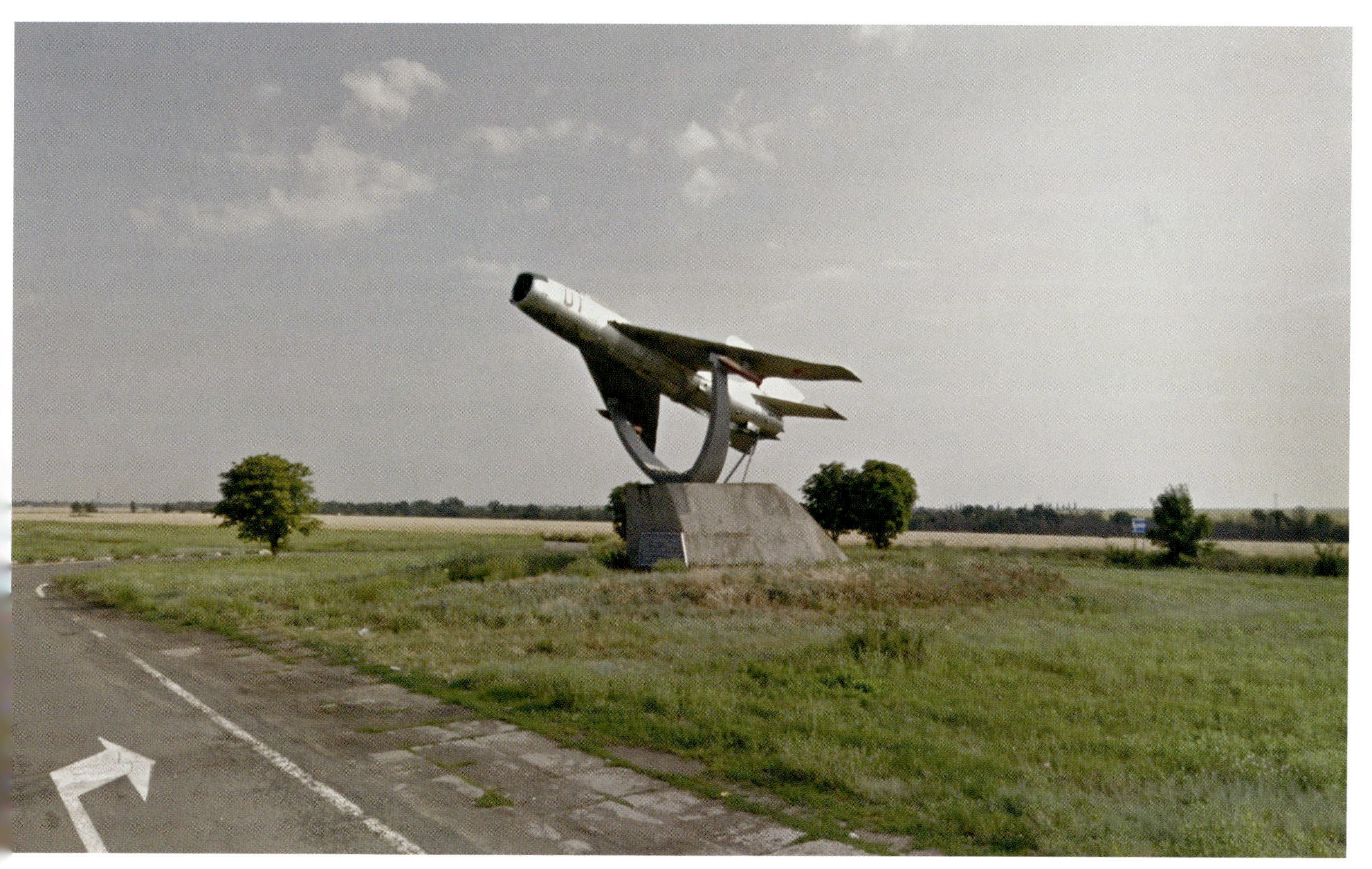

MYKOLAIV, UKRAINE

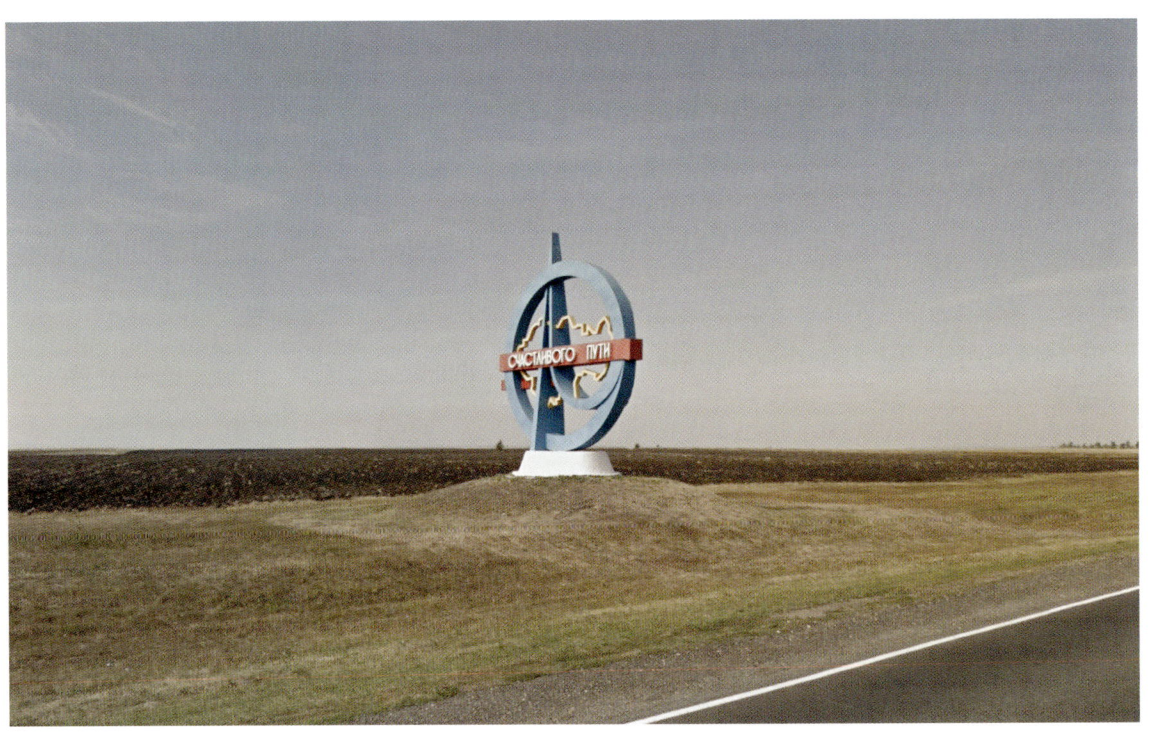

 SARATOV OBLAST, RUSSIA

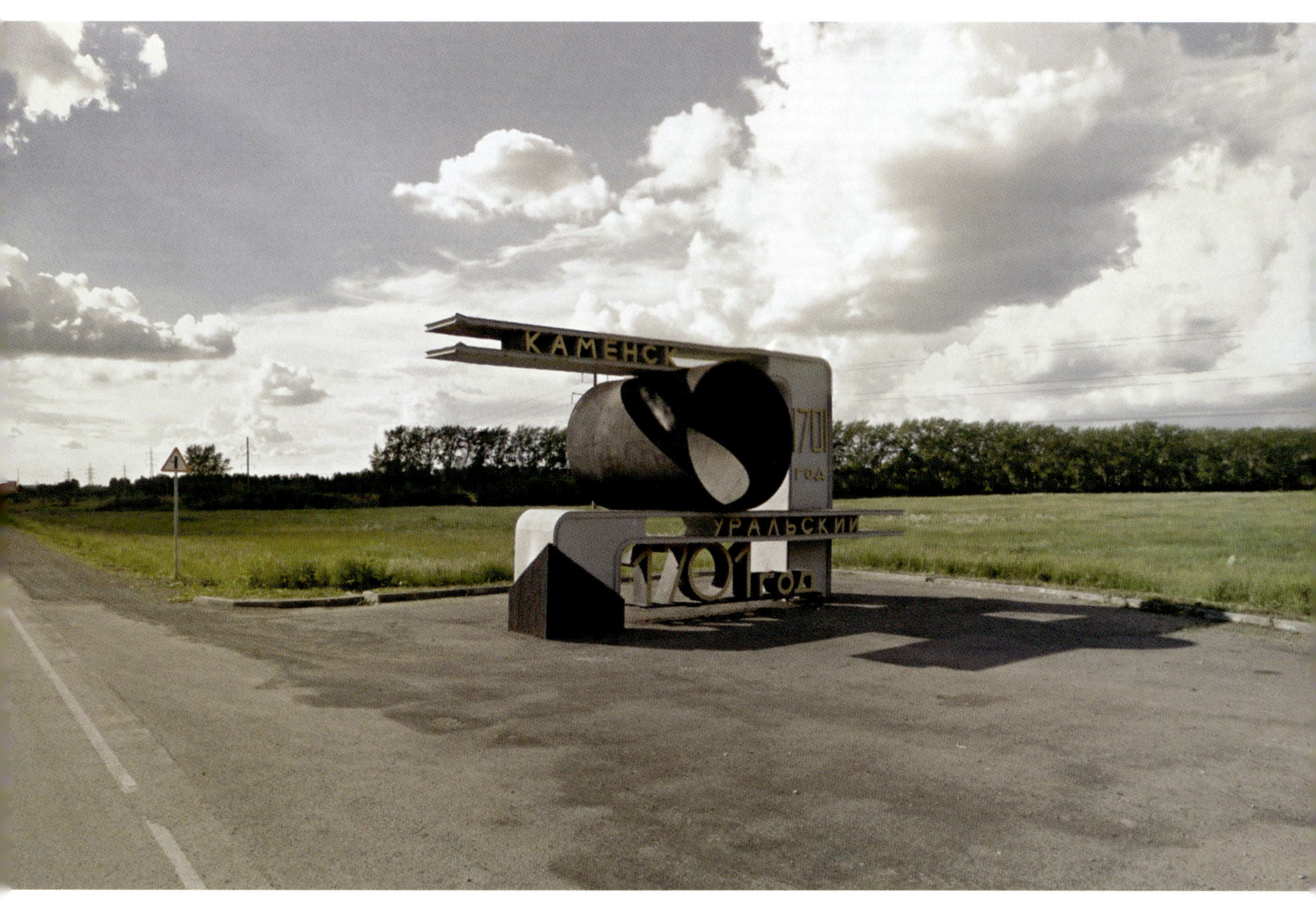

KAMENSK, RUSSIA

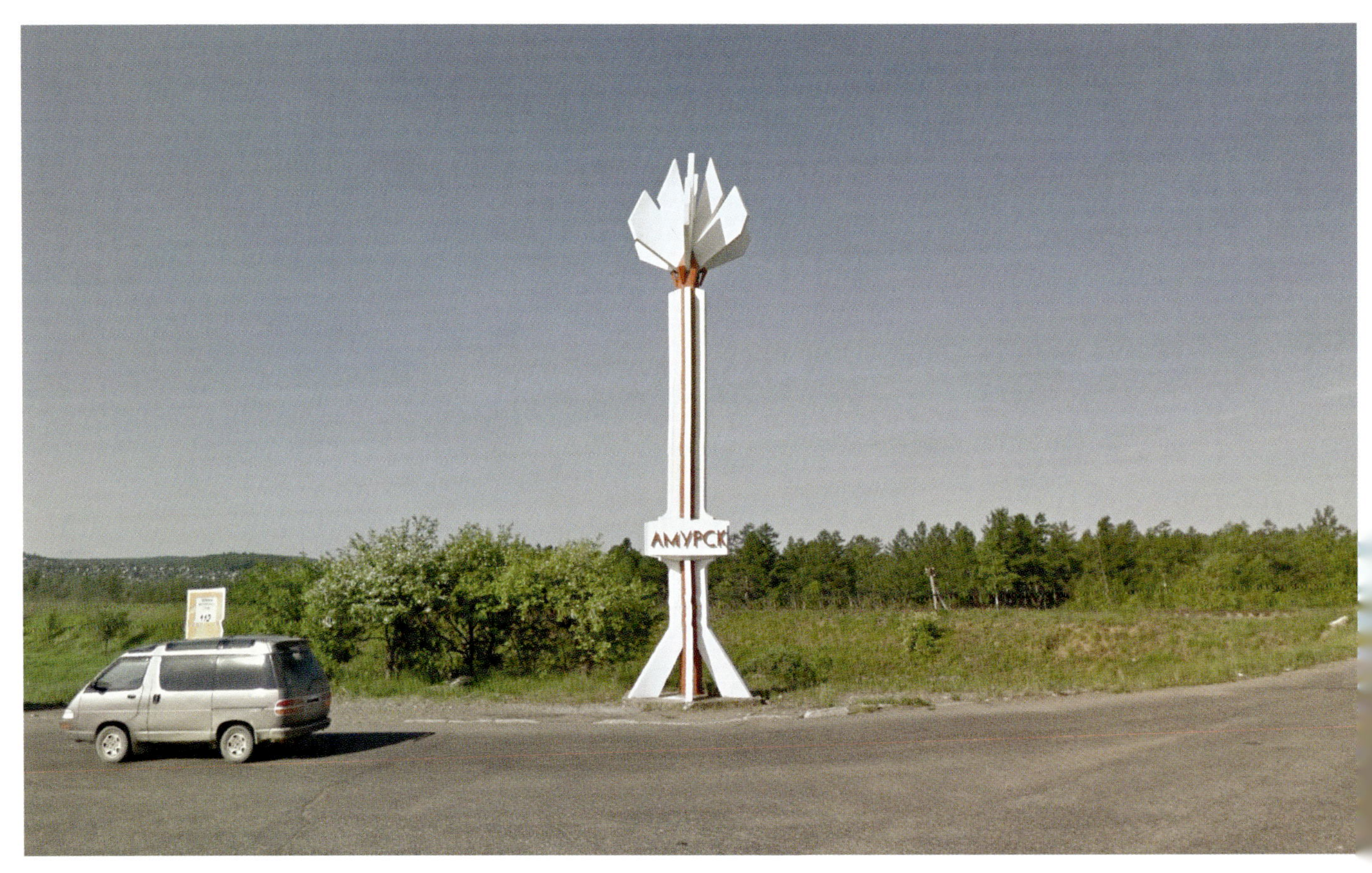

 AMURSK, RUSSIA

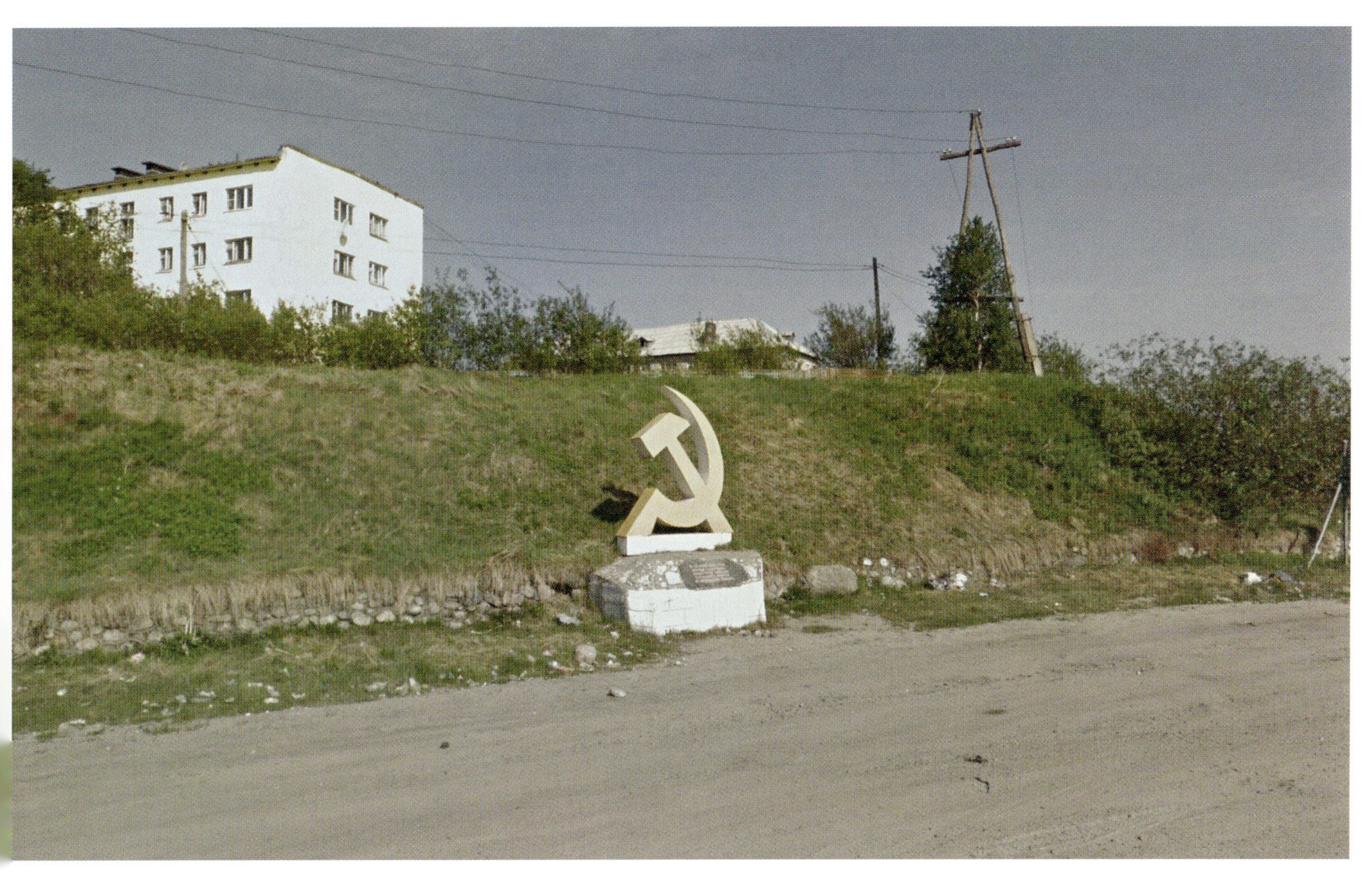

PECHENGA, RUSSIA

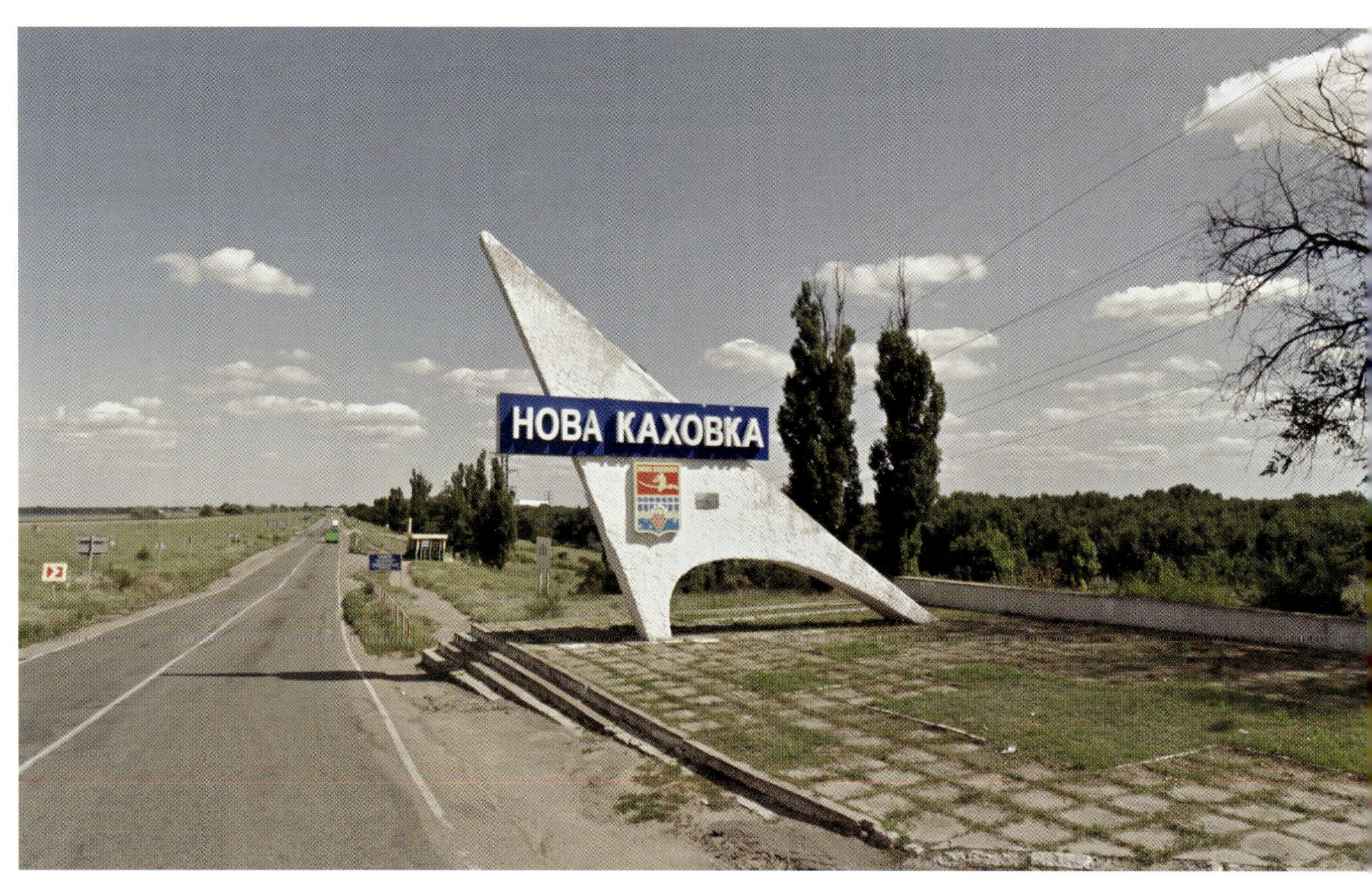

NOVA KAKHOVKA, UKRAINE

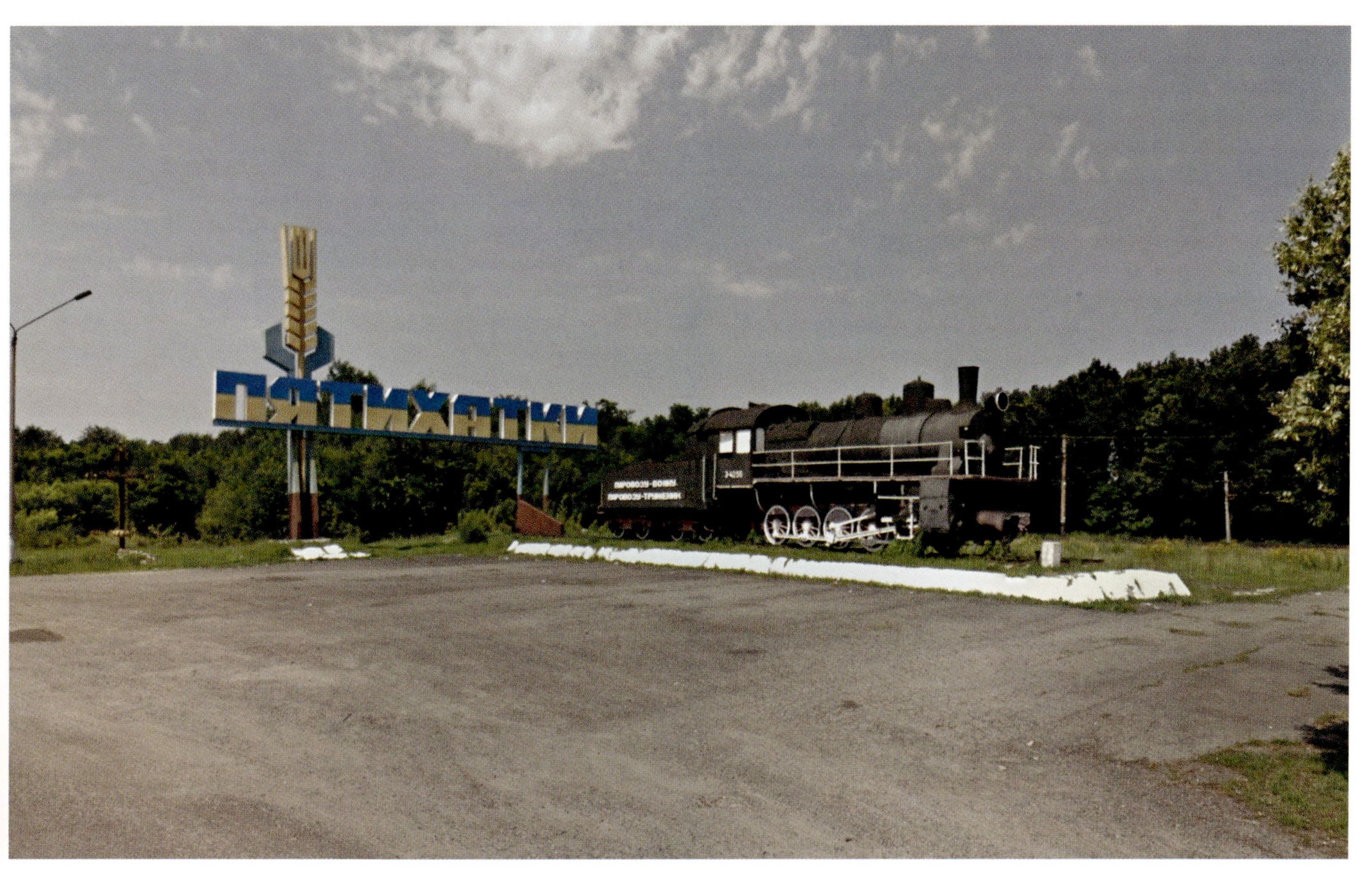

PIATYKHATKY, UKRAINE

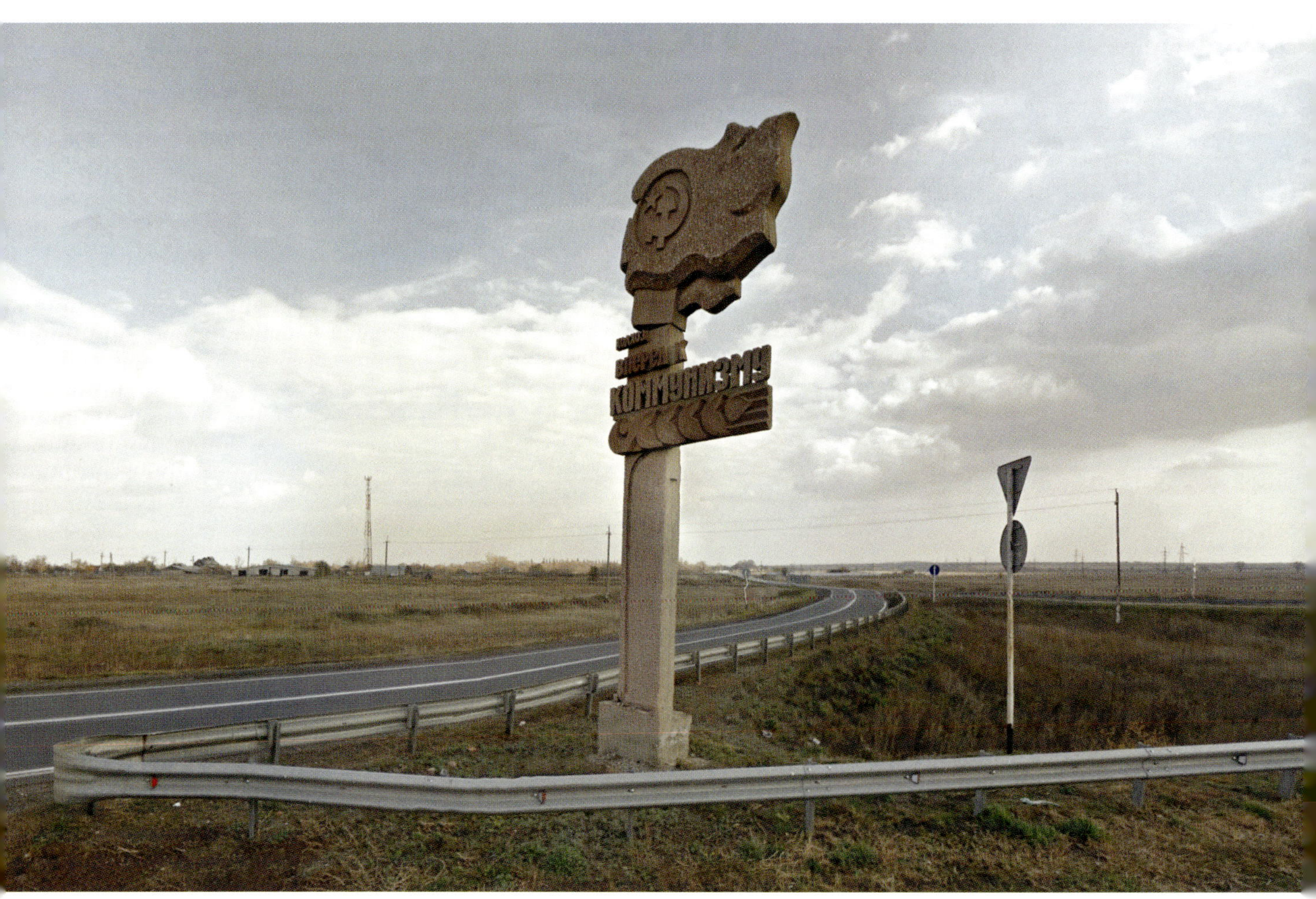

FORWARD TO COMMUNISM COLLECTIVE FARM, SAMARA, RUSSIA

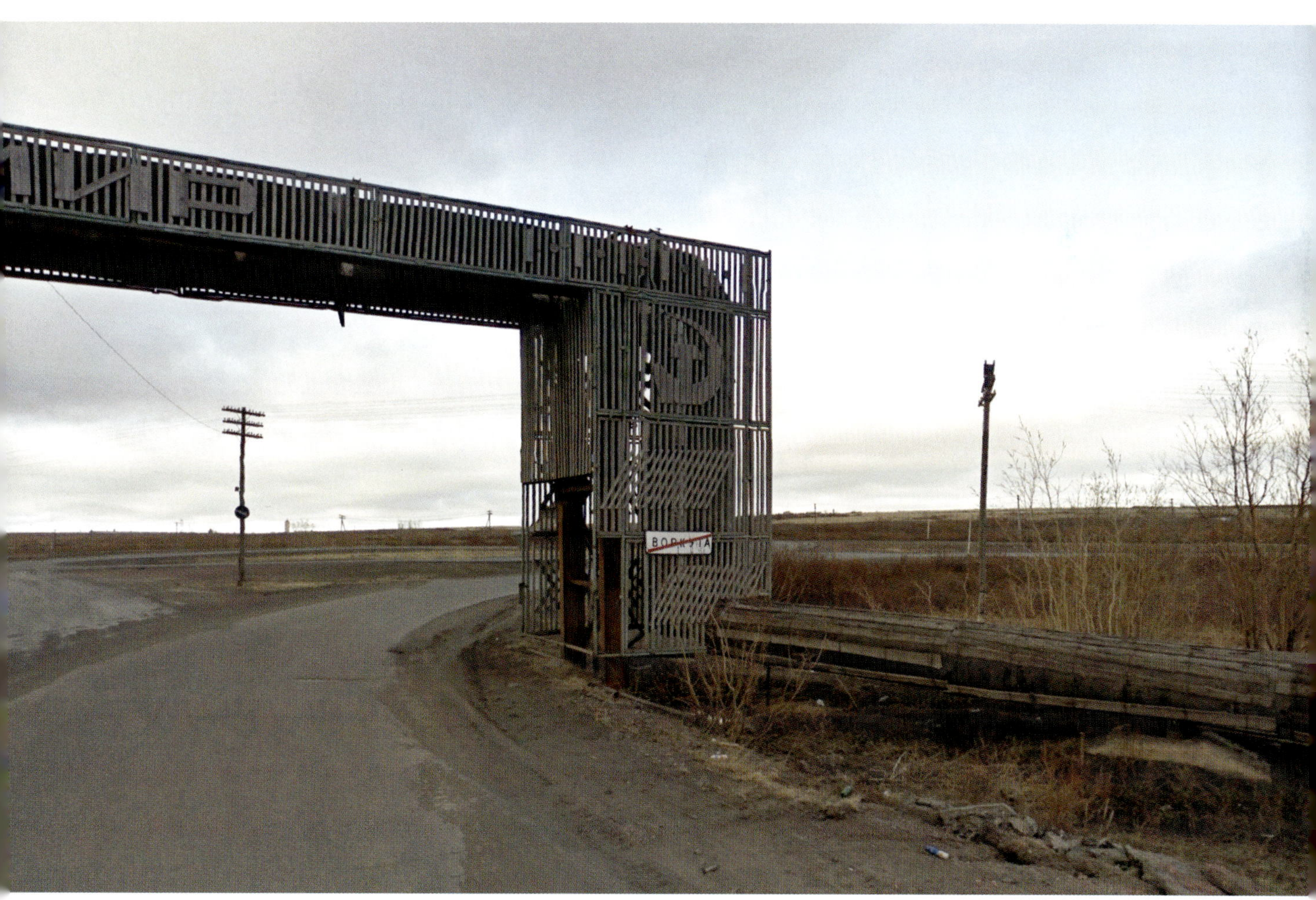

VORKUTA, RUSSIA

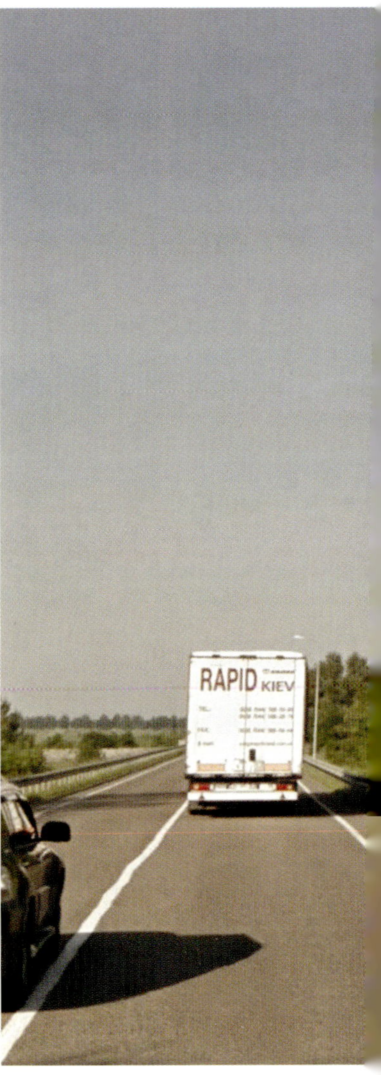

VOLODYMYRSKYI RAION, UKRAINE

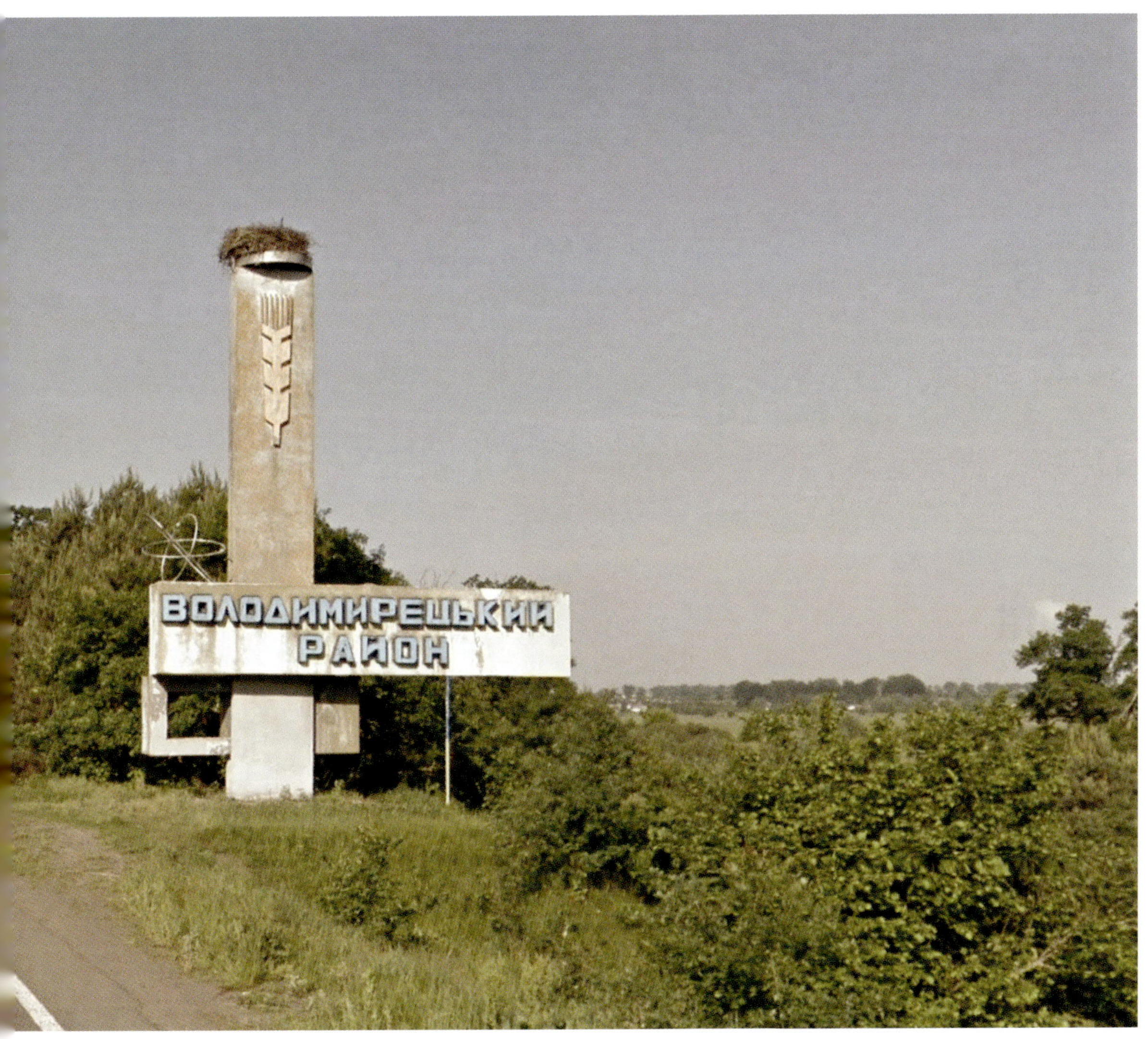
ВОЛОДИМИРЕЦЬКИЙ
РАЙОН

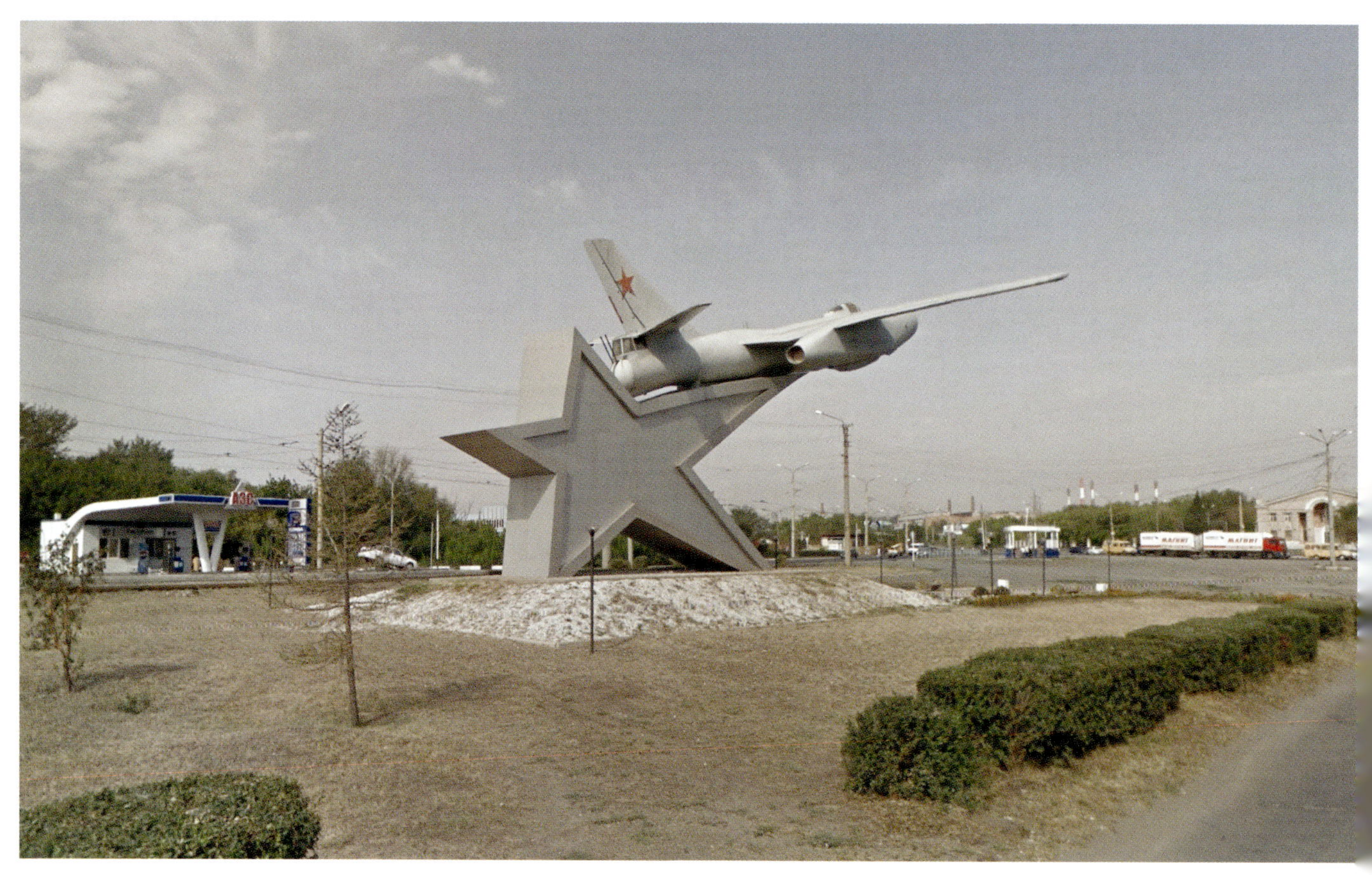

ORSK, RUSSIA

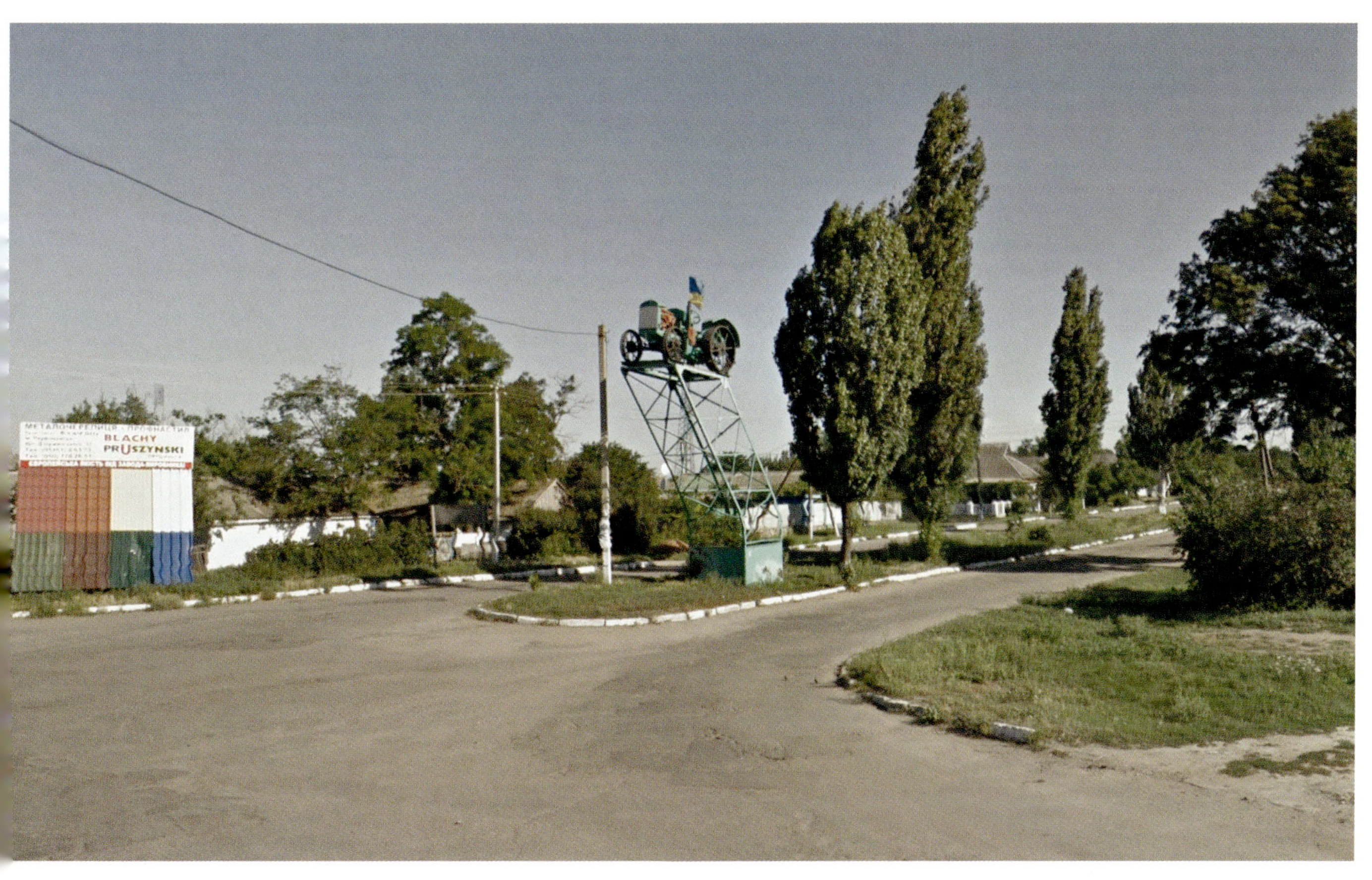
BLACHY
PRUSZYNSKI

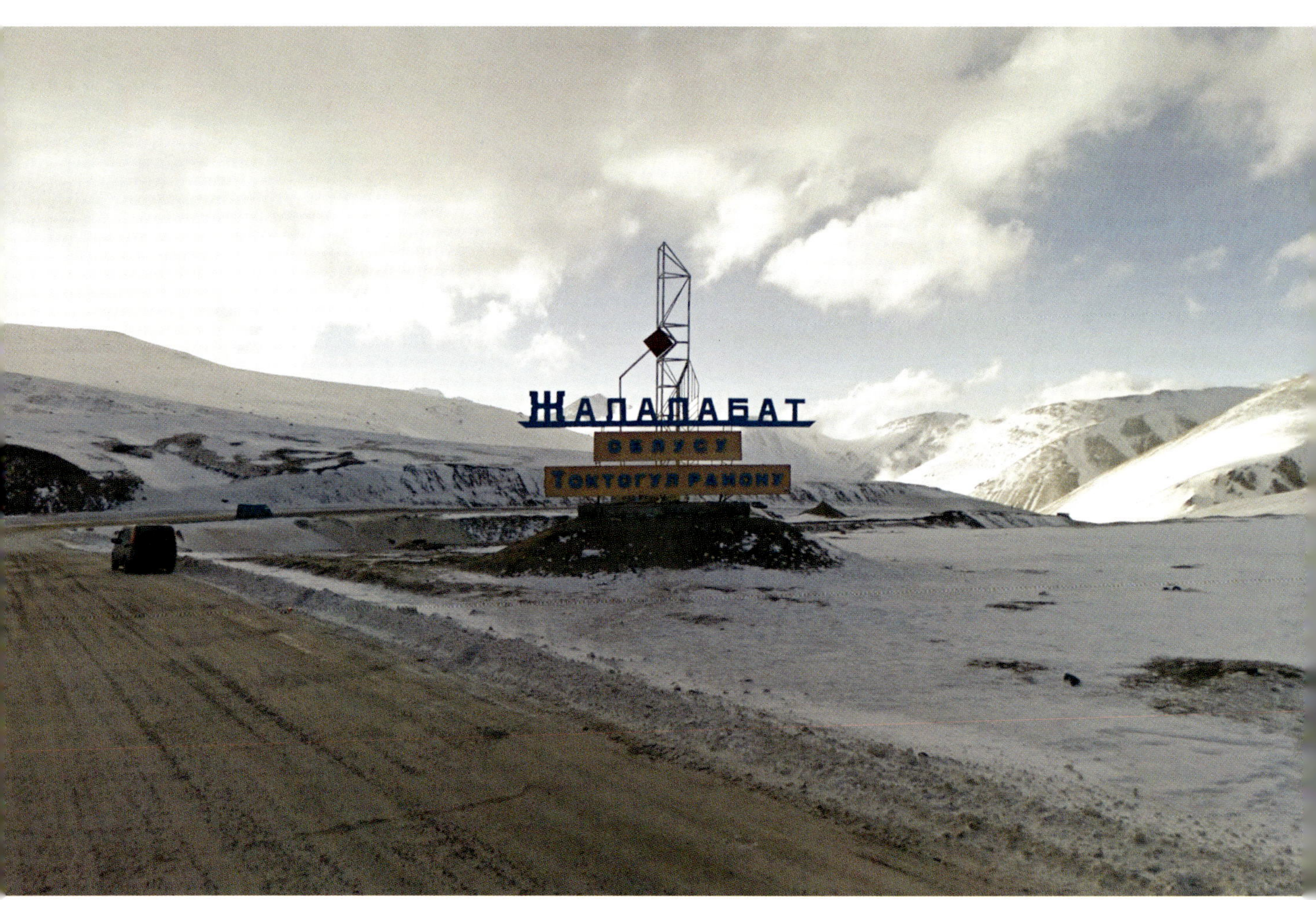

JALAL-ABAD, KYRGYZSTAN

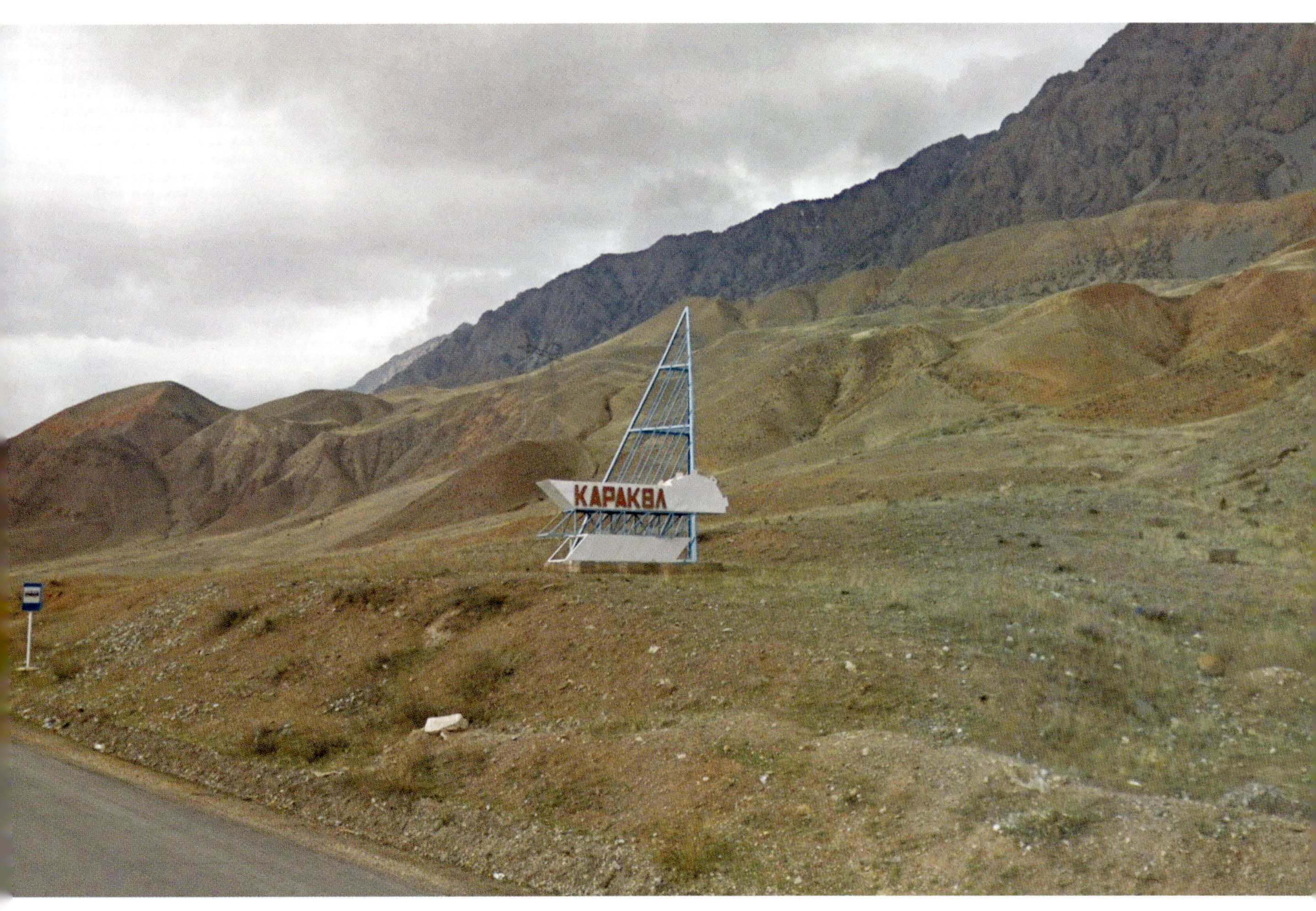

KARAKOL, KYRGYZSTAN

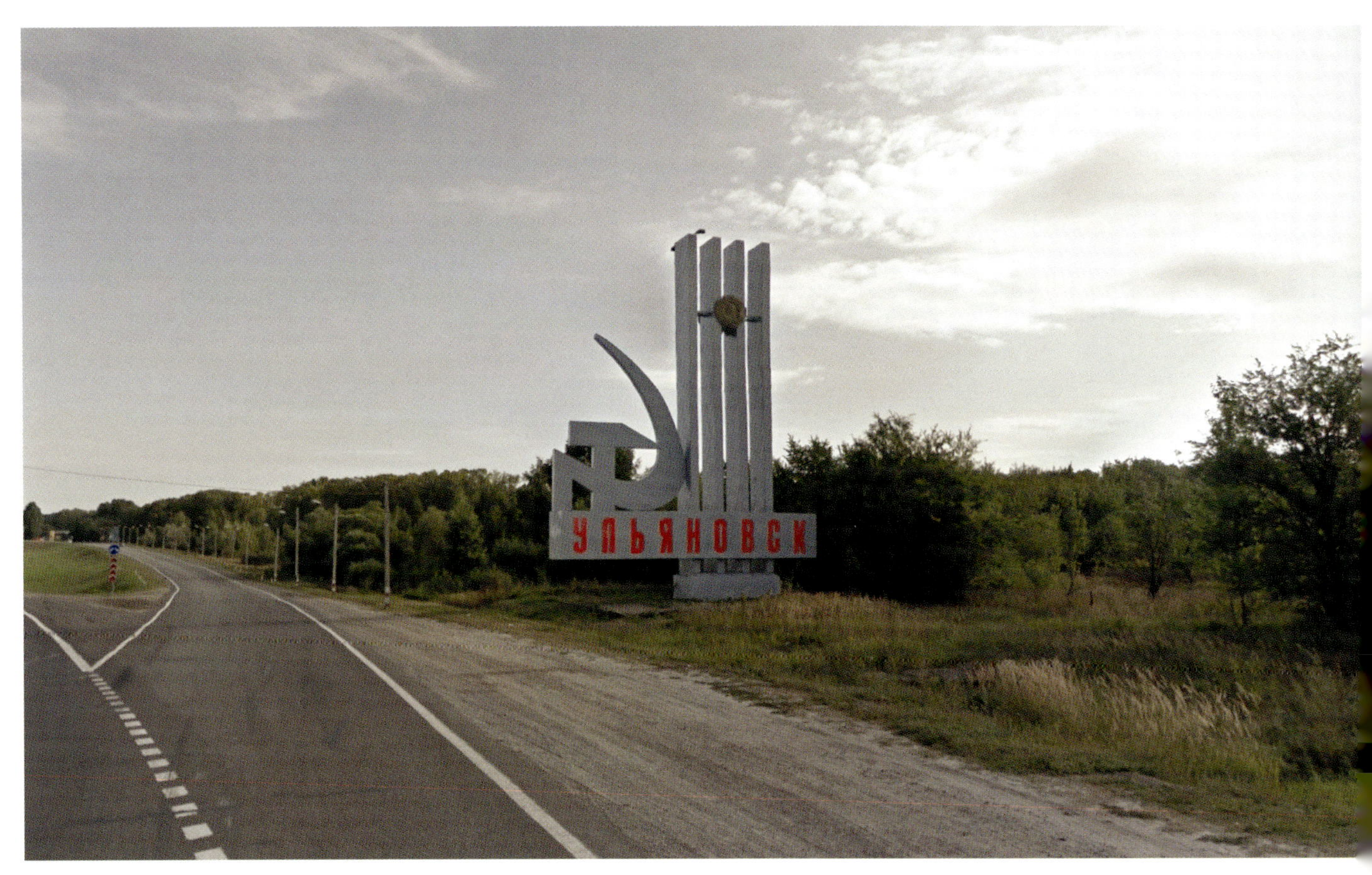

ULYANOVSK, RUSSIA

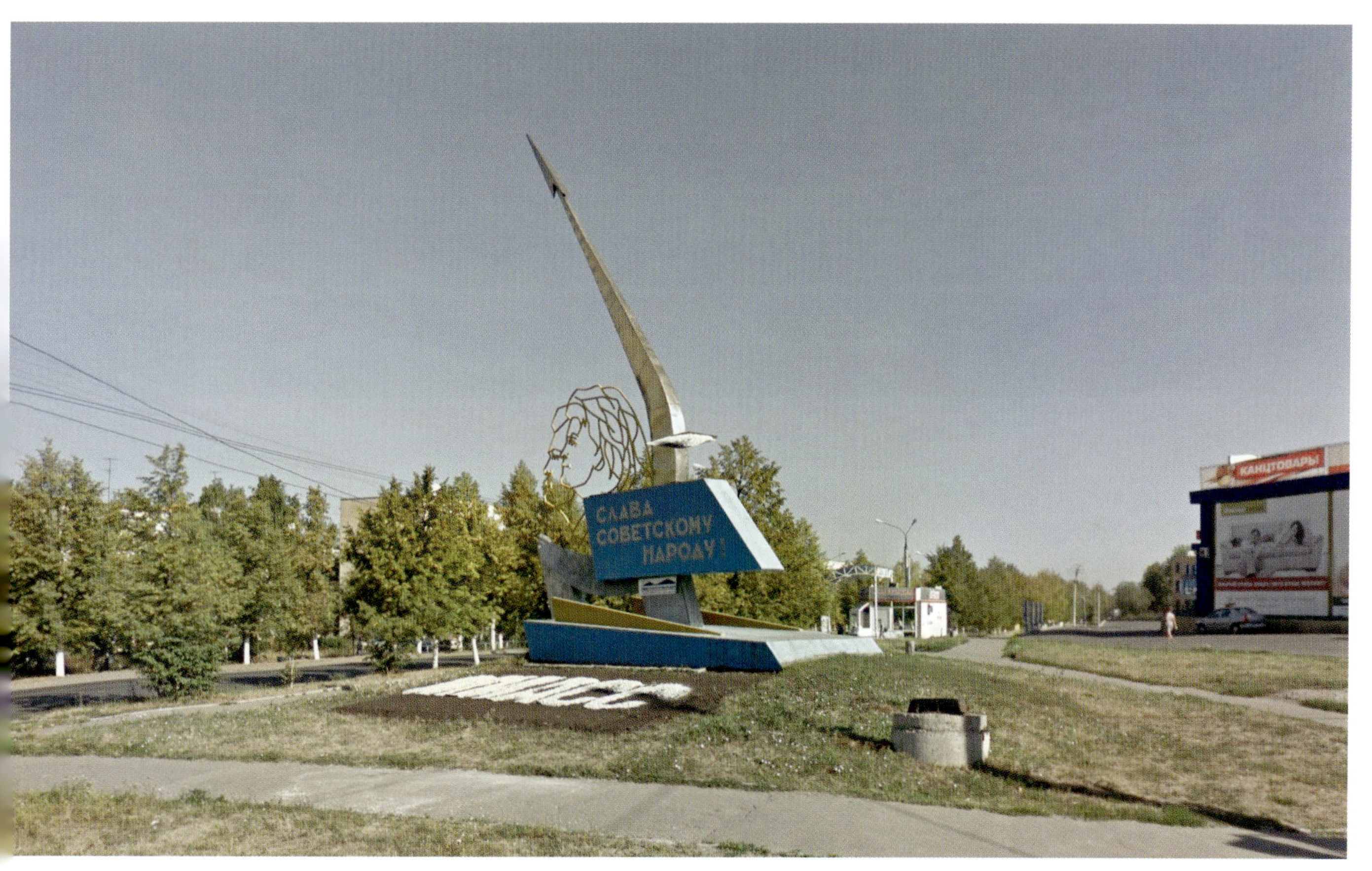

'GLORY TO THE SOVIET PEOPLE', MIASS, RUSSIA

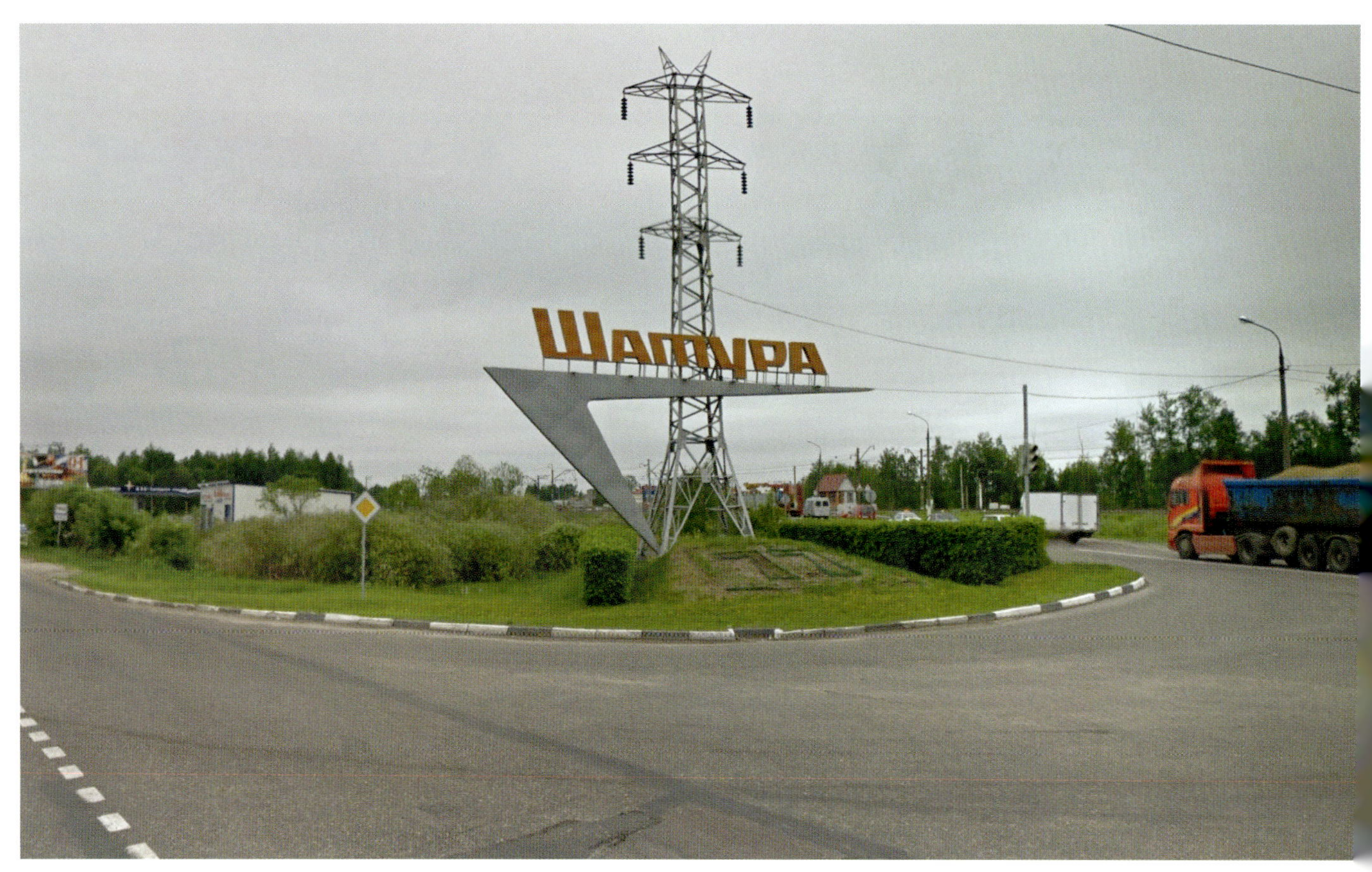

 SHATURA, RUSSIA

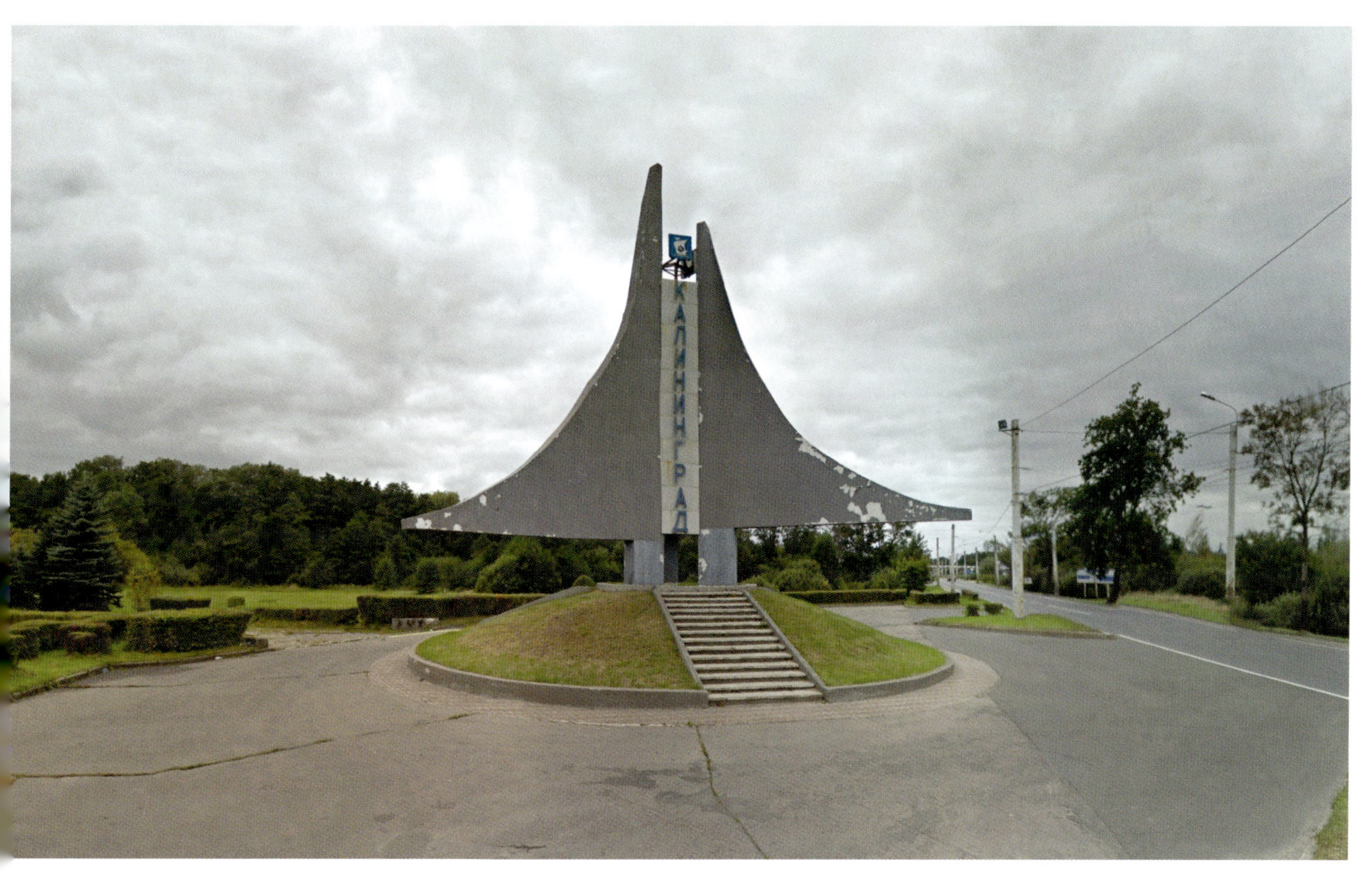

KALININGRAD, RUSSIA

 KALININGRAD, RUSSIA

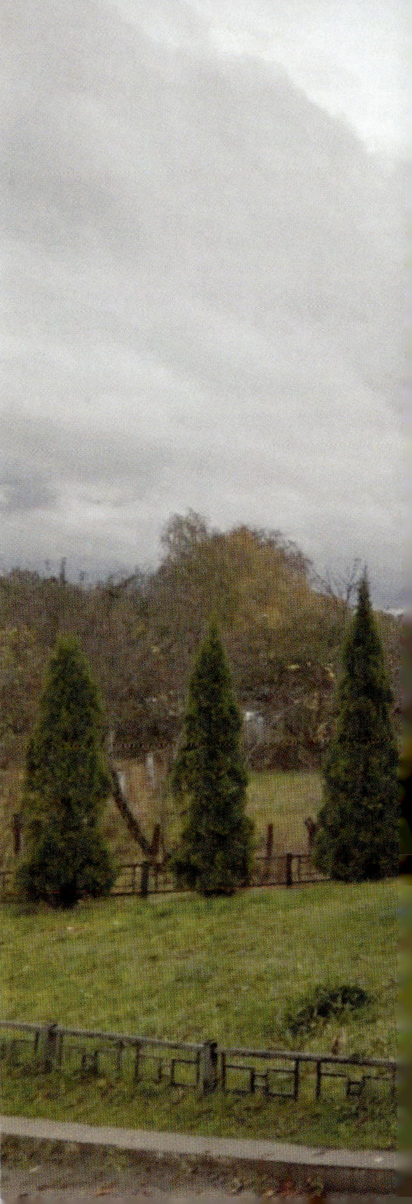

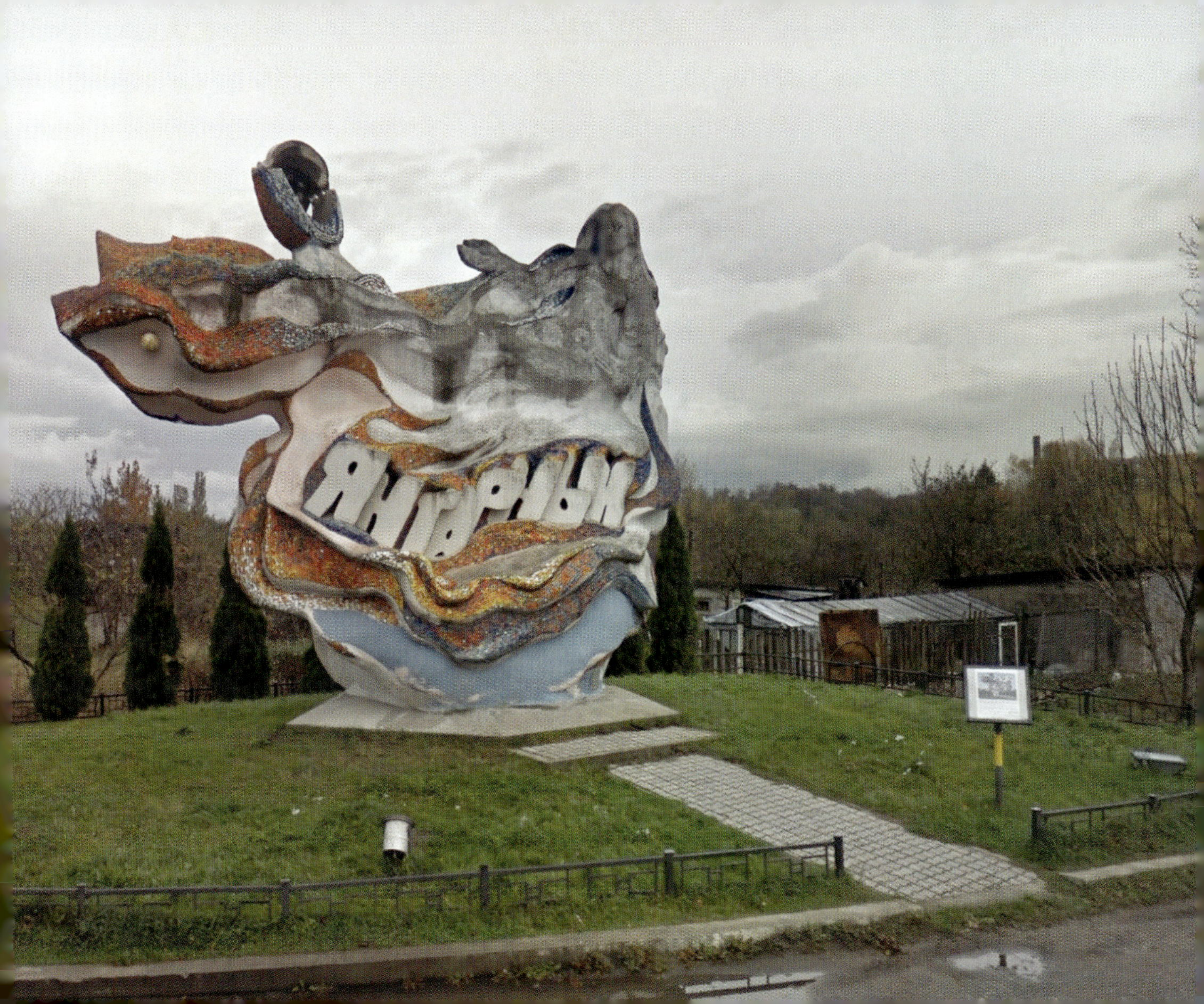

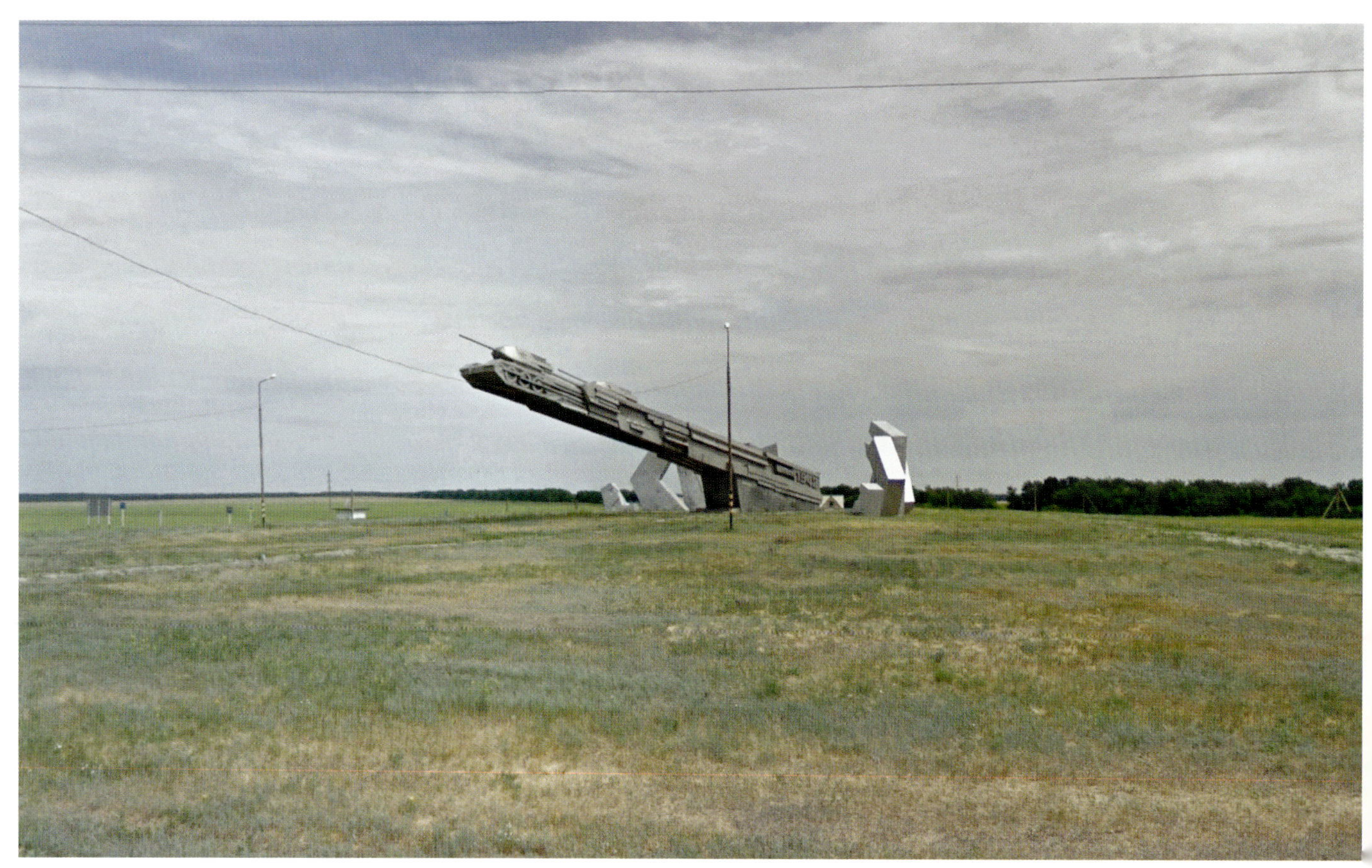

 VOLGOGRAD OBLAST, RUSSIA

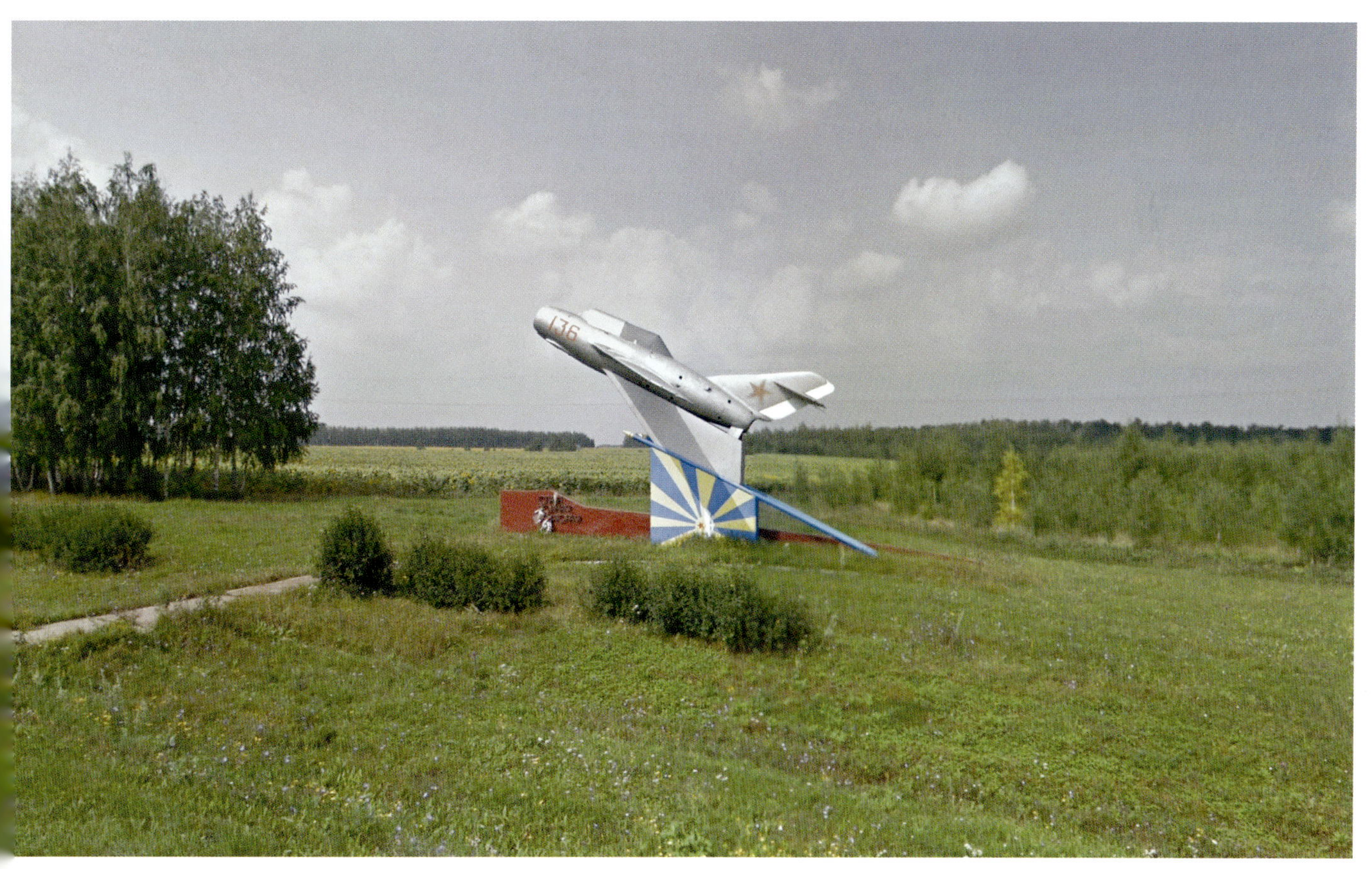

LIPETSK OBLAST, RUSSIA

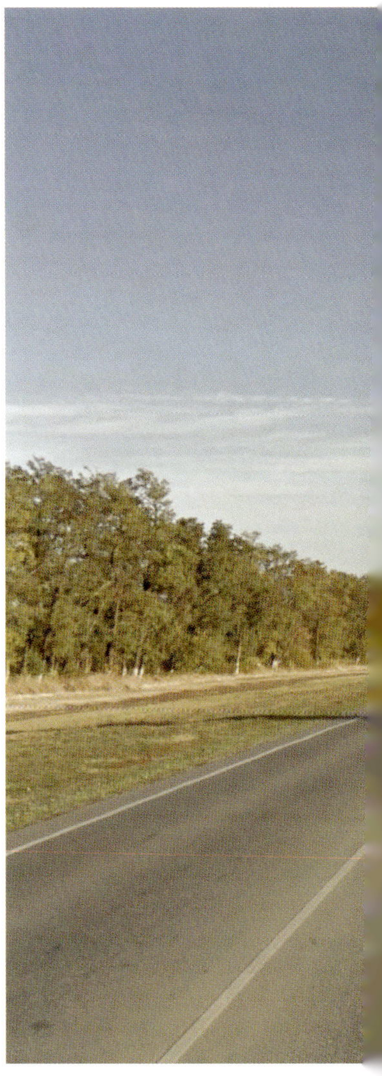

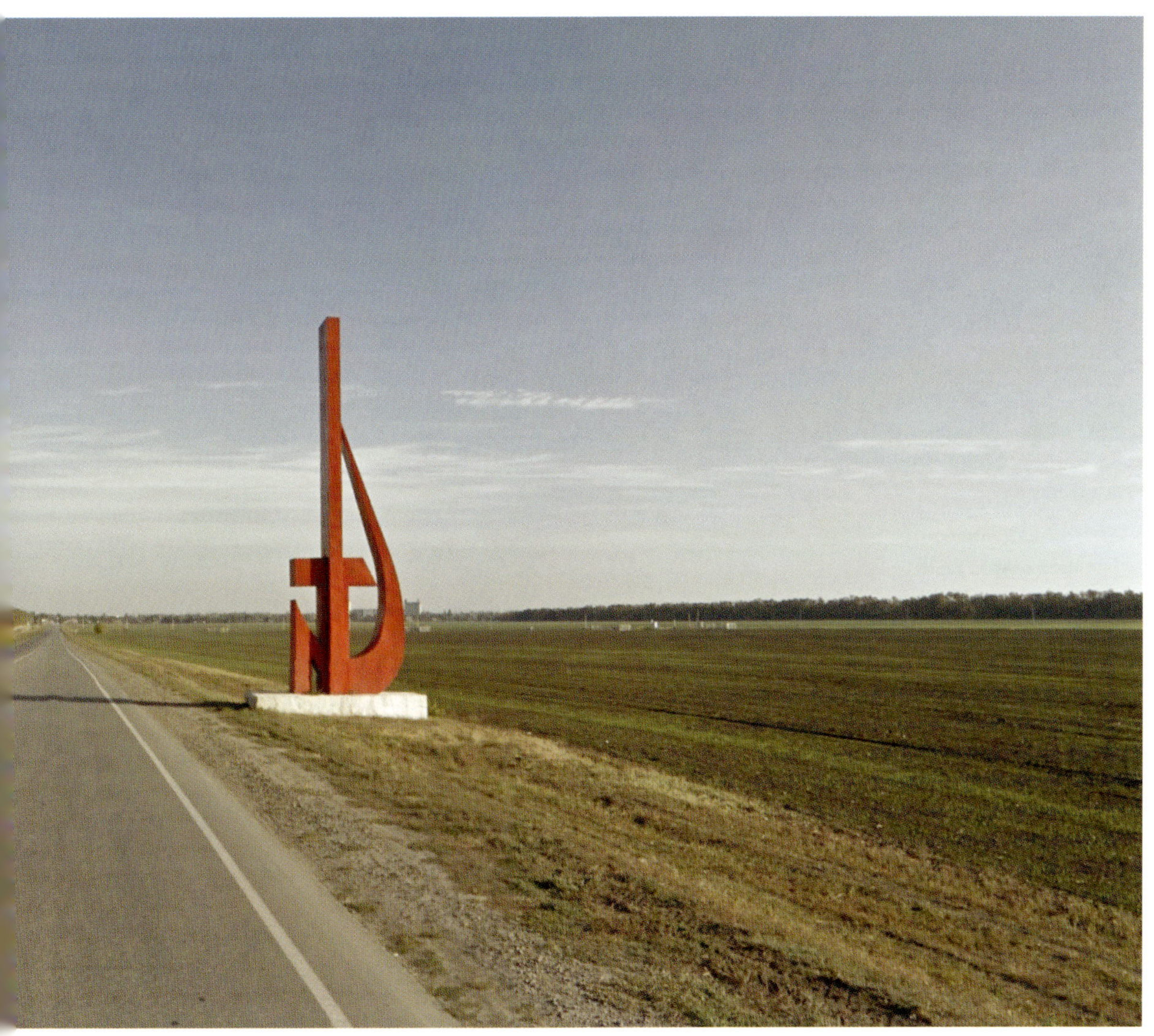

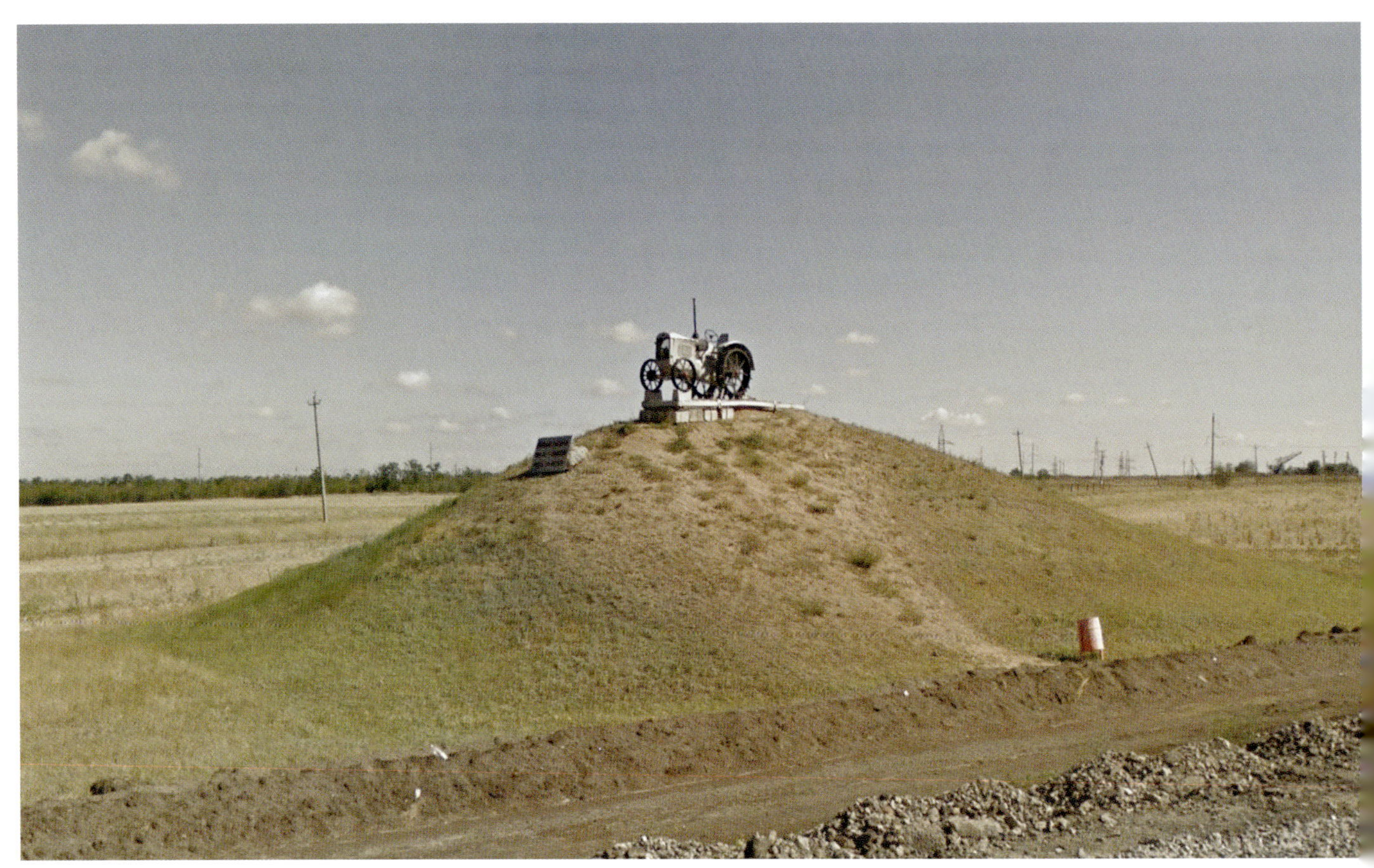

 SAMARA OBLAST, RUSSIA

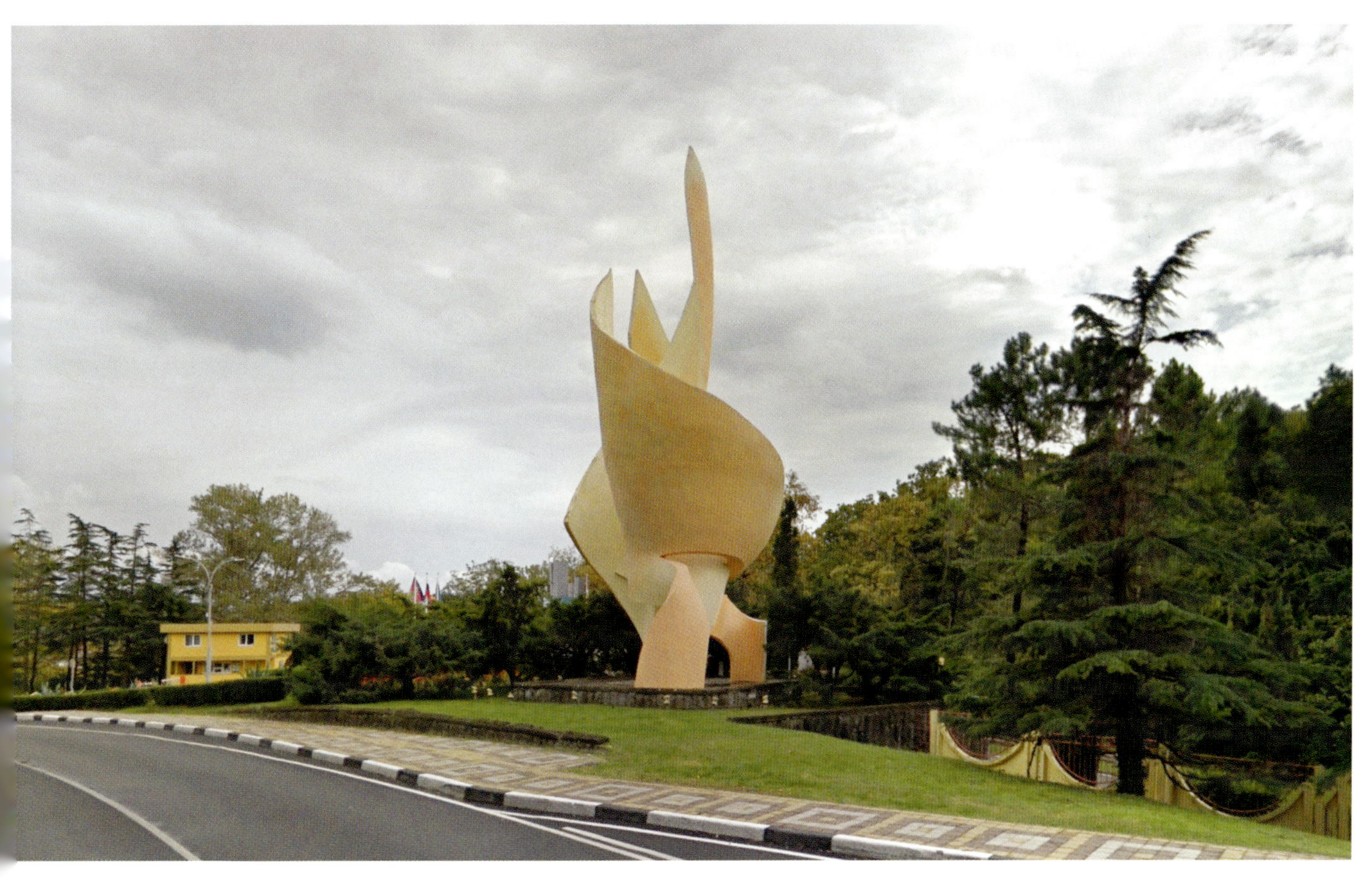

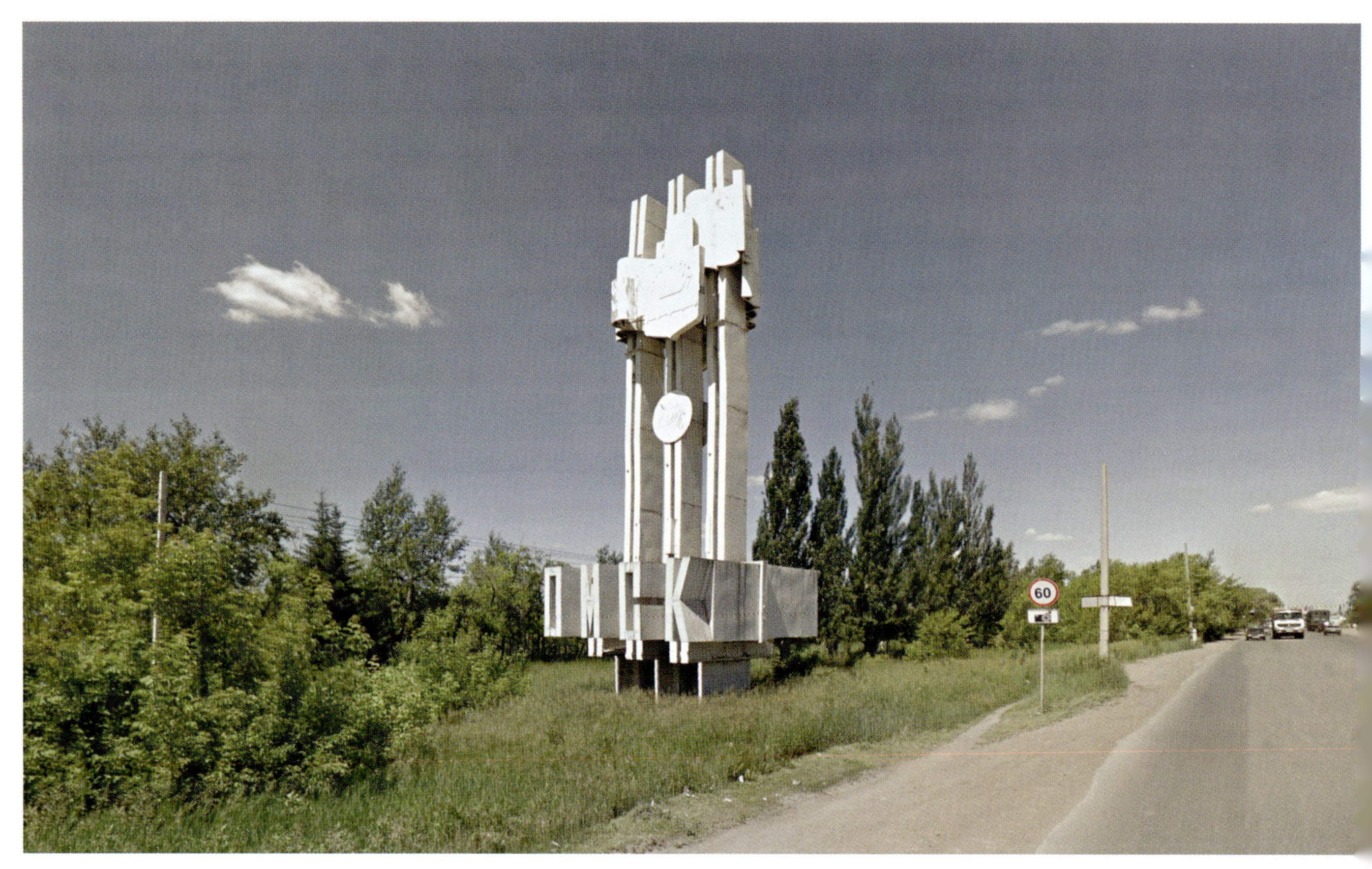

OMSK, RUSSIA

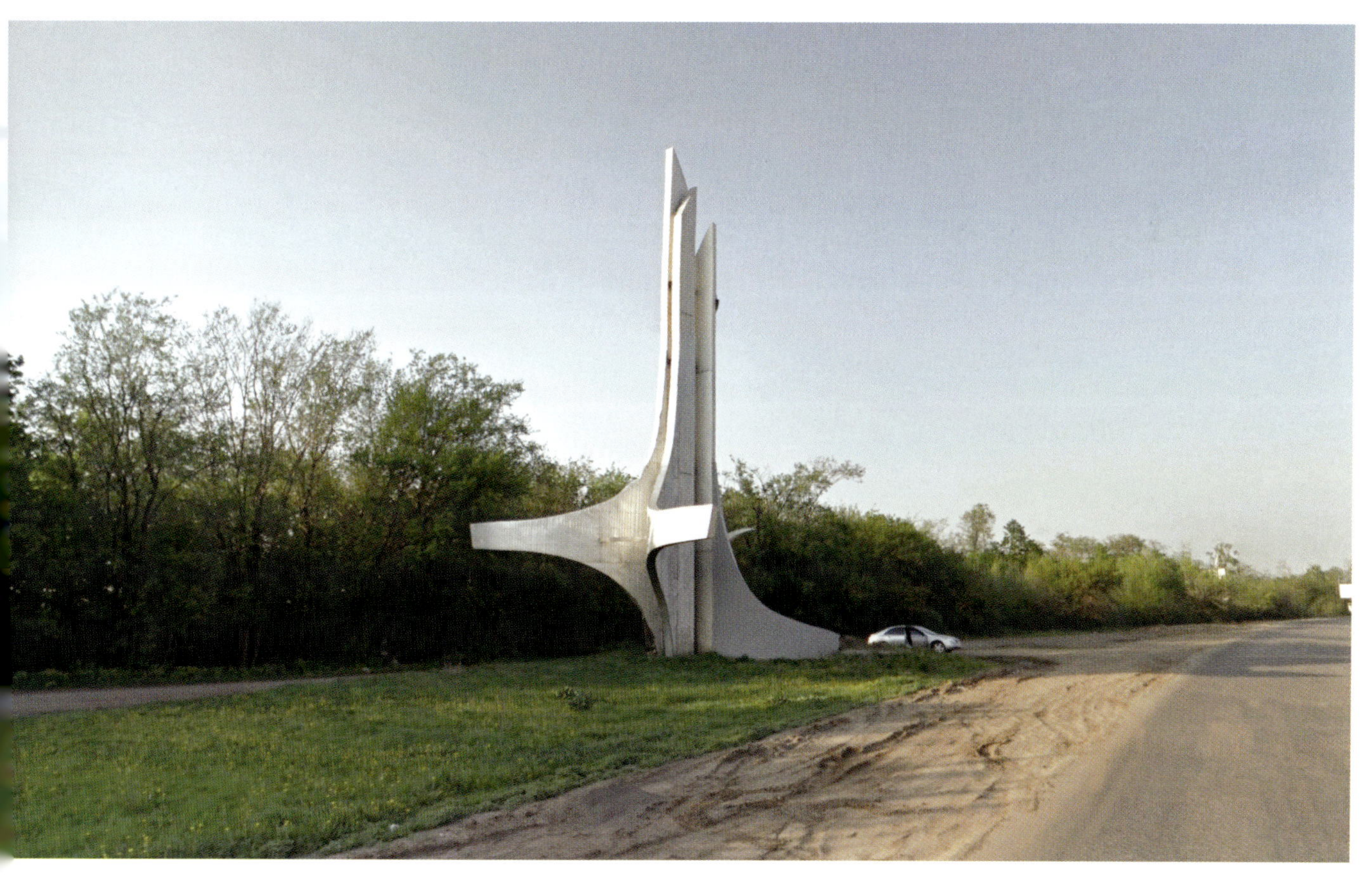

ULYANOVSK, RUSSIA

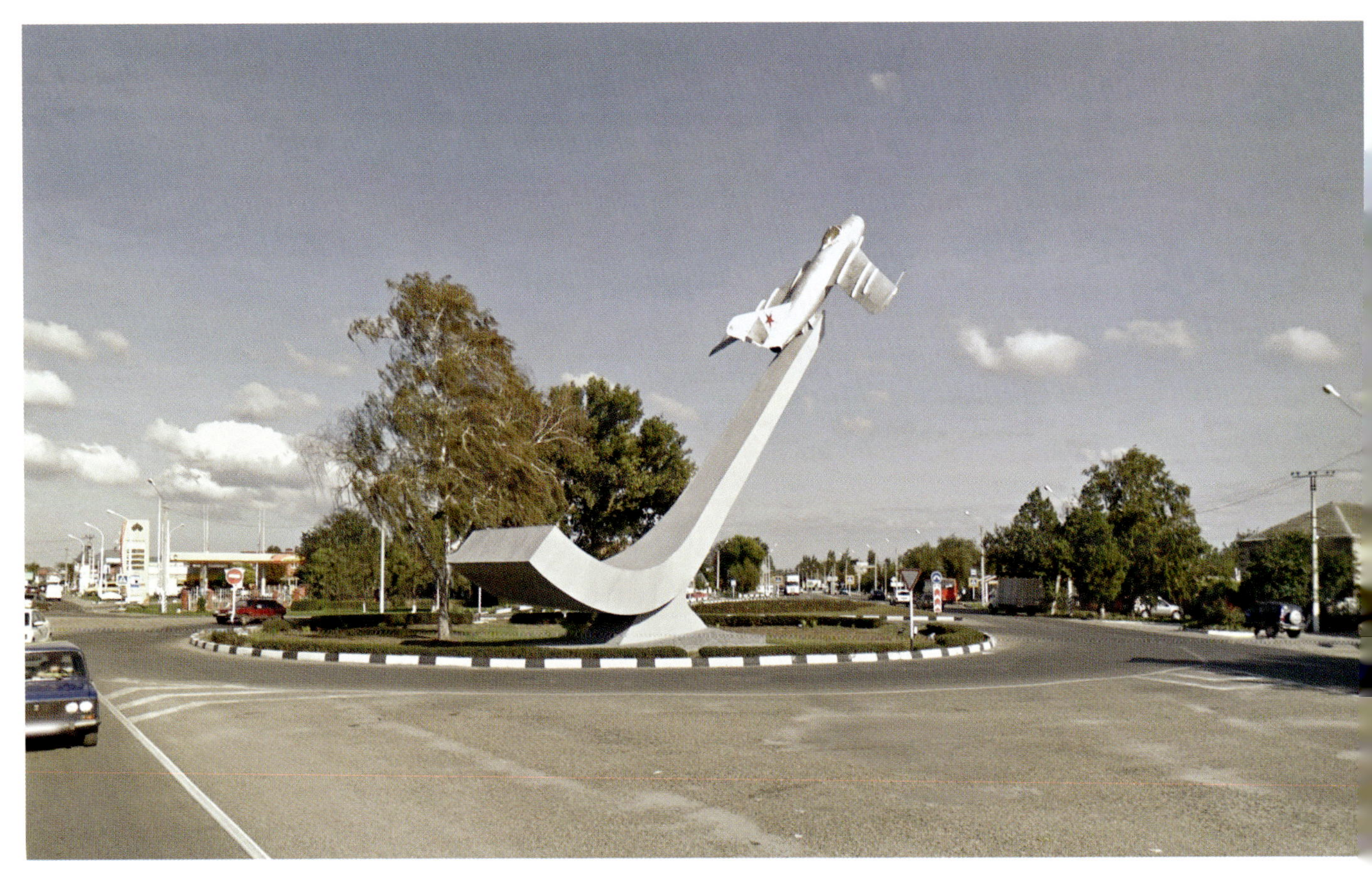

 PRIMORSKO-AKHTARSK, RUSSIA

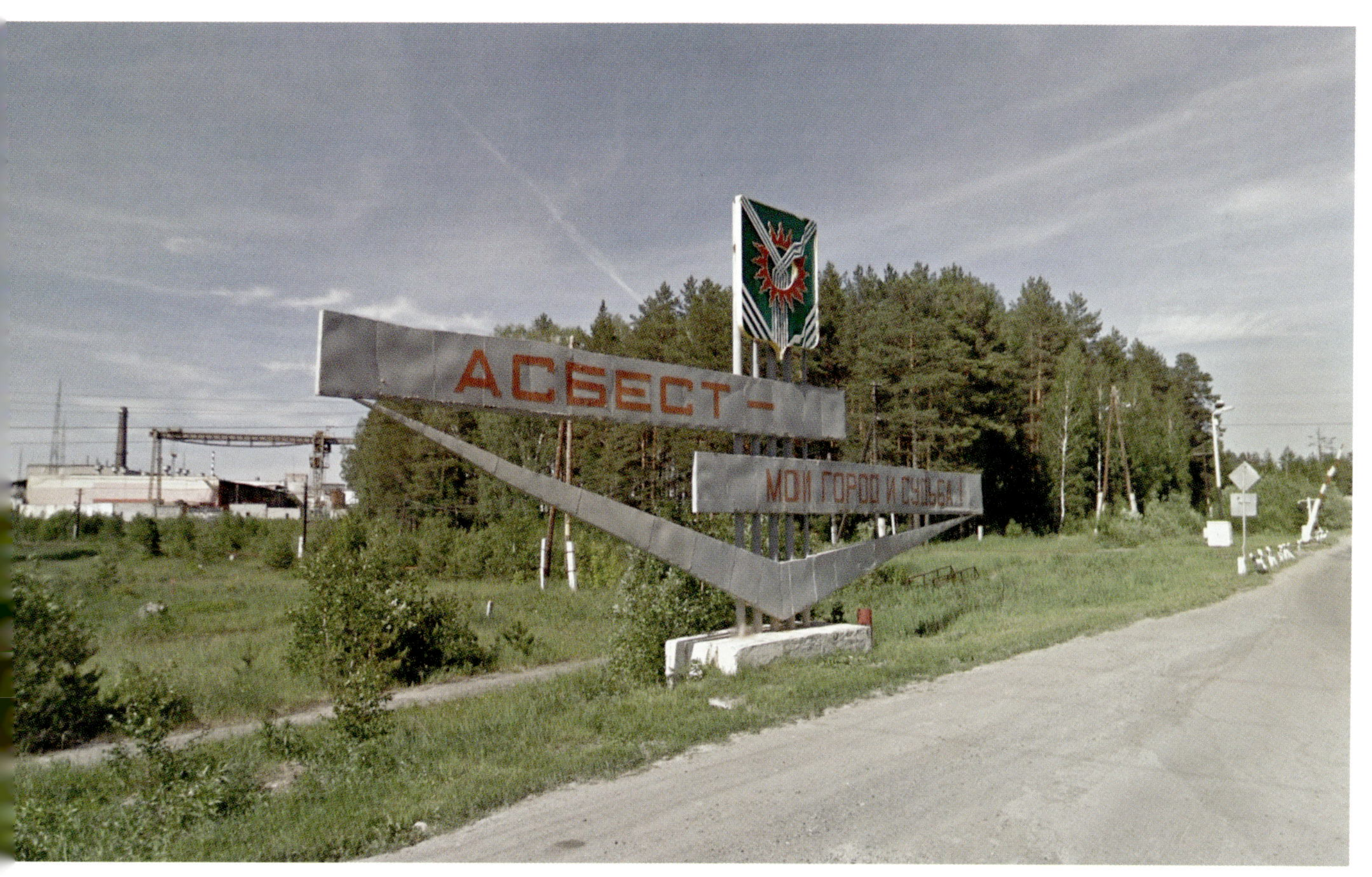

ASBEST, RUSSIA

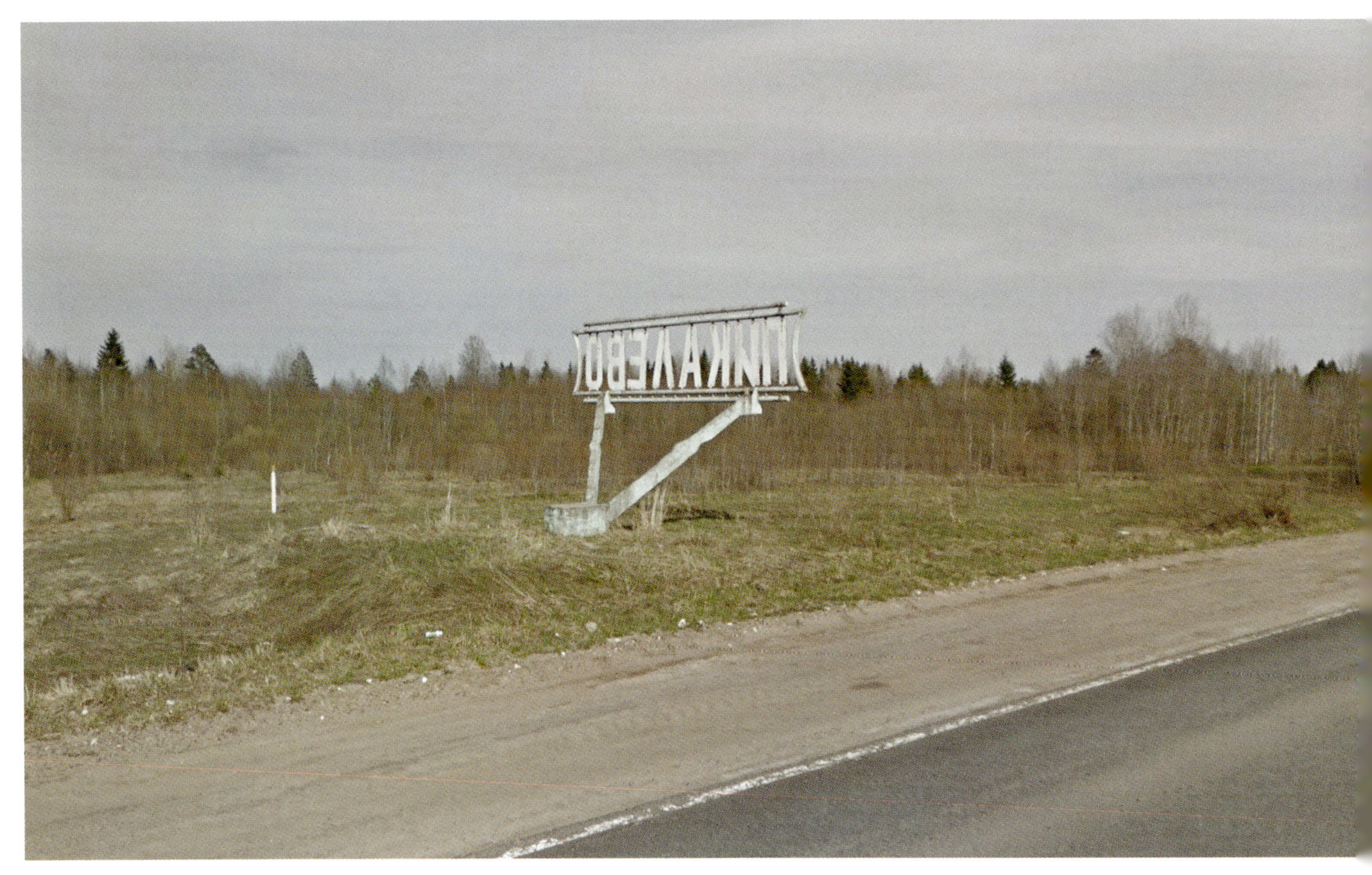

PIKALYOVO, RUSSIA

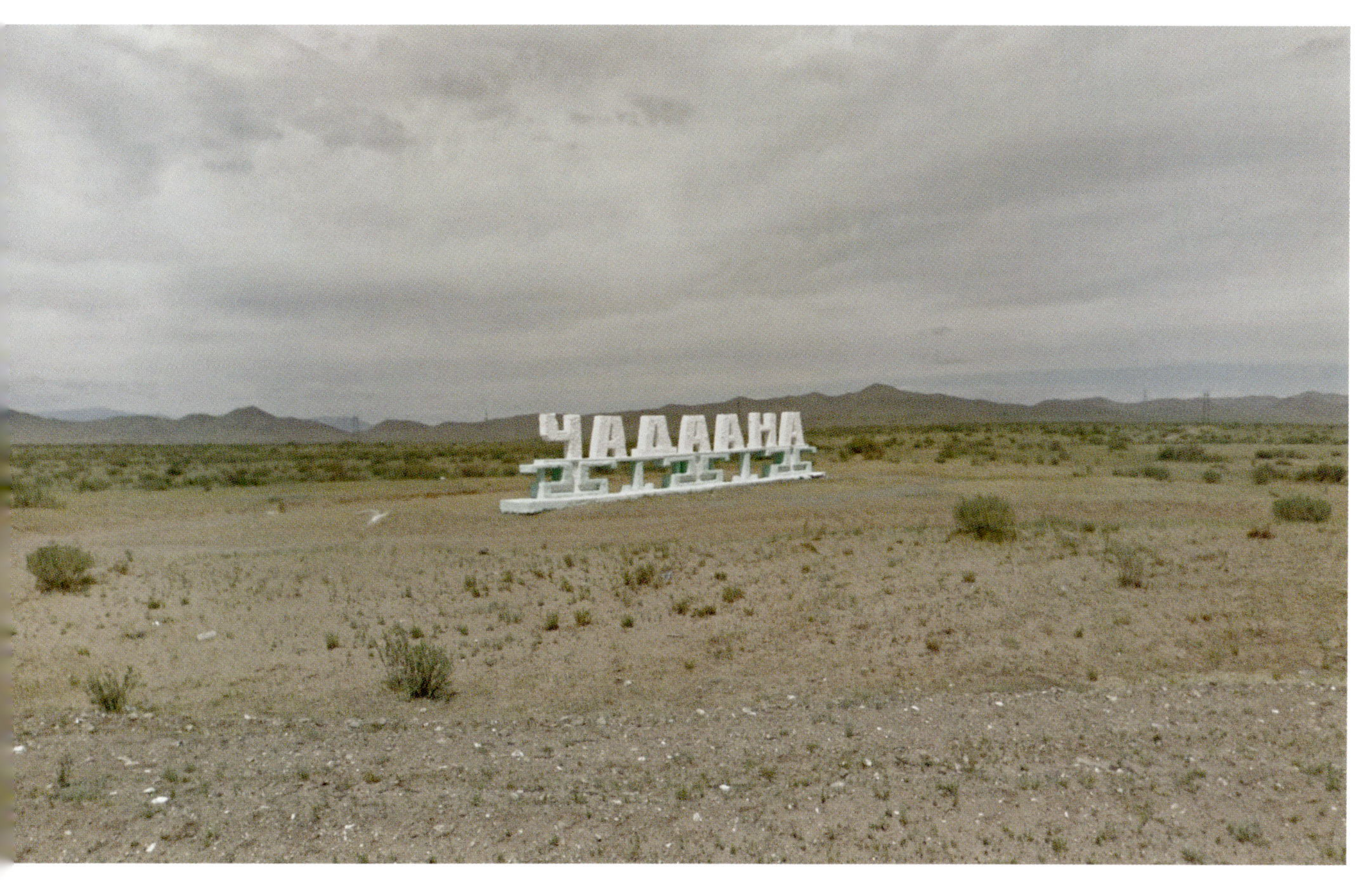

CHADAN, RUSSIA

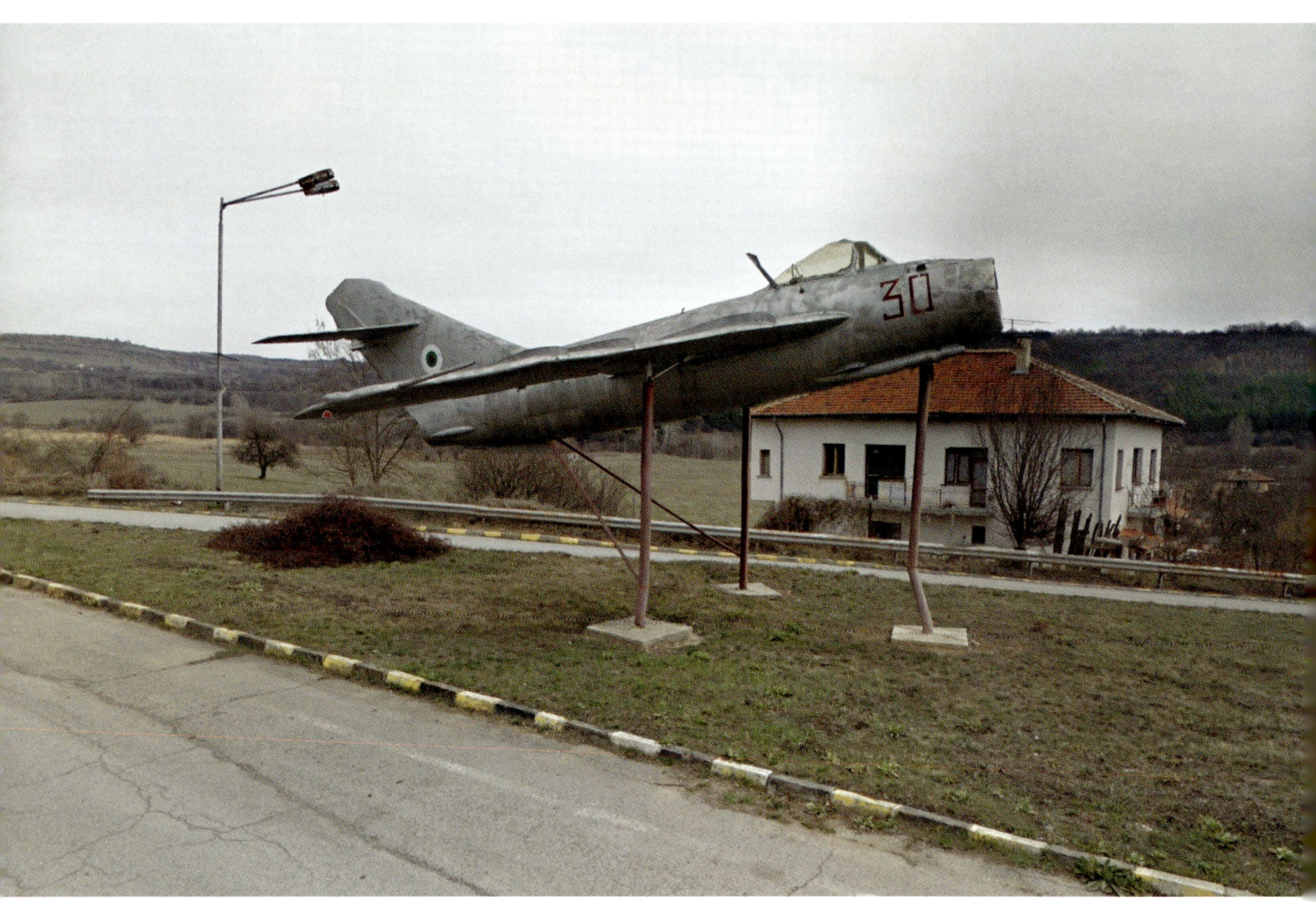

PERNIK, BULGARIA

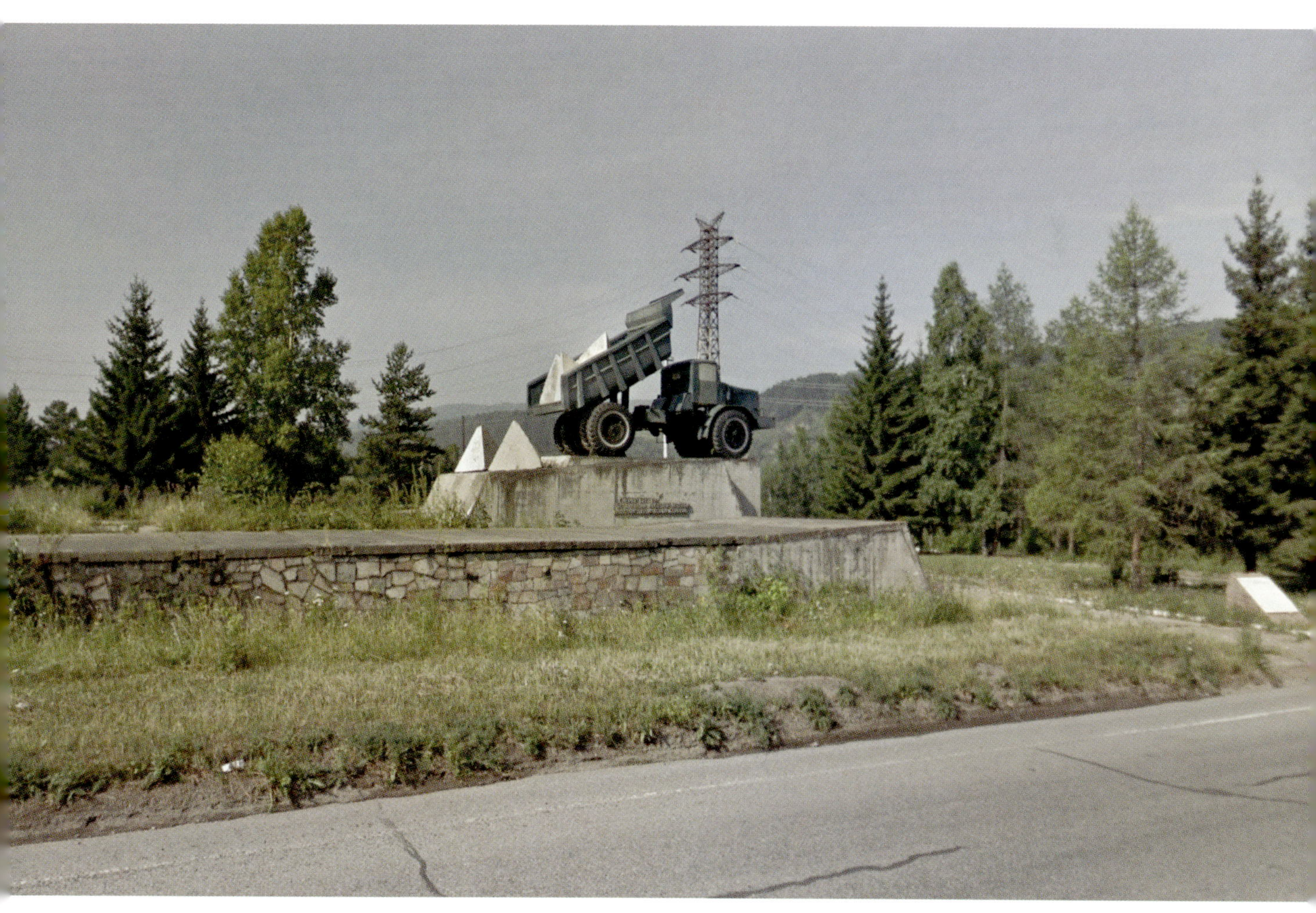

KRASNOYARSK, RUSSIA

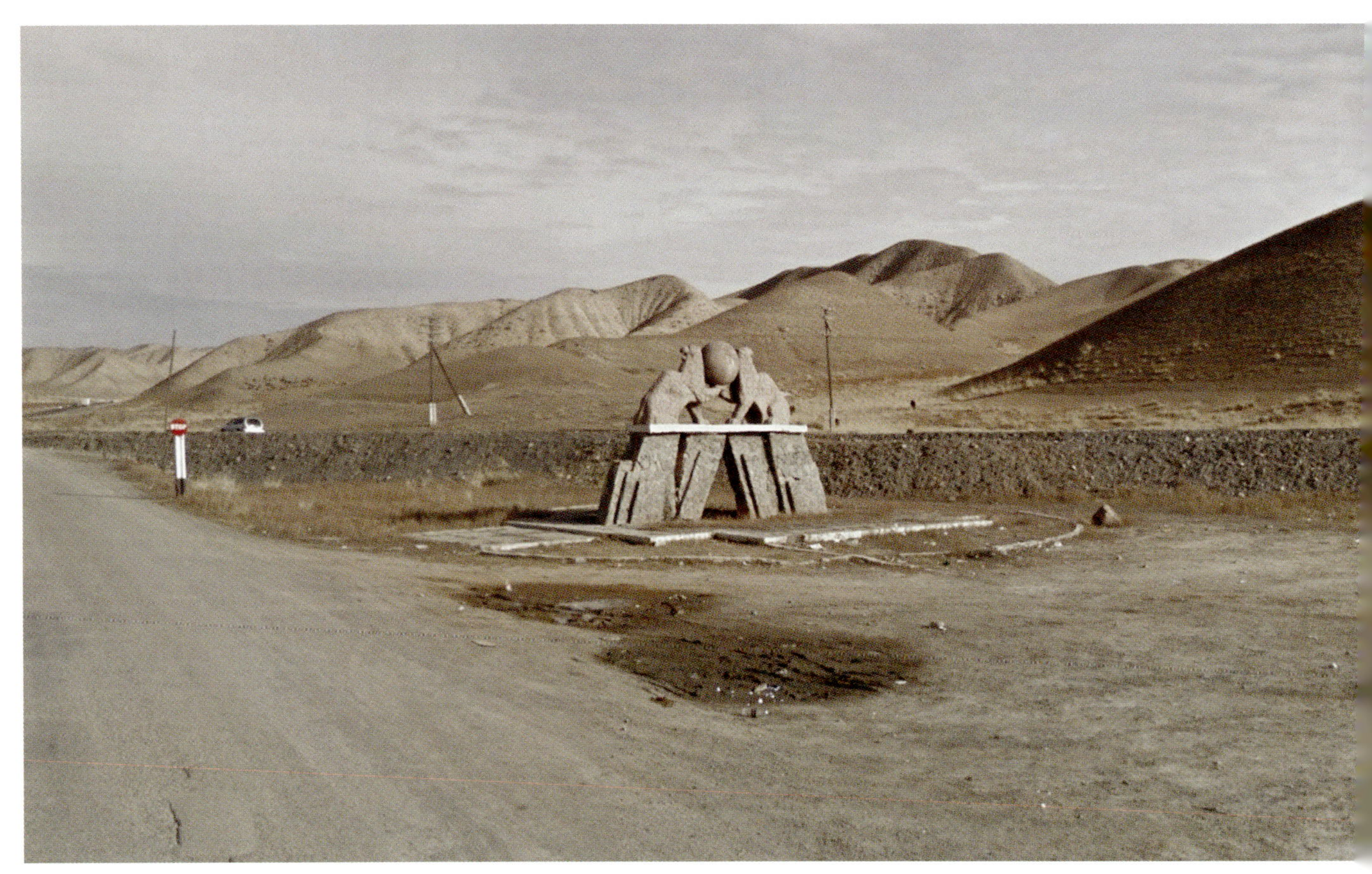

 NARYN PROVINCE, KYRGYZSTAN

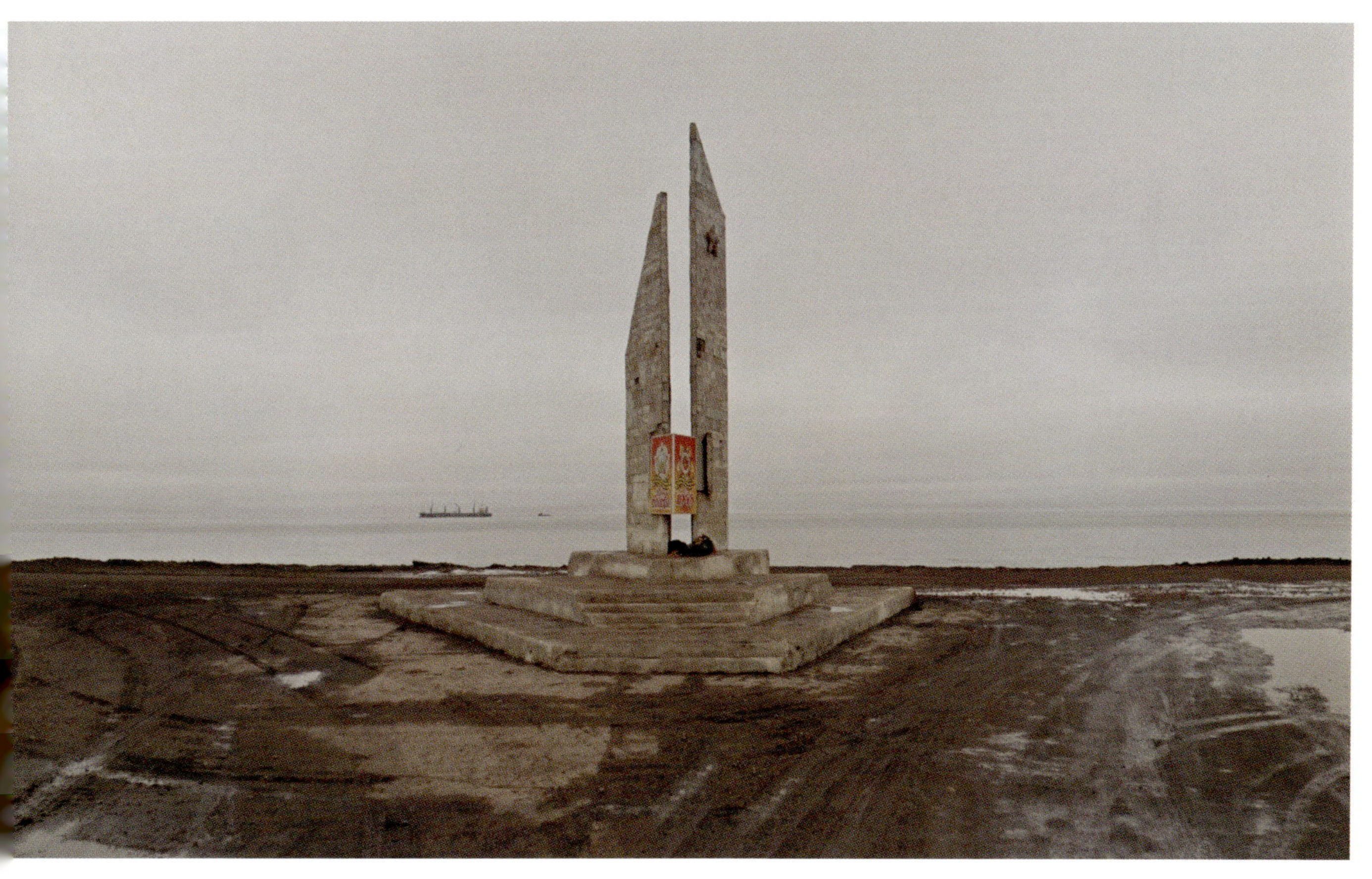

SAKHALIN ISLAND, RUSSIA

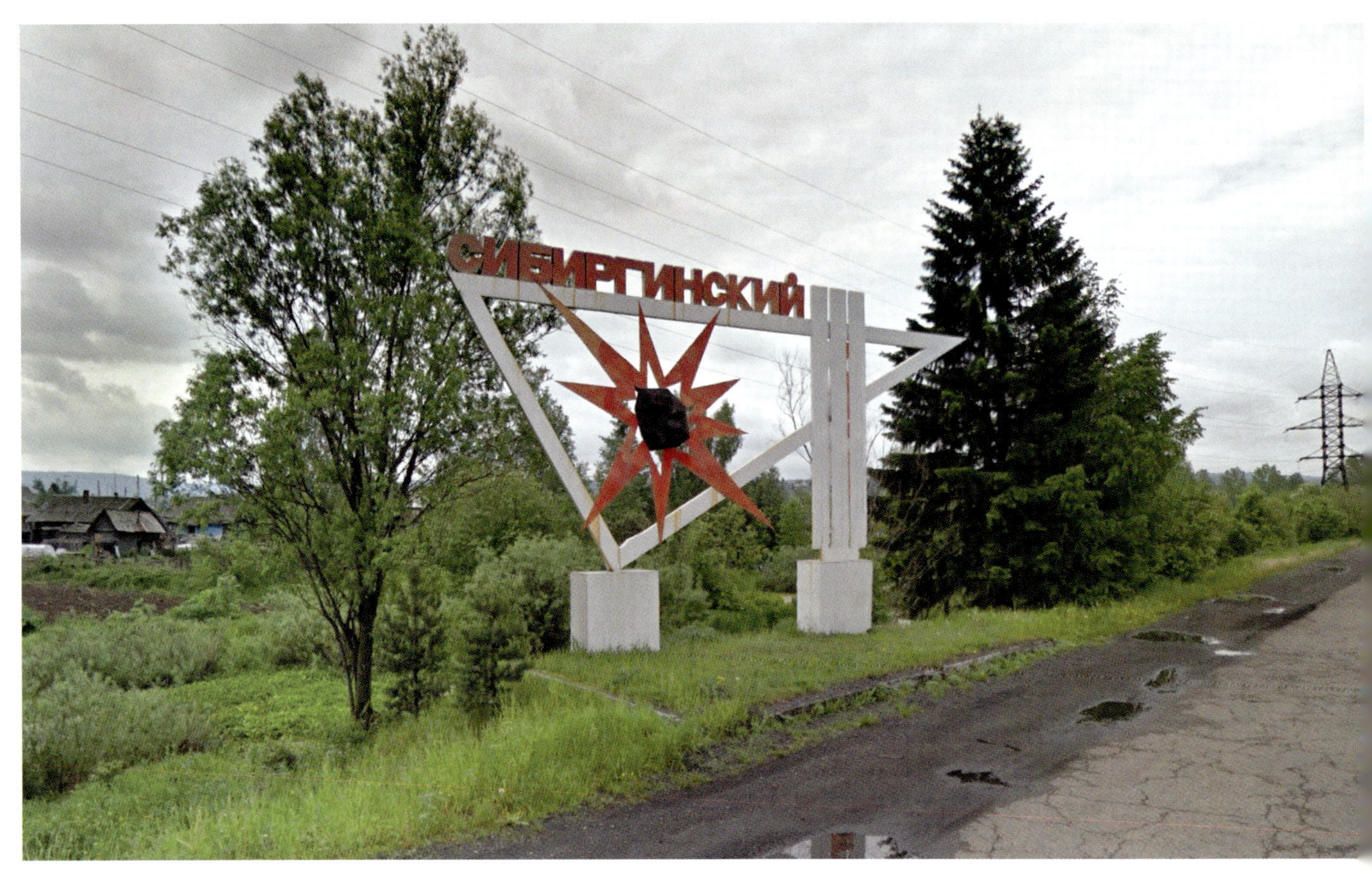

 SIBIRGINSKI OPEN CAST MINE, KEMEROVO OBLAST, RUSSIA

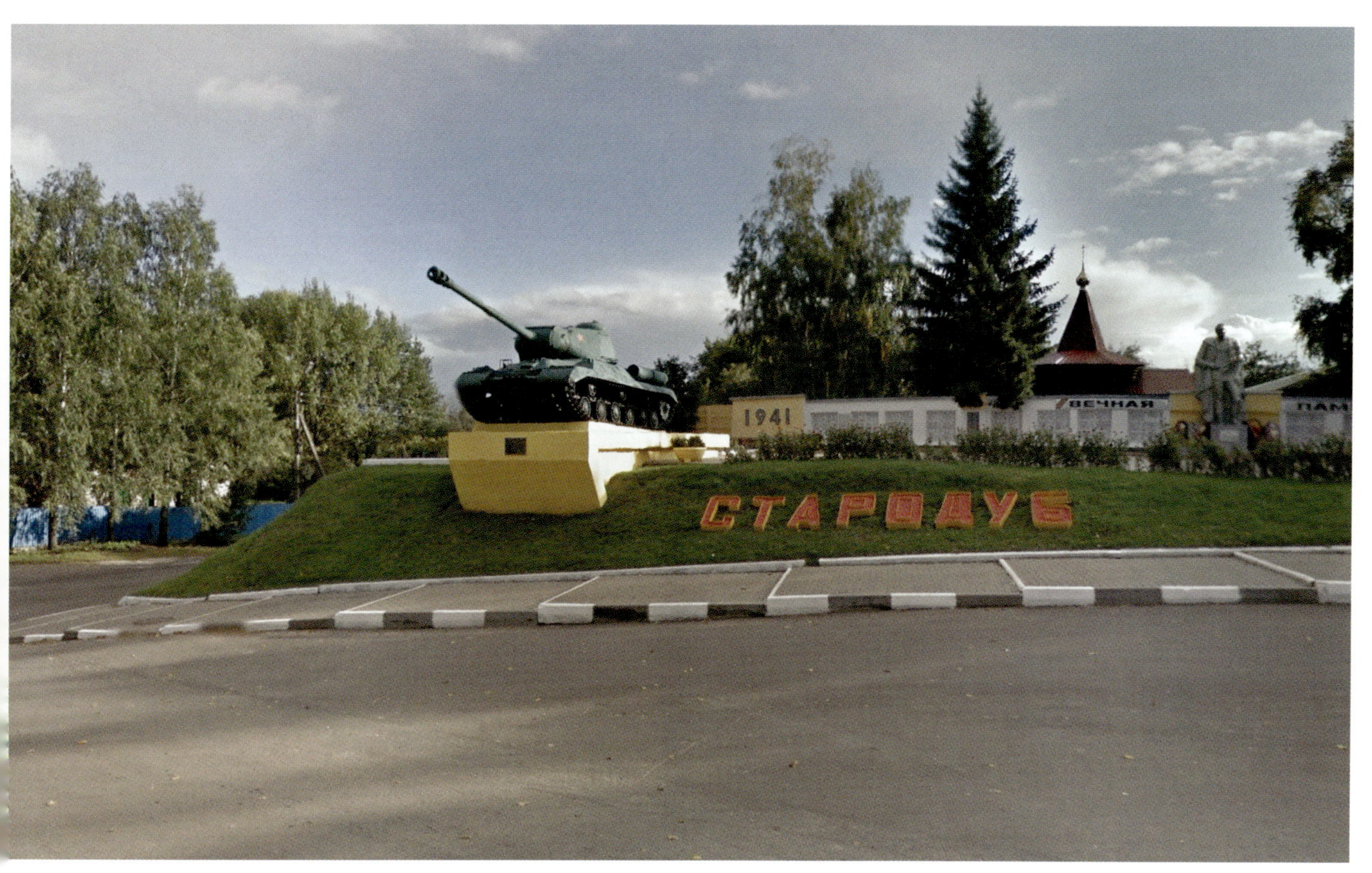

STARODUB, RUSSIA

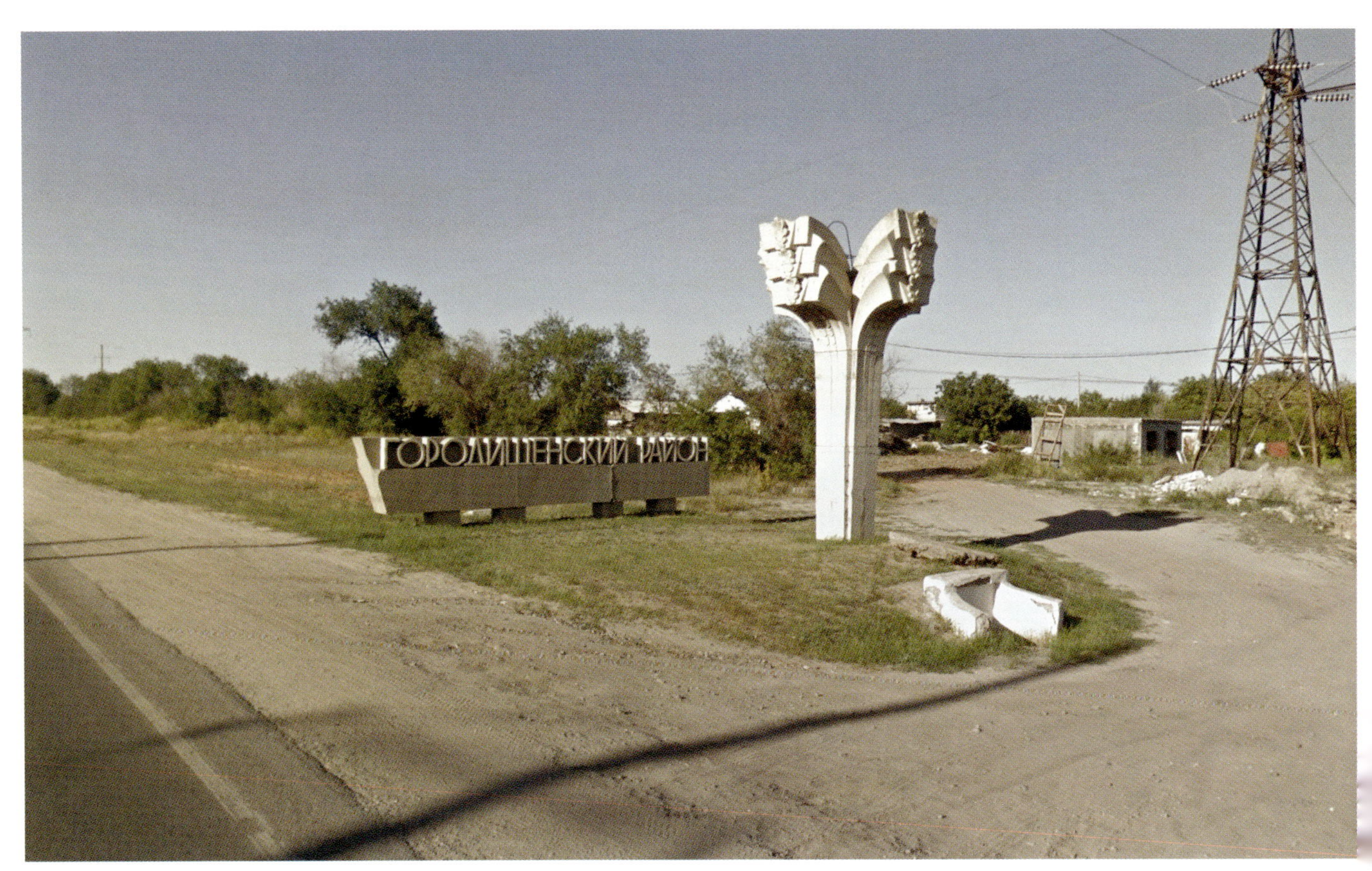

 GORODISHENSKI RAION, RUSSIA

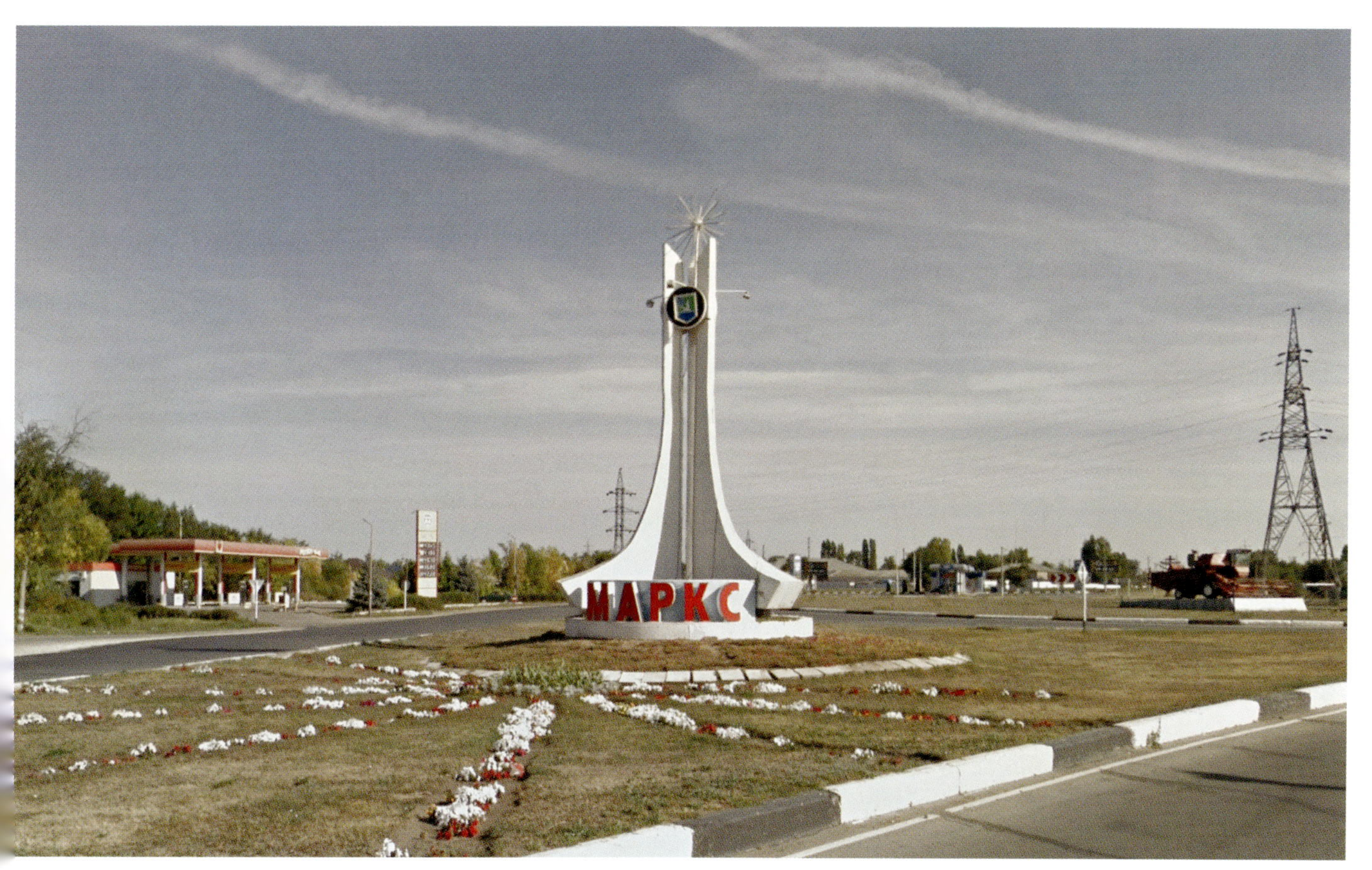

MARX, RUSSIA

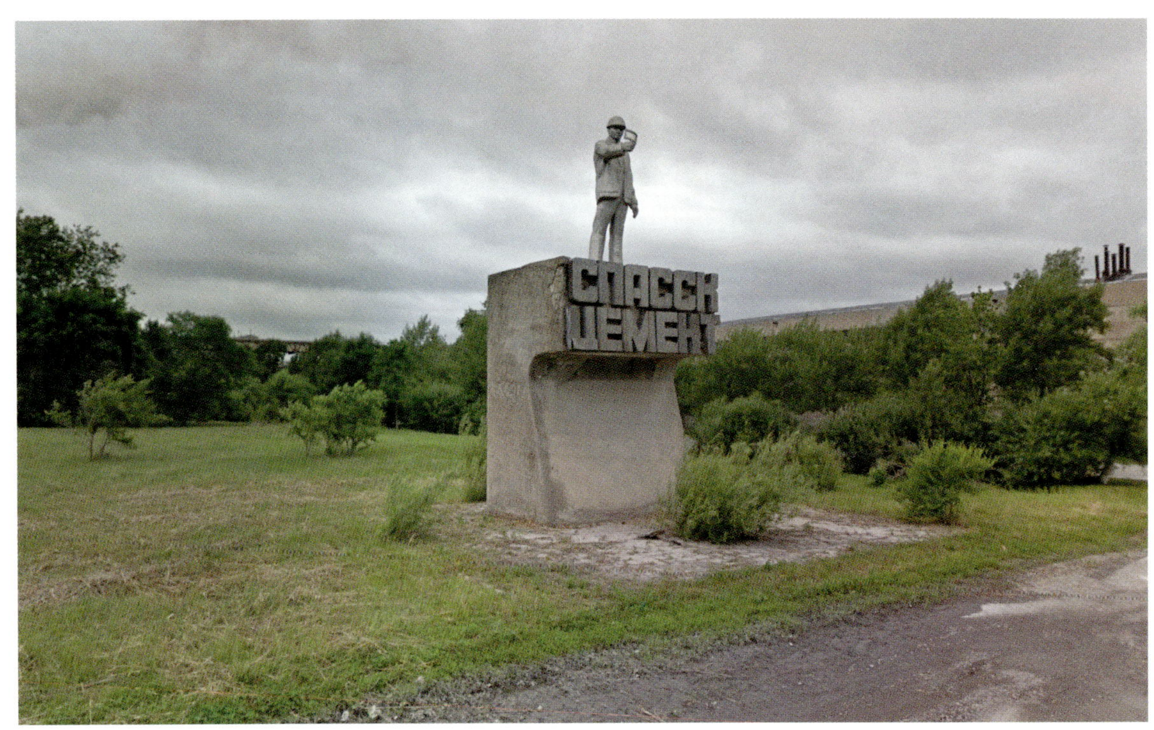

 SPASSK CEMENT, PRIMORSKY KRAI, RUSSIA

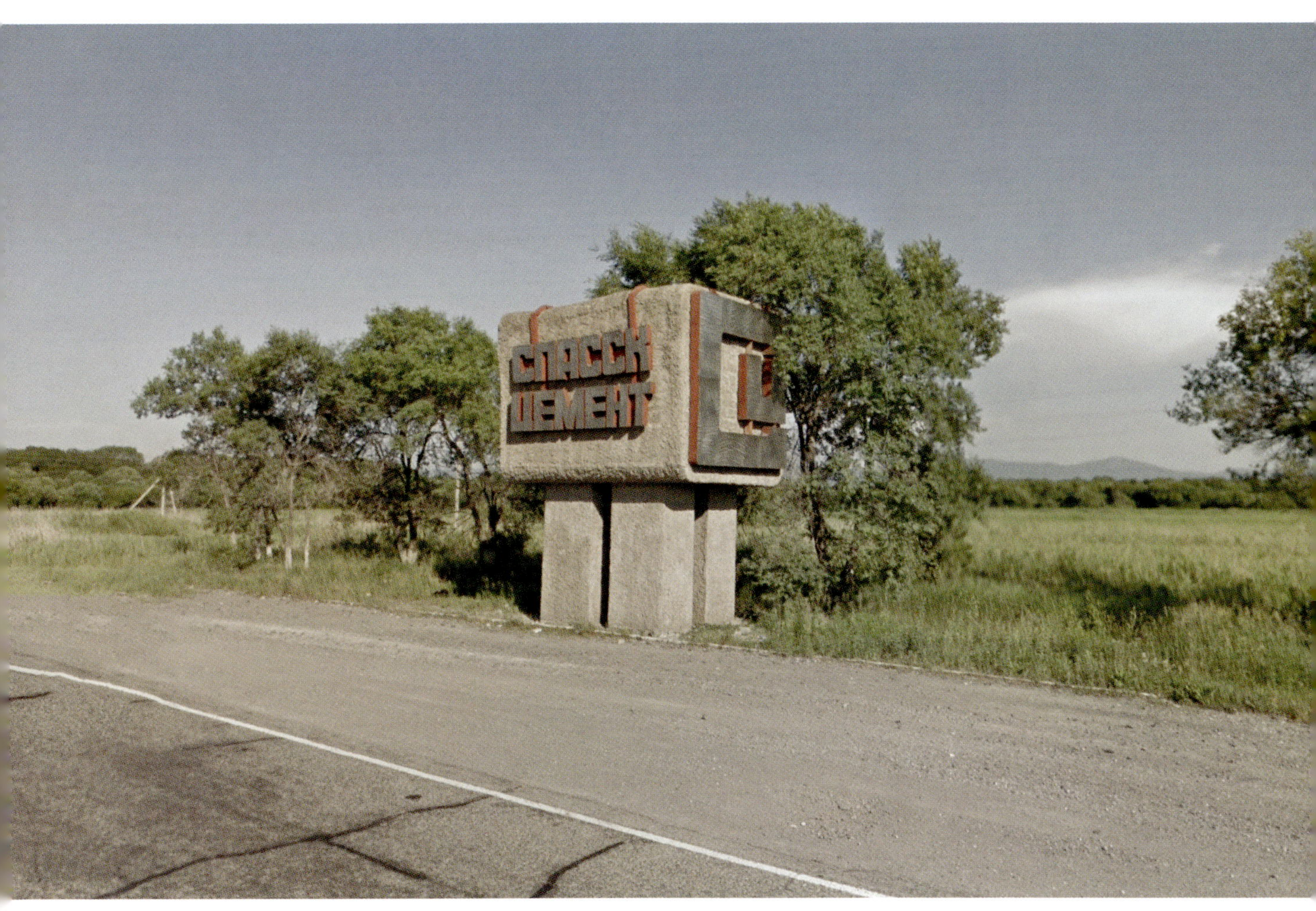

SPASSK CEMENT, PRIMORSKY KRAI, RUSSIA

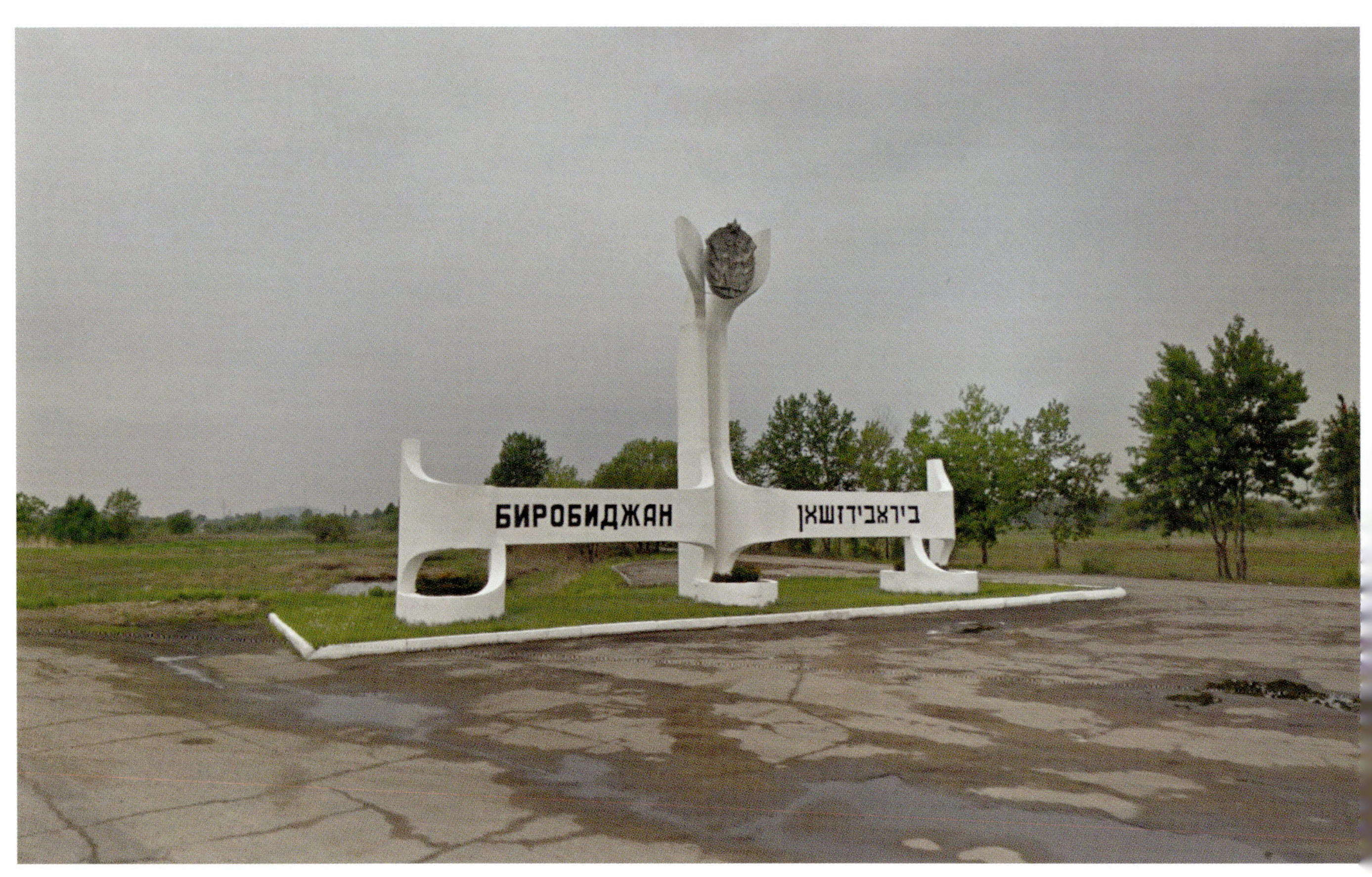

BIROBIDZHAN, RUSSIA

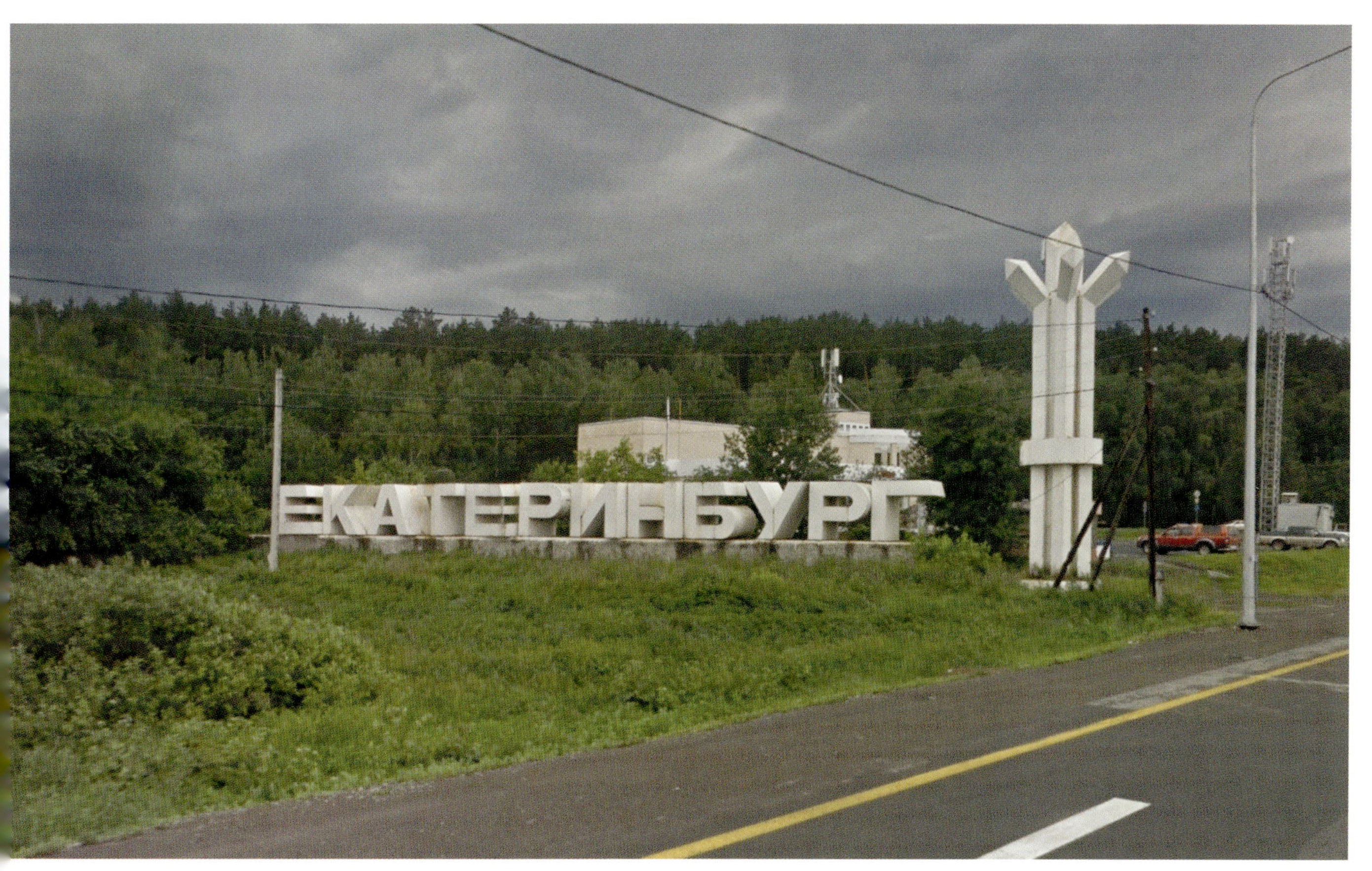
ЕКАТЕРИНБУРГ

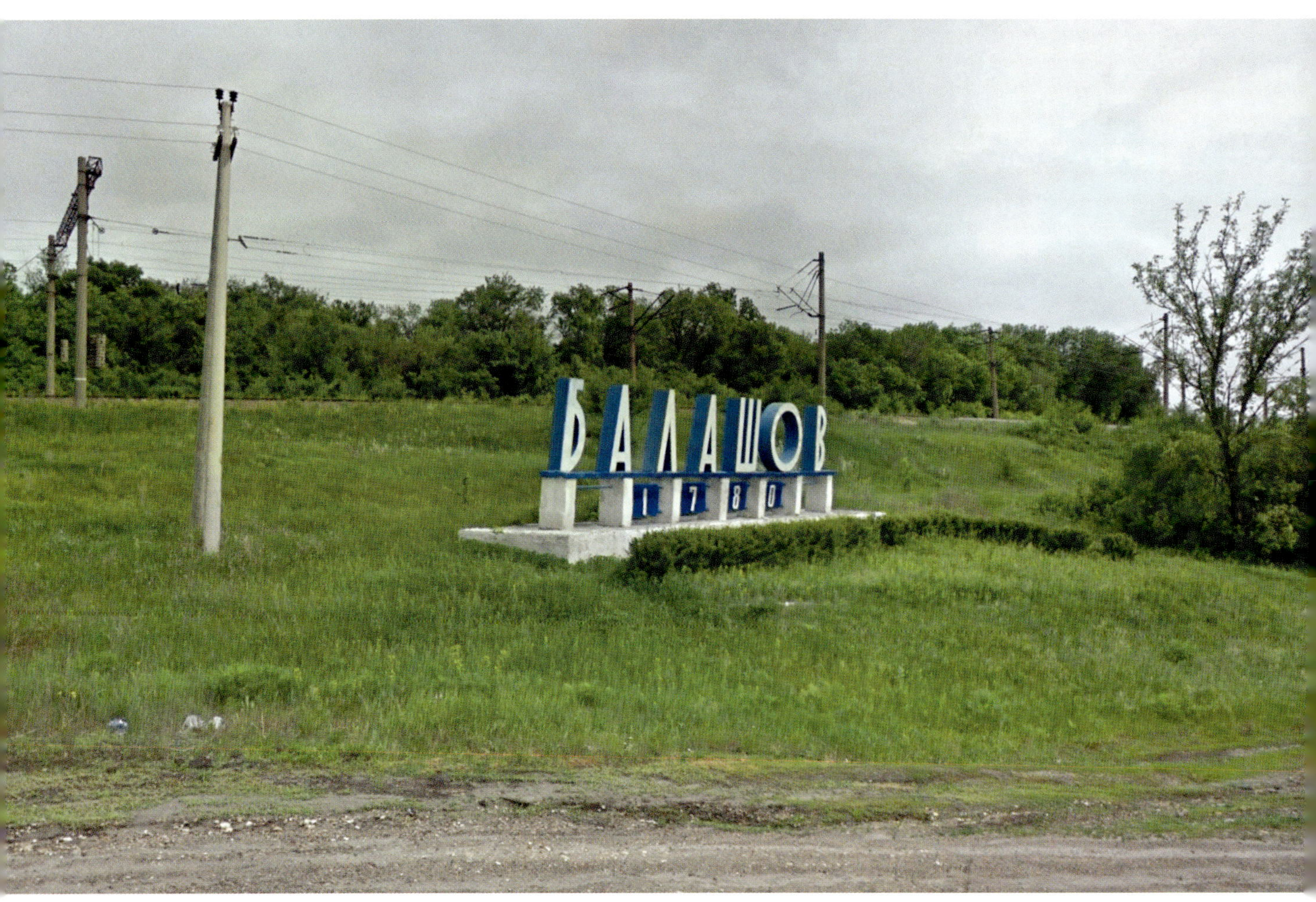

 BALASHOV, RUSSIA

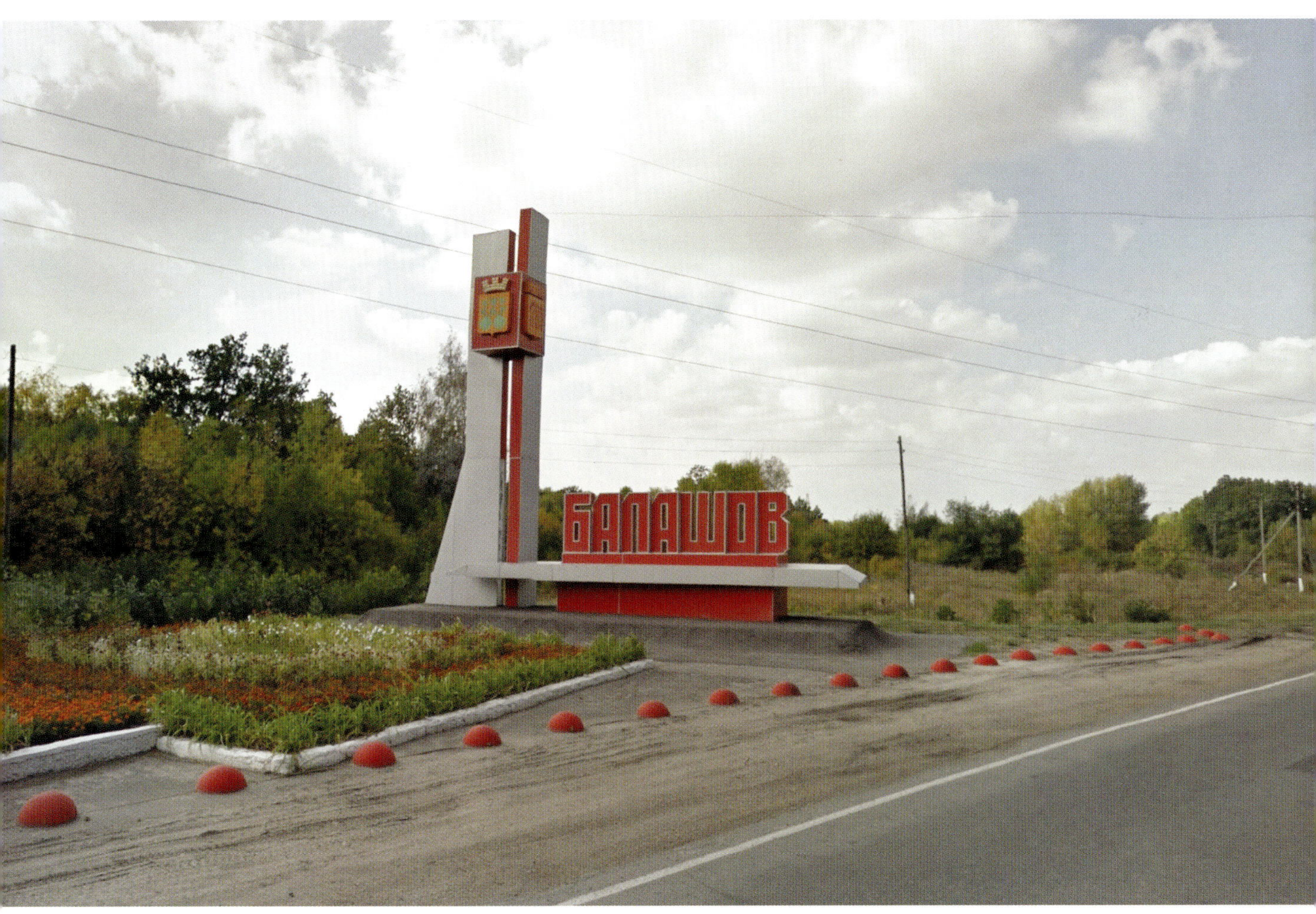

BALASHOV, RUSSIA

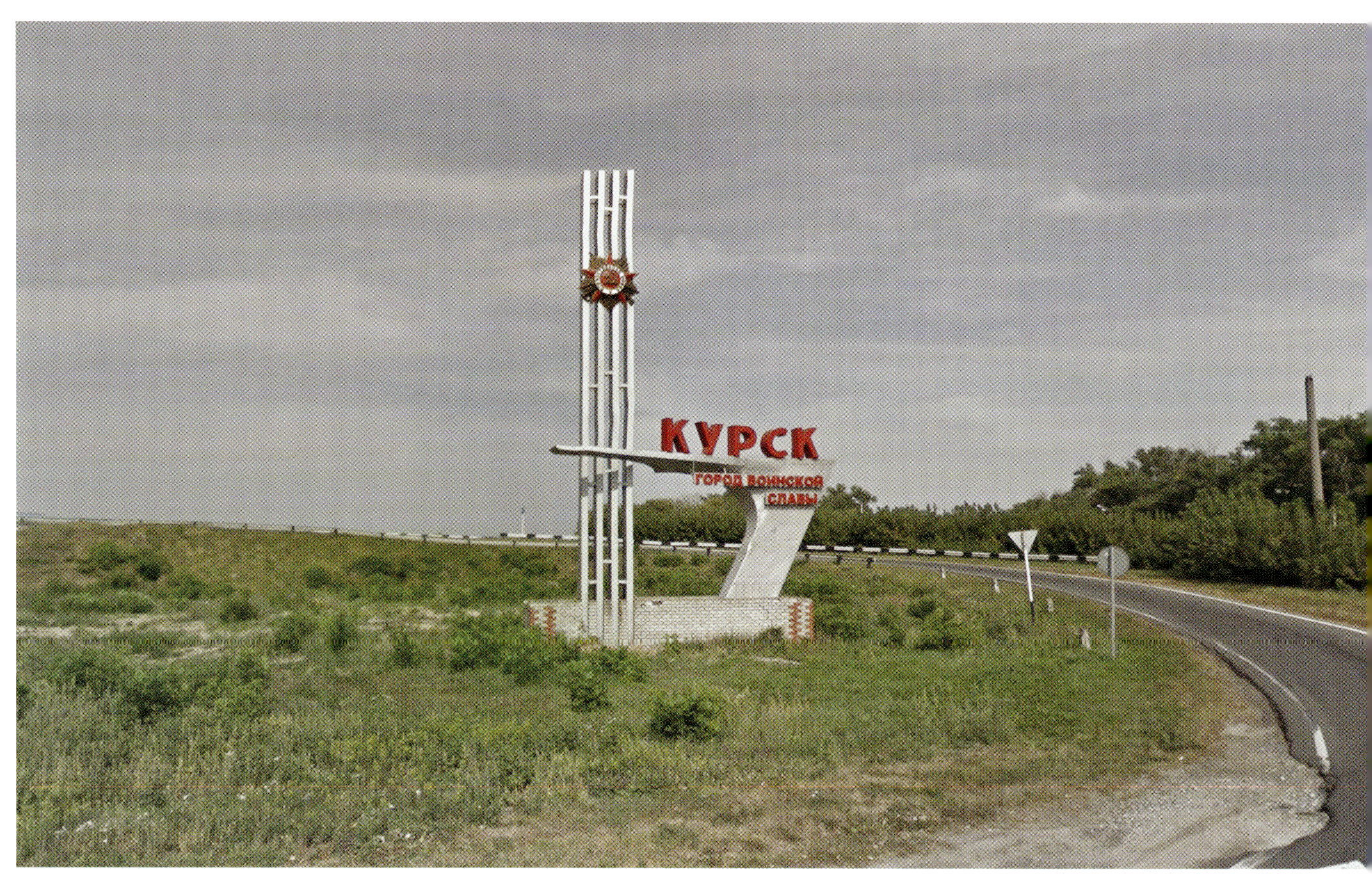

 KURSK, RUSSIA

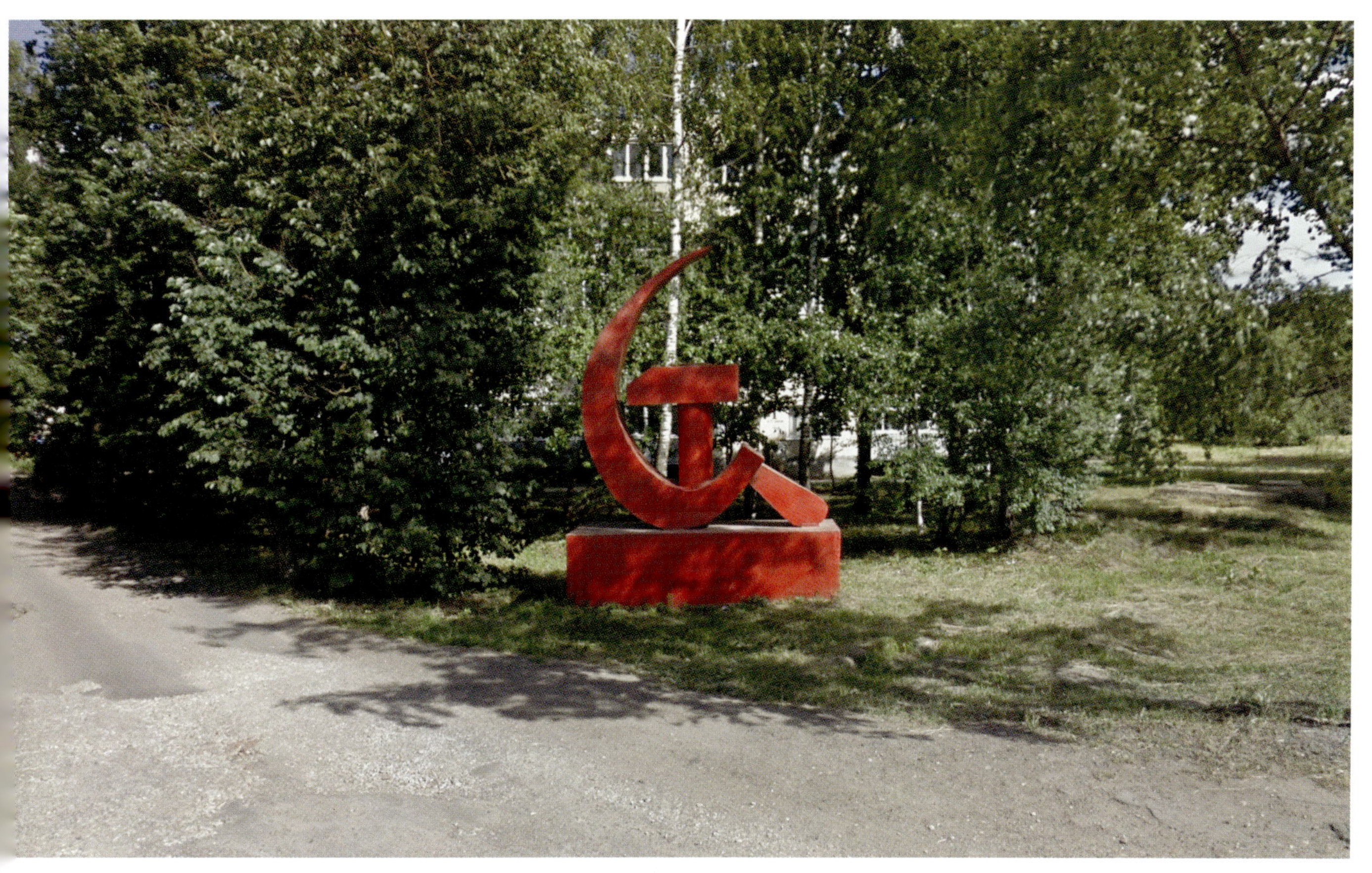

SAINT PETERSBURG, RUSSIA

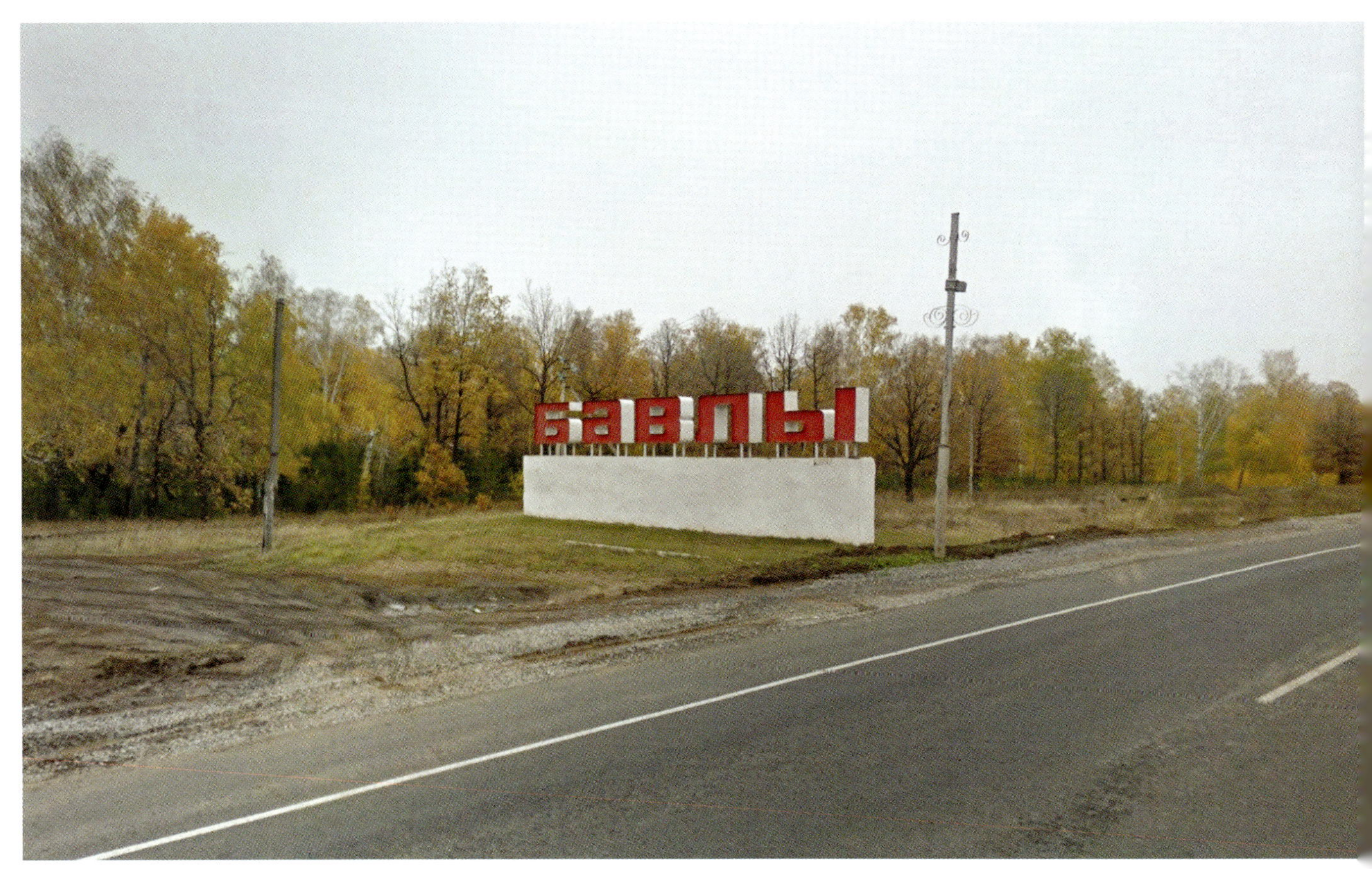

 BAVLY, RUSSIA

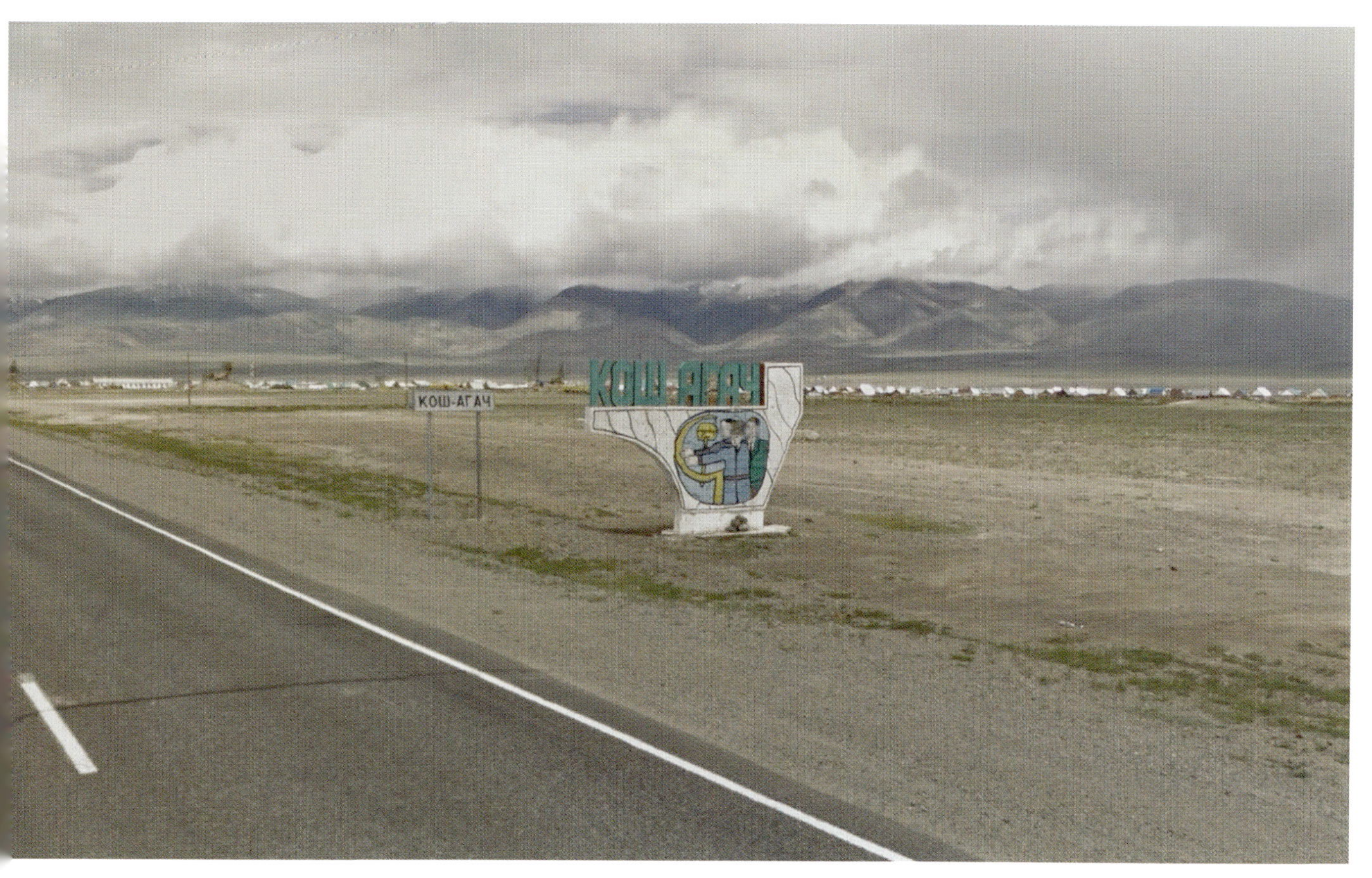

KOSH-AGACH, RUSSIA

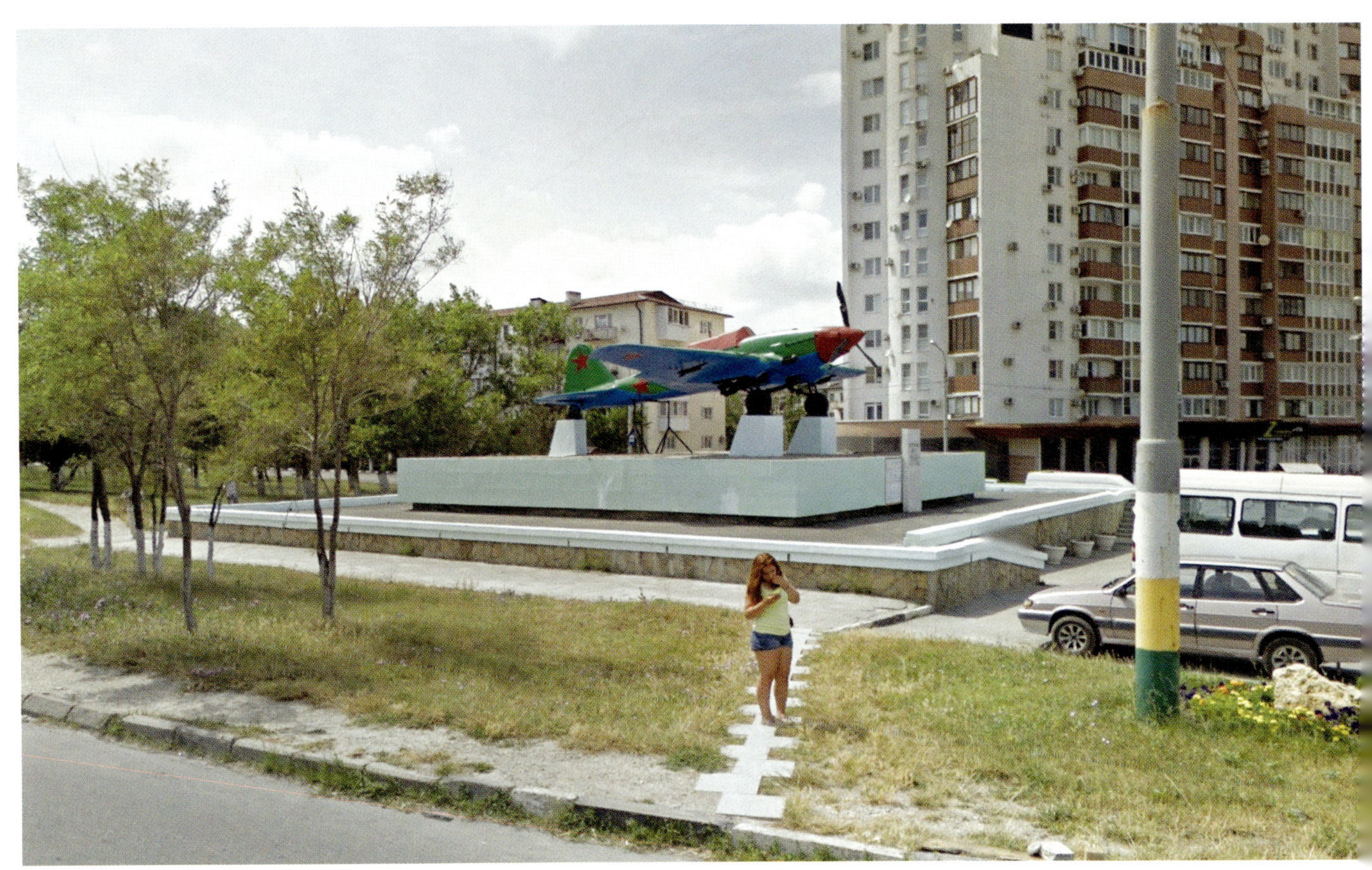

 NOVOSIBIRSK, RUSSIA

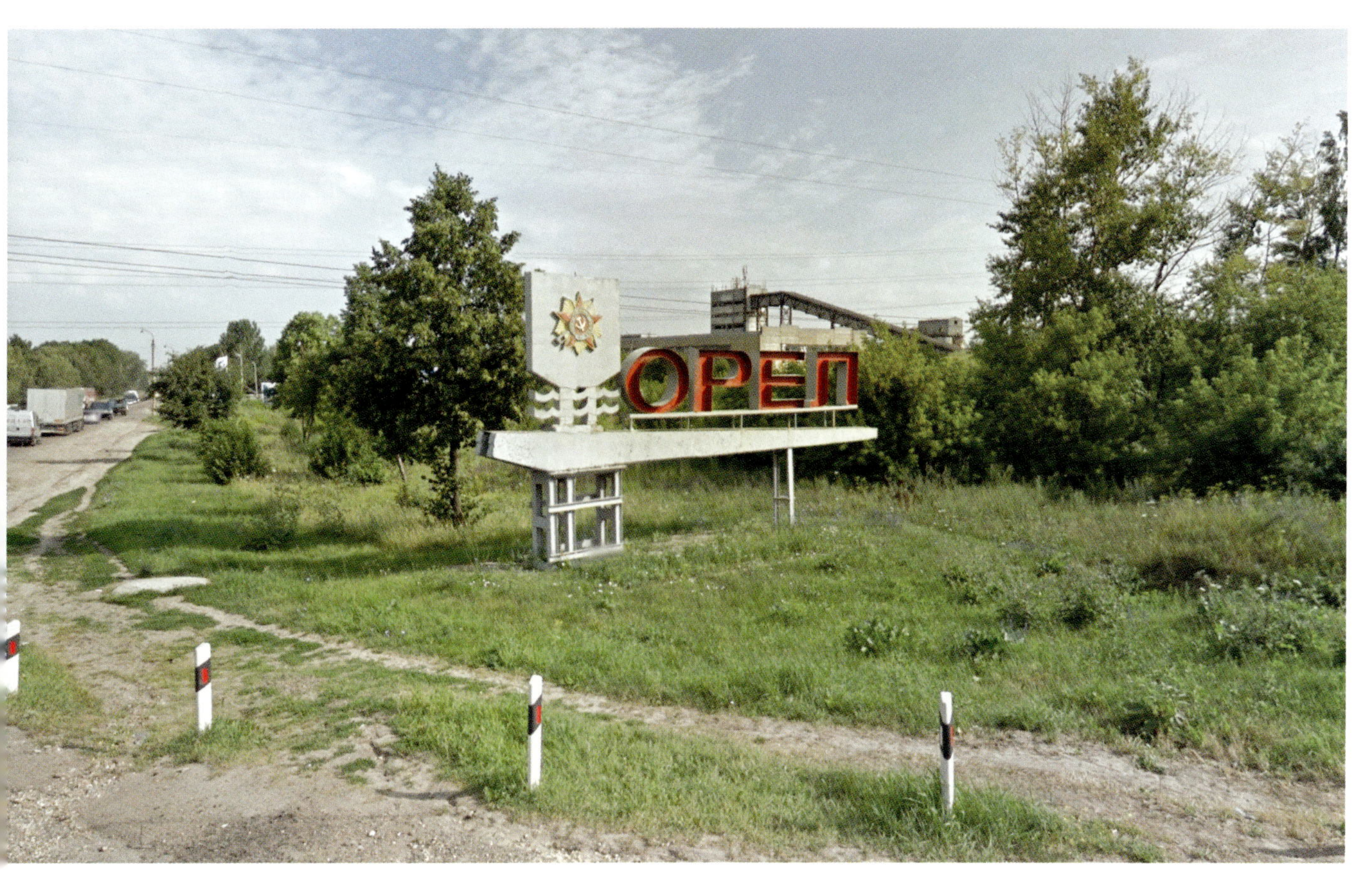

ORYOL, RUSSIA

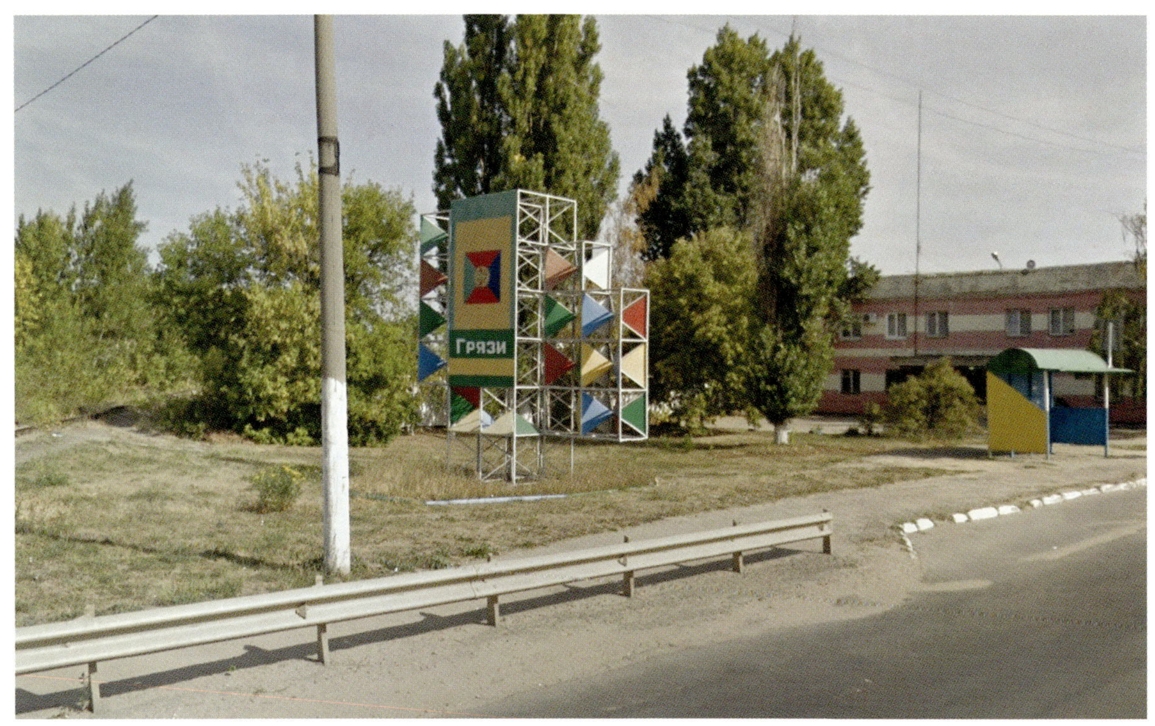

 GRYAZI, RUSSIA

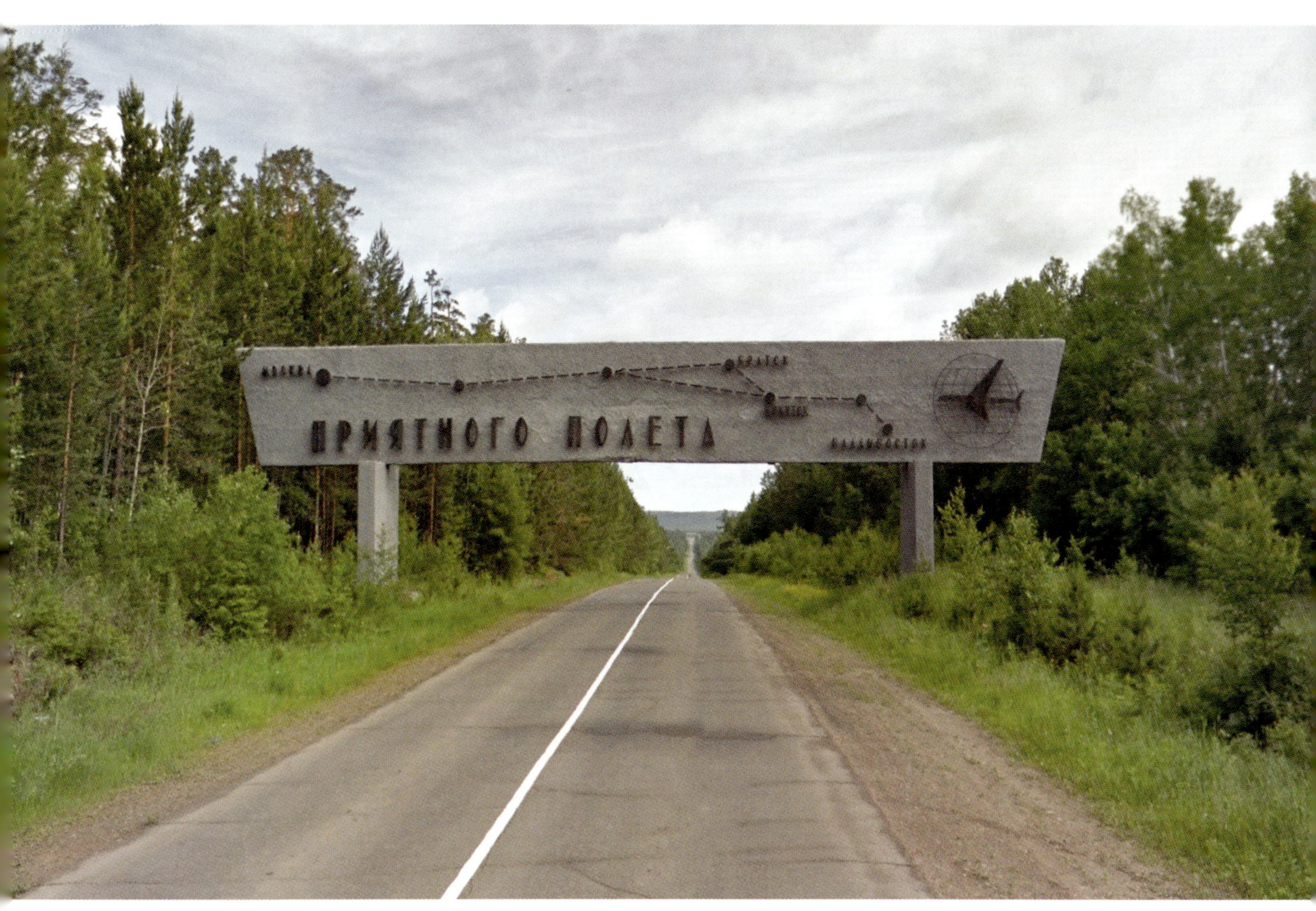

BRATSK, RUSSIA

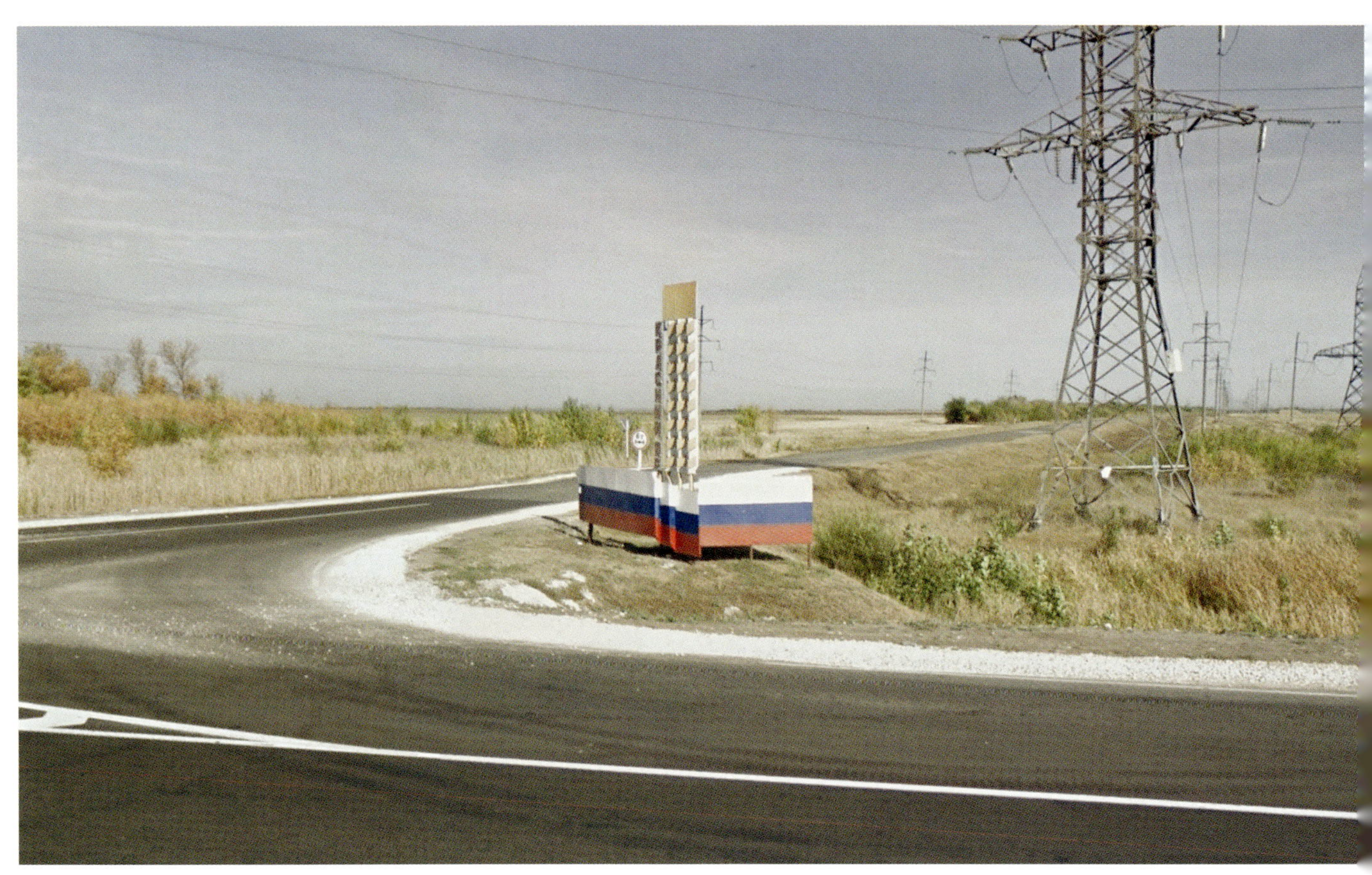

 VOLGOGRAD OBLAST, RUSSIA

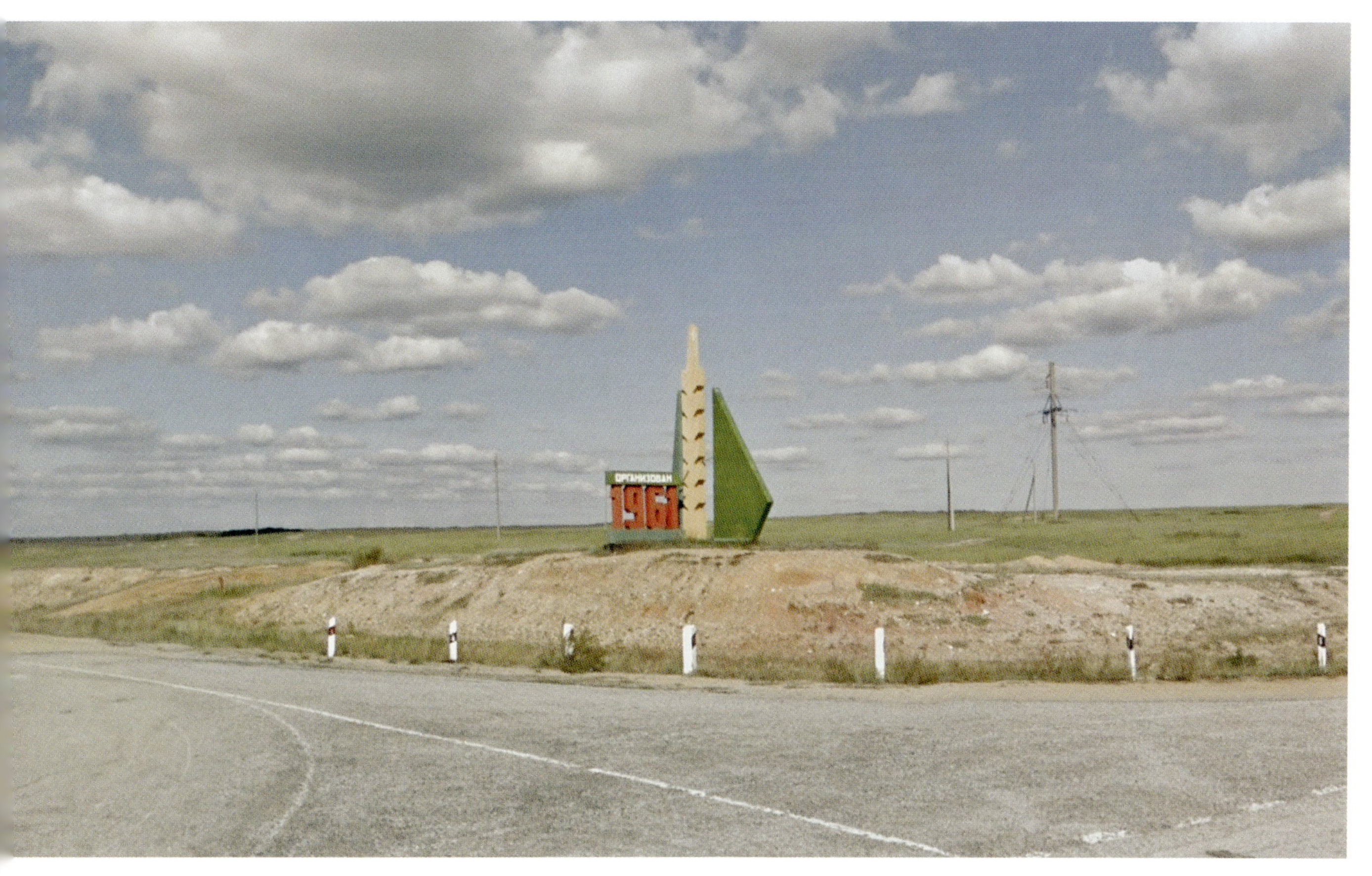

CHELYABINSK OBLAST, RUSSIA

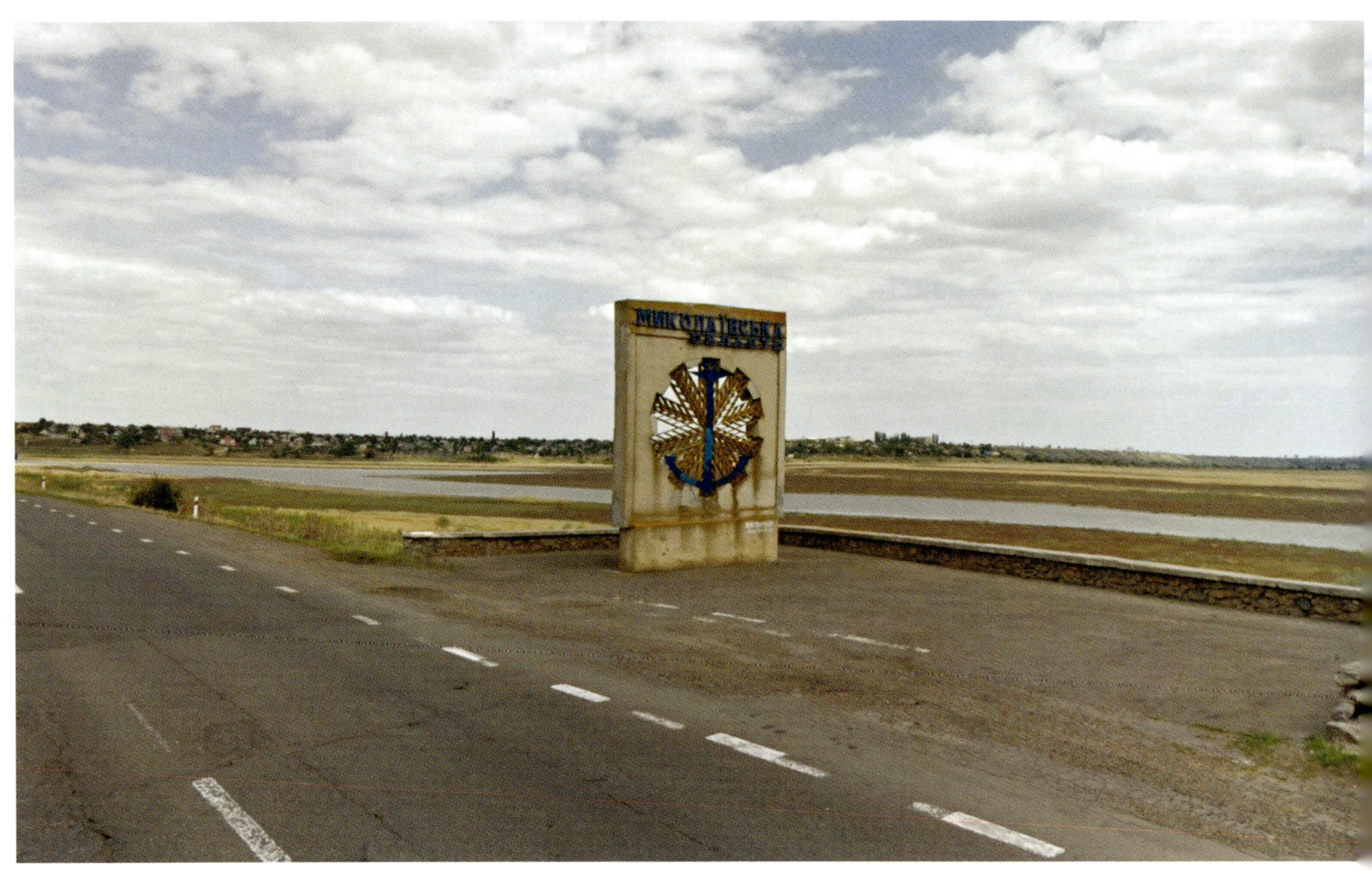

 MYKOLAIV OBLAST, UKRAINE

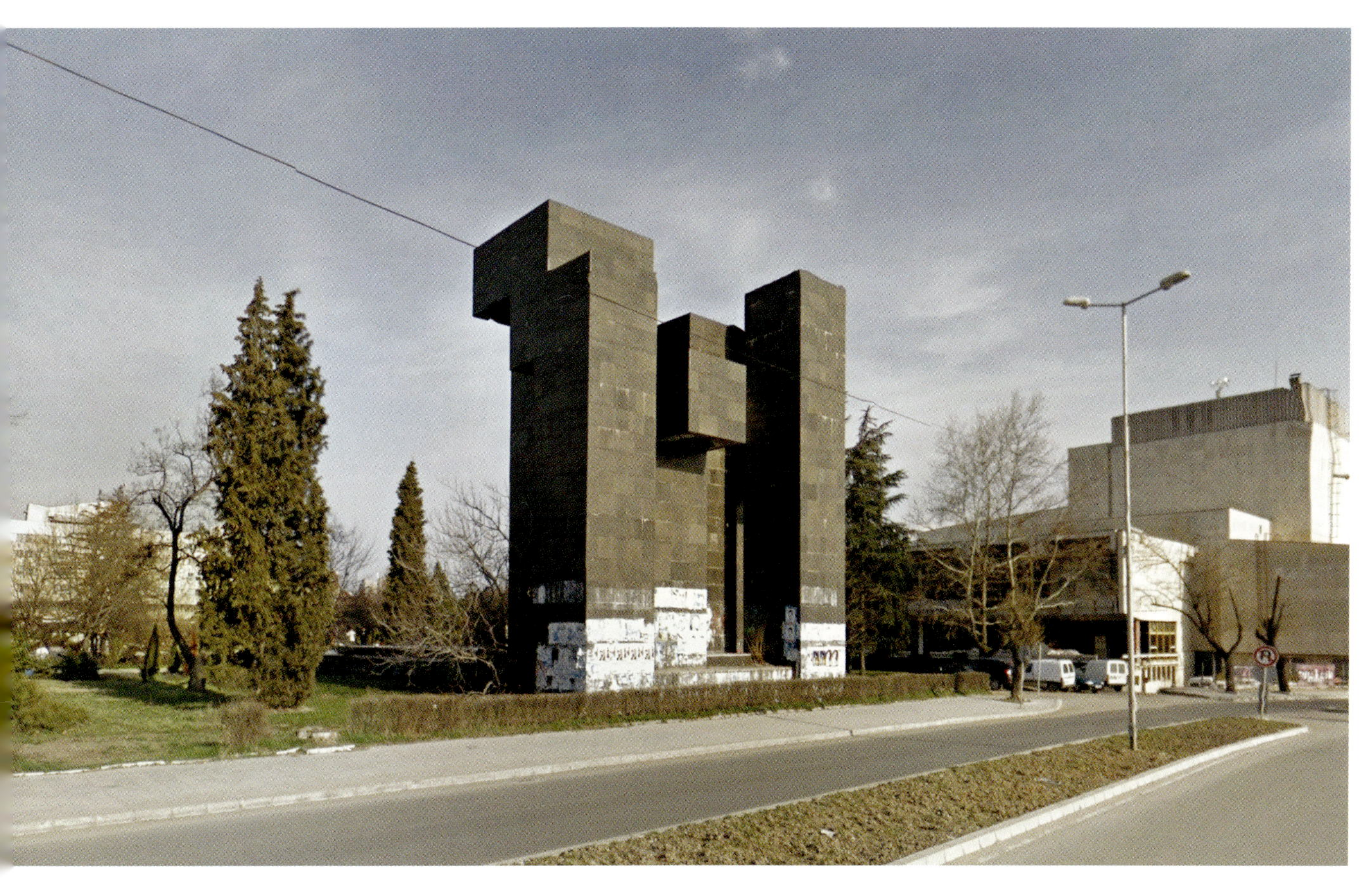

KARDZHALI, BULGARIA

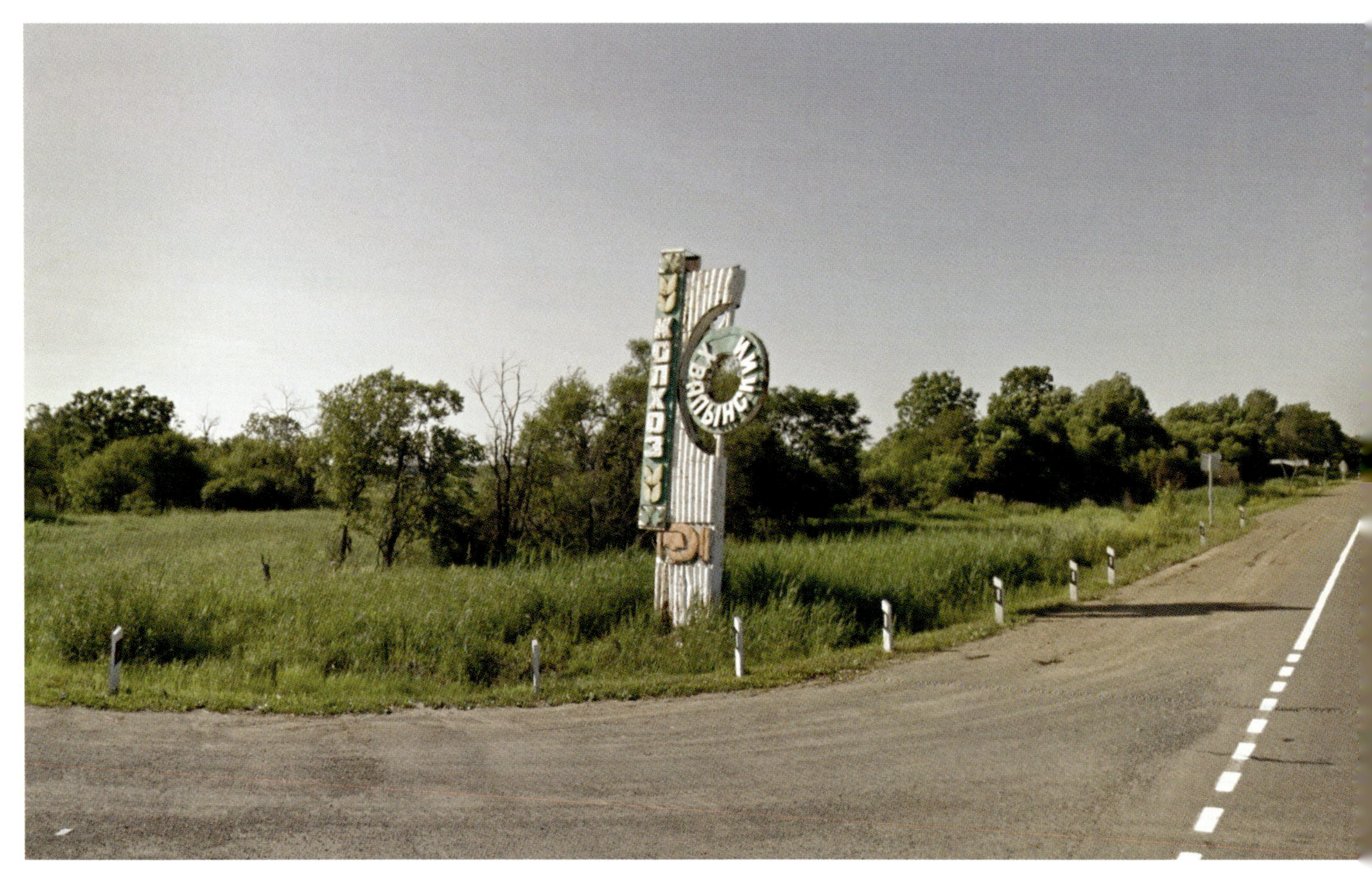

KHVALYNSK COLLECTIVE FARM, PRIMORSKY KRAI, RUSSIA

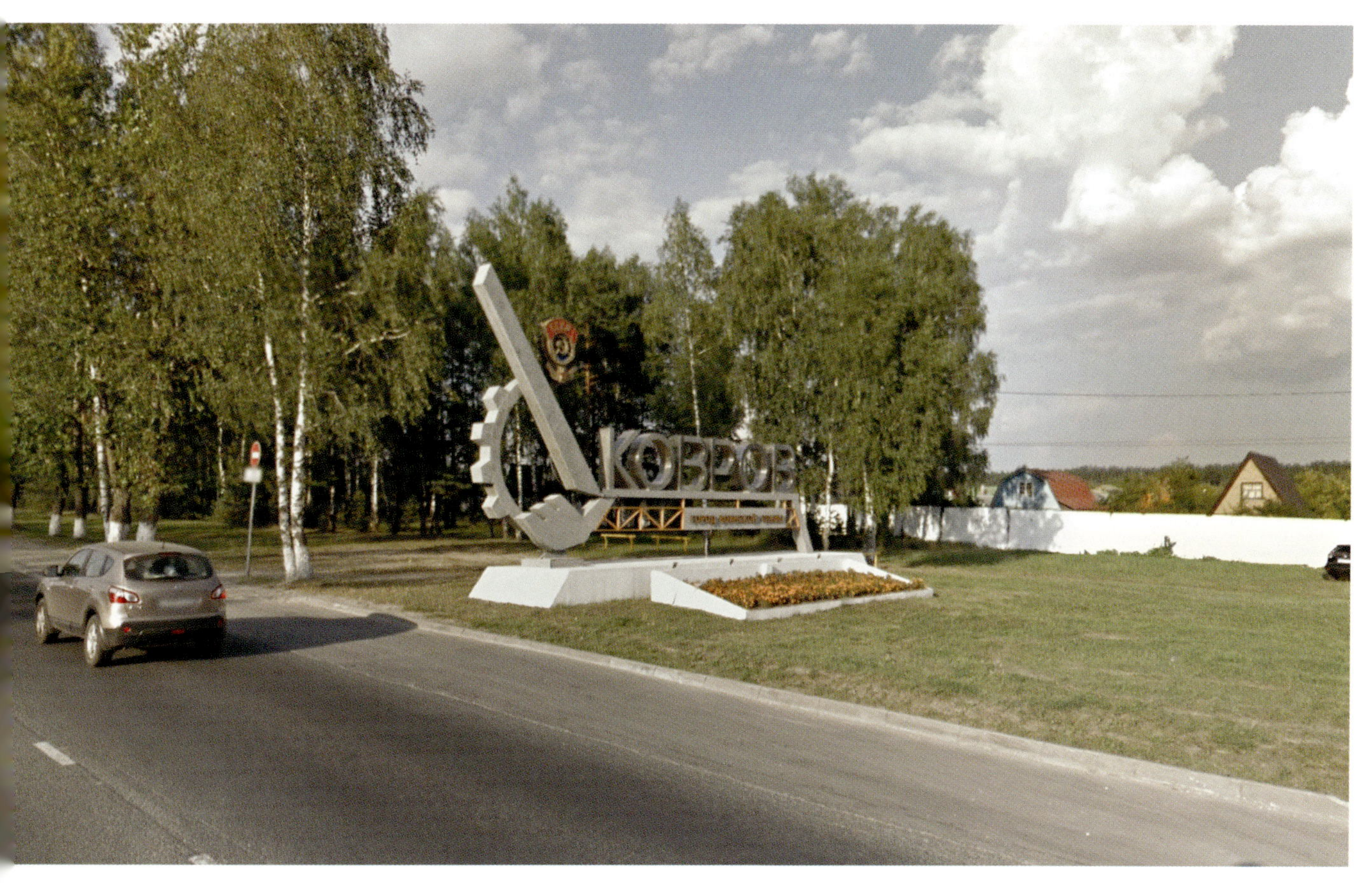

KOVROV, RUSSIA

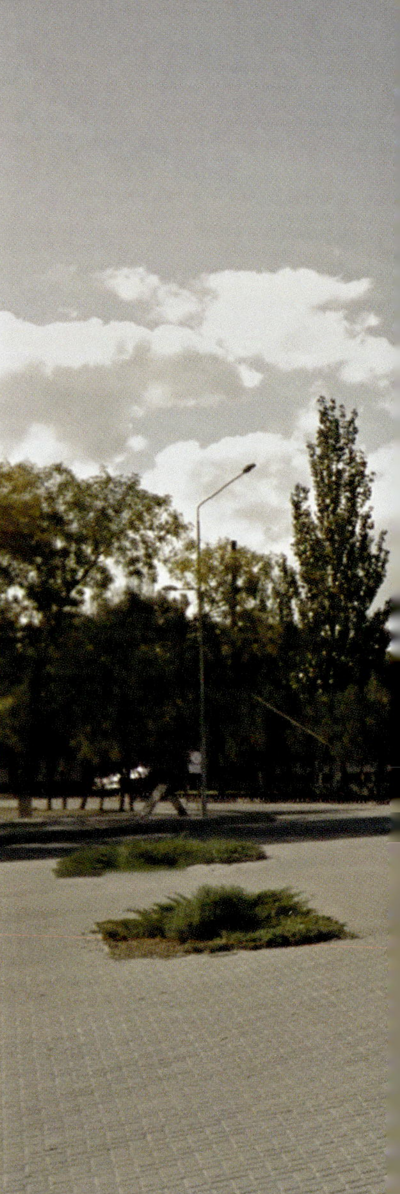

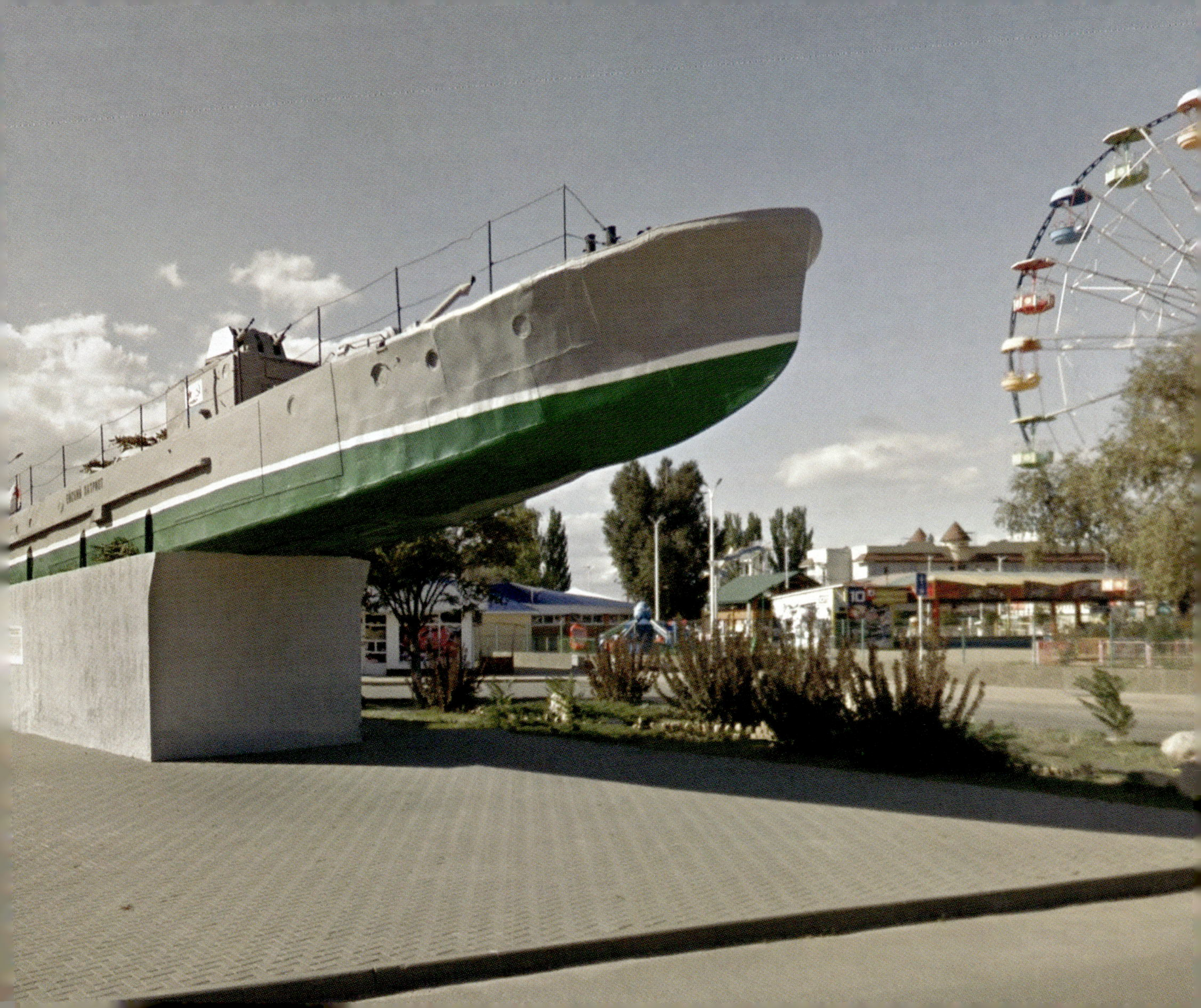

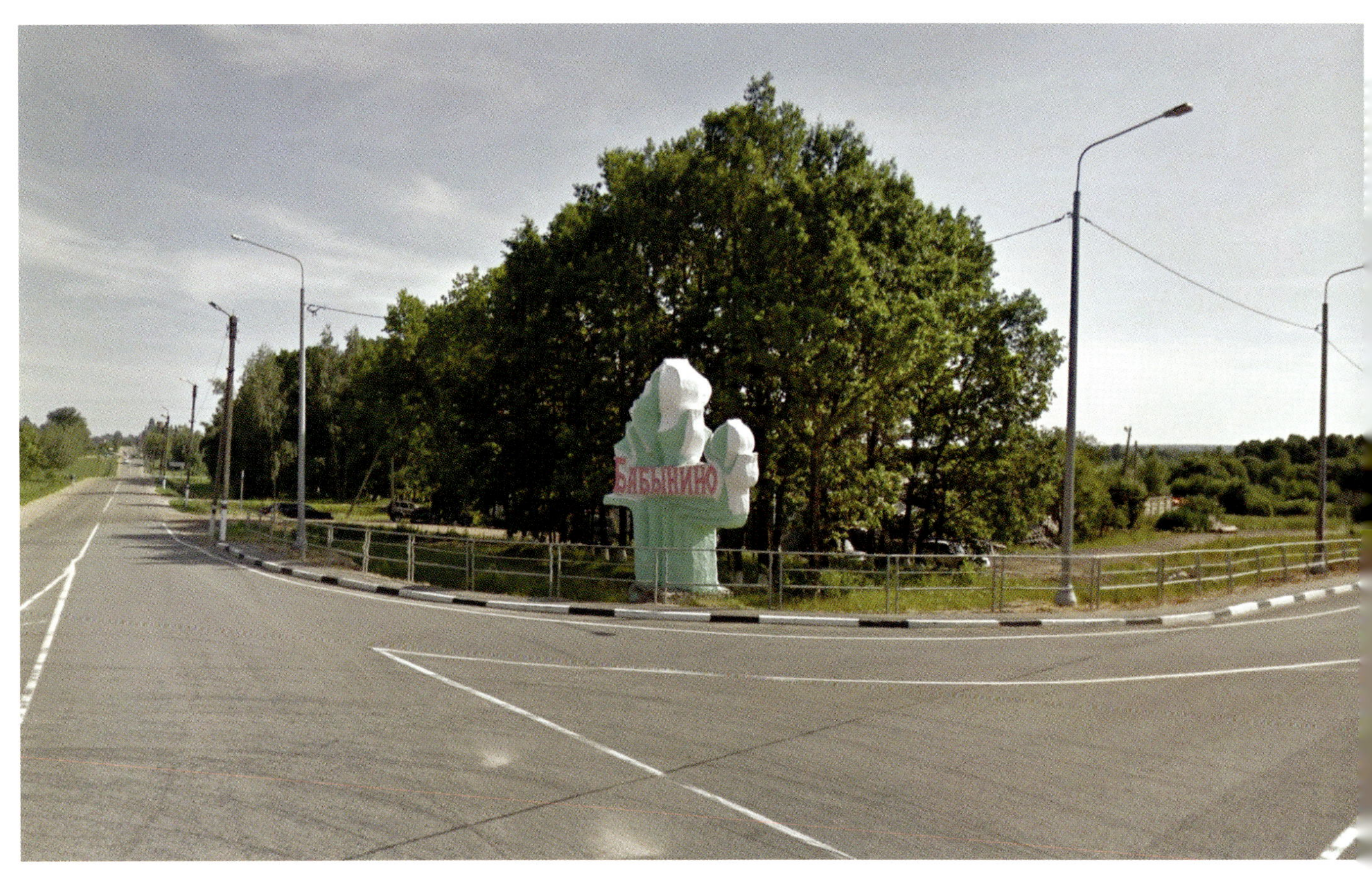

BABYNINO, RUSSIA

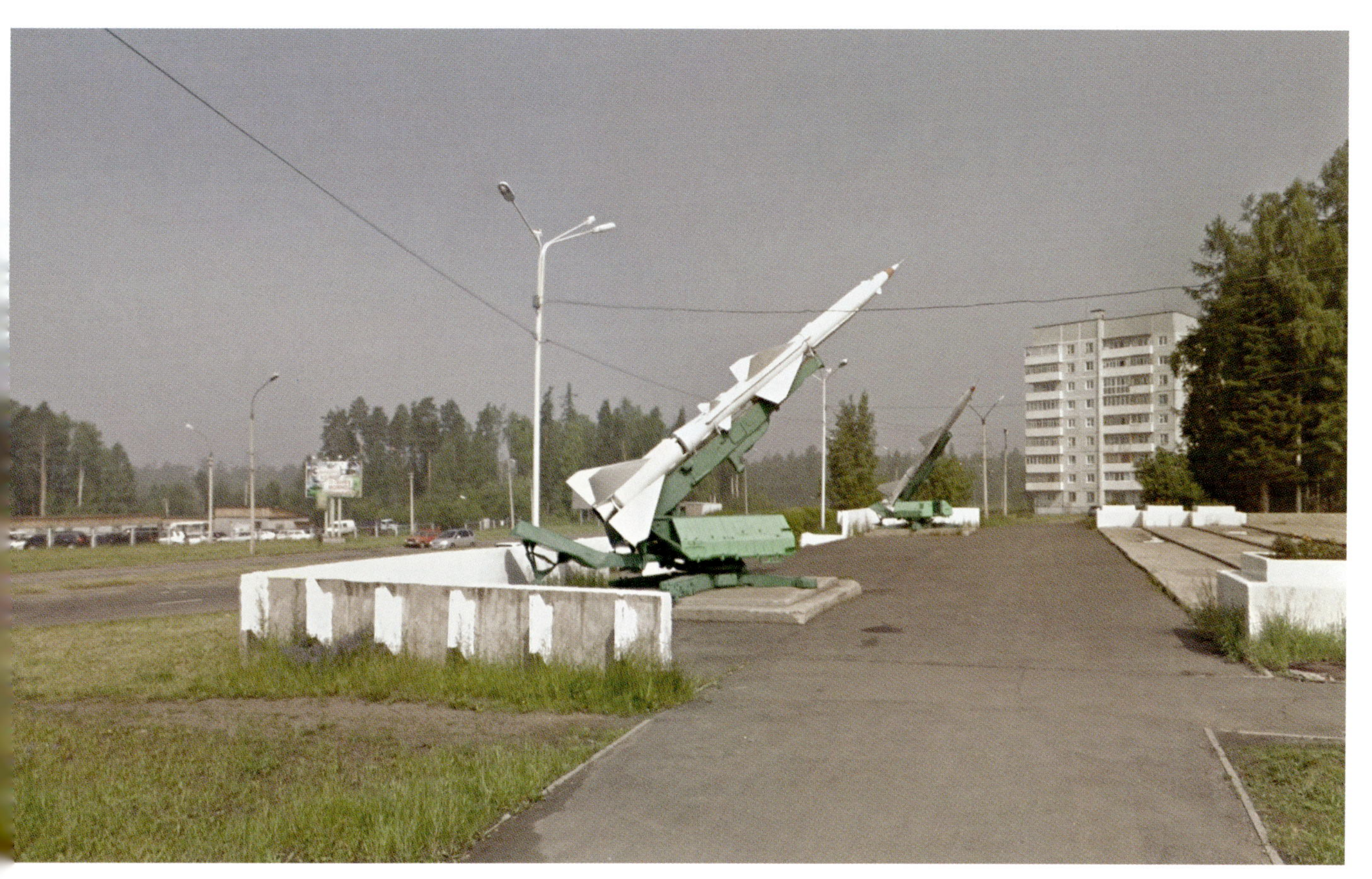

UST-ILIMSK, RUSSIA

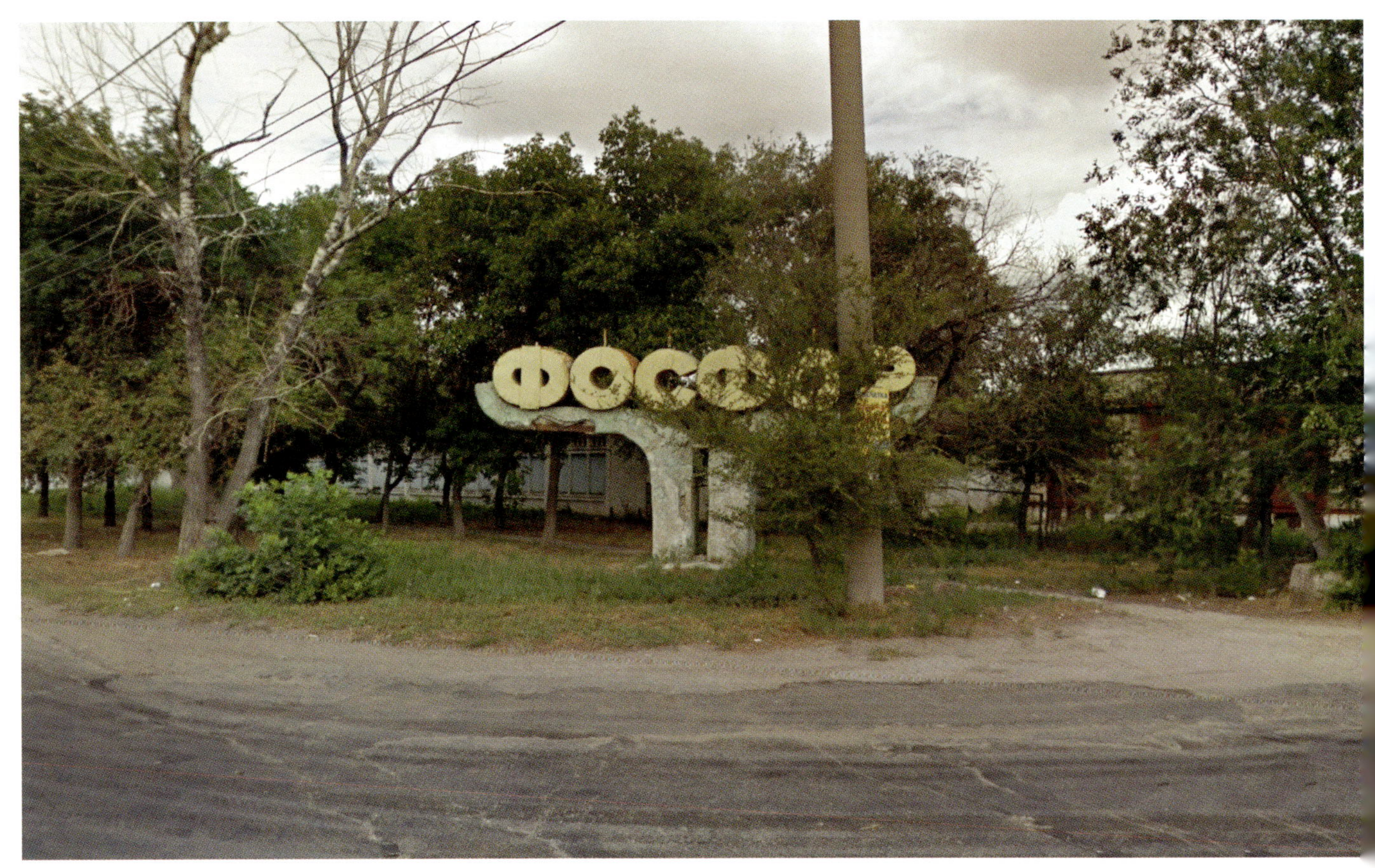

TOLYATTI, RUSSIA

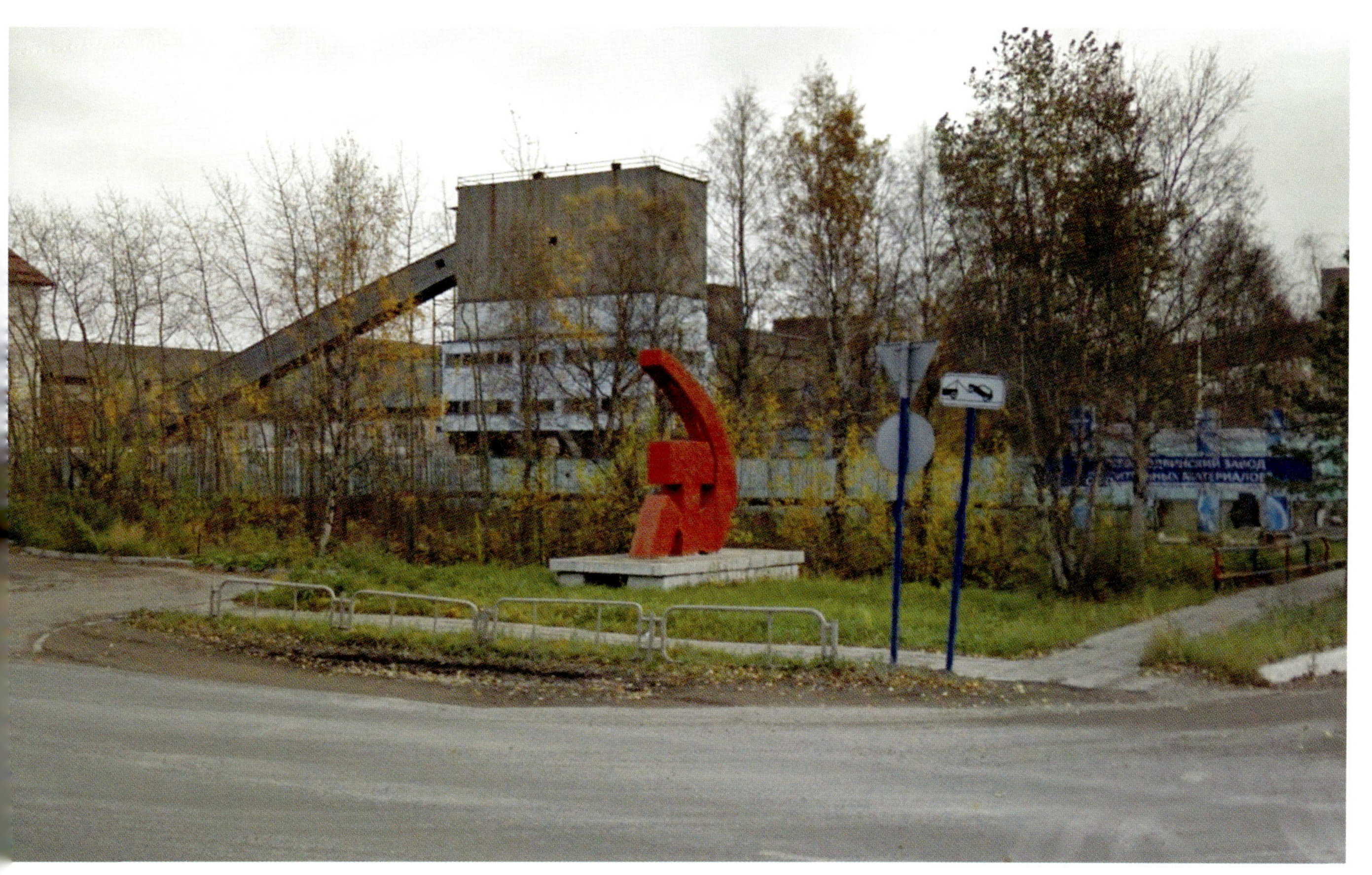

SEVERODVINSK, RUSSIA

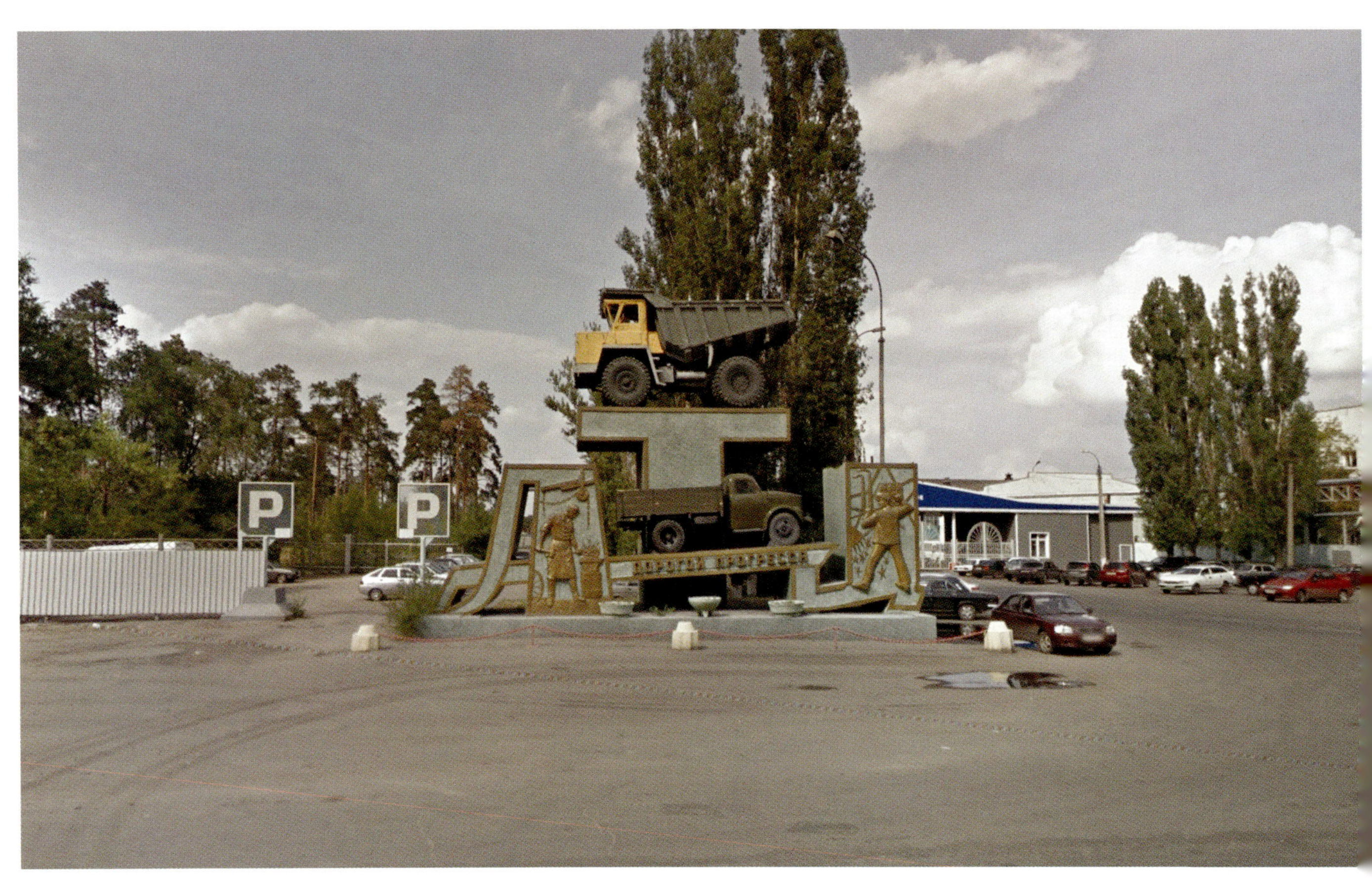

LIPETSK, RUSSIA

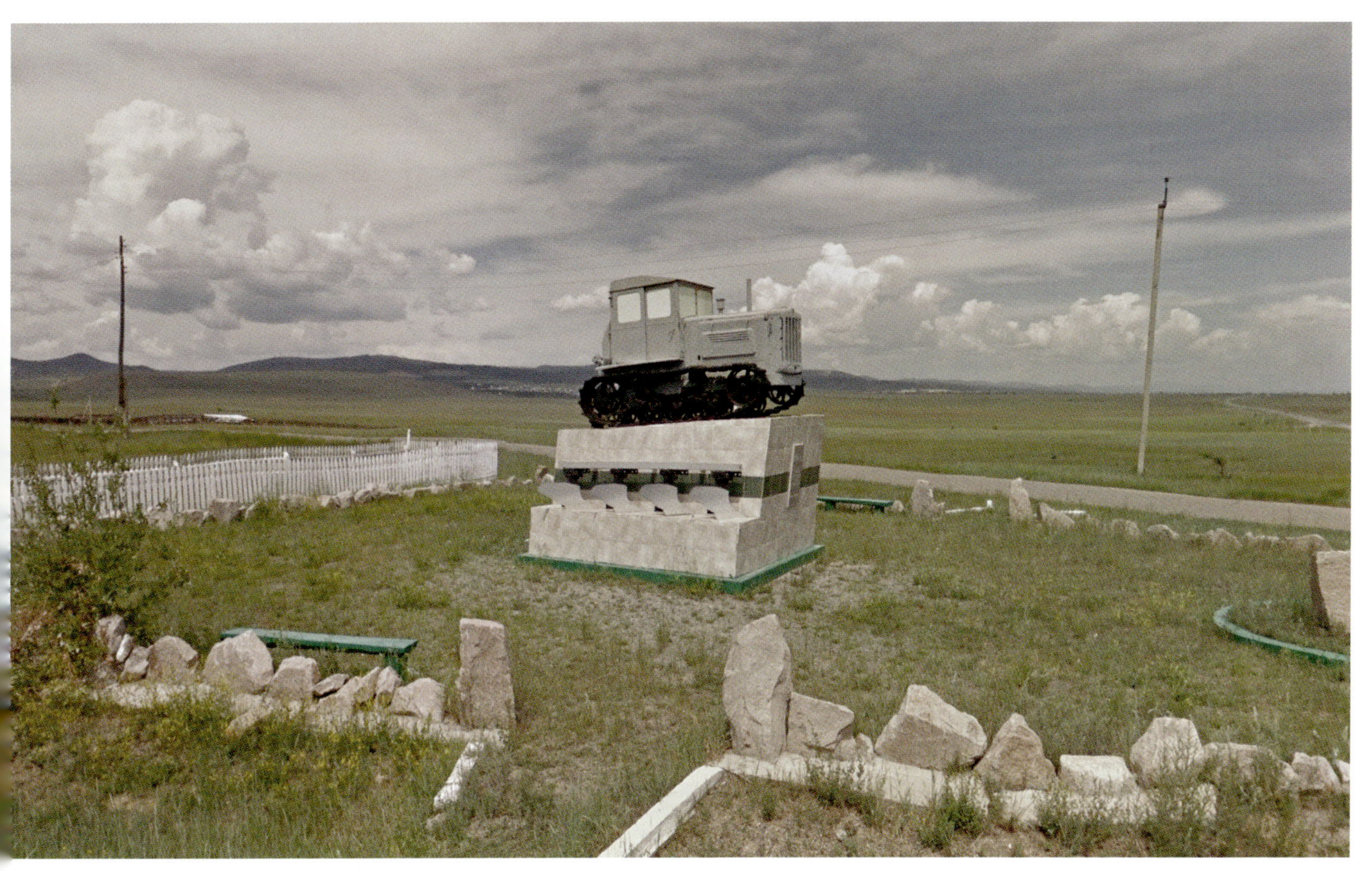

ZABAYKALSKY KRAI, RUSSIA

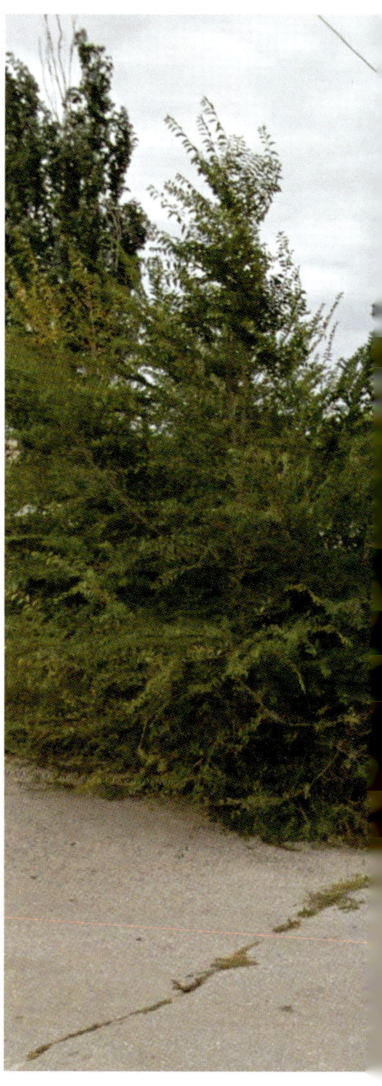

POULTRY FARM OF ARMY No.62, GORODISHCHE, RUSSIA

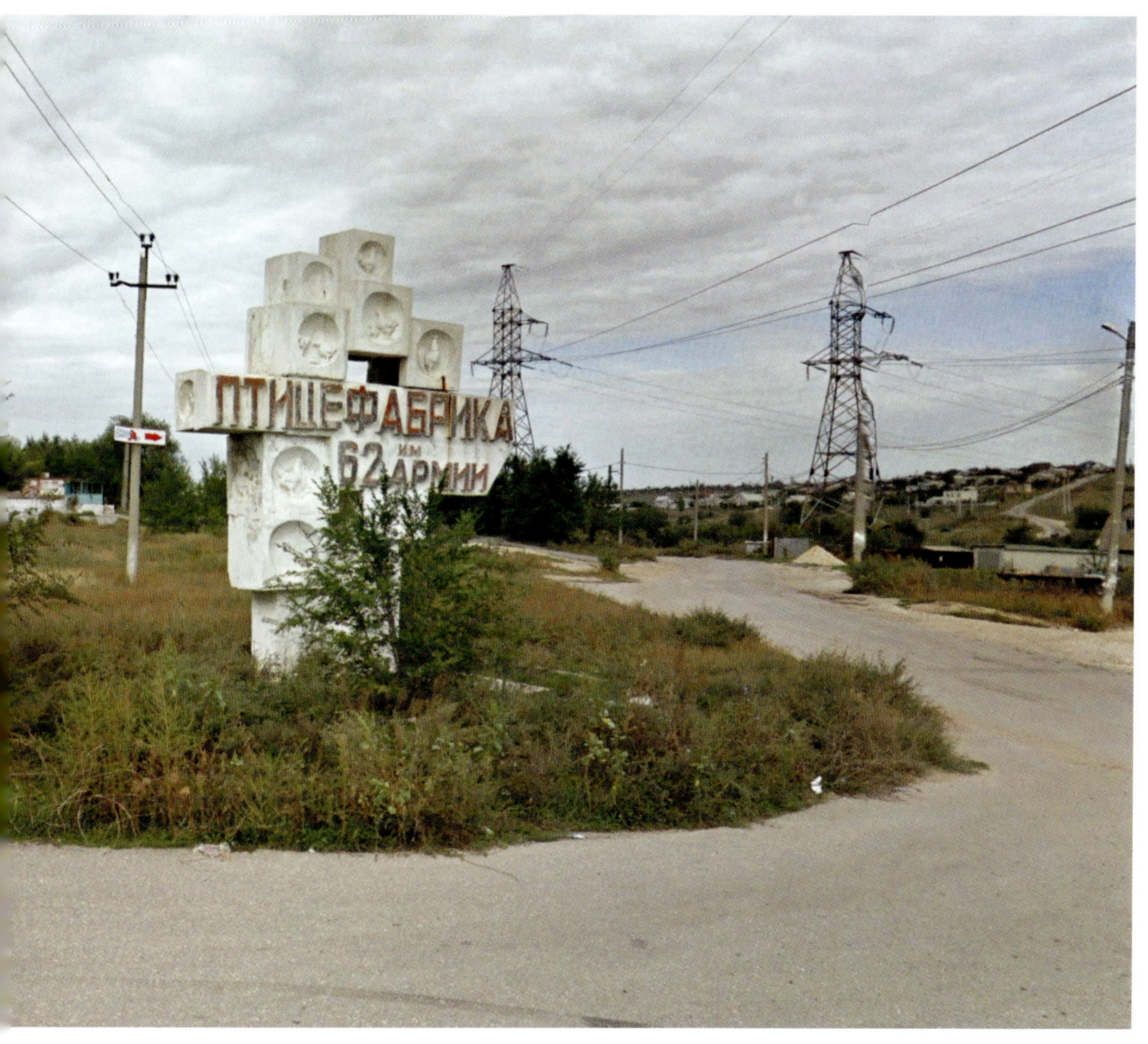
ПТИЦЕФАБРИКА
им
62 АРМИИ

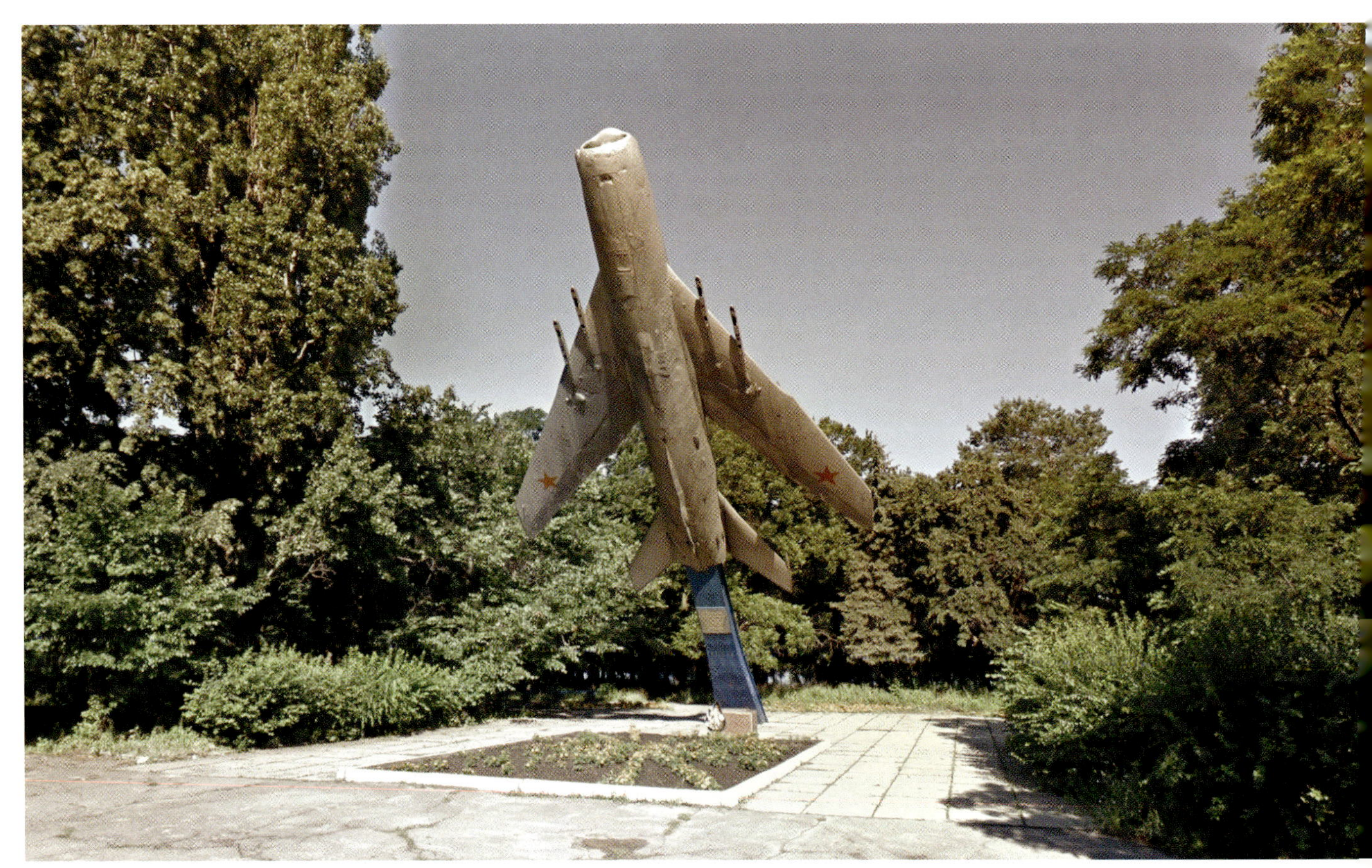

 SVITLOVODSK, UKRAINE

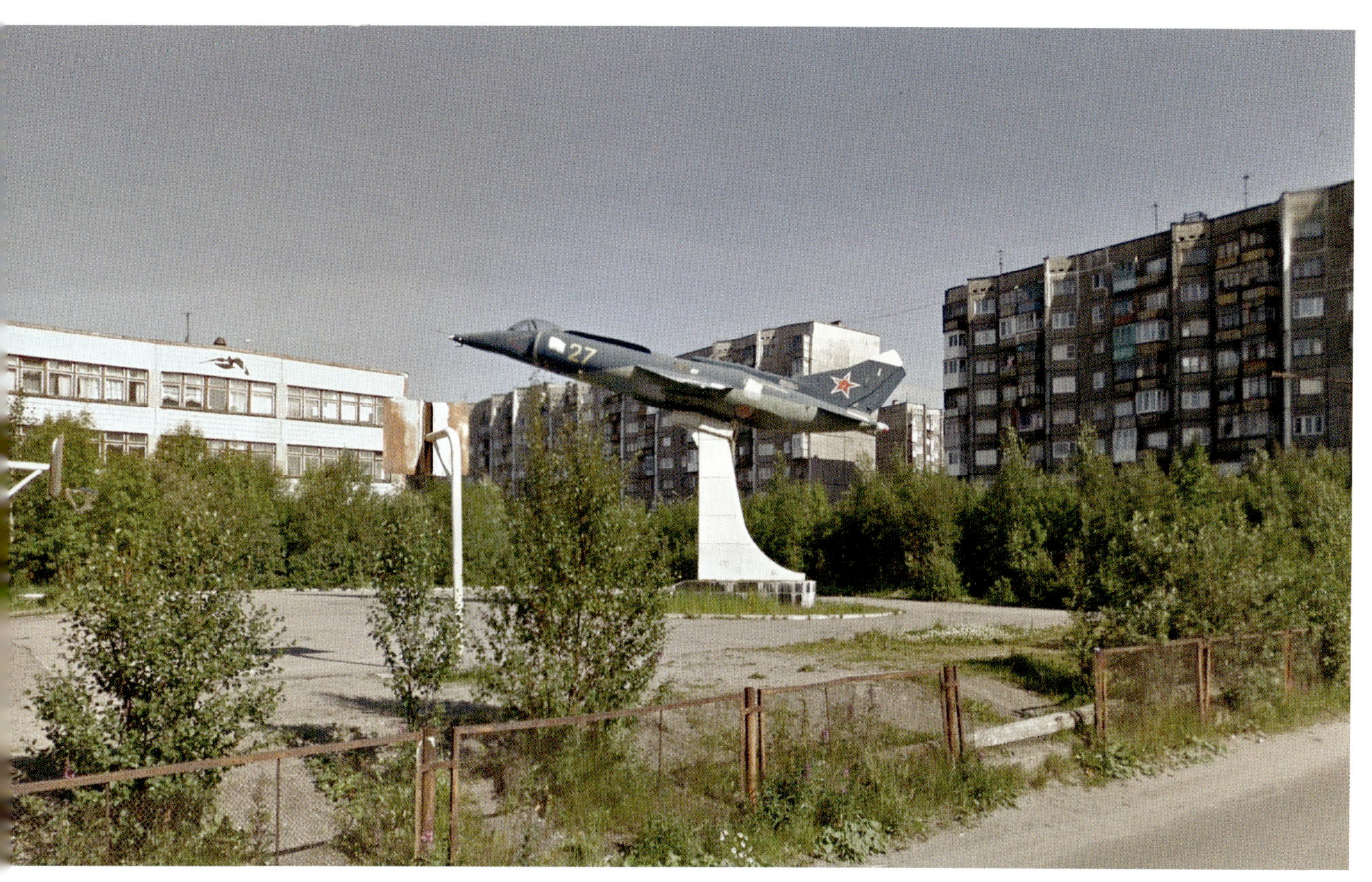

MURMANSK, RUSSIA

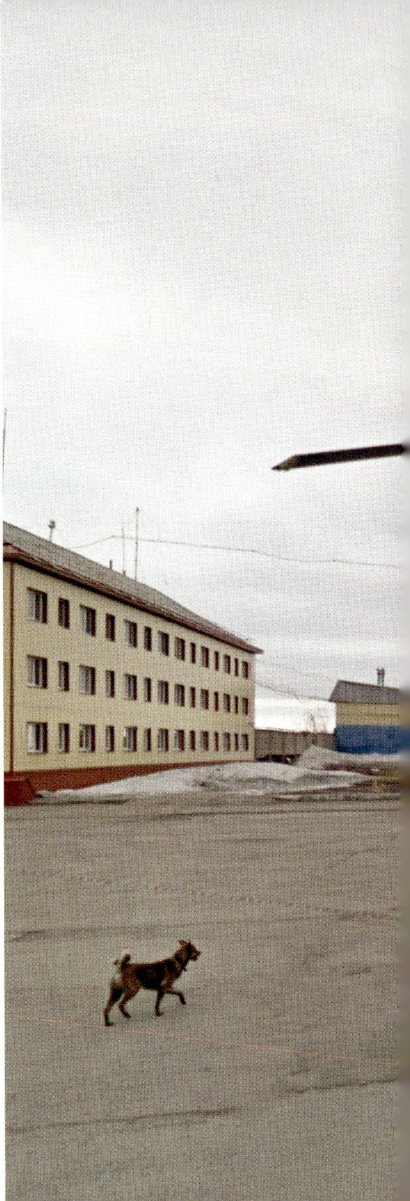

VORKUTA, RUSSIA

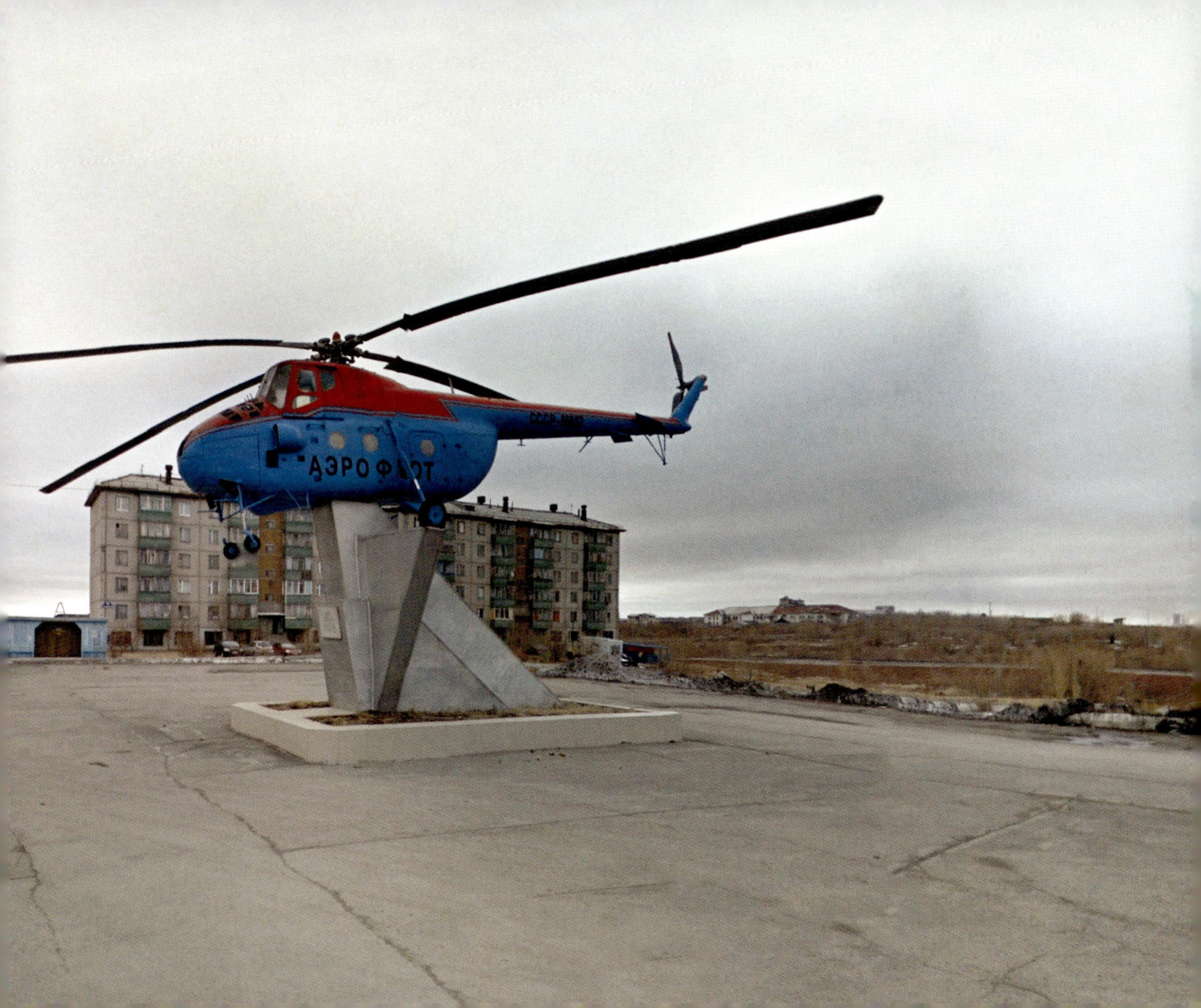

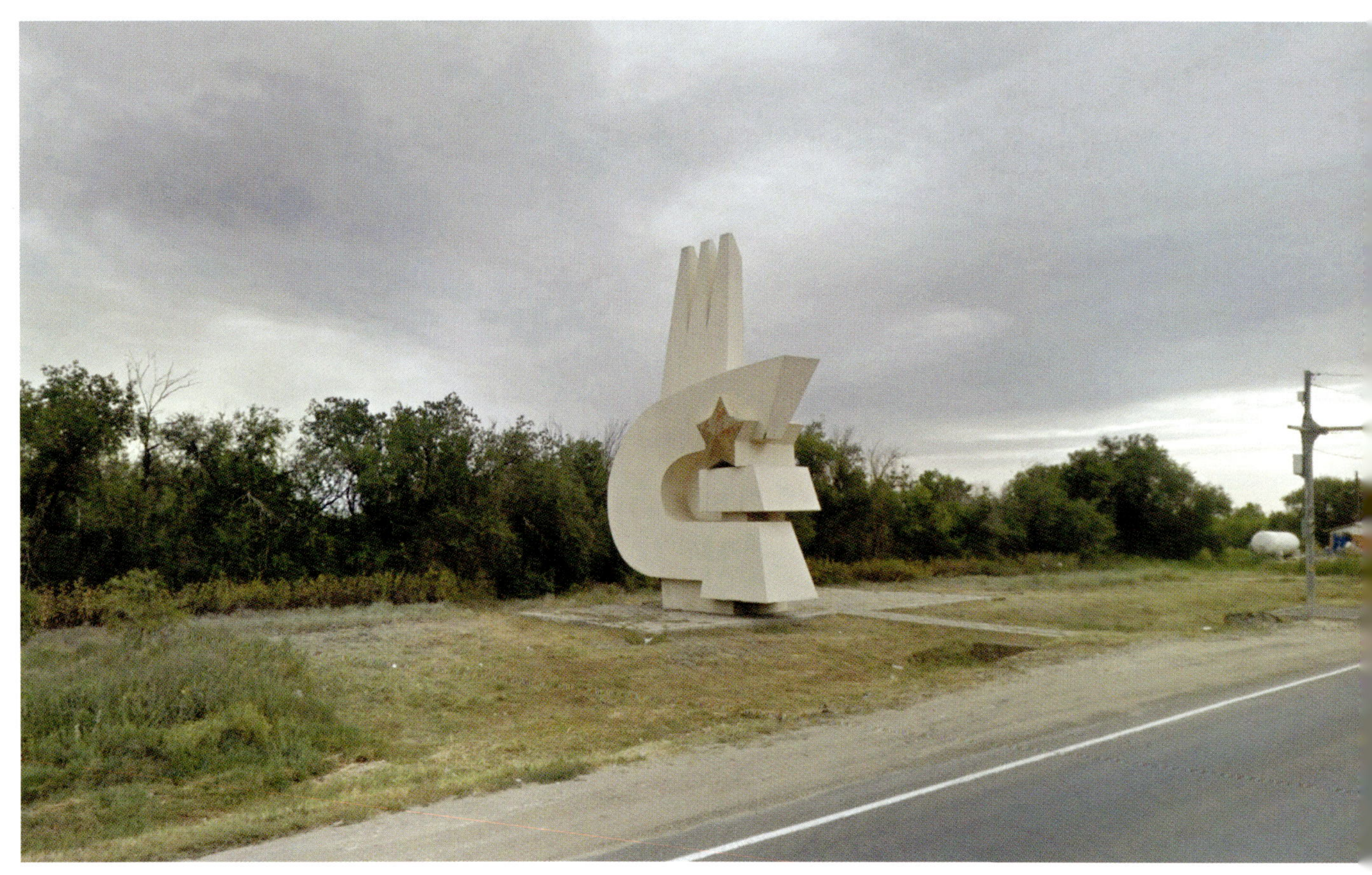

 VOLGOGRAD, RUSSIA

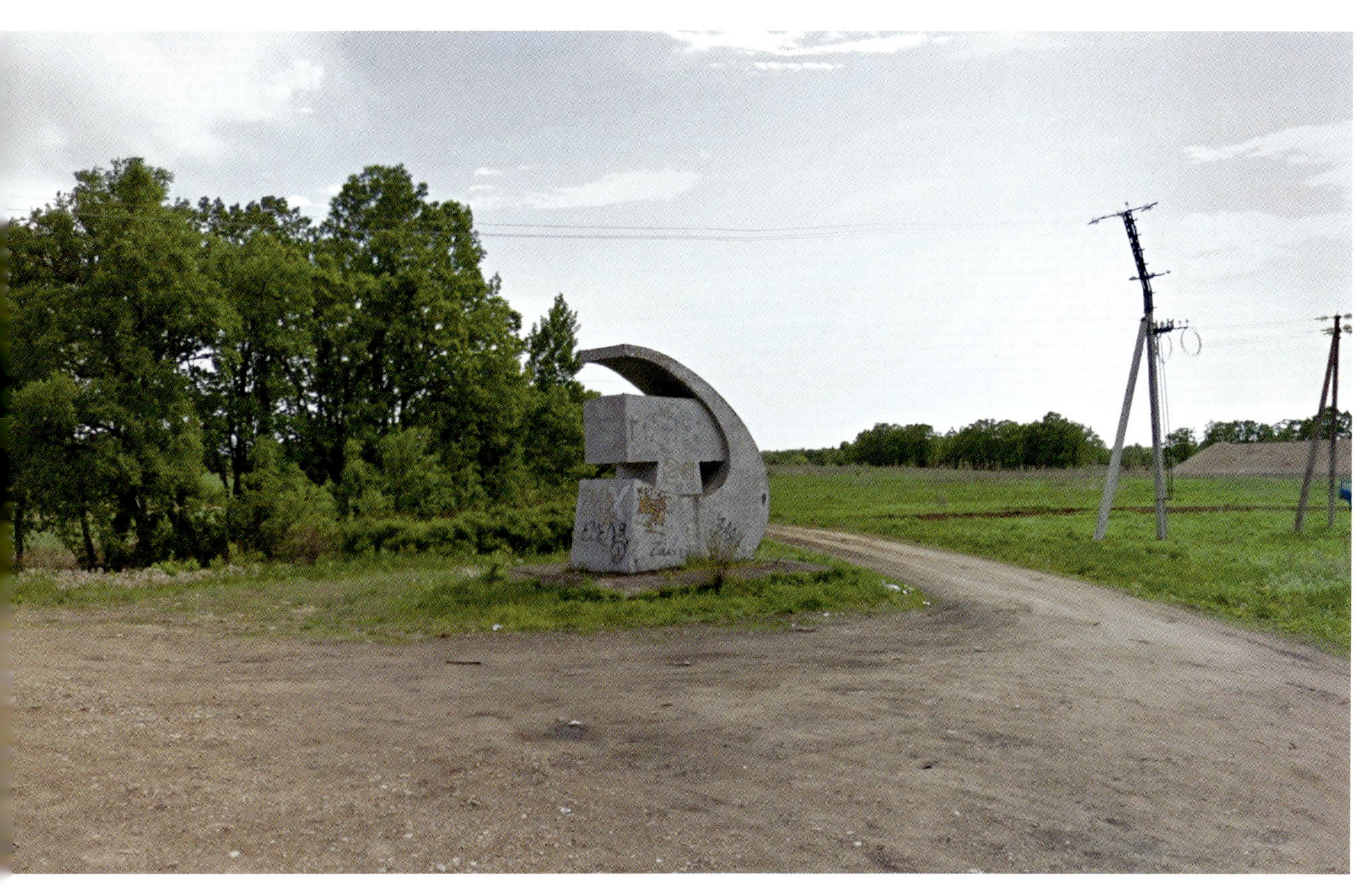

BIROBIDZHAN, RUSSIA

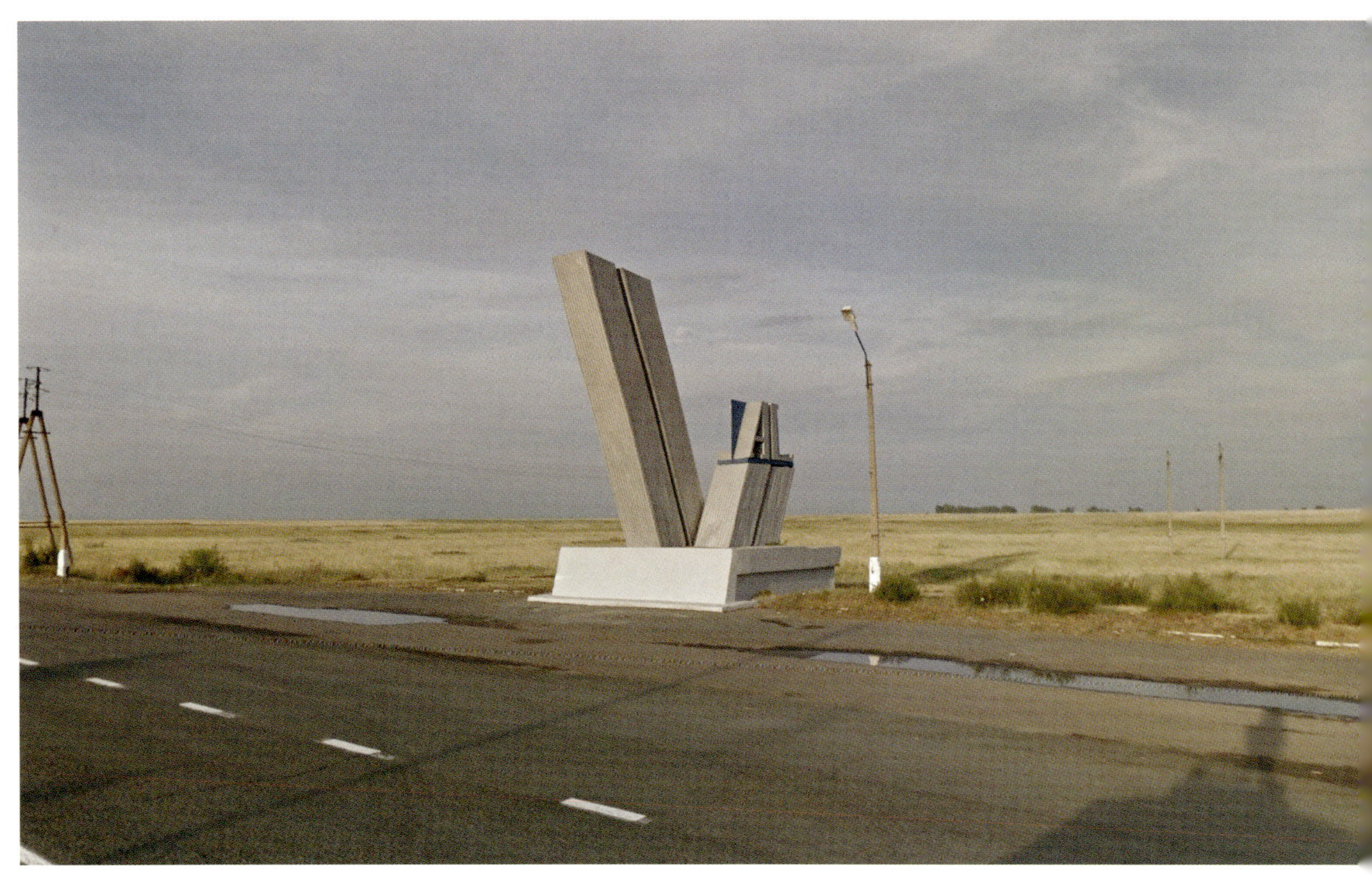

 KHAKASSIA, RUSSIA

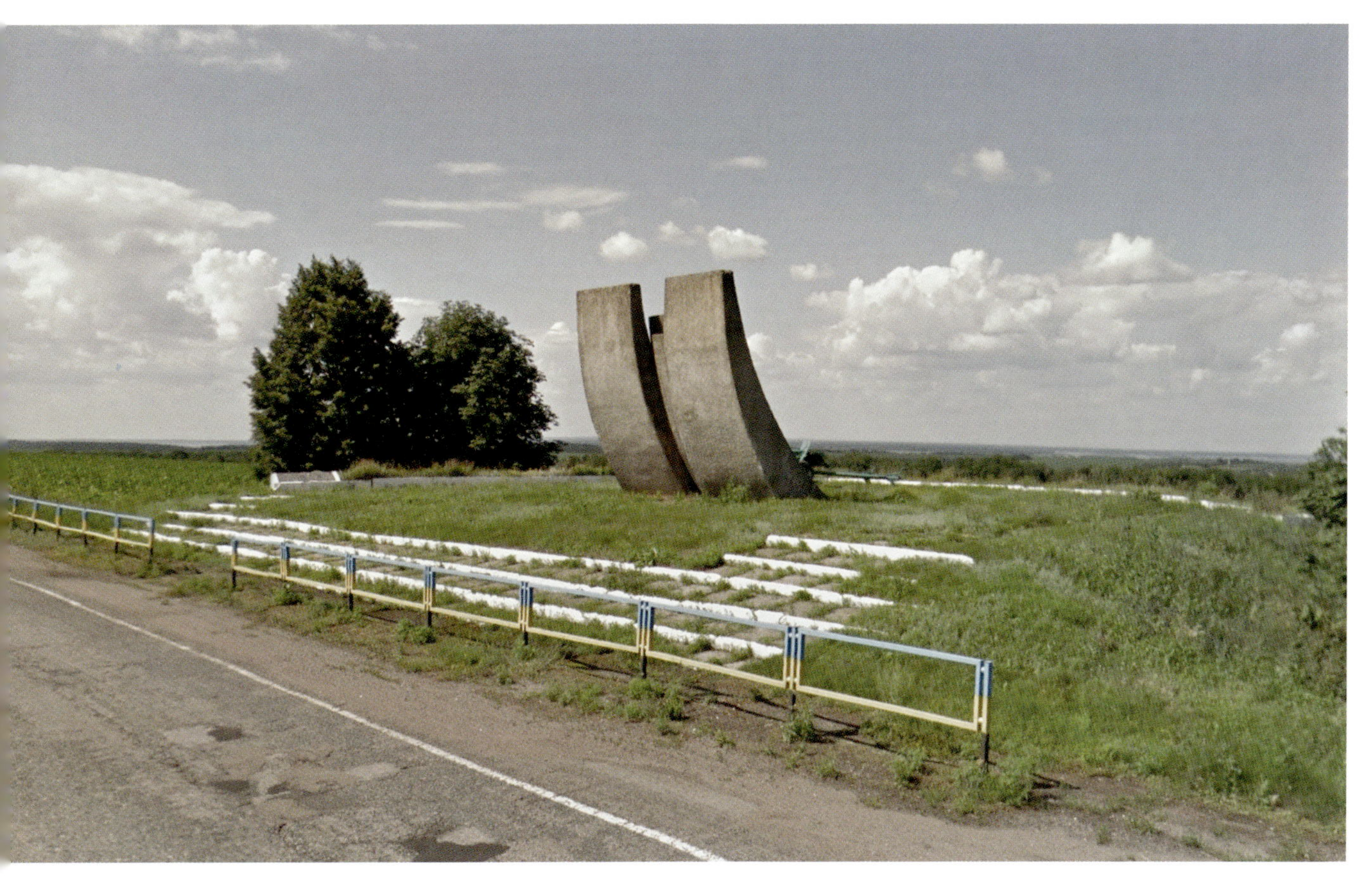

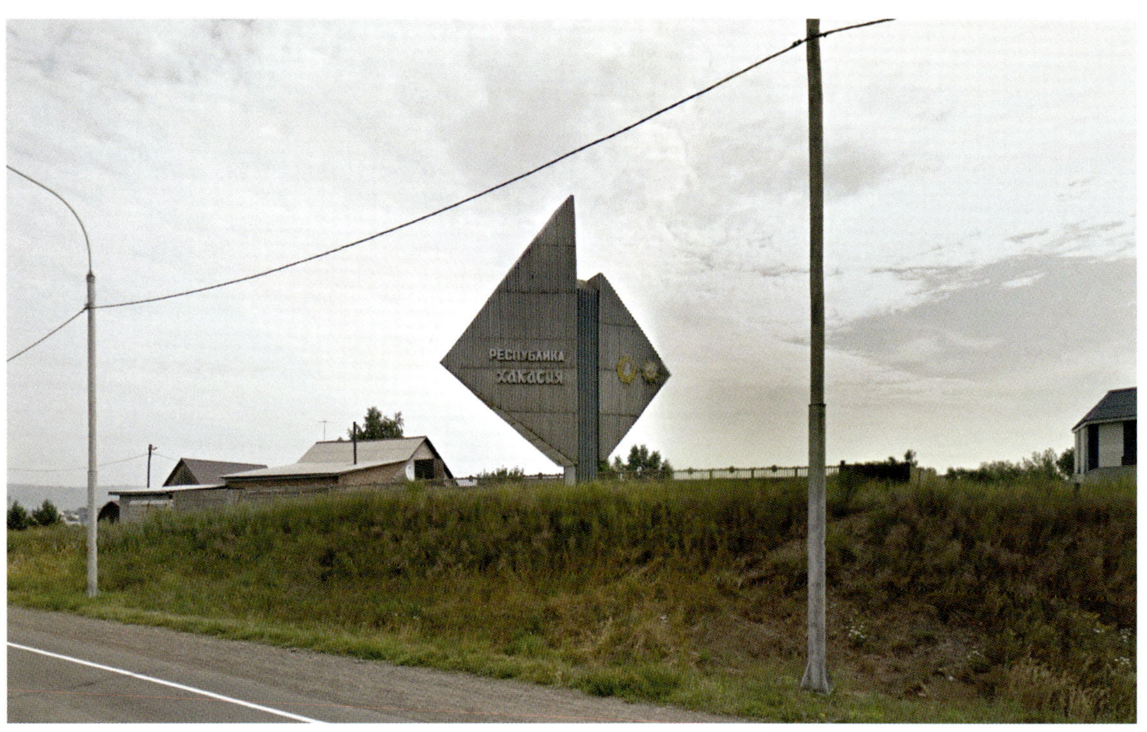

 KHAKASSIA, RUSSIA

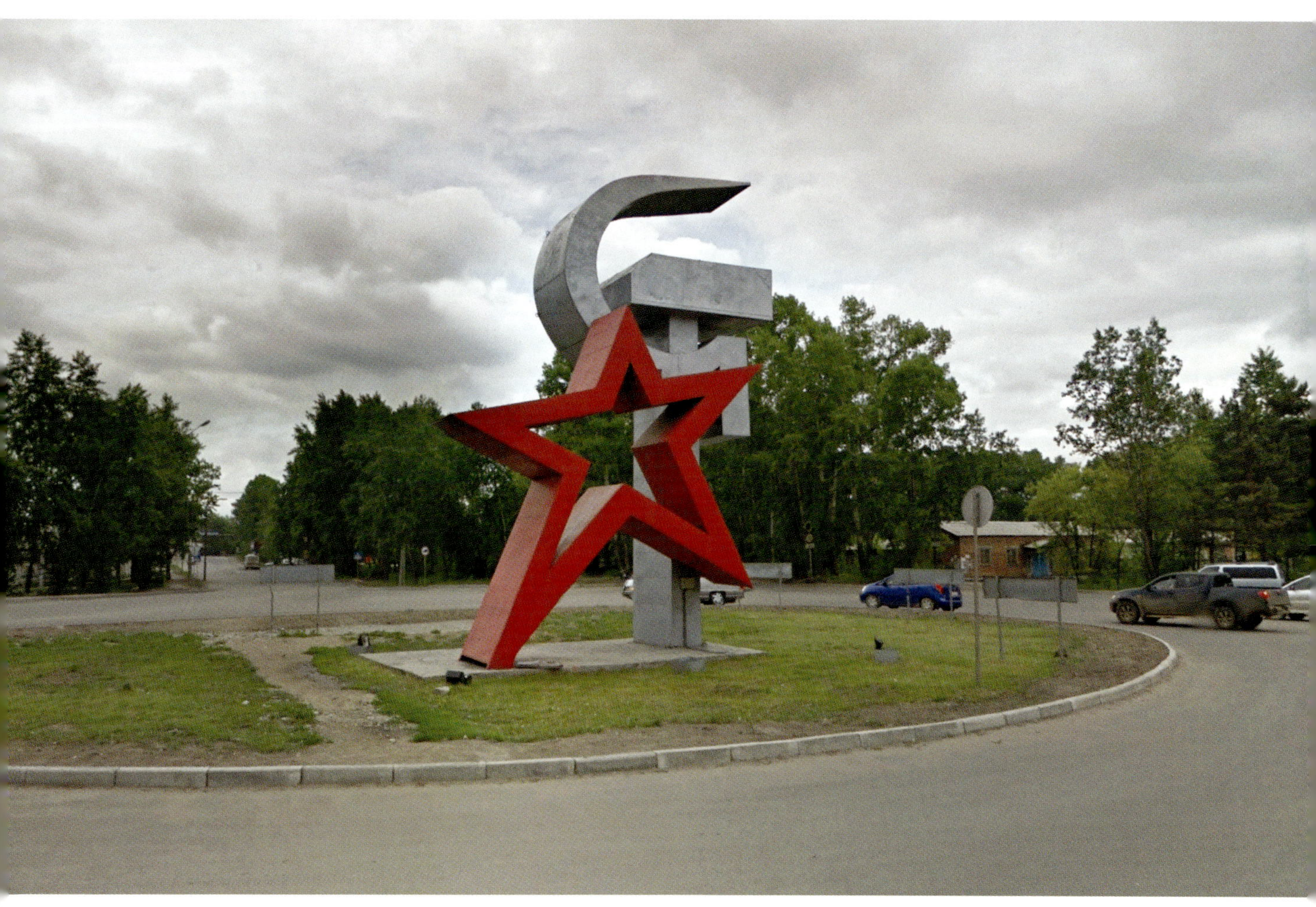

SHELEKHOV, RUSSIA

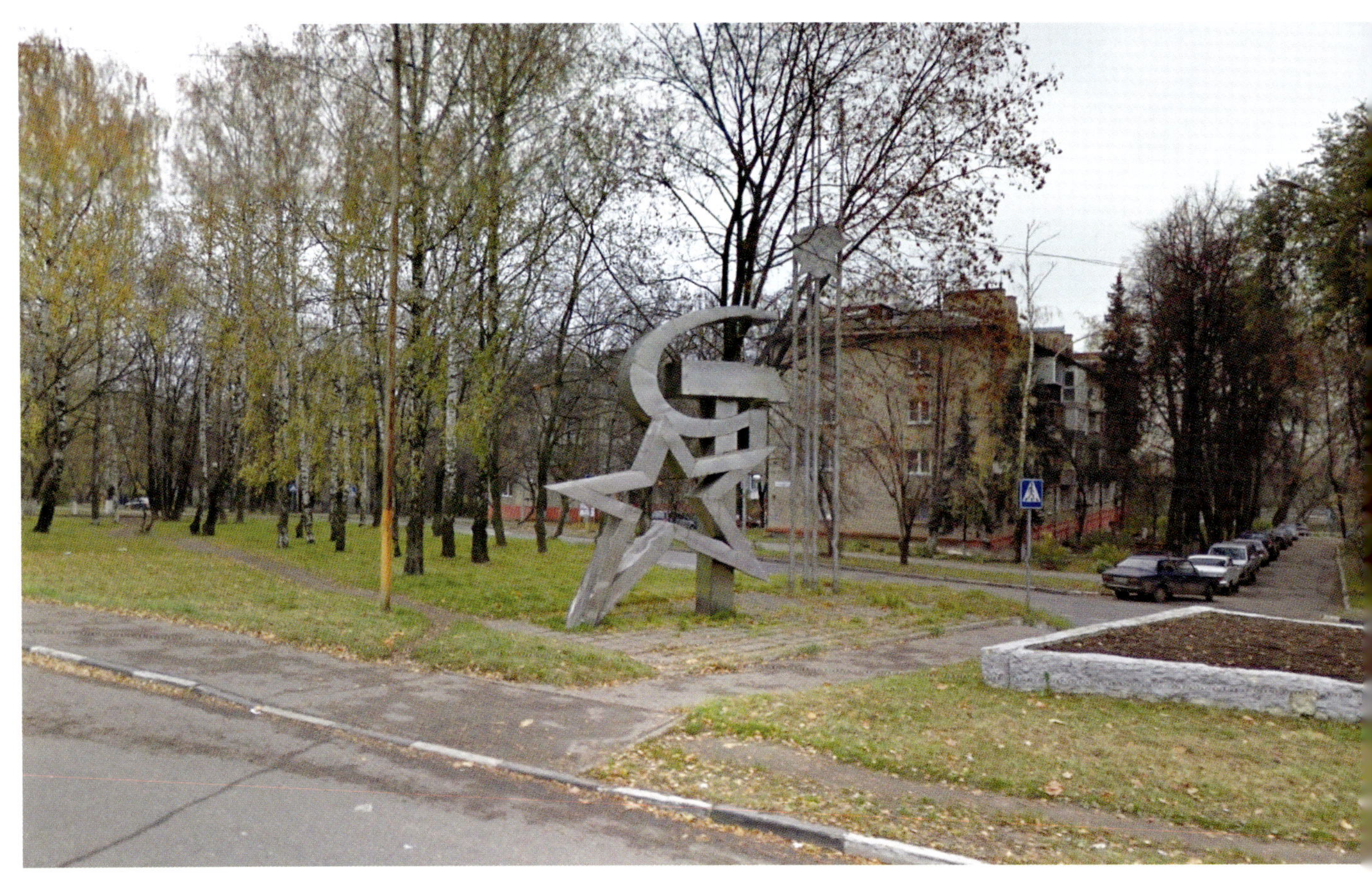

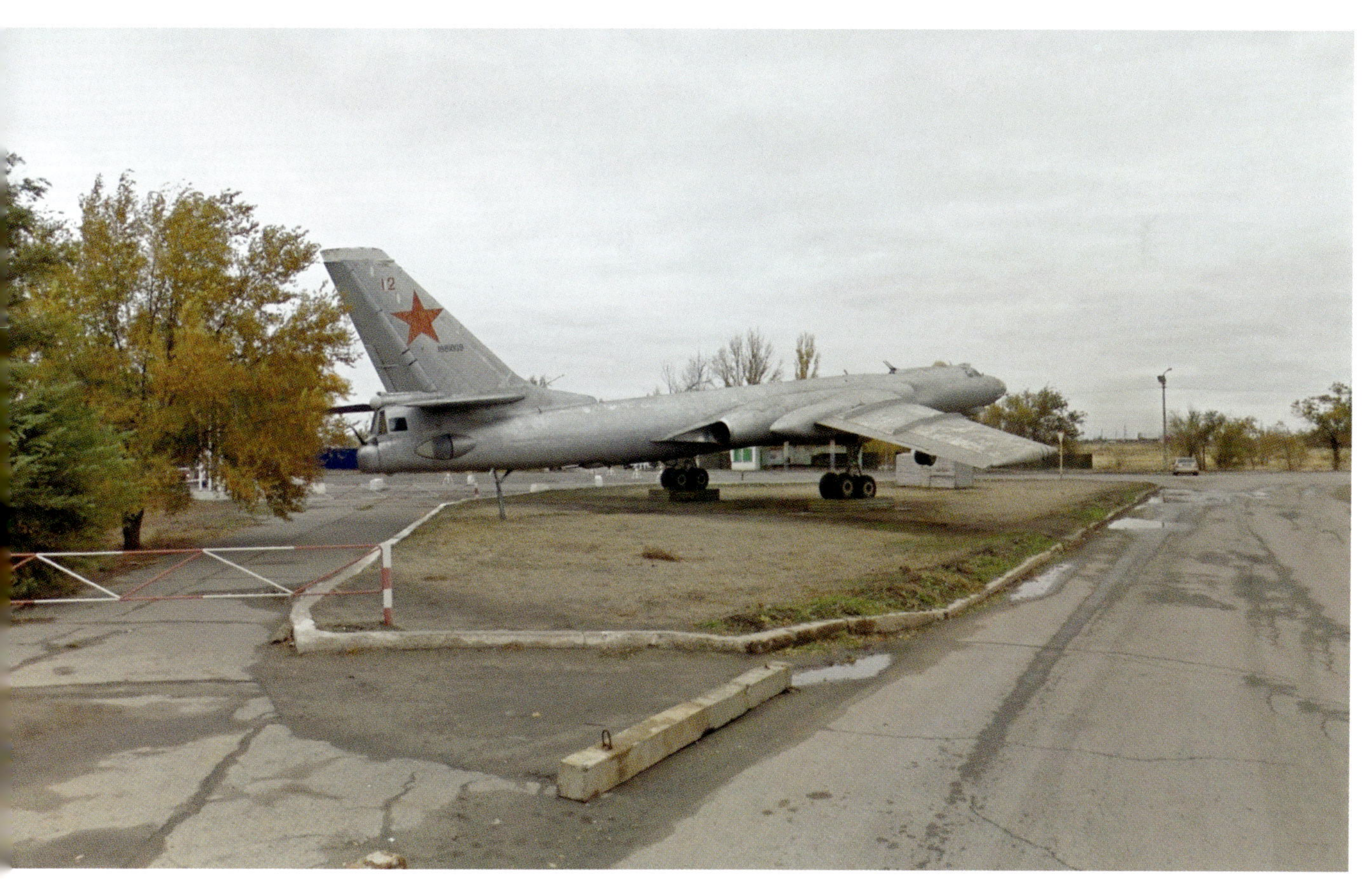

AKHTUBINSK, RUSSIA

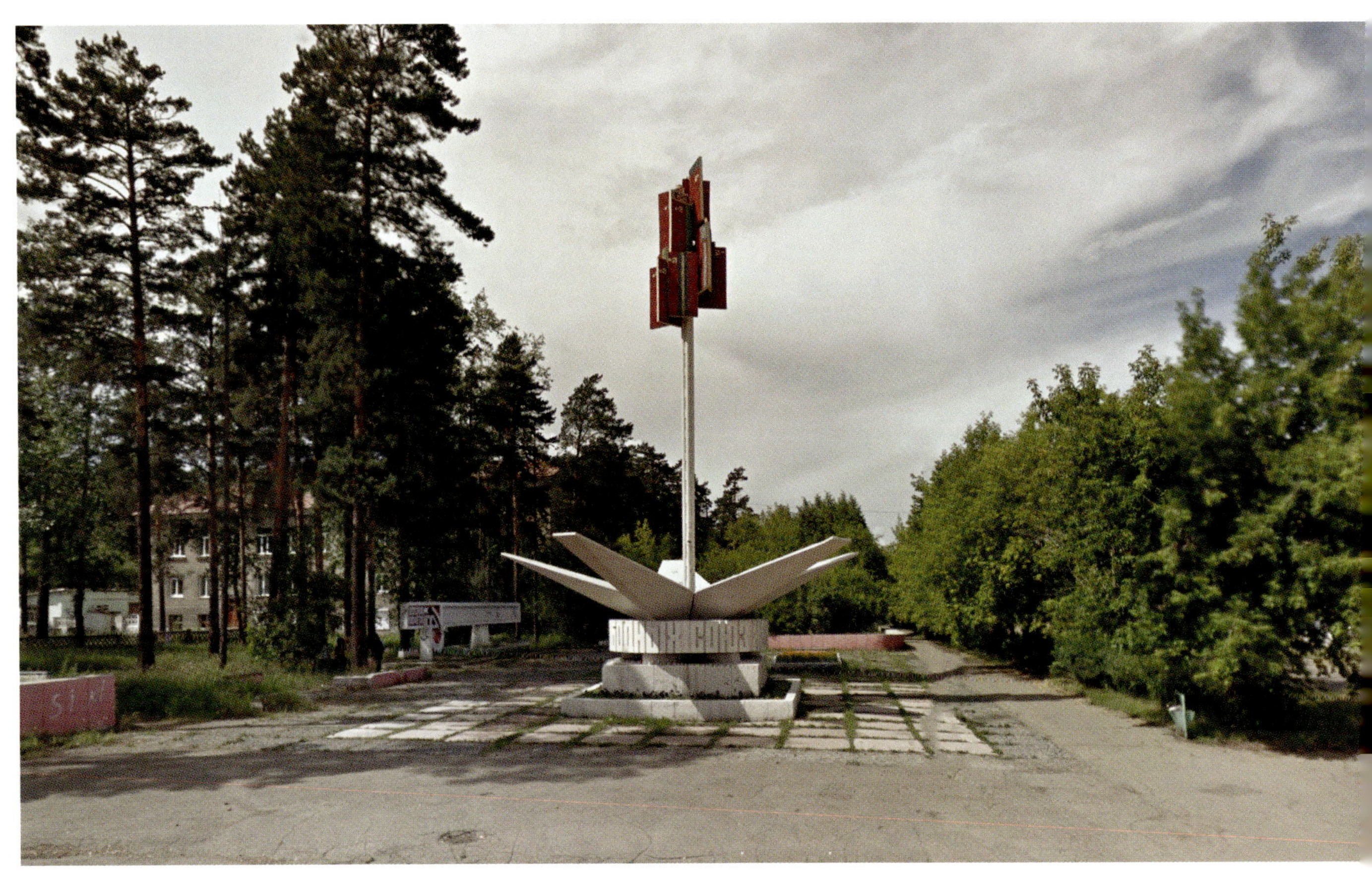

 ANGARSK, RUSSIA

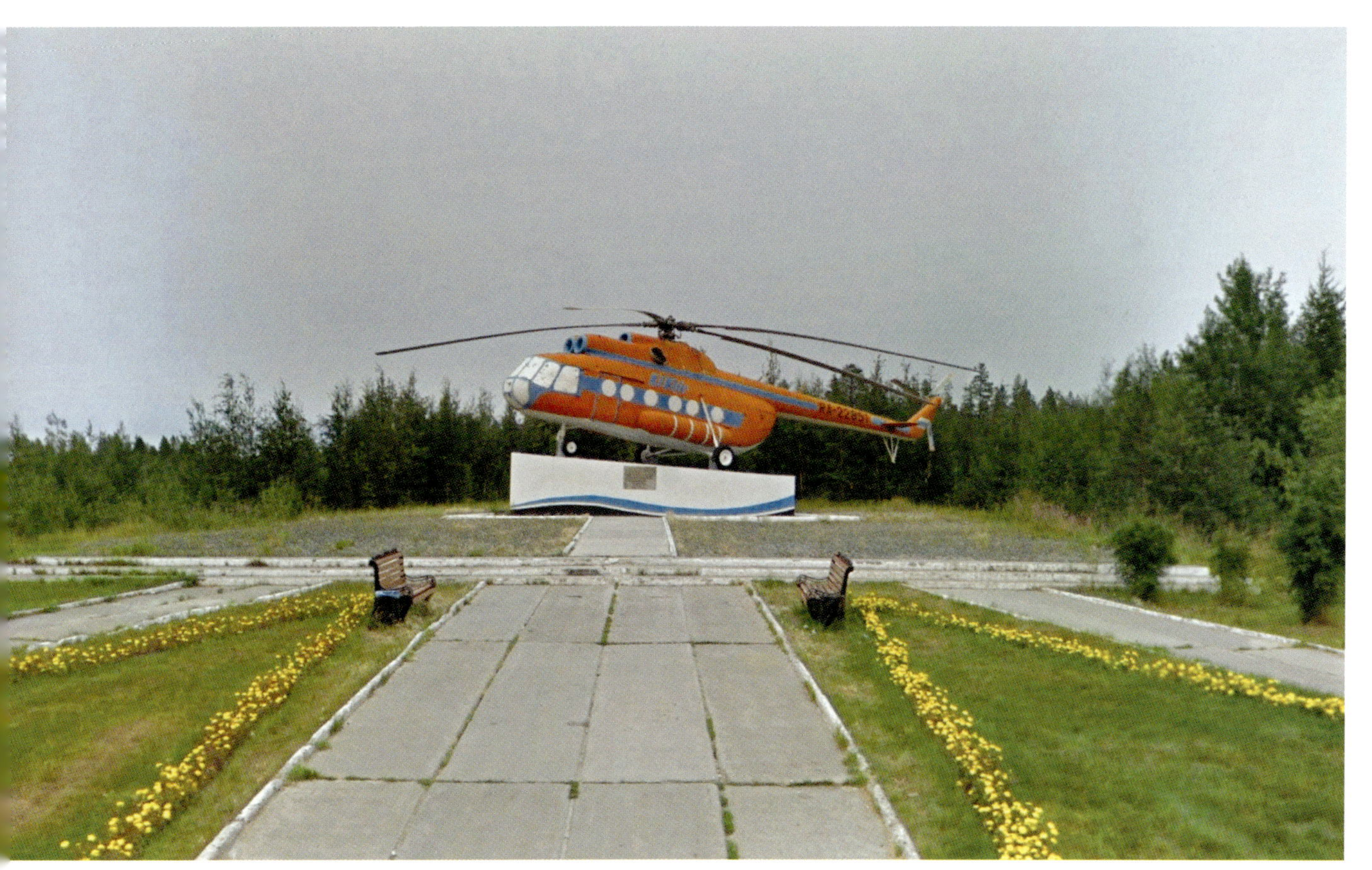

NOYABRSK, RUSSIA

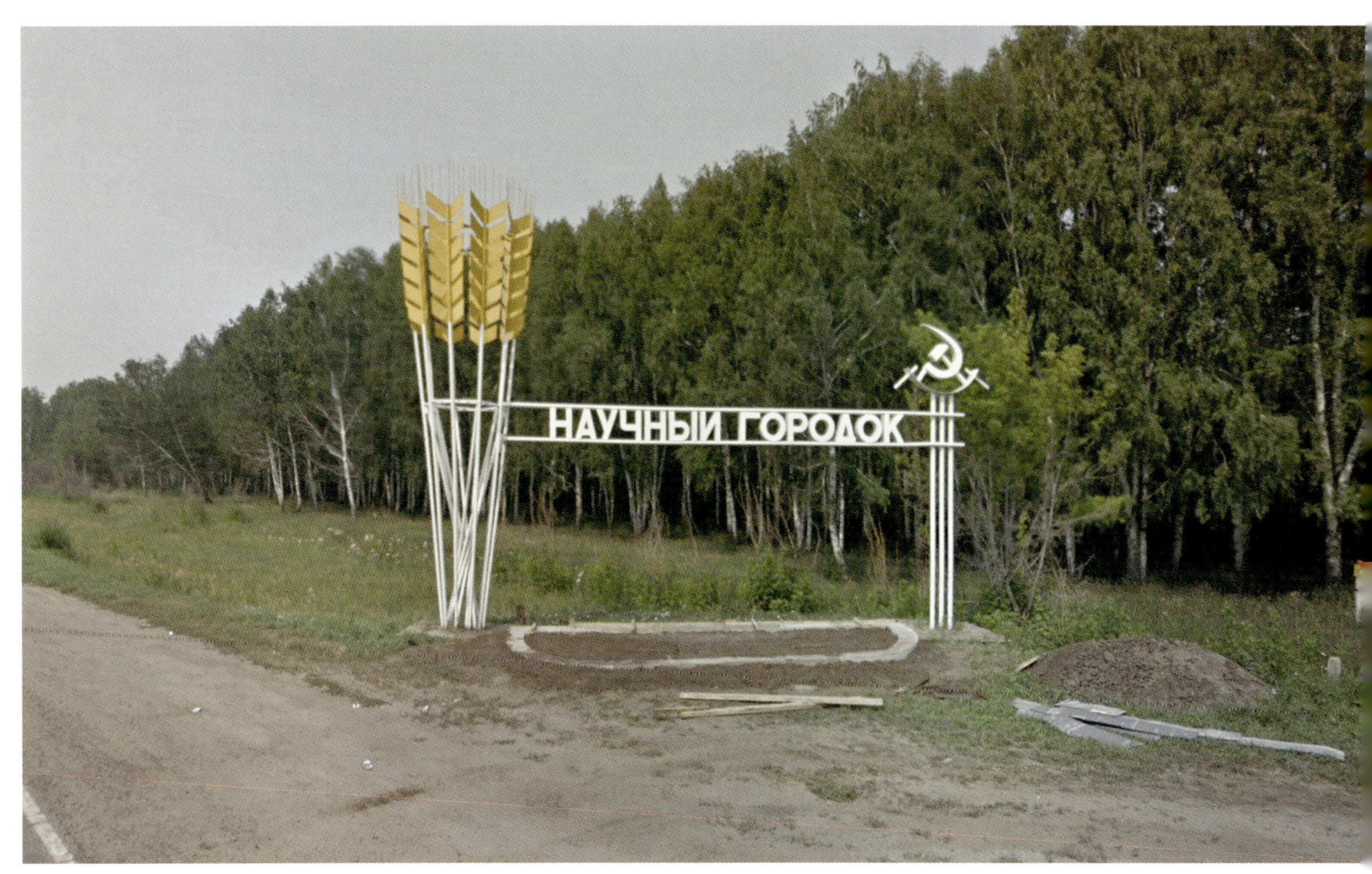

 NAUCHNY GORODOK, RUSSIA

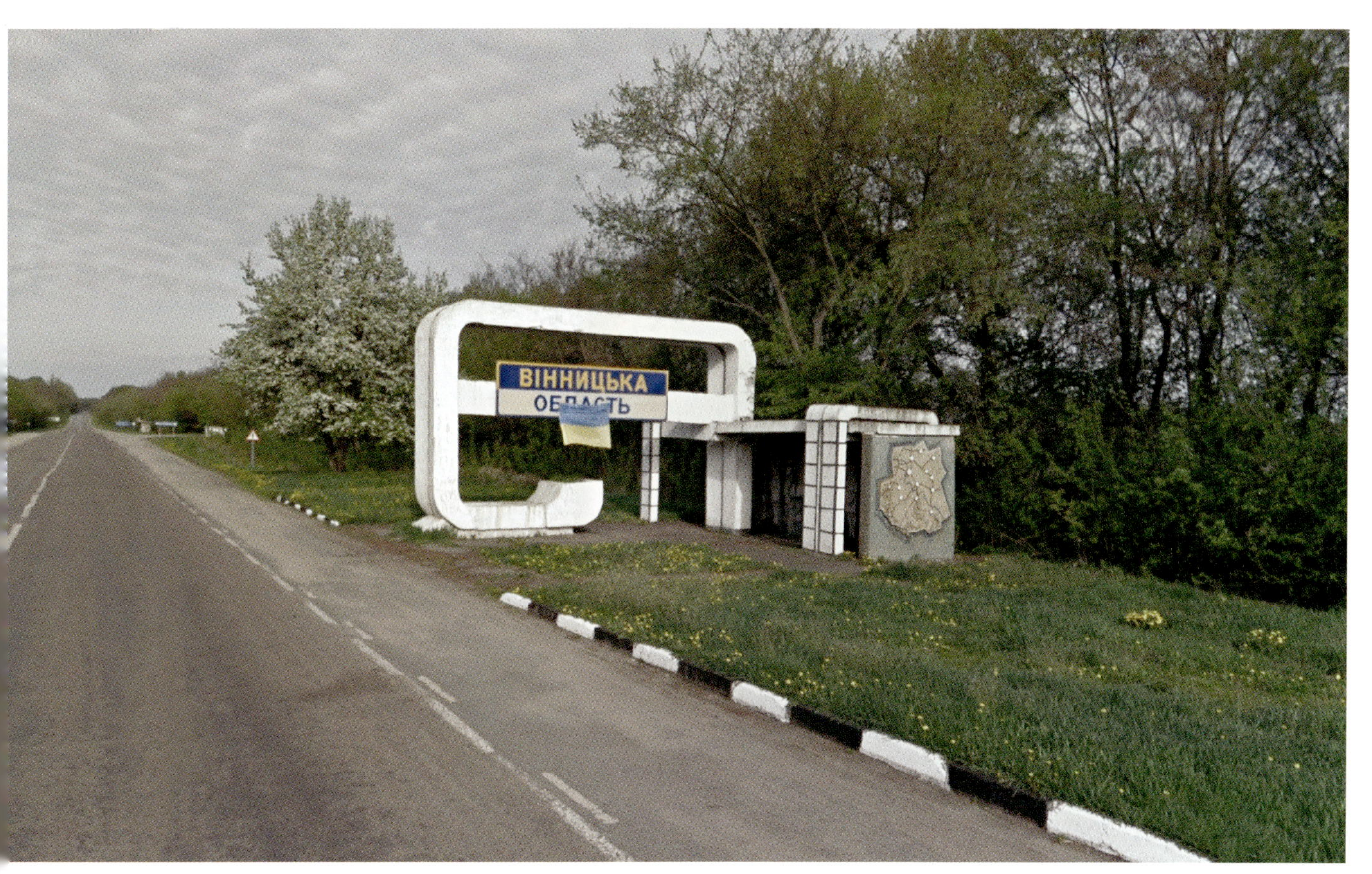

VINNYTSIA, UKRAINE

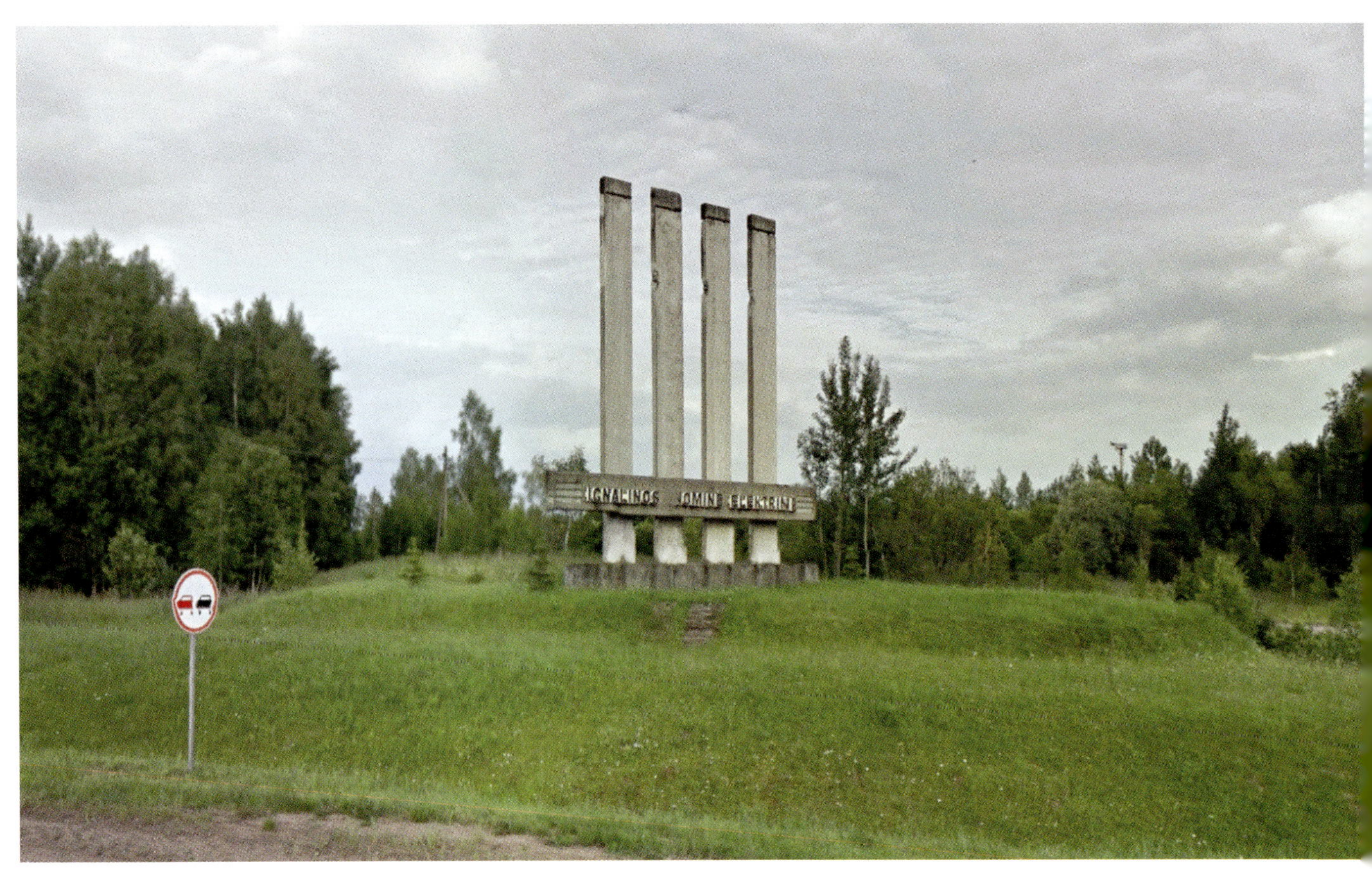

 IGNALINA NUCLEAR POWER PLANT, VISAGINAS, LITHUANIA

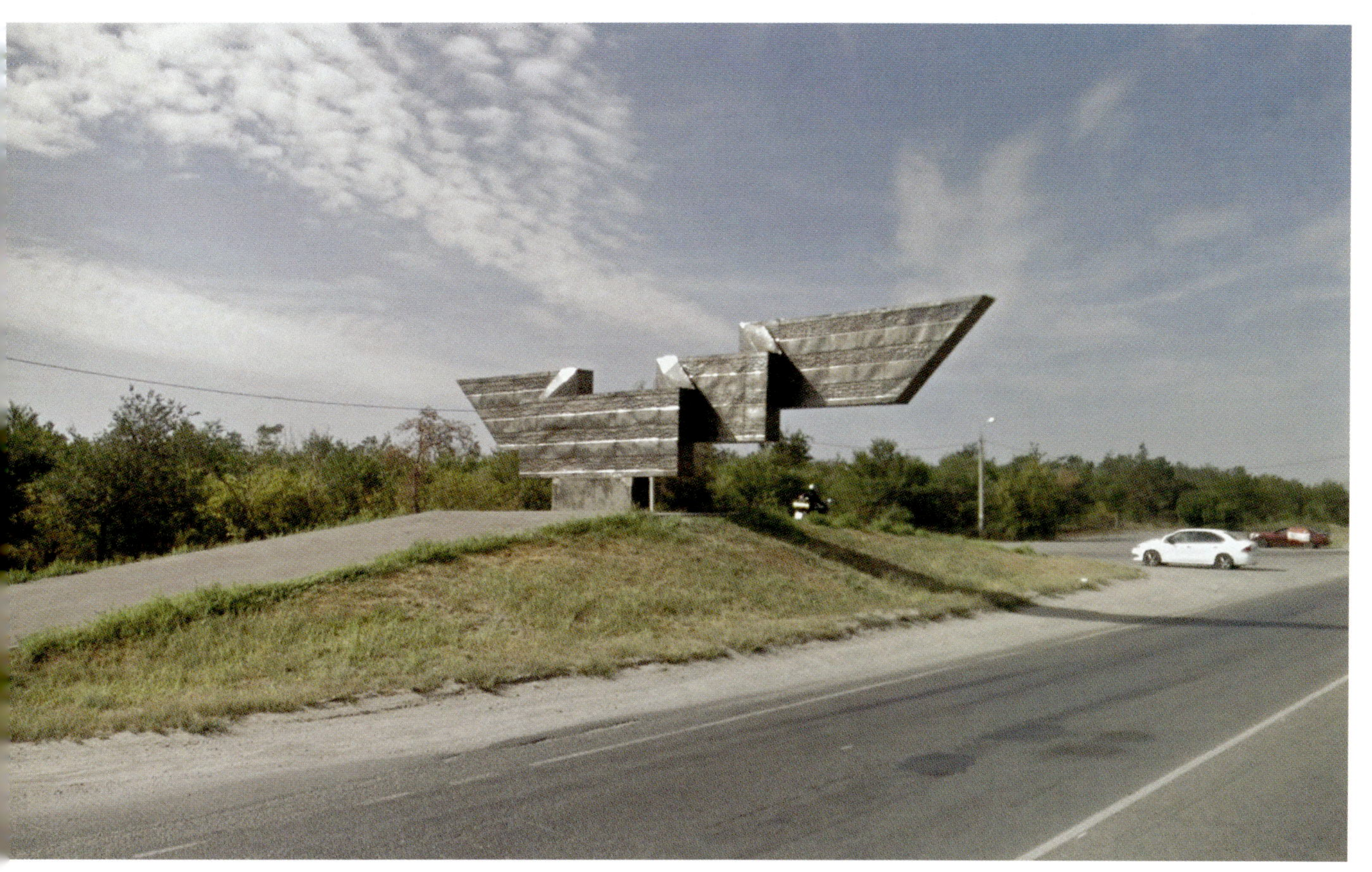

VOLGOGRAD, RUSSIA

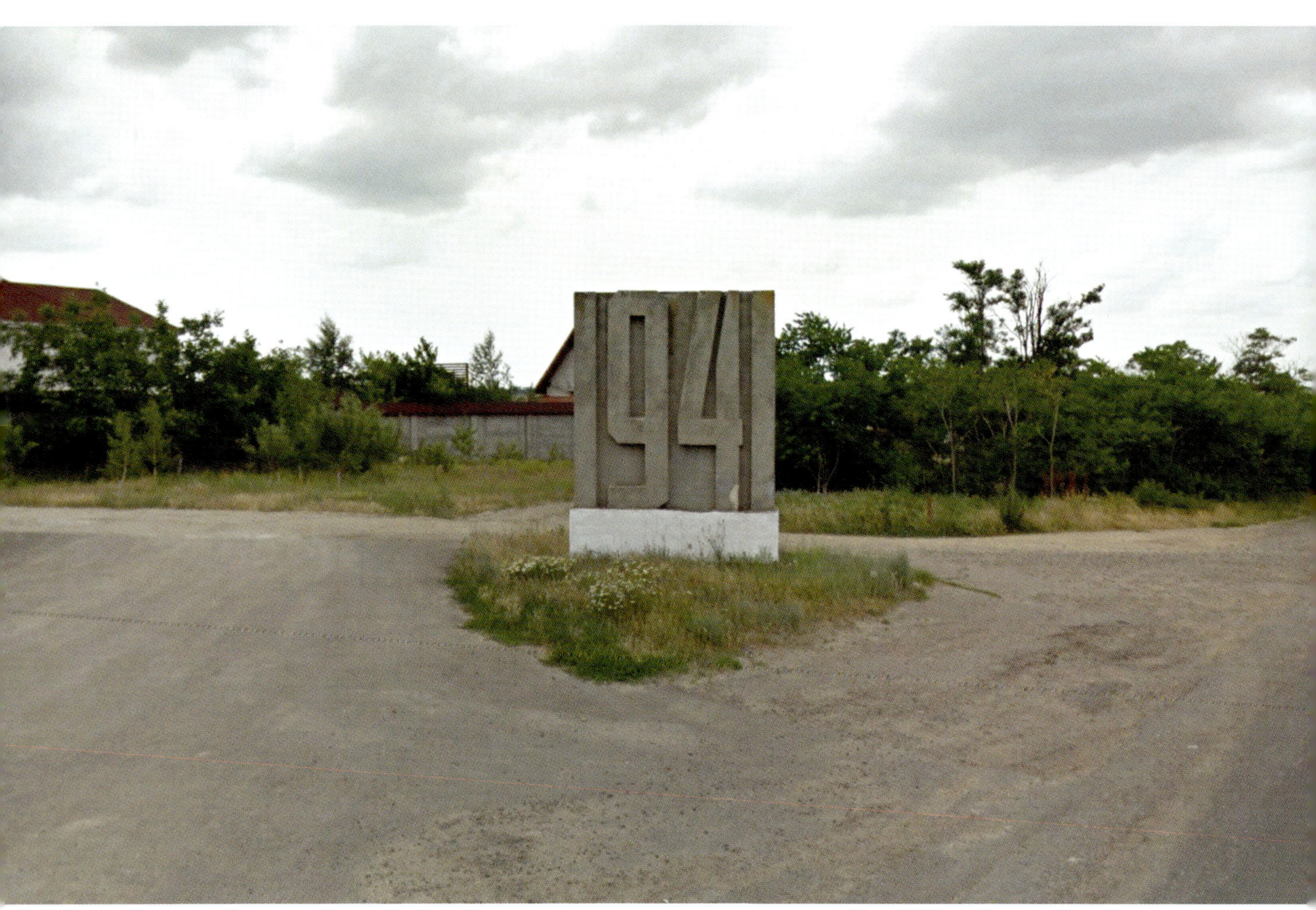

ODESSA OBLAST, UKRAINE

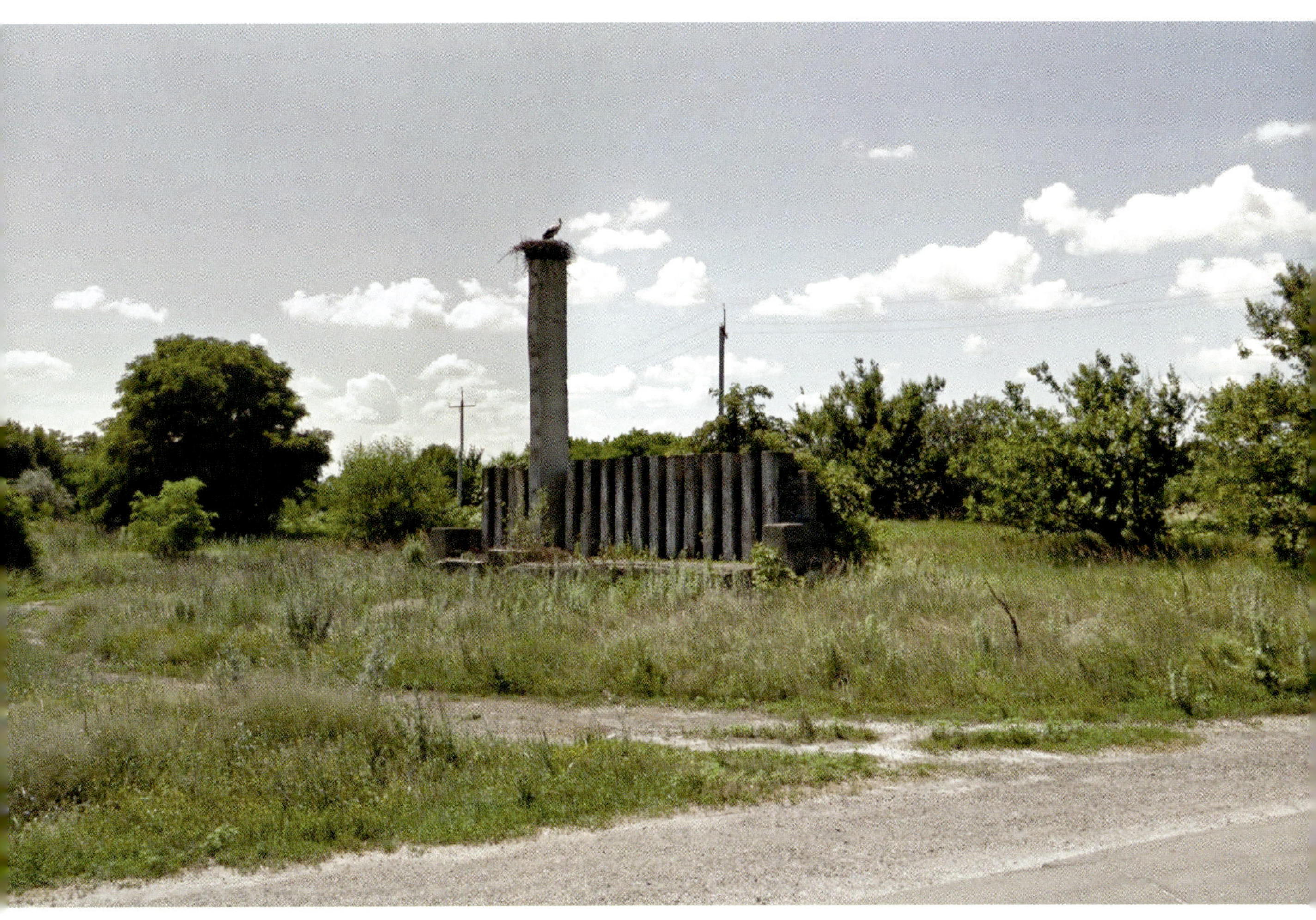

POLTAVA OBLAST, UKRAINE

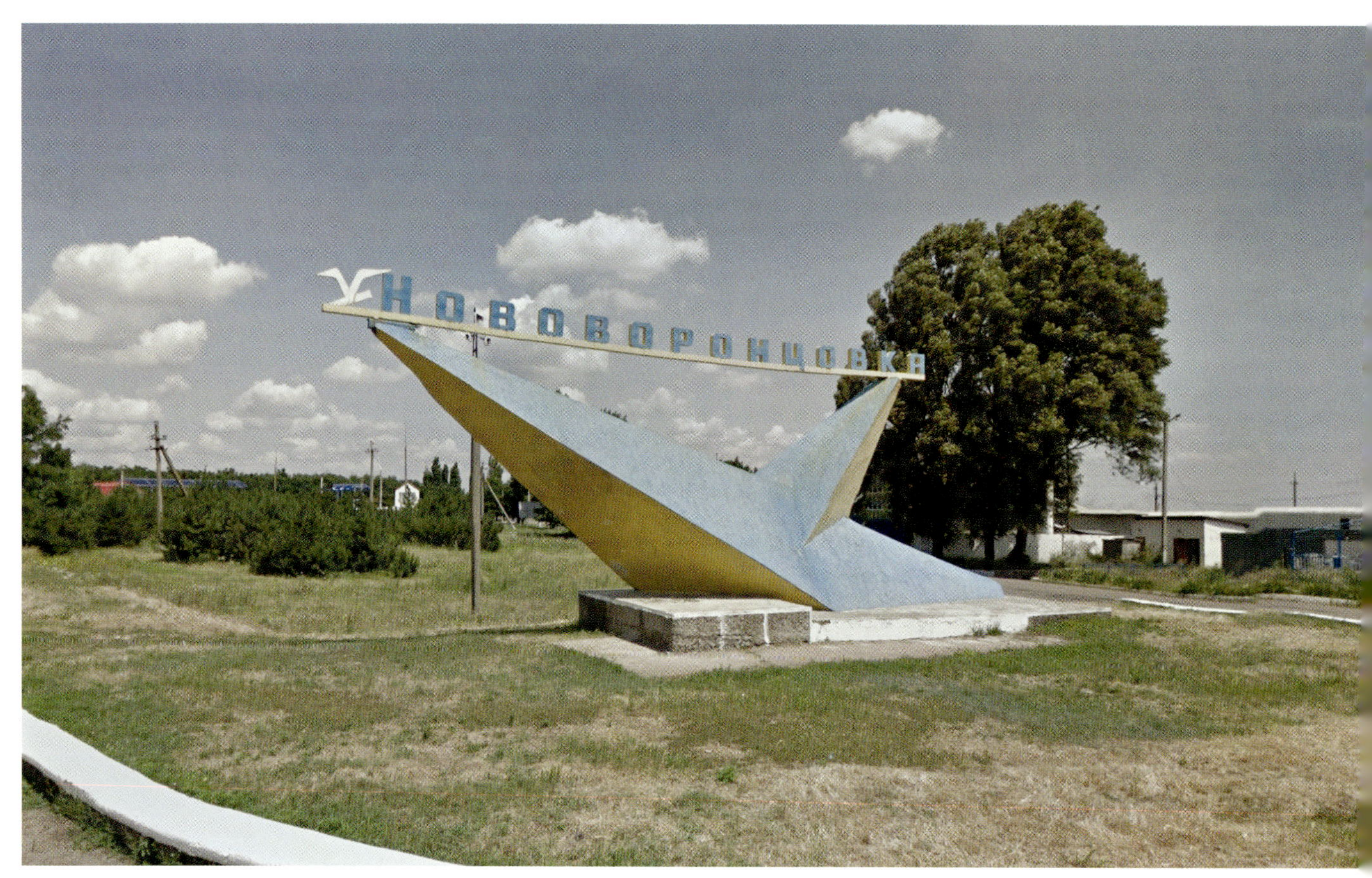

NOVOVORONTSOVKA, UKRAINE

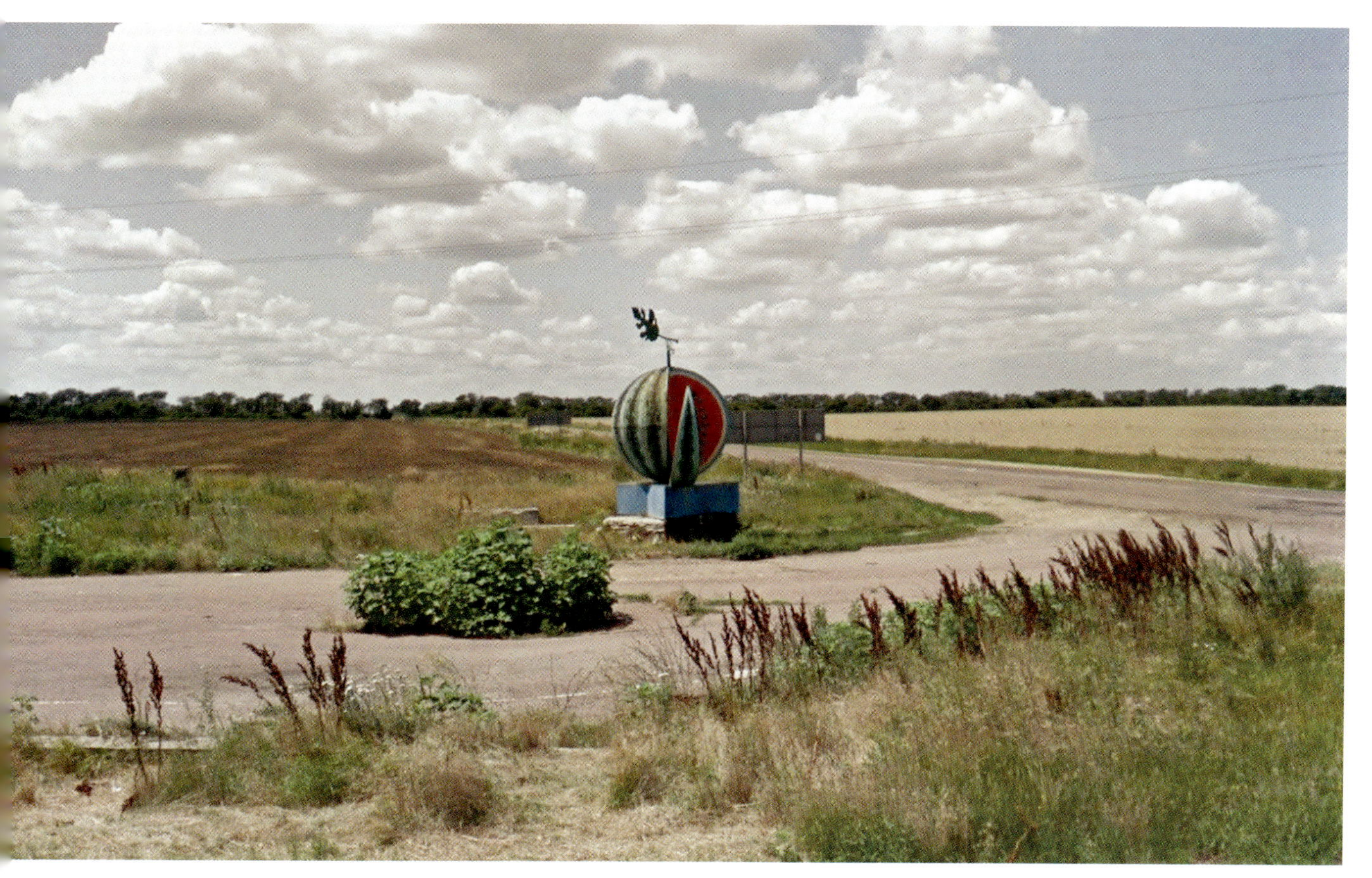

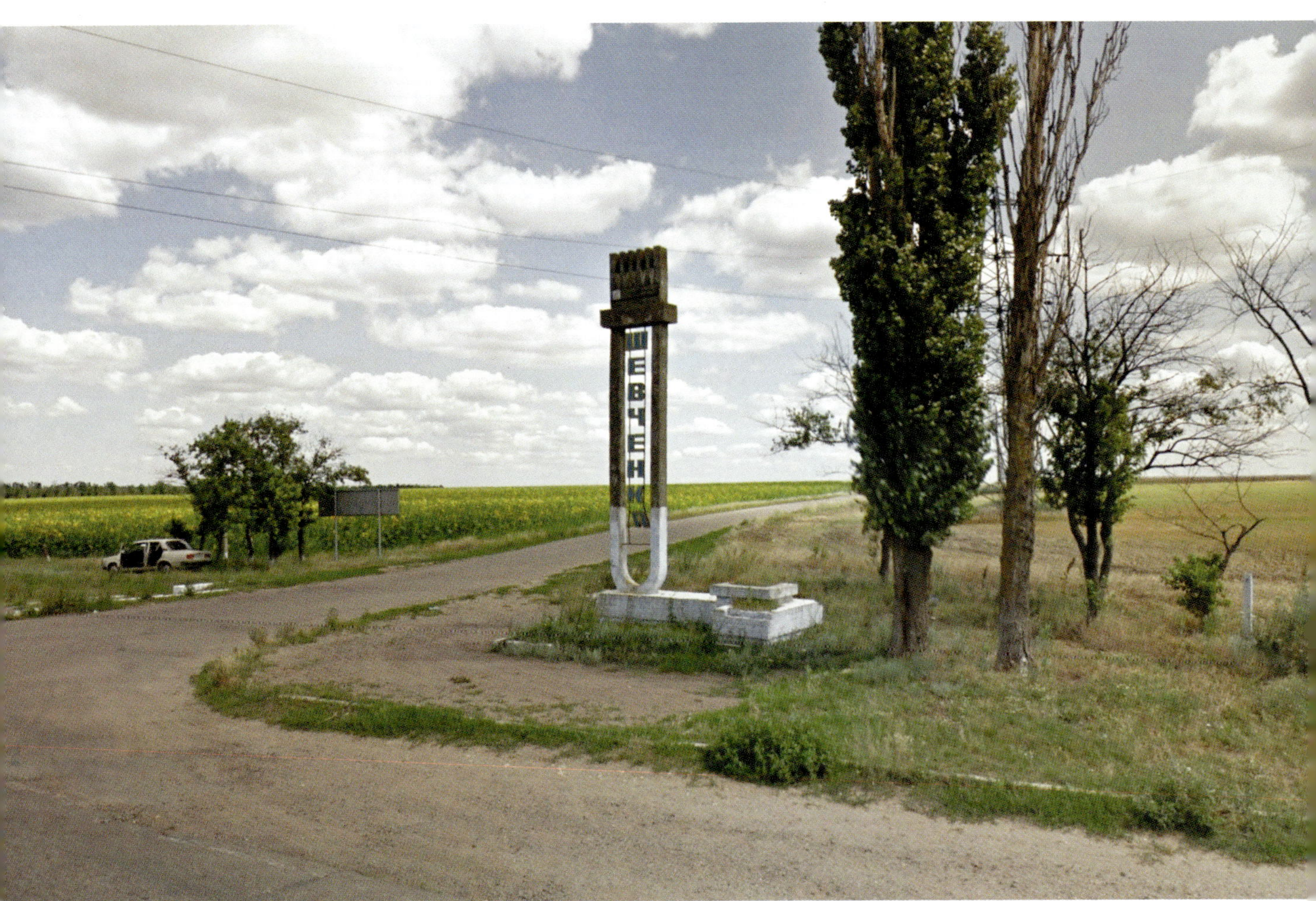

SHEVCHENKA, UKRAINE

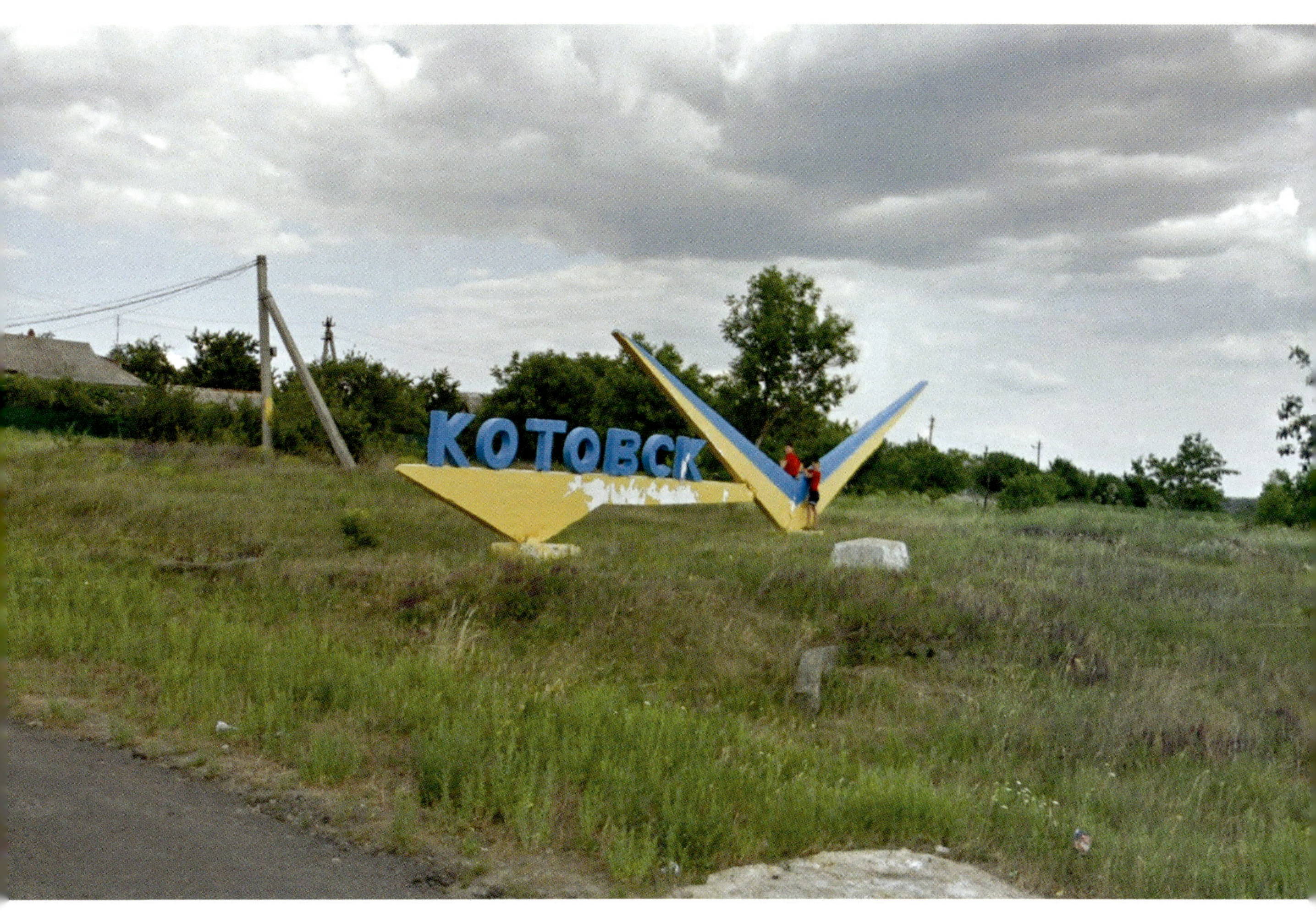

KOTOVSK, UKRAINE

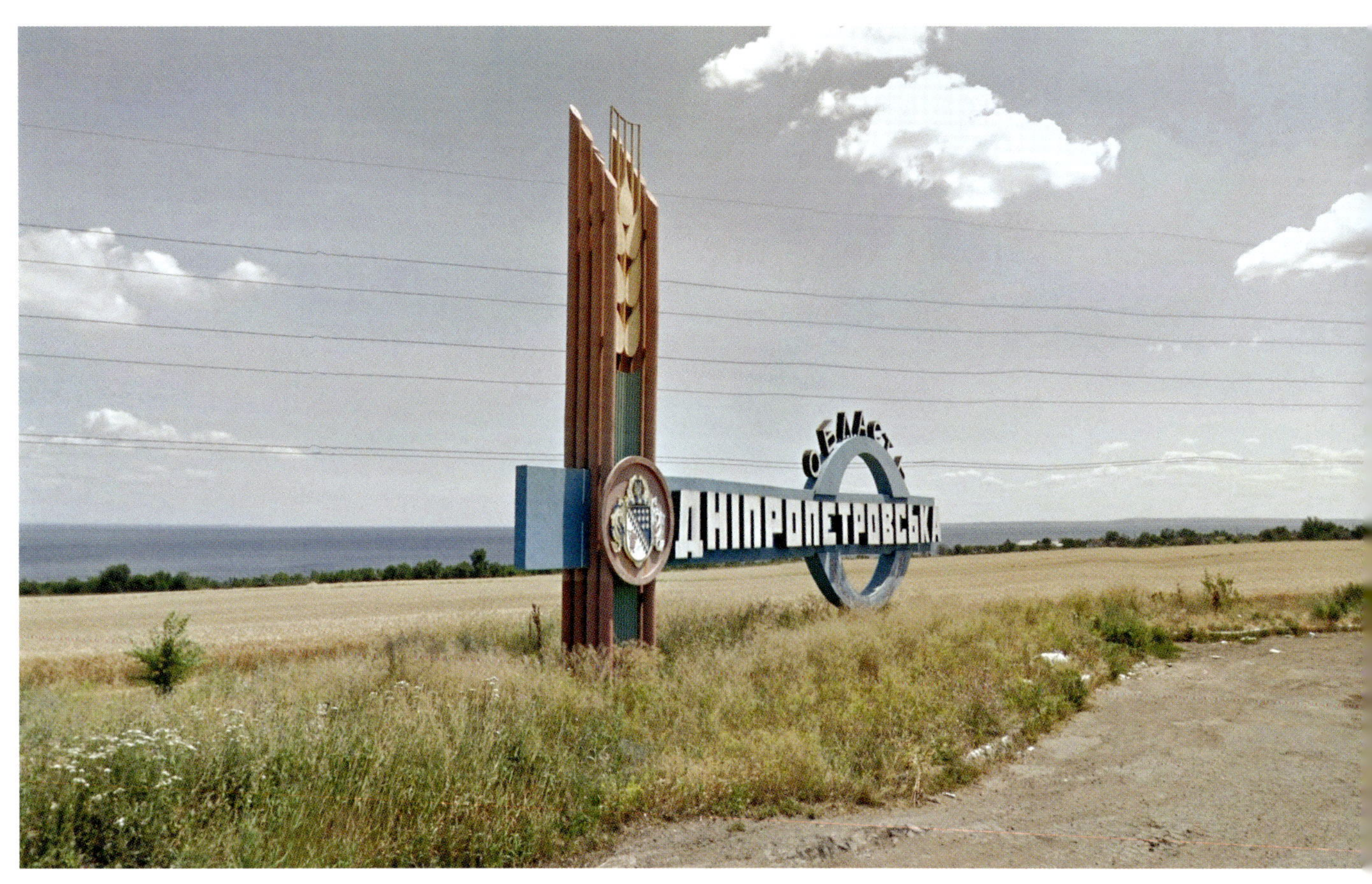

DNIPROPETROVSK OBLAST, UKRAINE

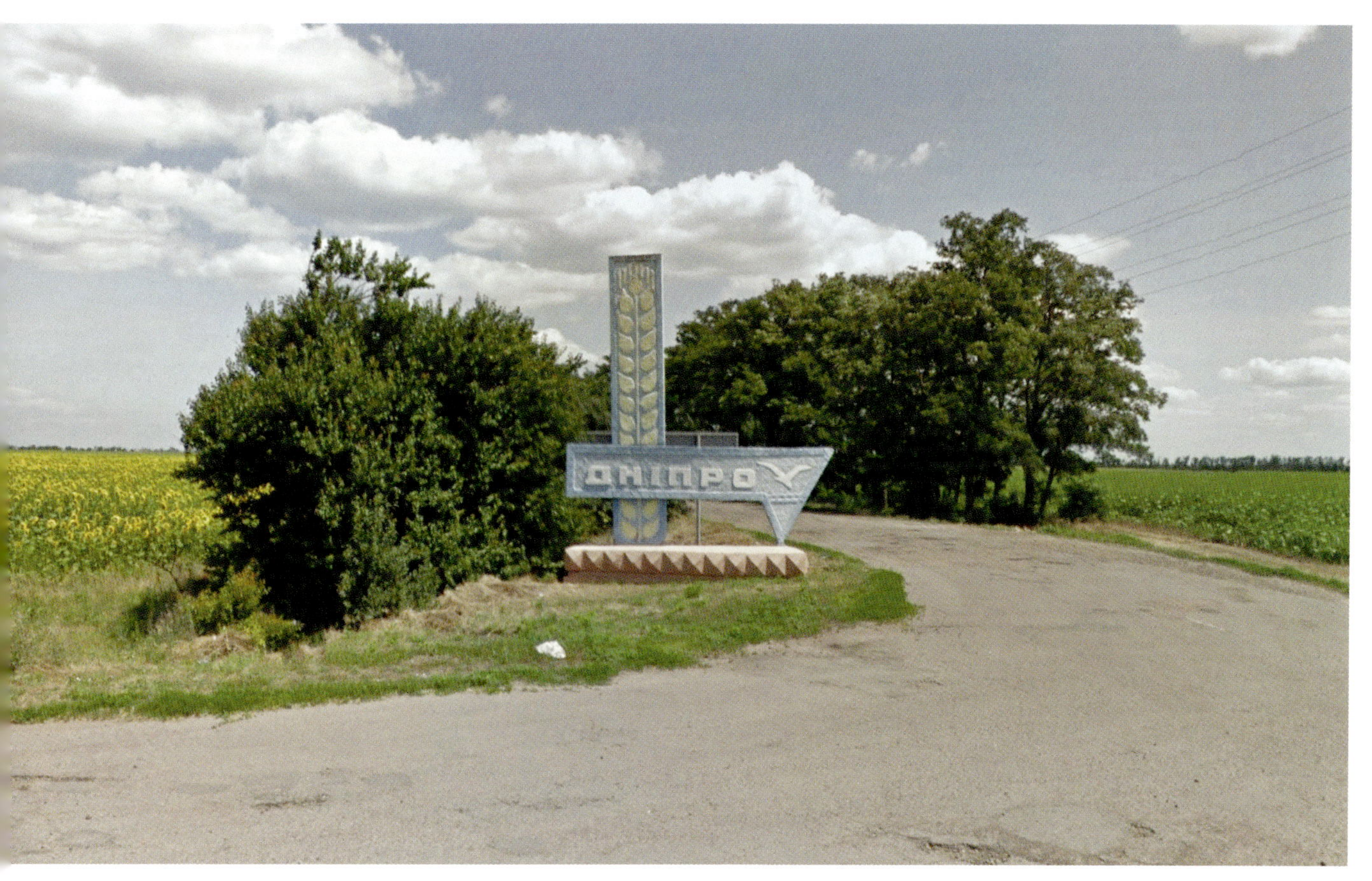

DNIPRO, UKRAINE

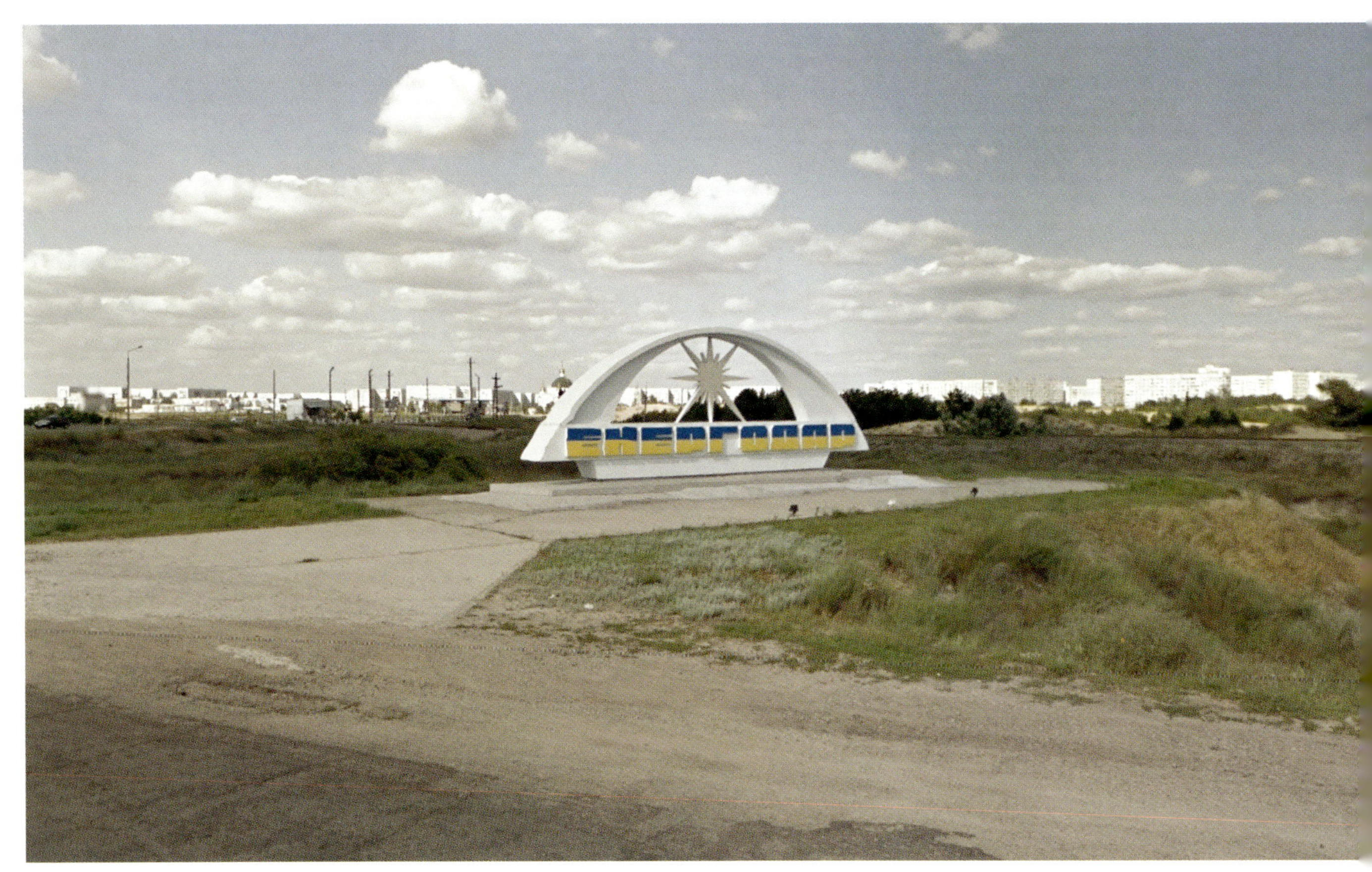

 ENERHODAR, UKRAINE

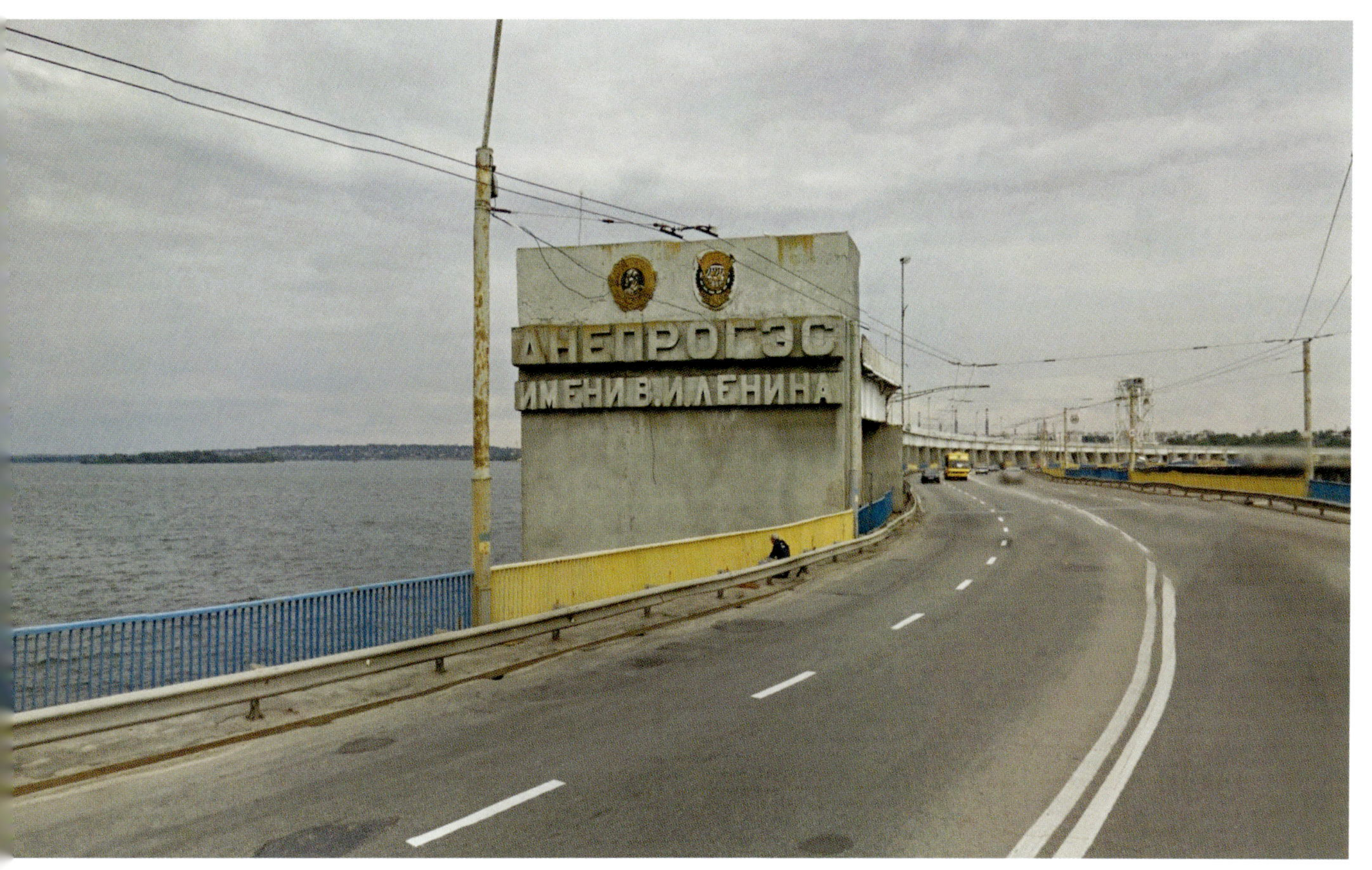

ZAPORIZHZHIA, UKRAINE

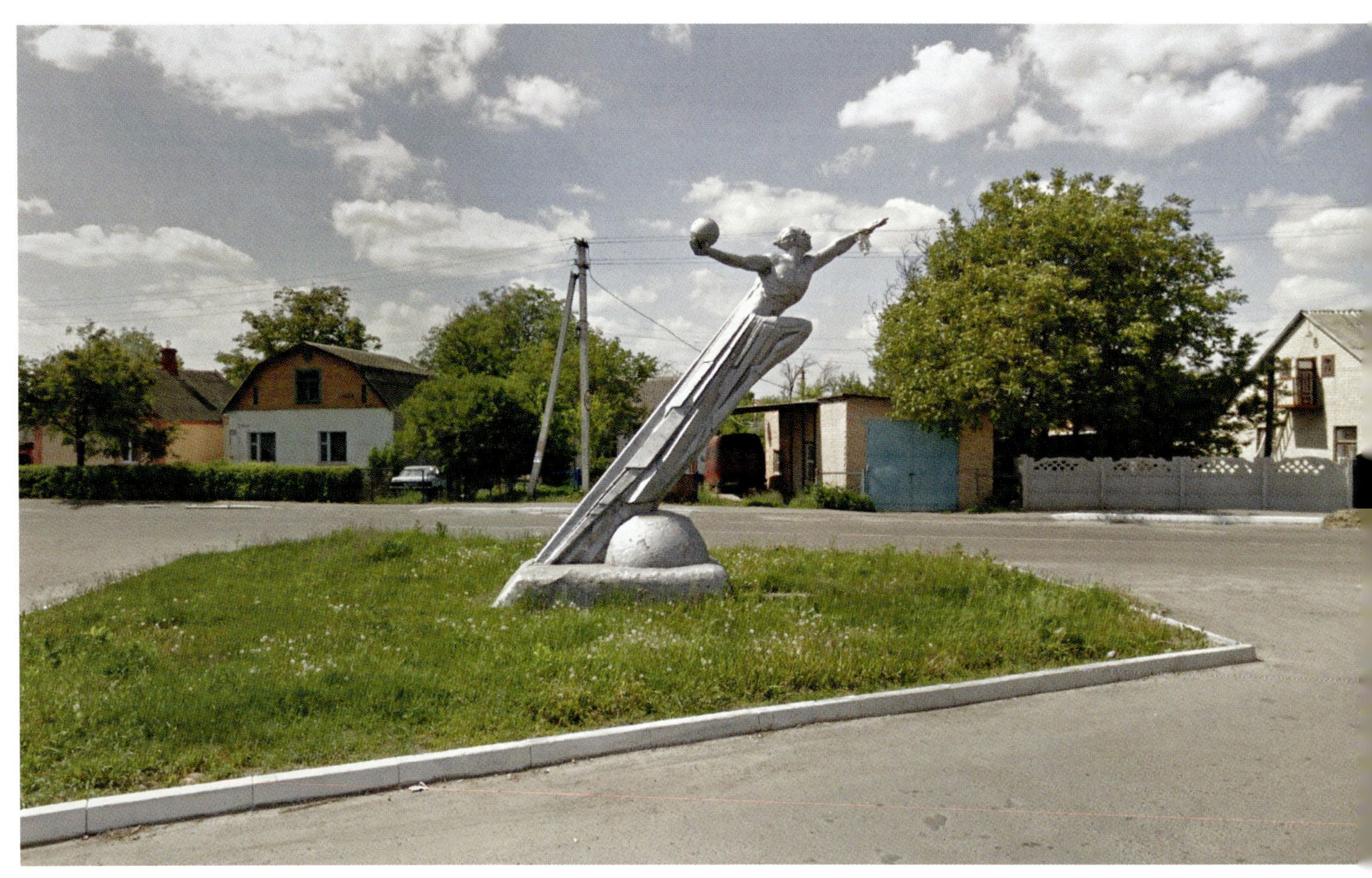

RIVNE, RUSSIA

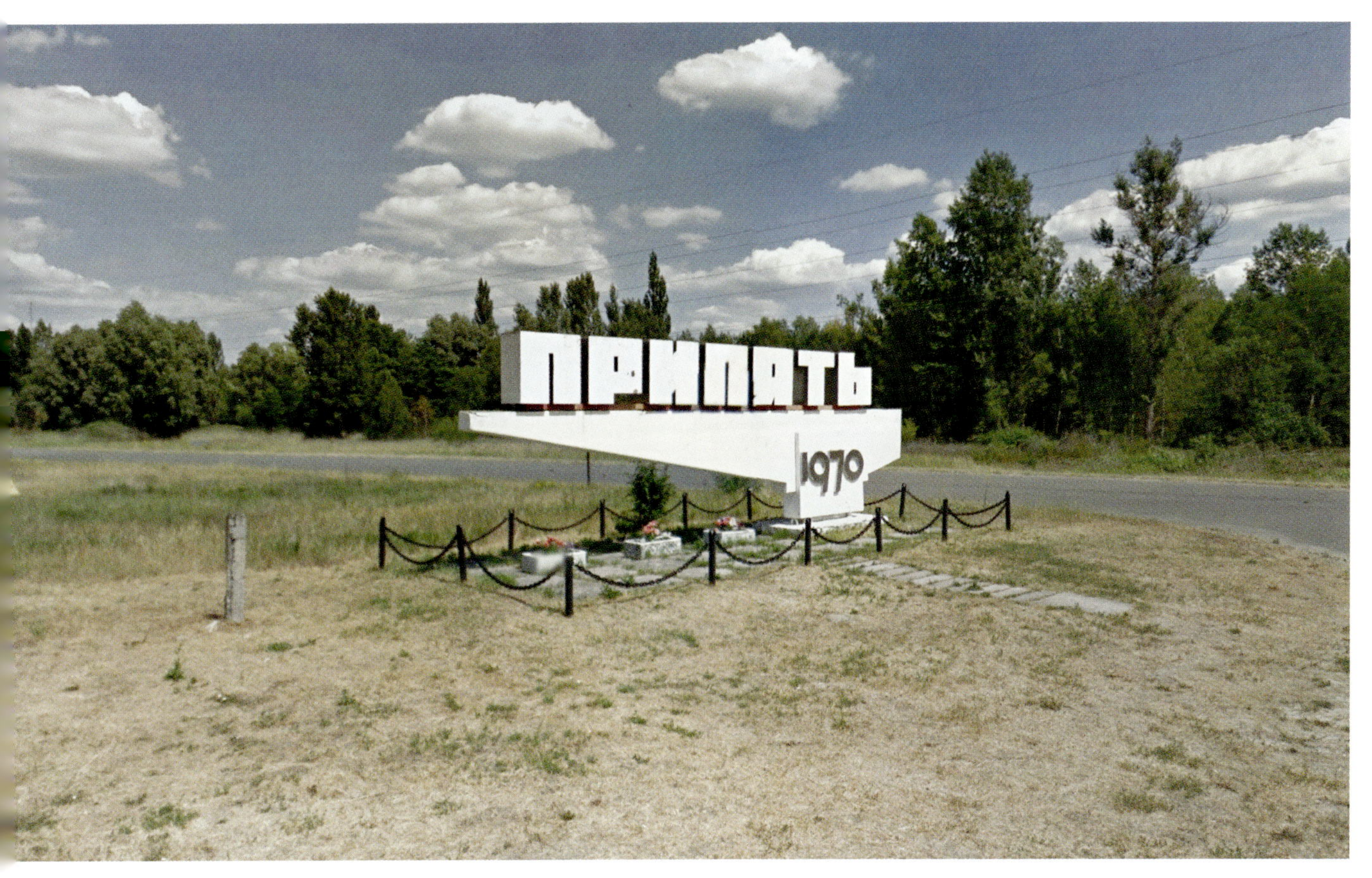

PRIPYAT, UKRAINE

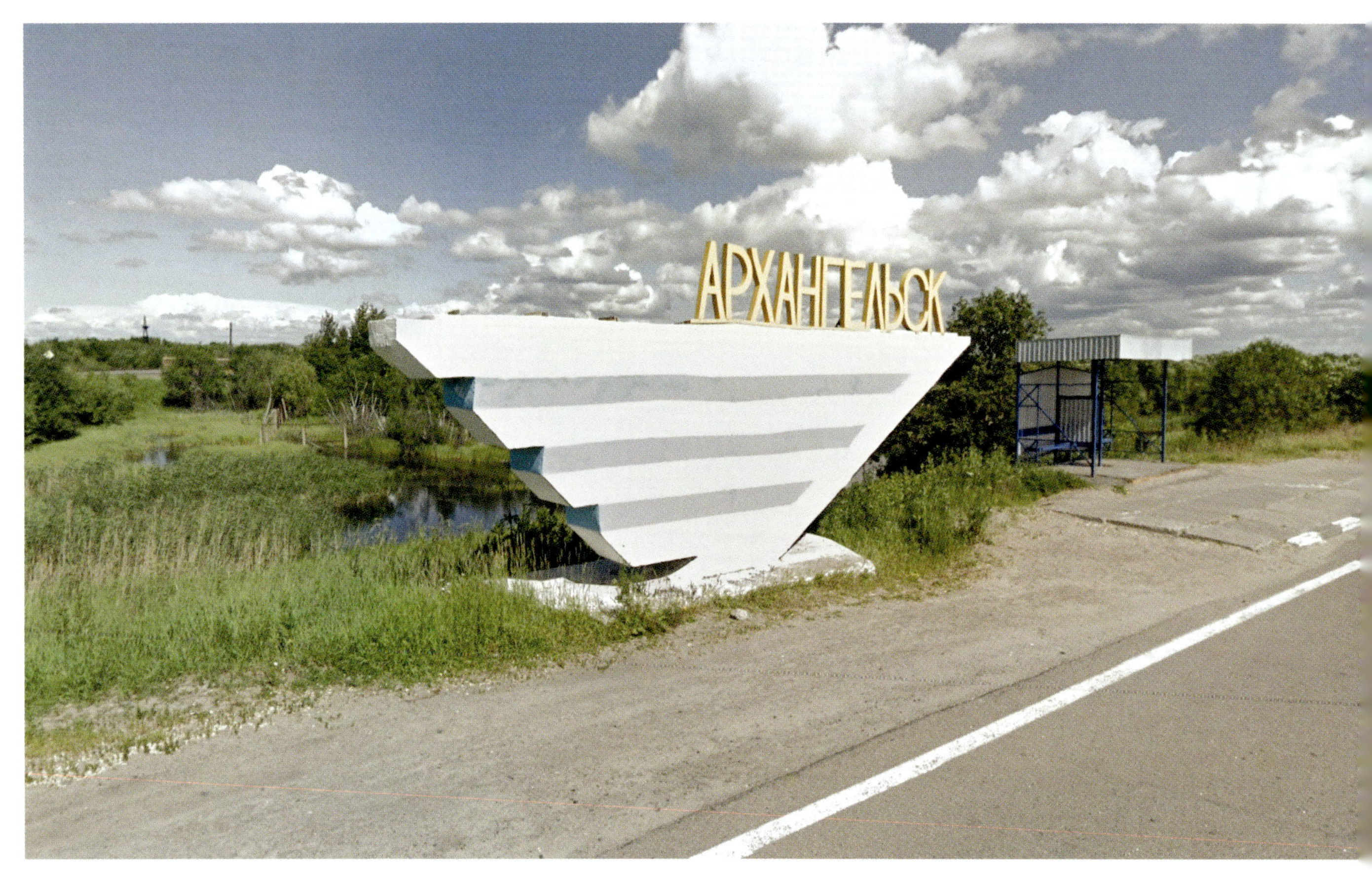

 ARKHANGELSK, RUSSIA

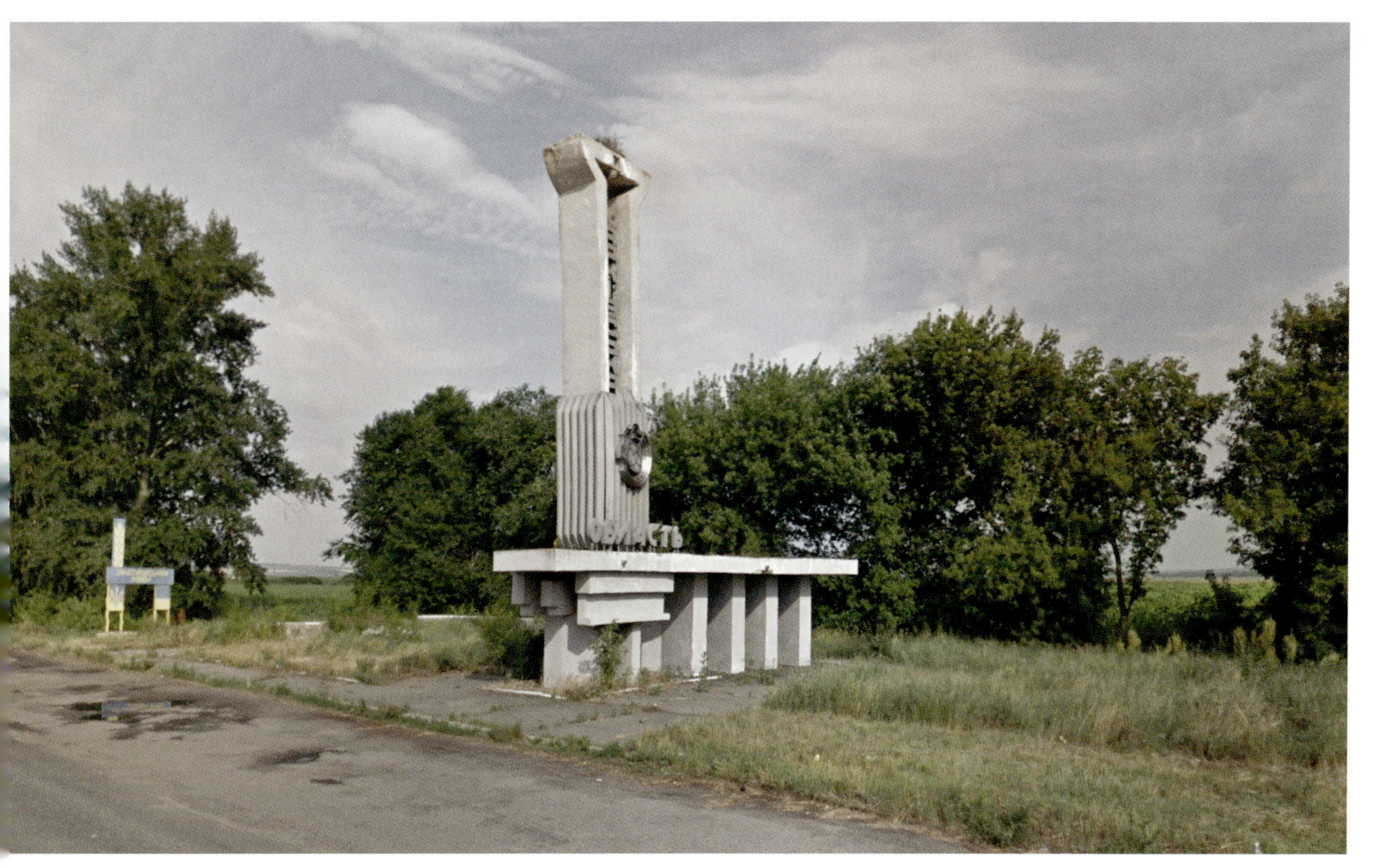

KHARKIV OBLAST, UKRAINE

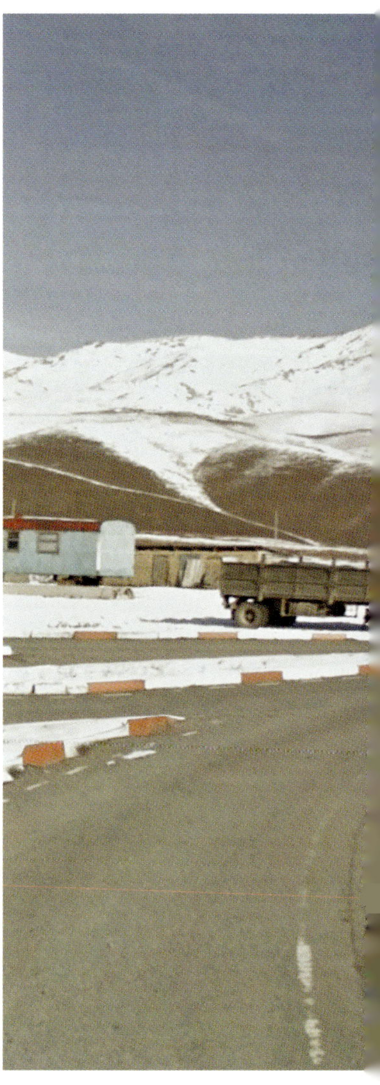

 CHUY PROVINCE, KYRGYZSTAN

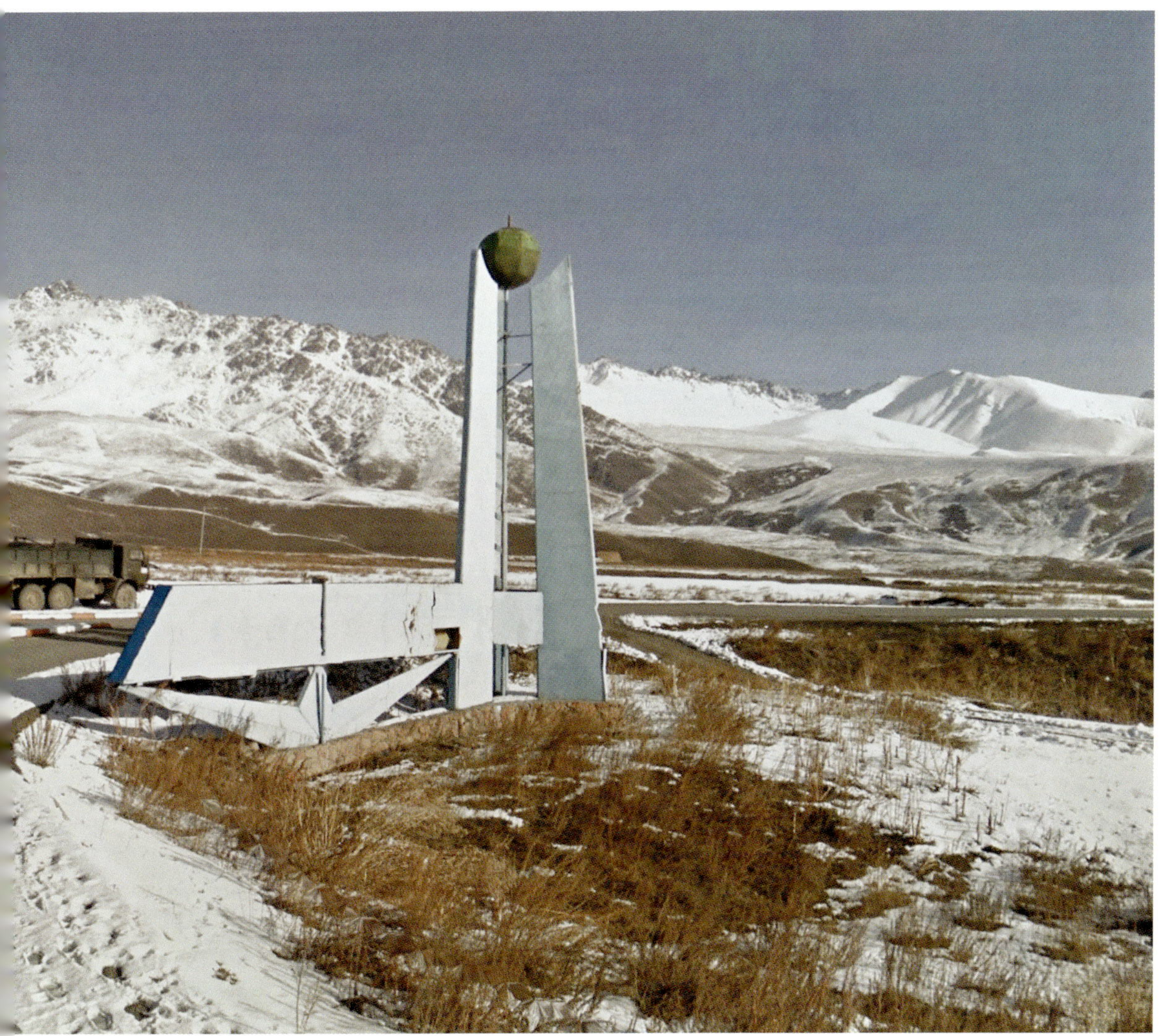

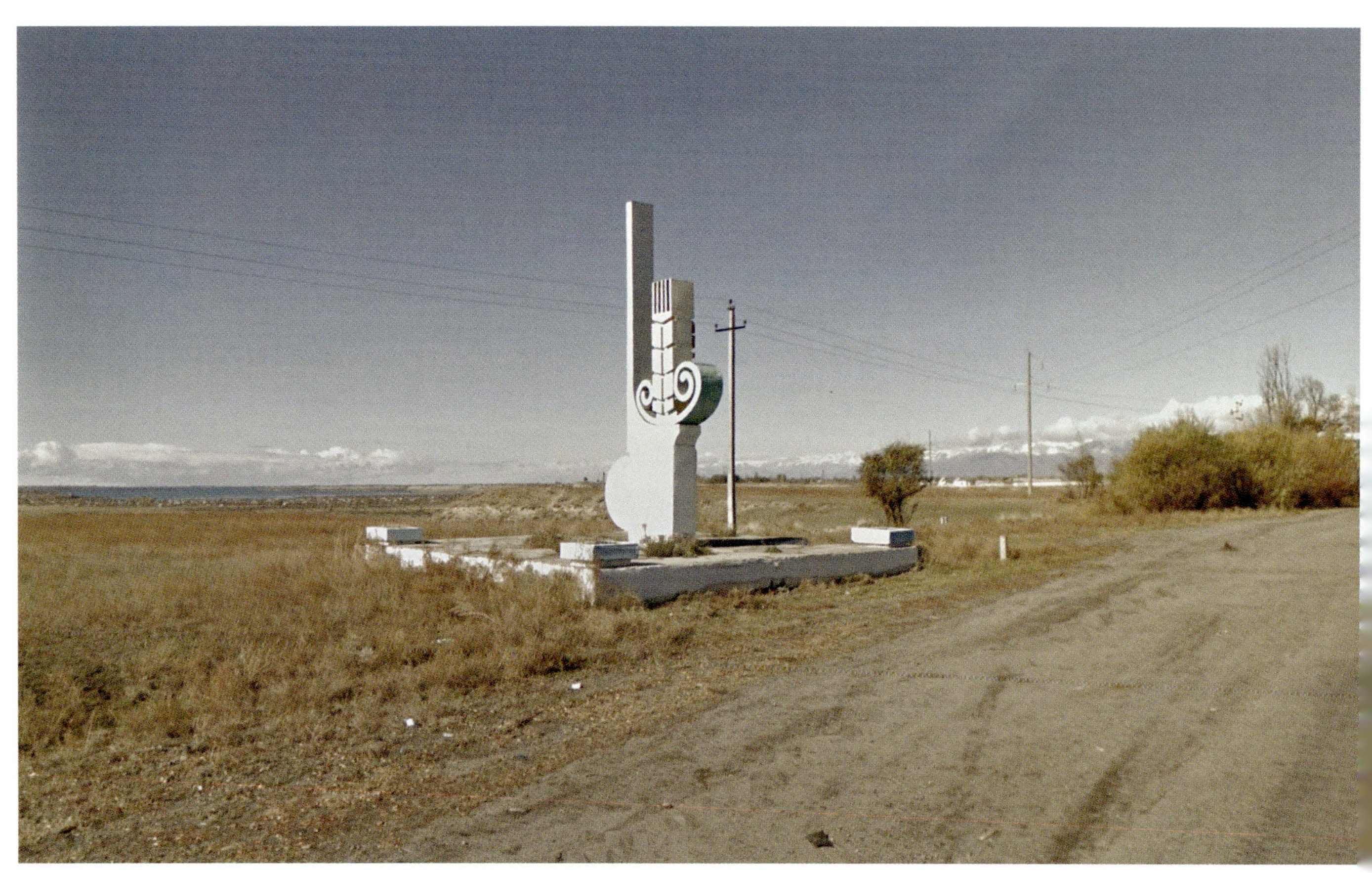

 KARAKOL, KYRGYZSTAN

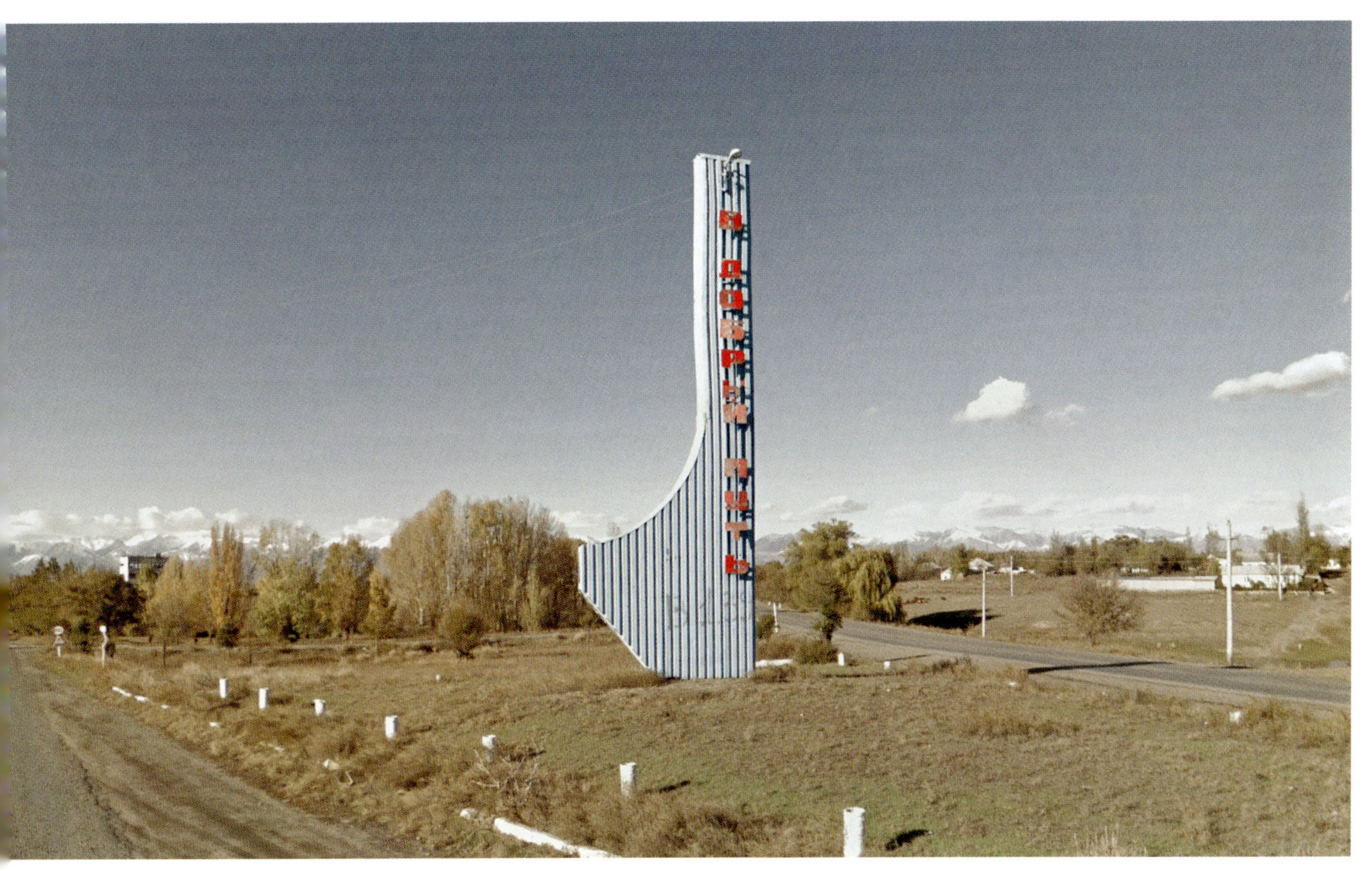

KARAKOL, KYRGYZSTAN

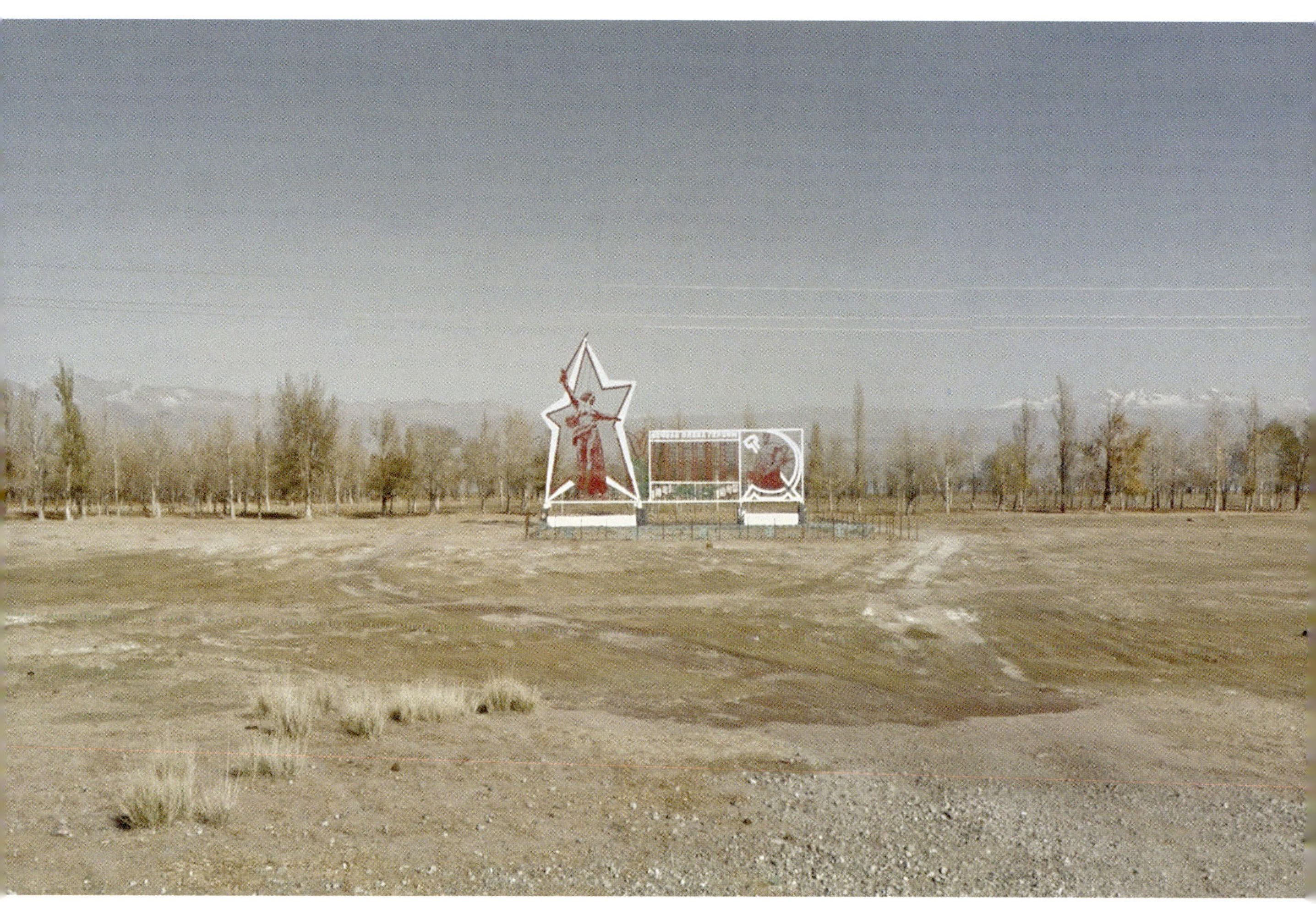

 OTTUK, KYRGYZSTAN

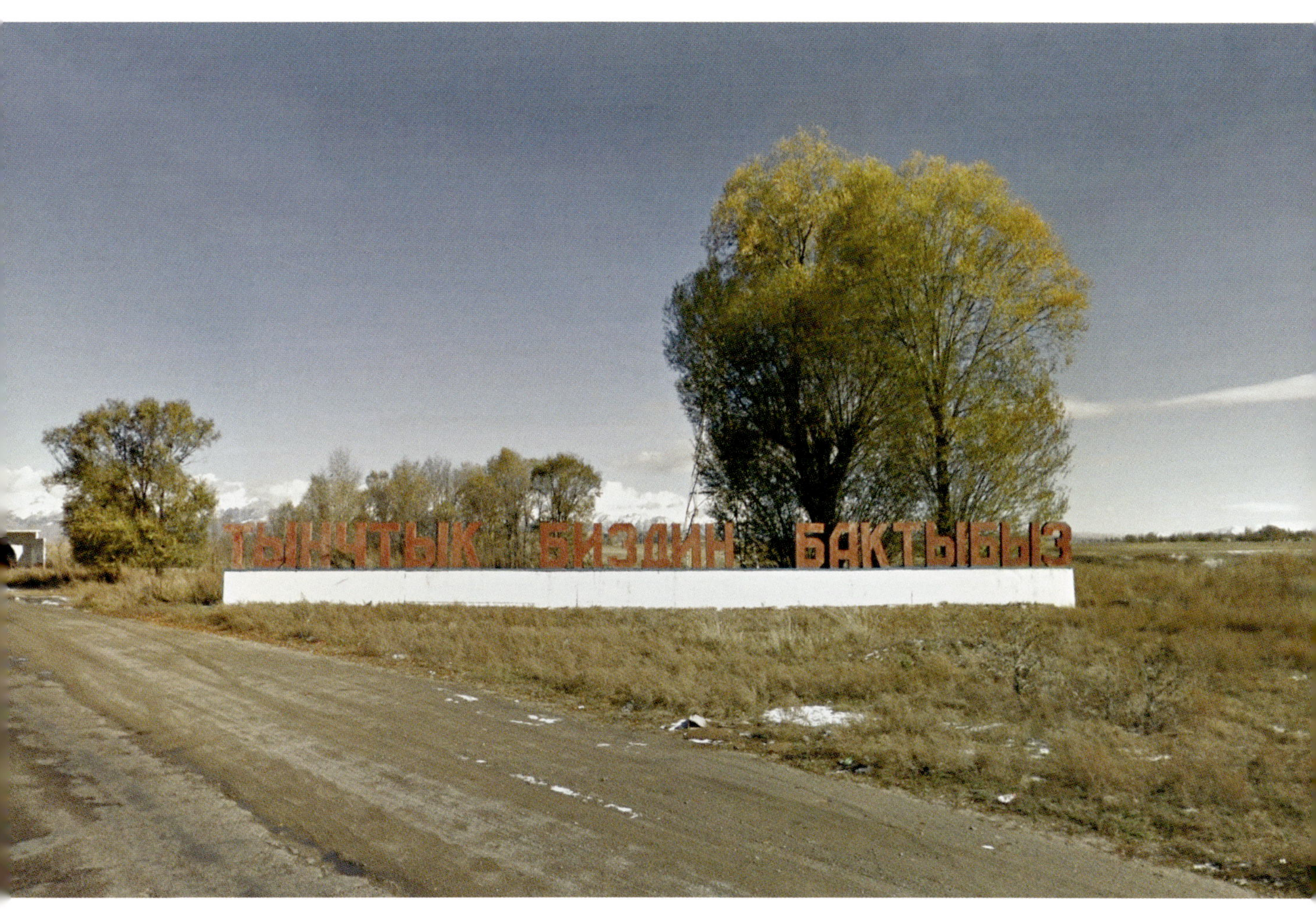

'PEACE IS UPON US', TÜP, KYRGYZSTAN

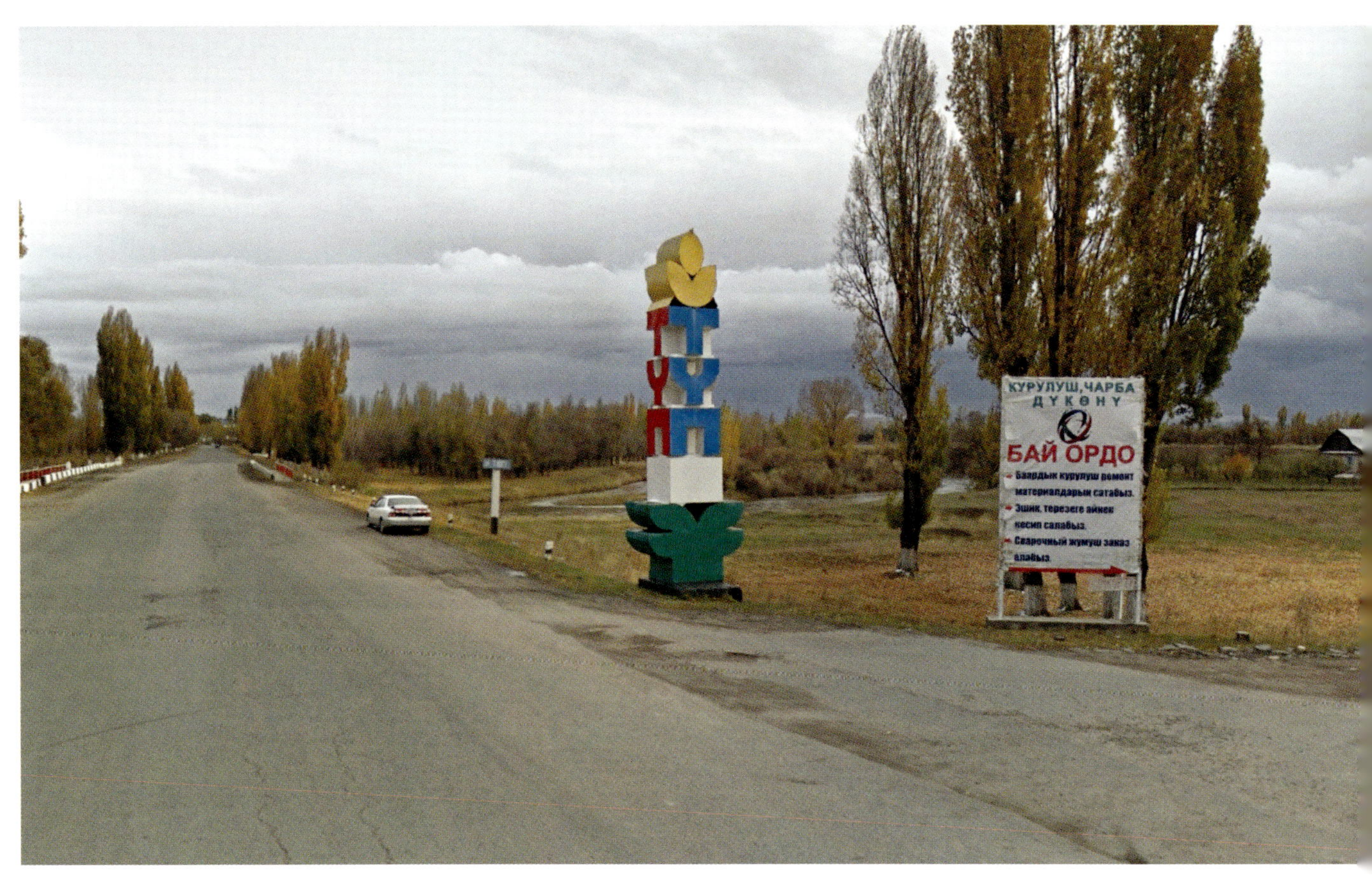
ТҮП
КУРУЛУШ,ЧАРБА
ДҮКӨНҮ
БАЙ ОРДО

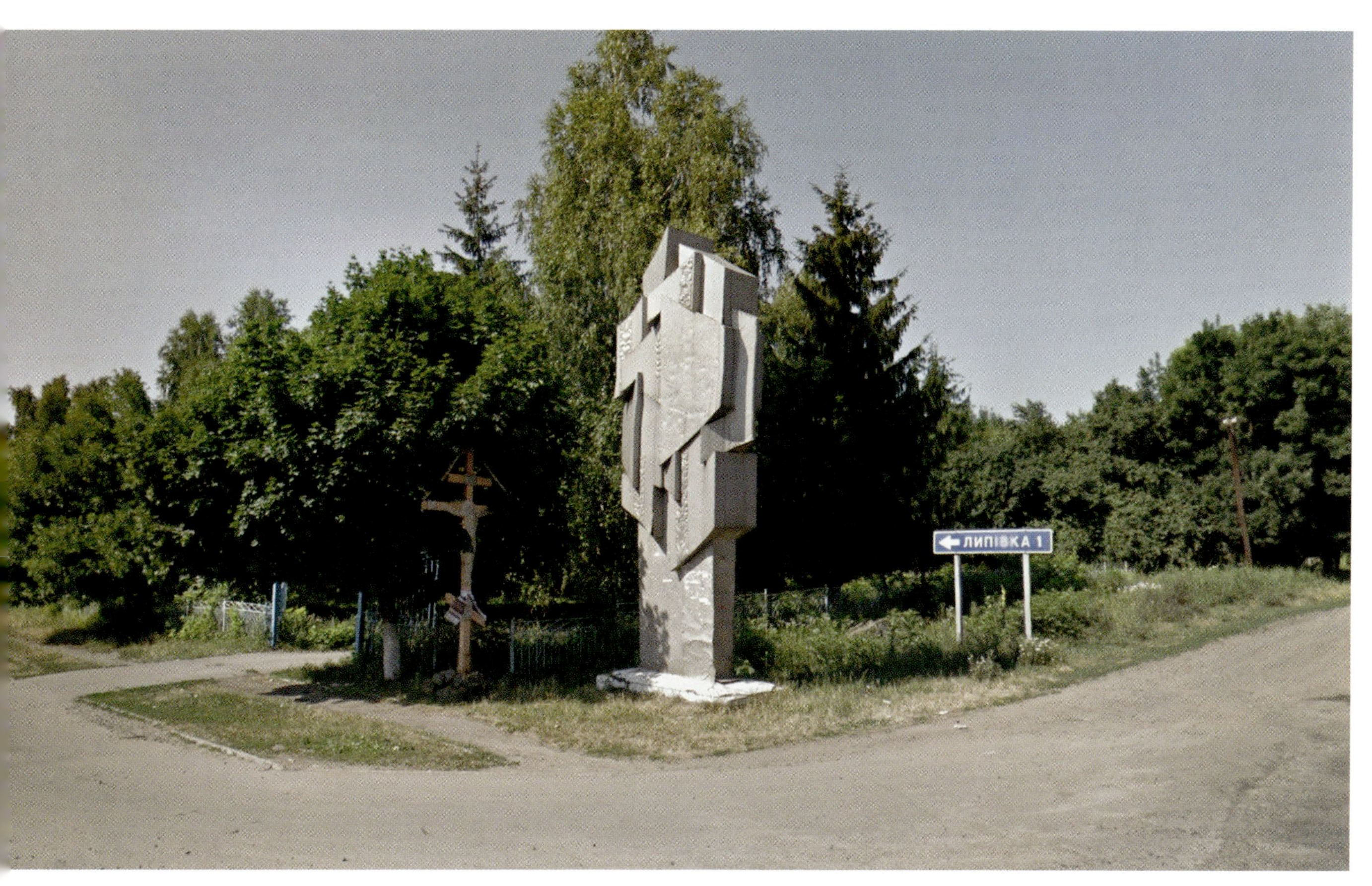

VINNYTSIA OBLAST, UKRAINE

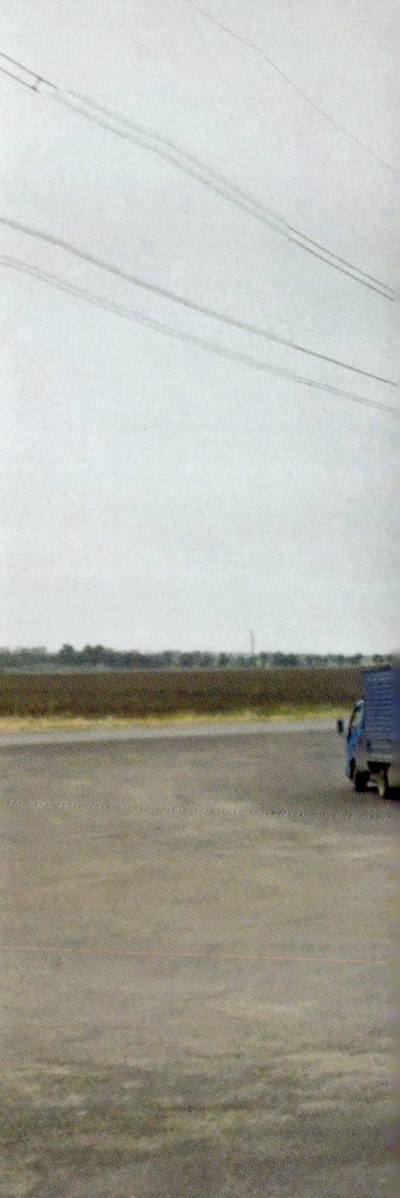

ORDZHONIKIDZE, UKRAINE

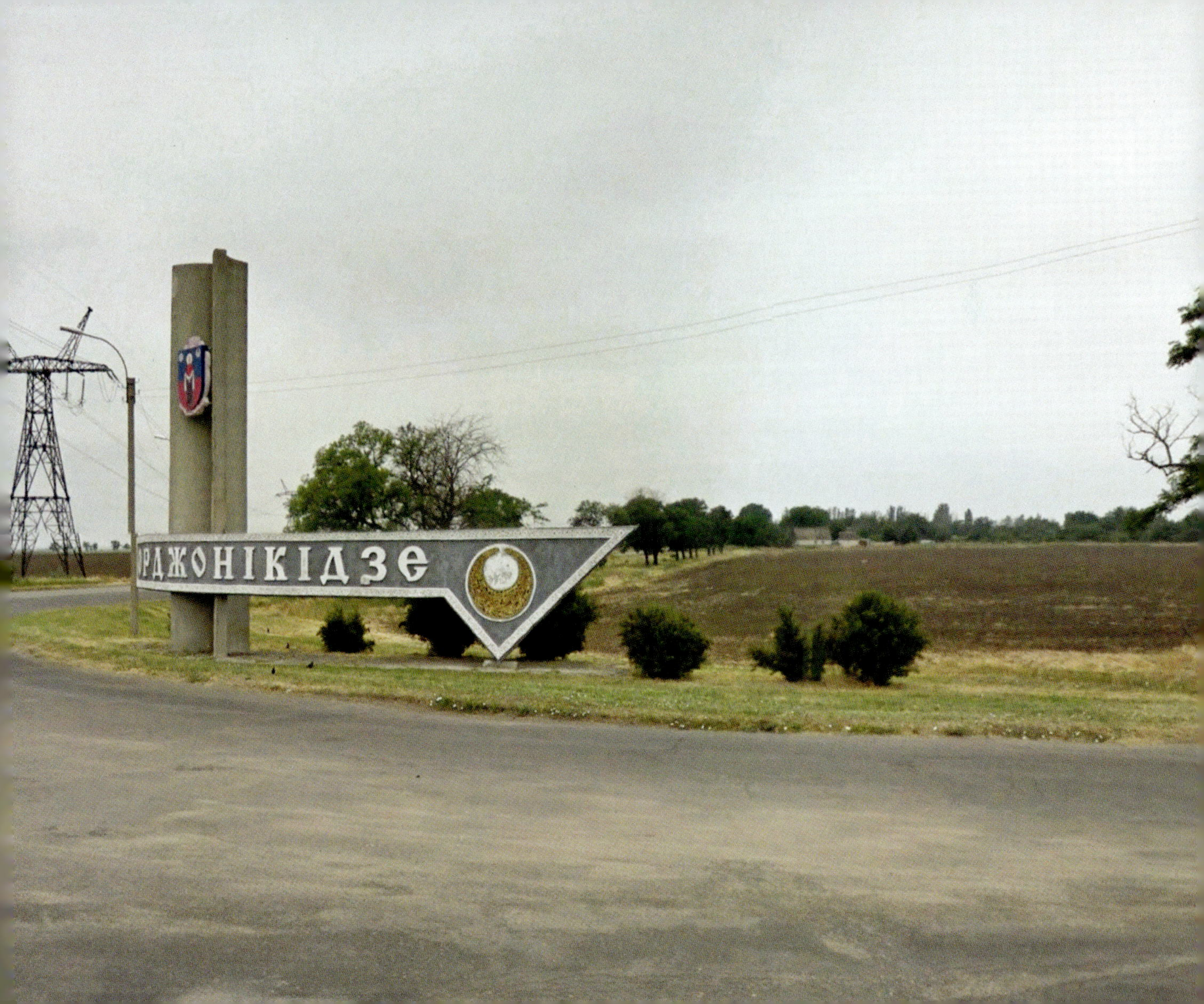
ОРДЖОНІКІДЗЕ

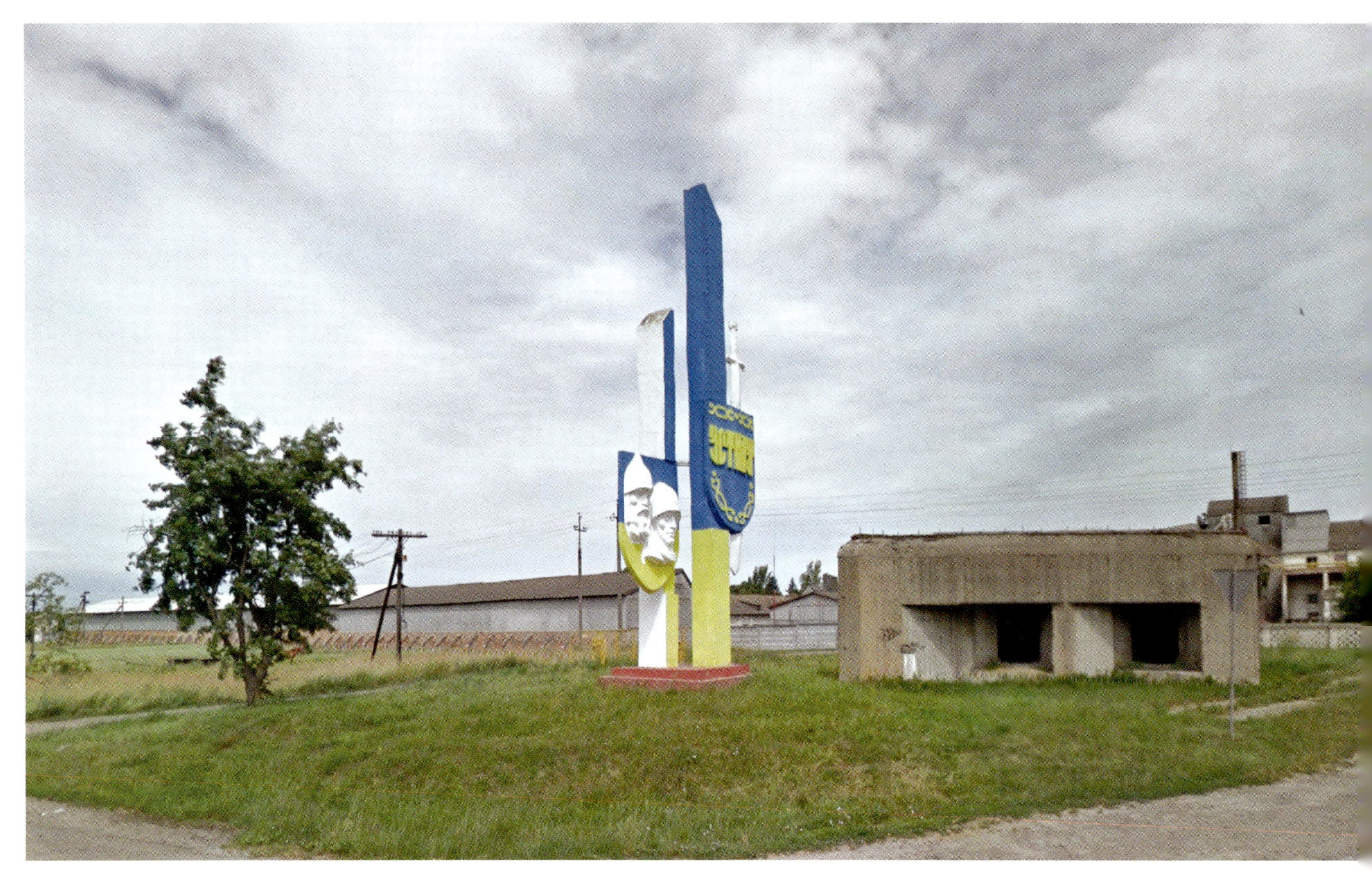

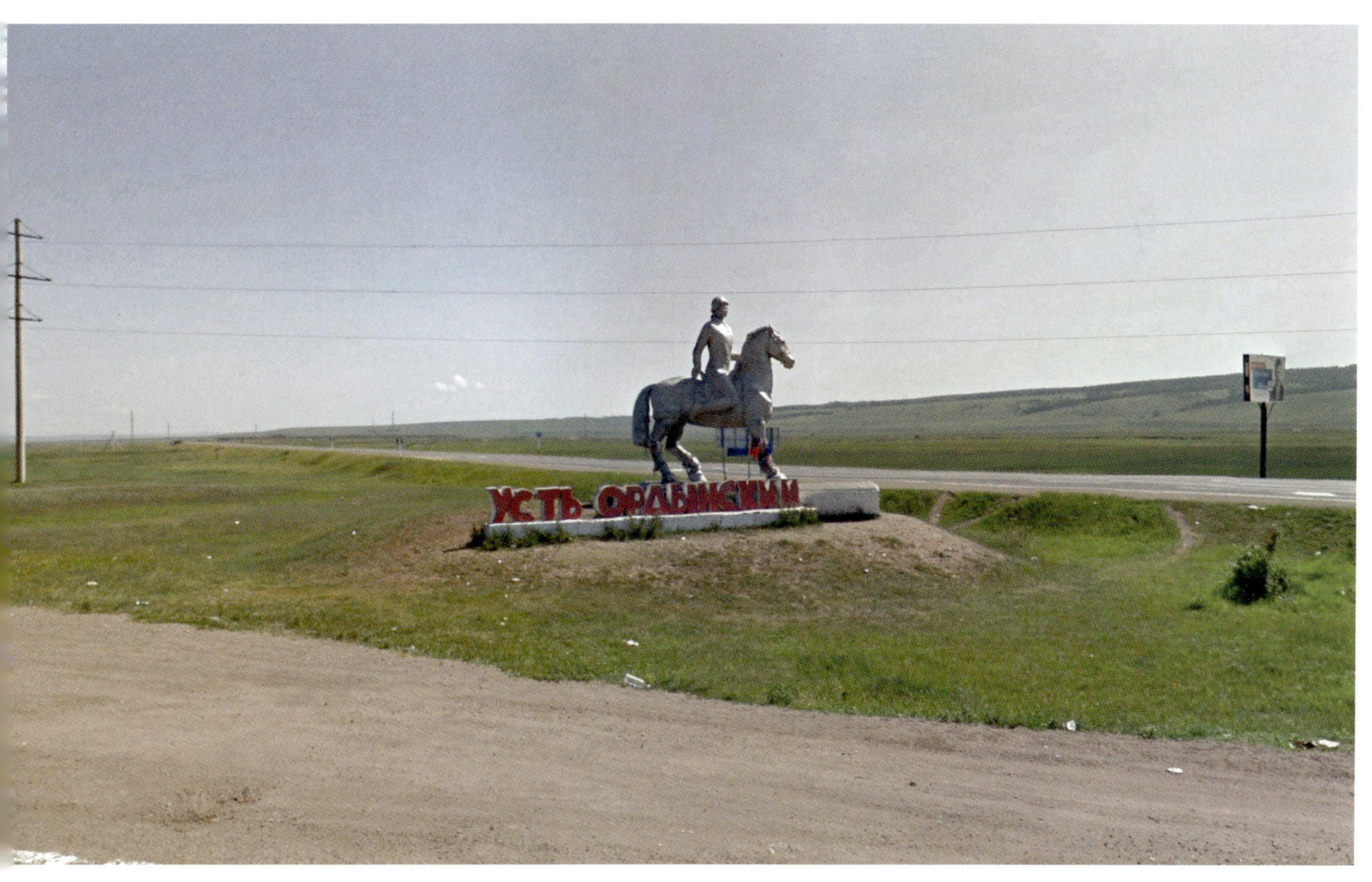

UST-ORDYNSKY, RUSSIA

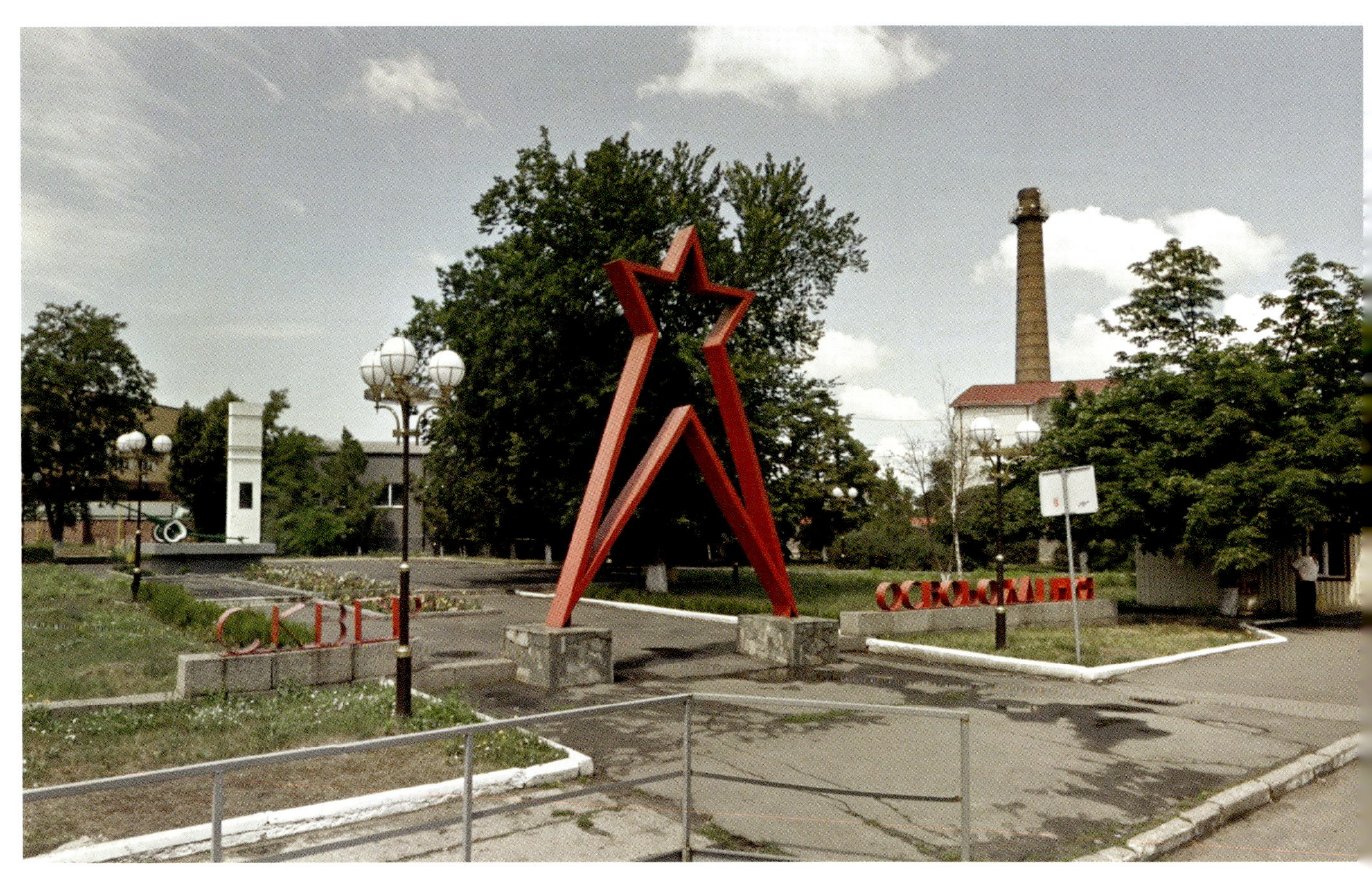

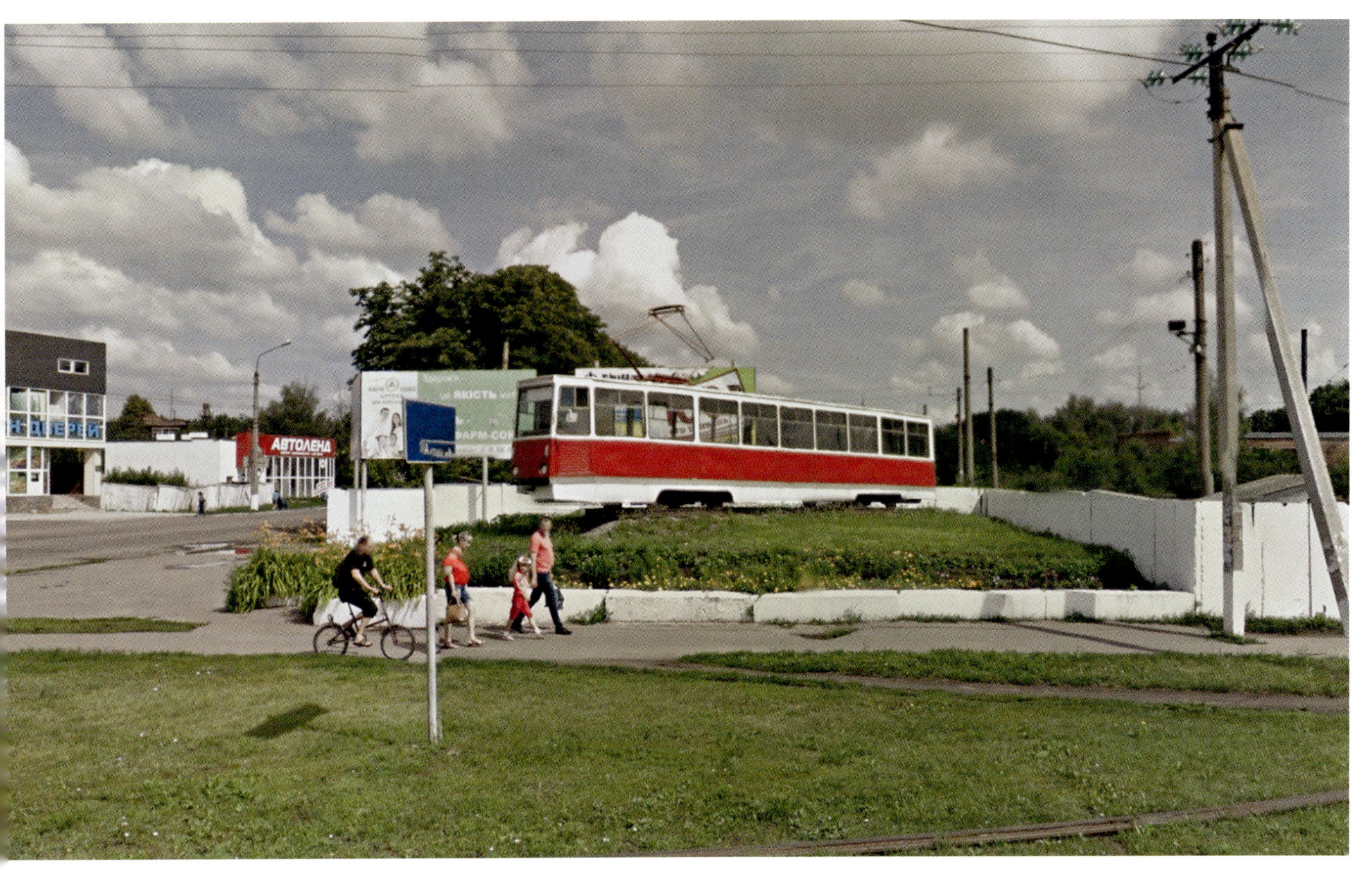

KRYVYI RIH, UKRAINE

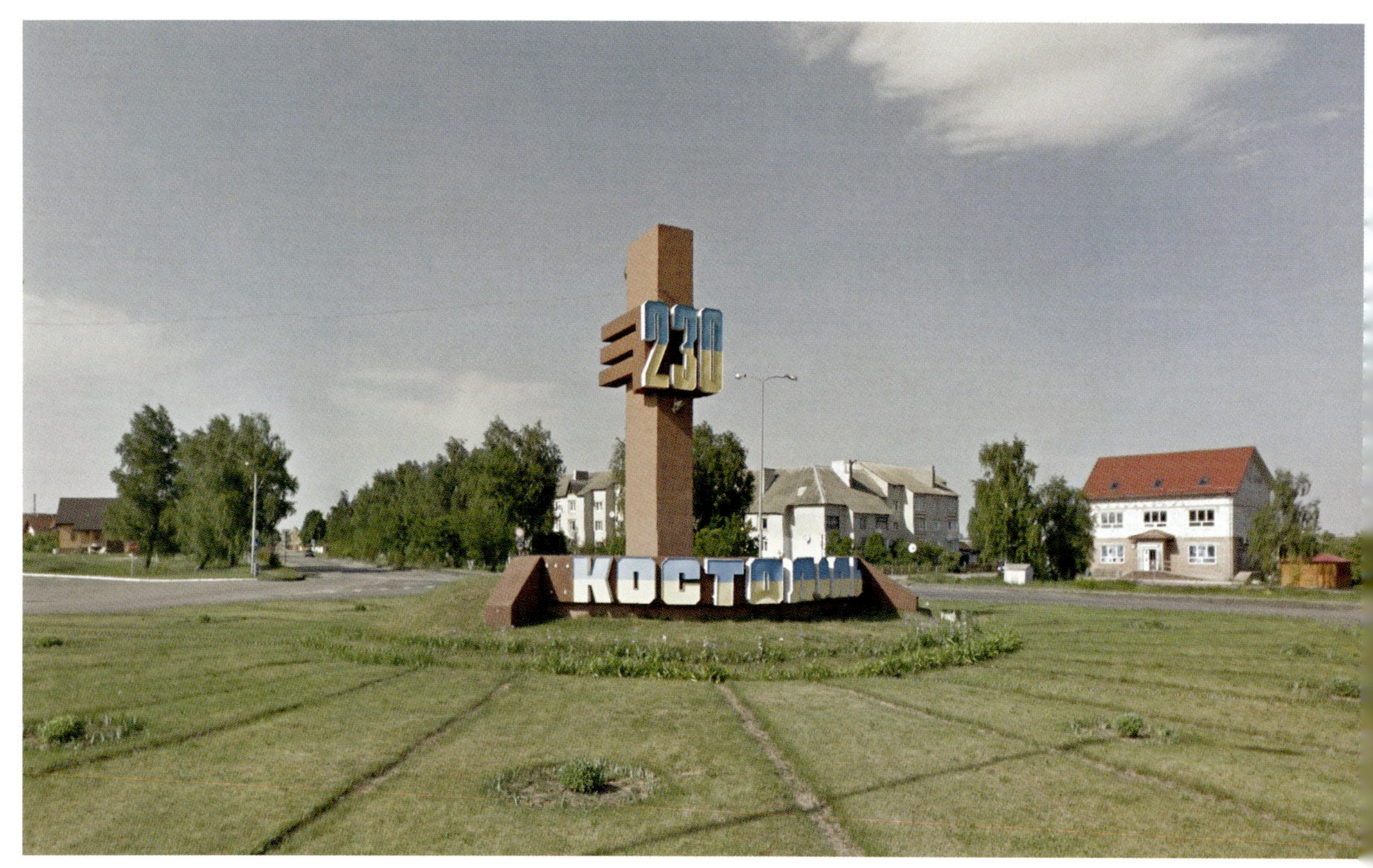

 KOSTOPIL, UKRAINE

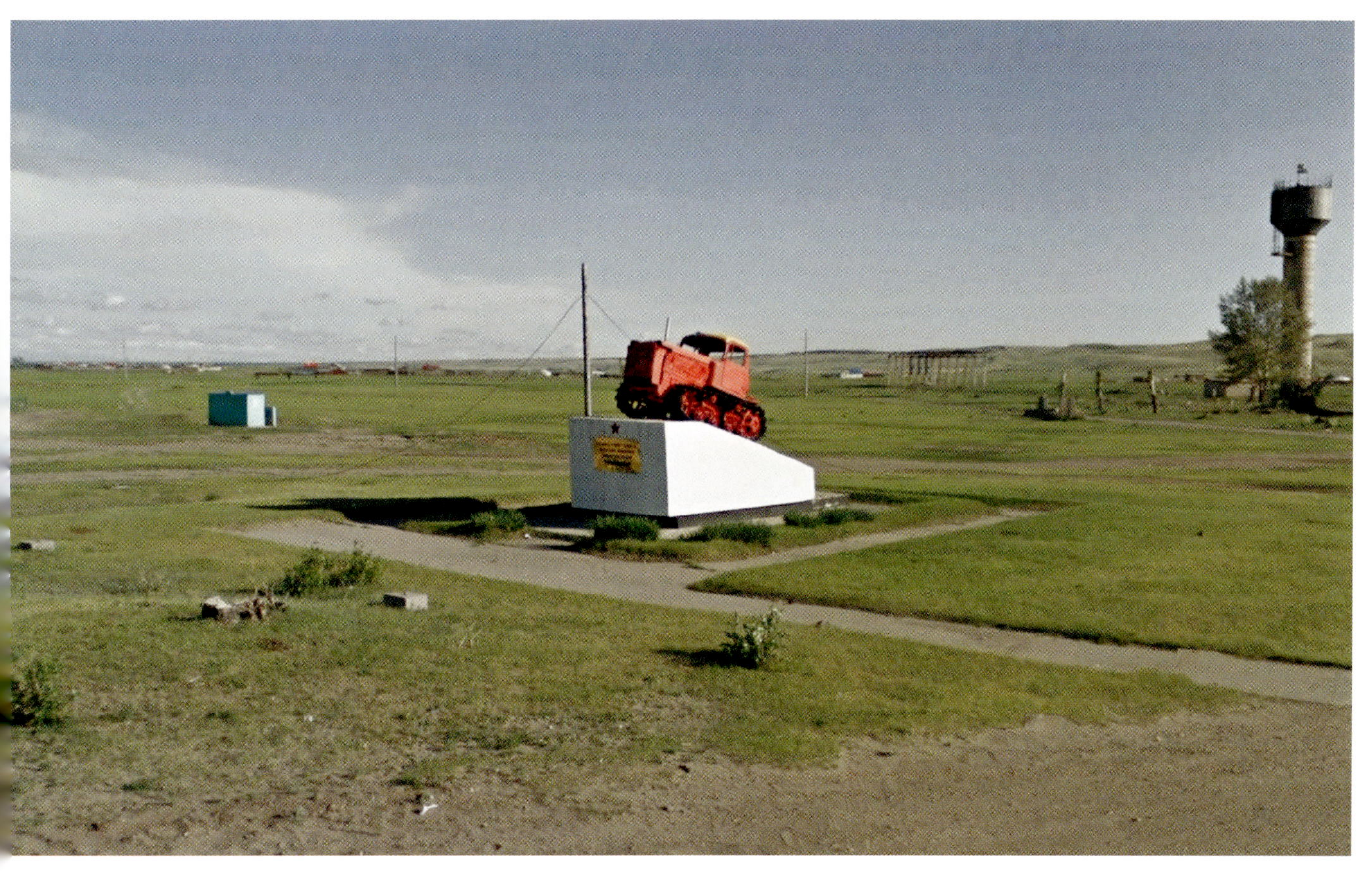

DORNOD, MONGOLIA

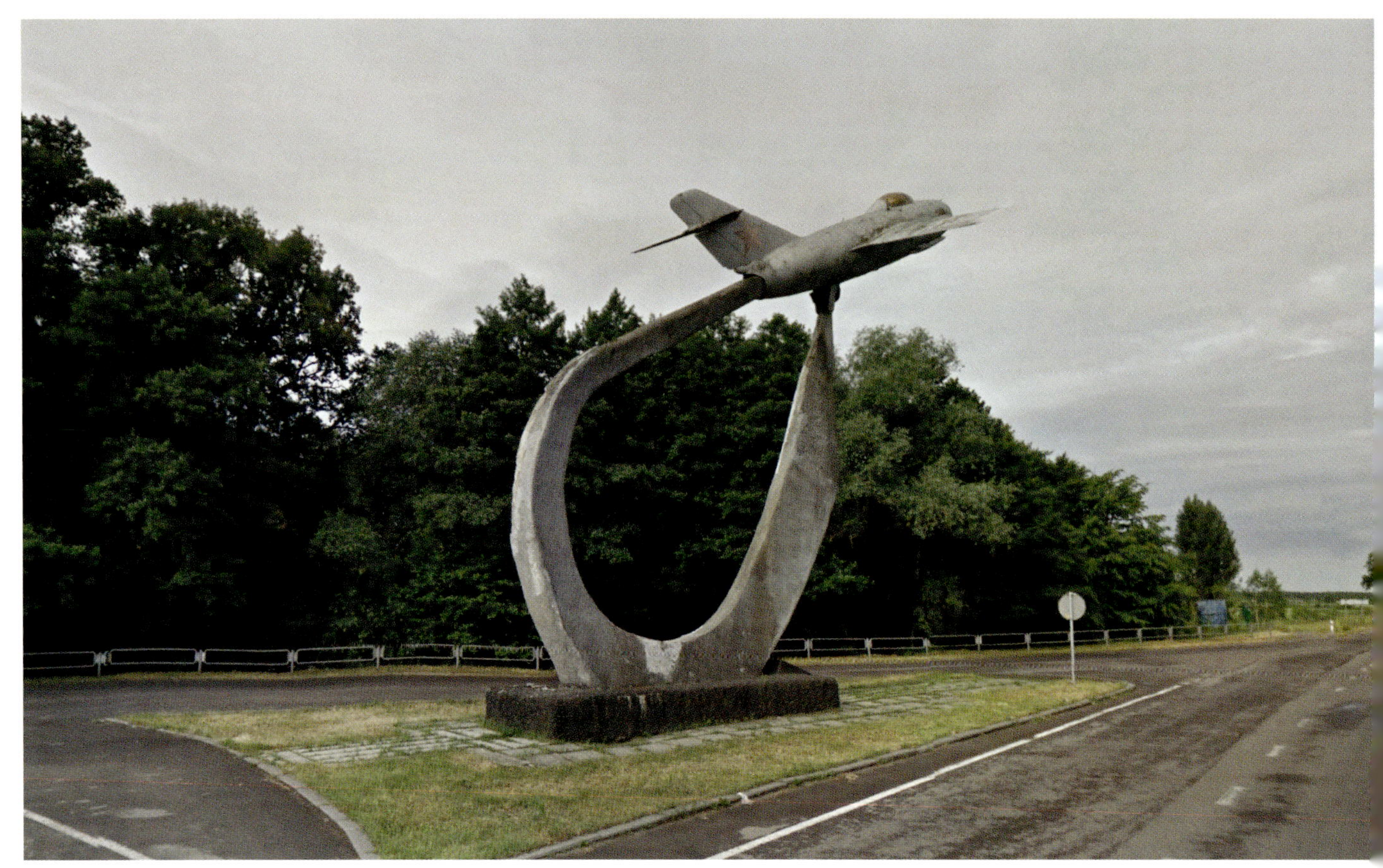

 RIVNE, UKRAINE

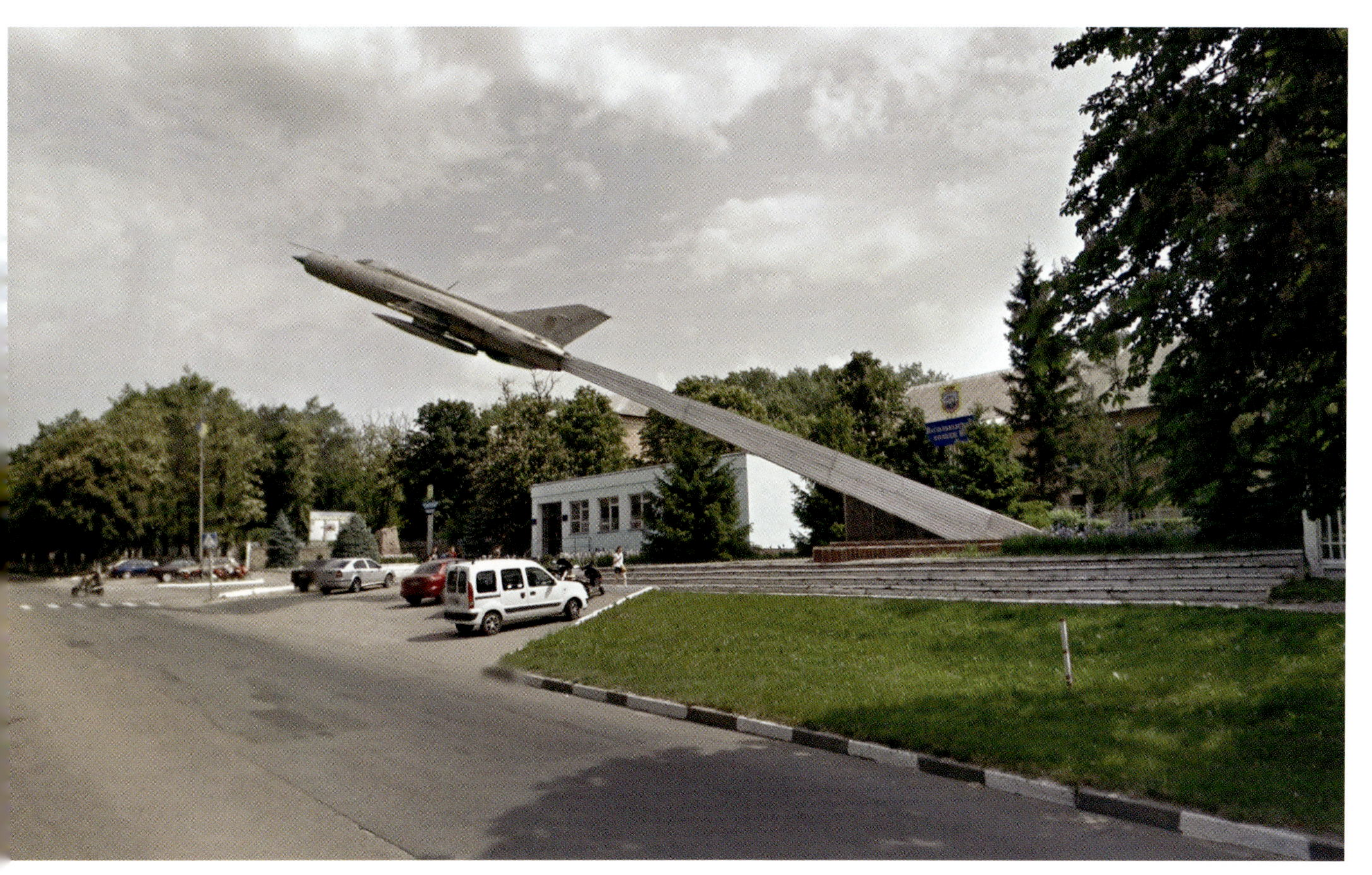

VASYLKIV, UKRAINE

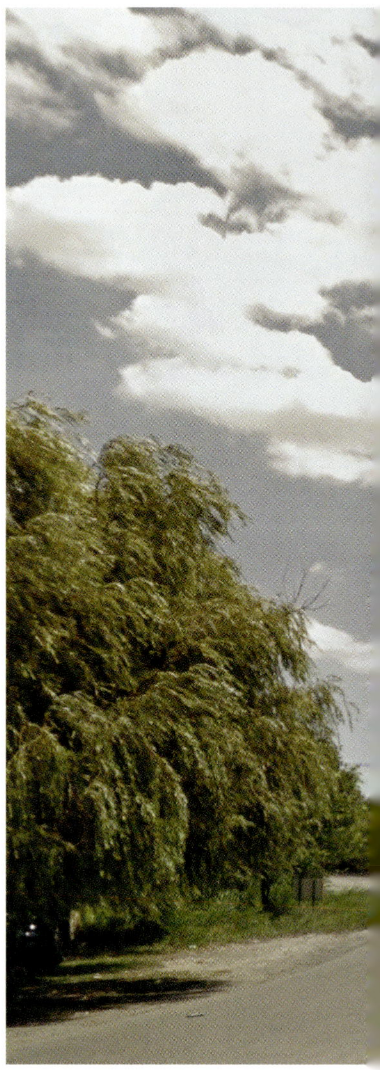

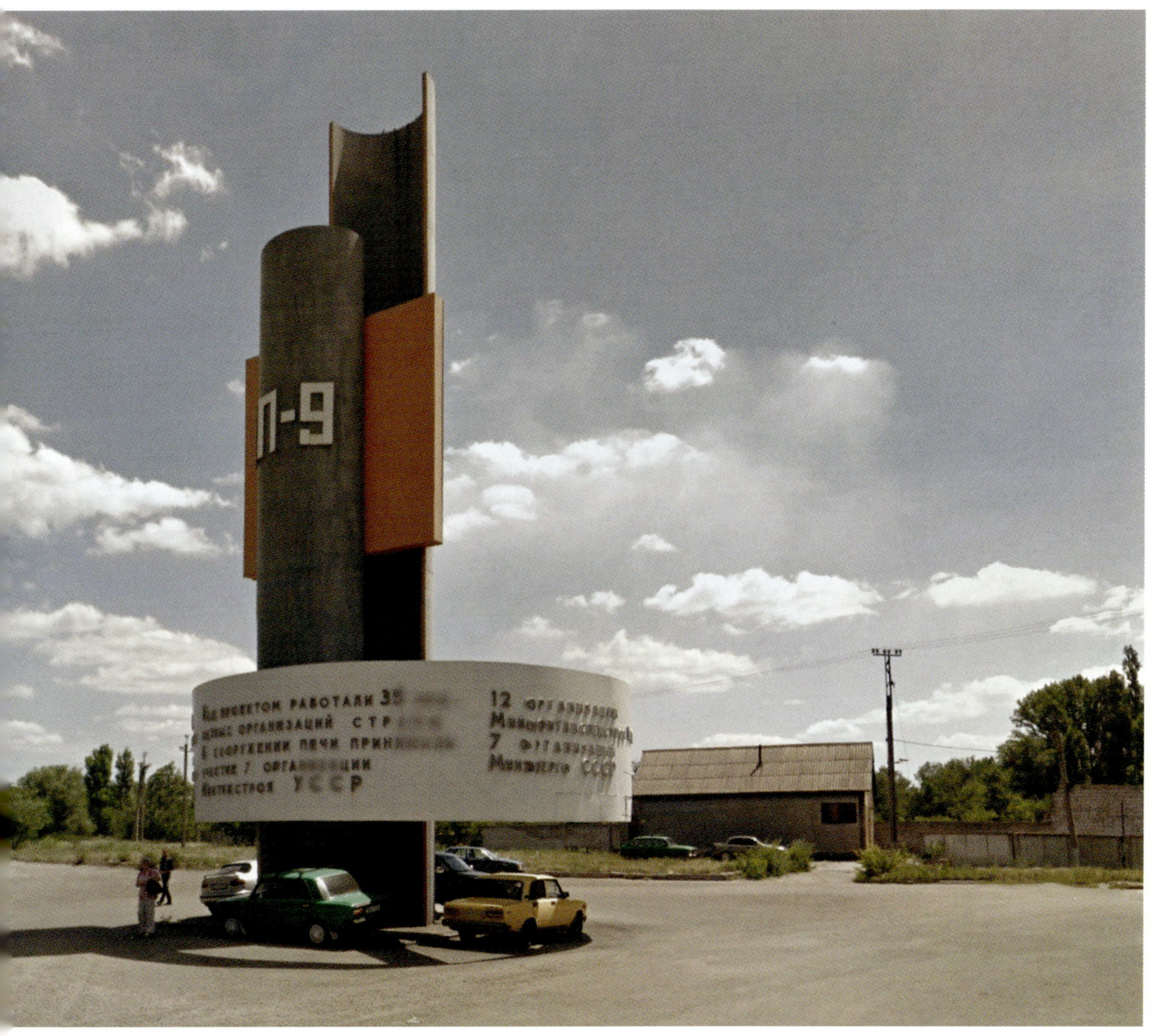
П-9
УССР
СССР

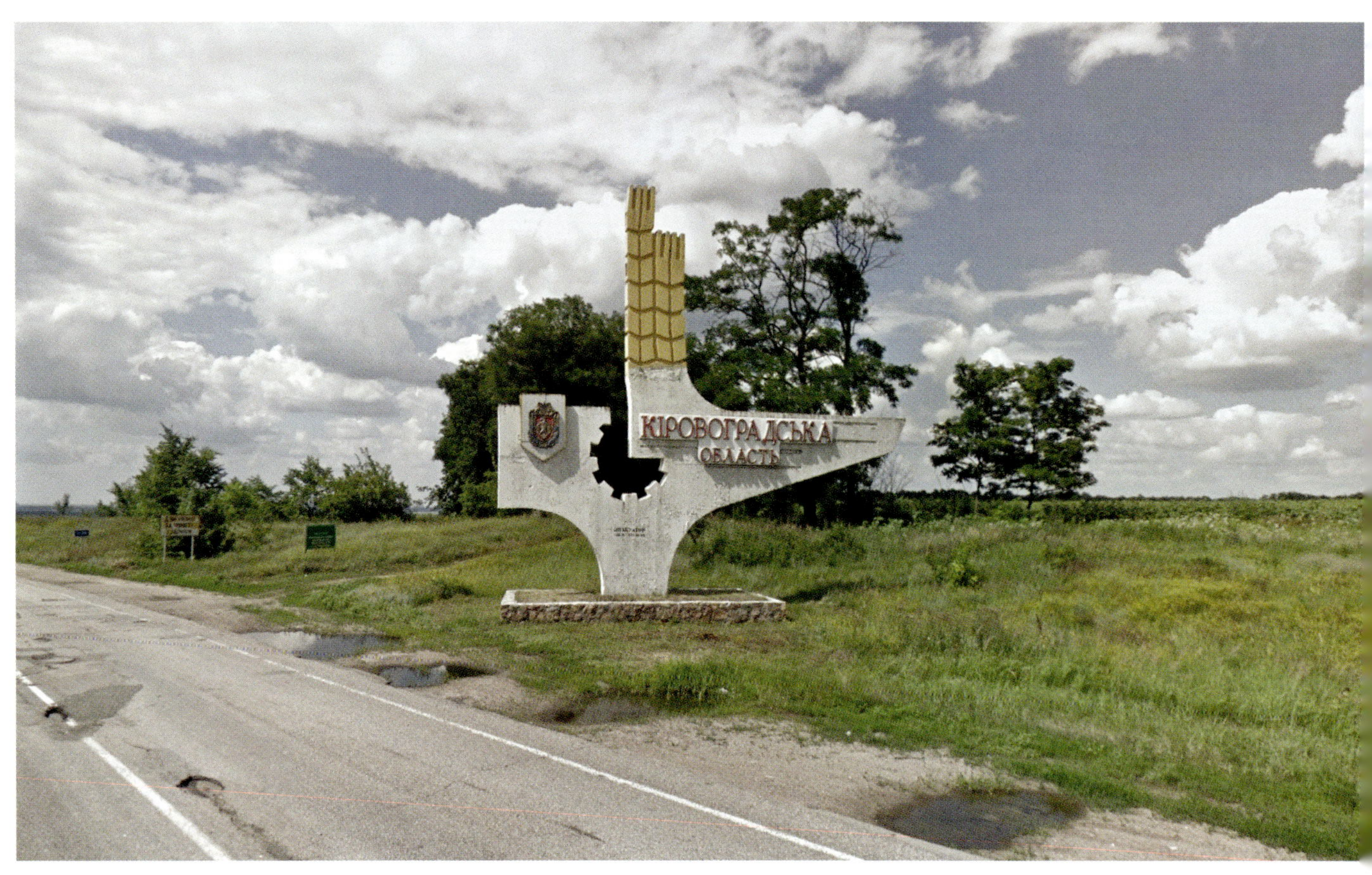

 KIROVOHRAD OBLAST, UKRAINE

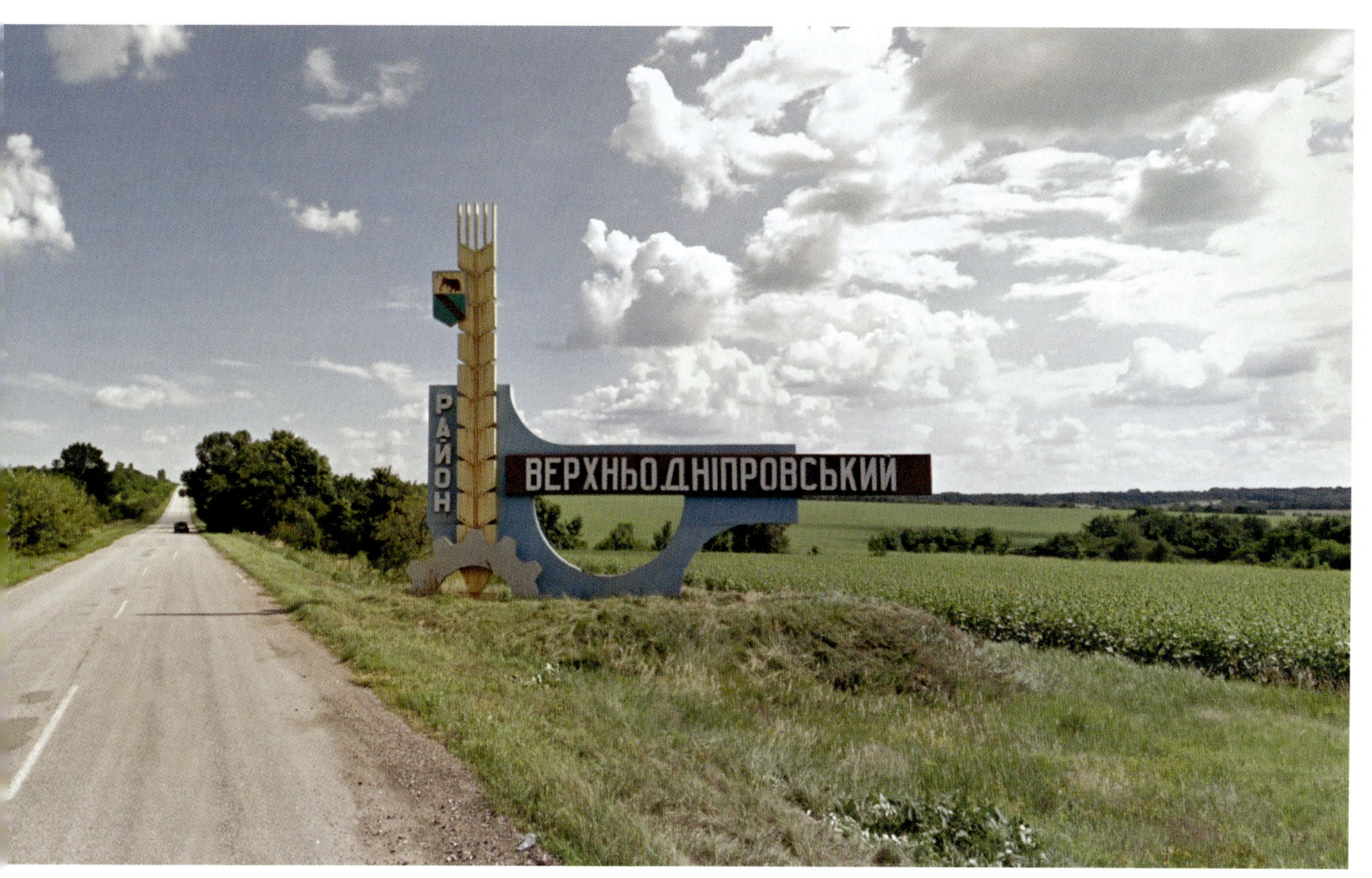

VERKHNODNIPROVSK RAION, UKRAINE

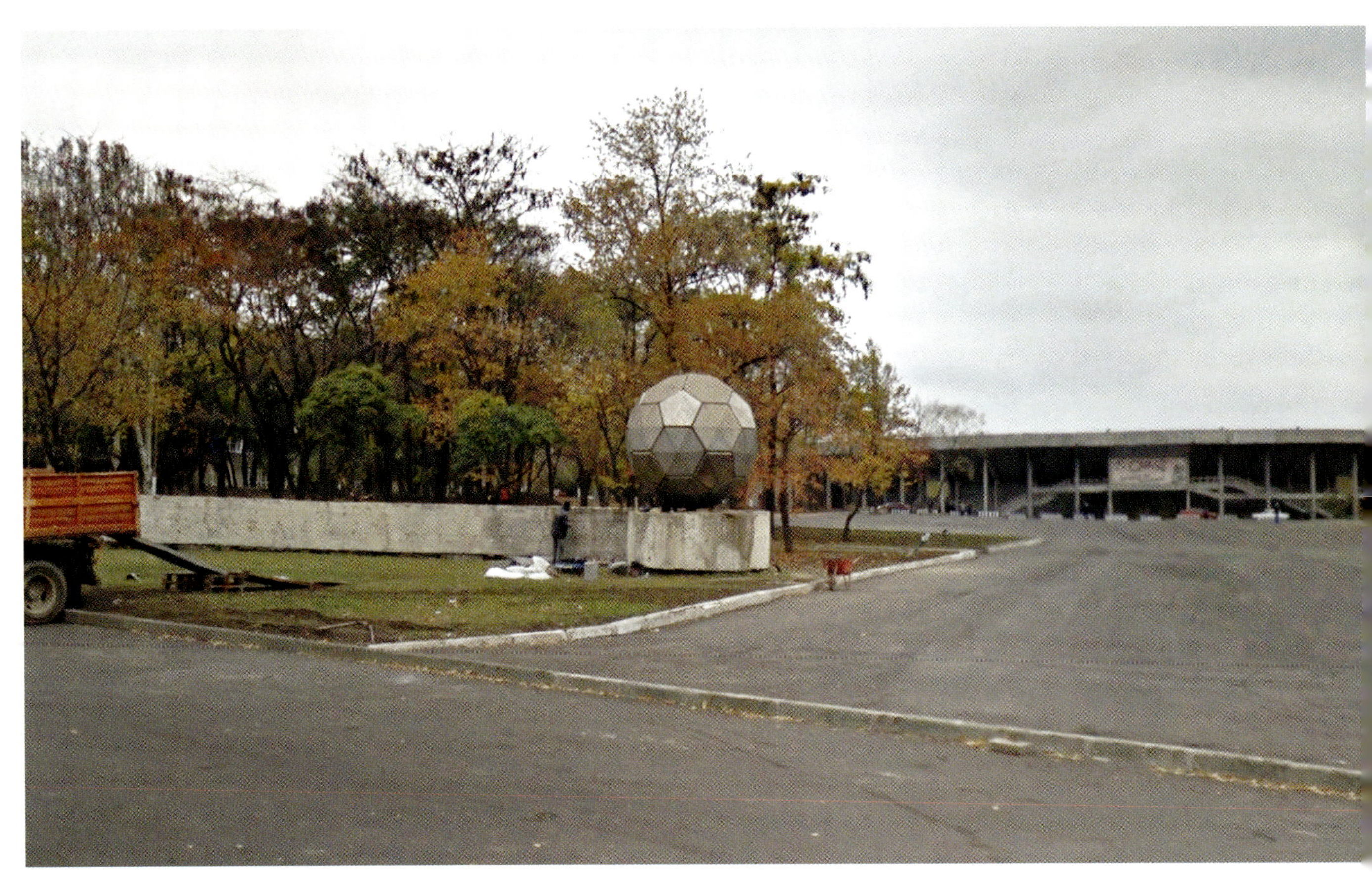

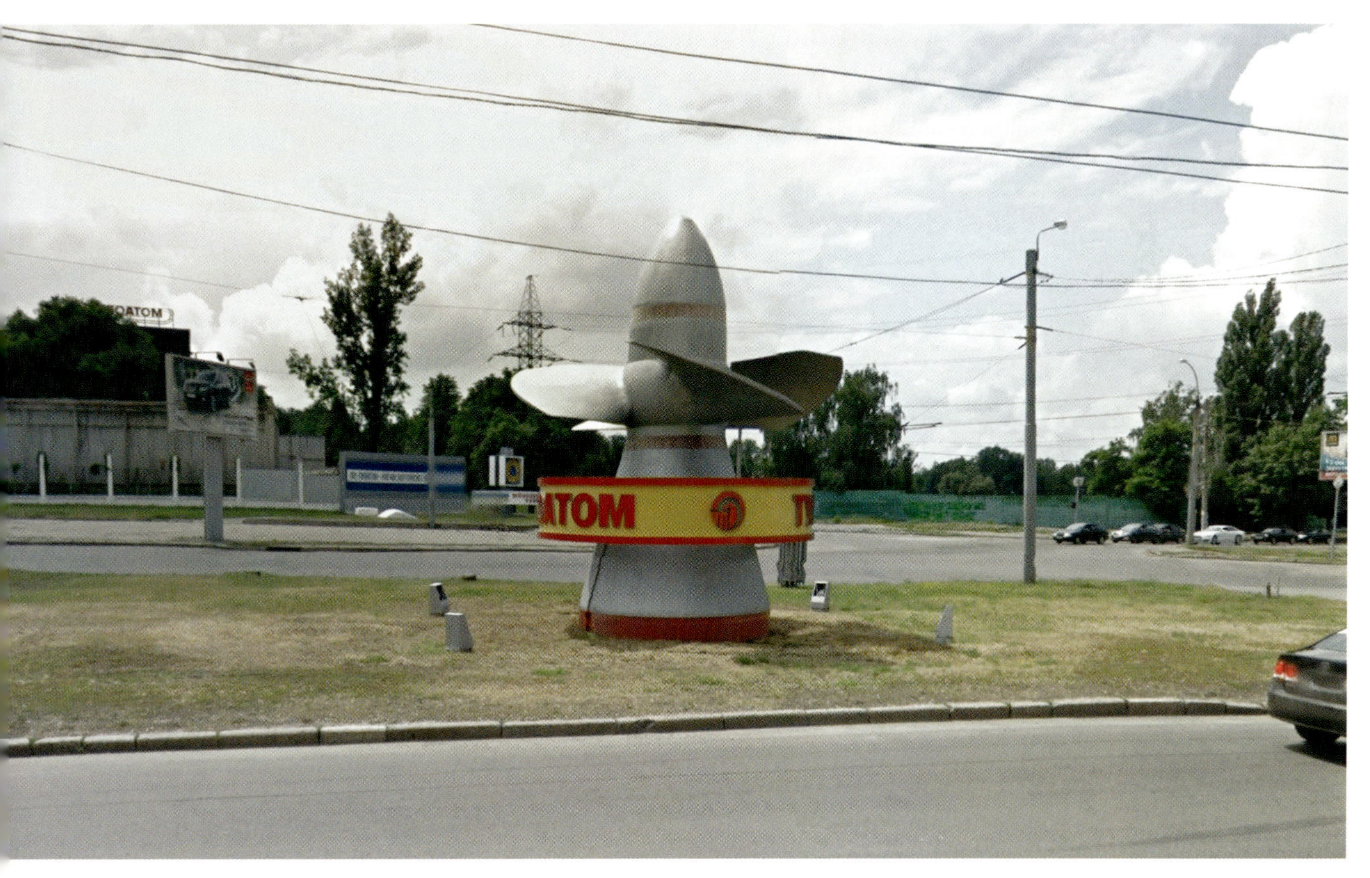
ATOM
ОАТОМ

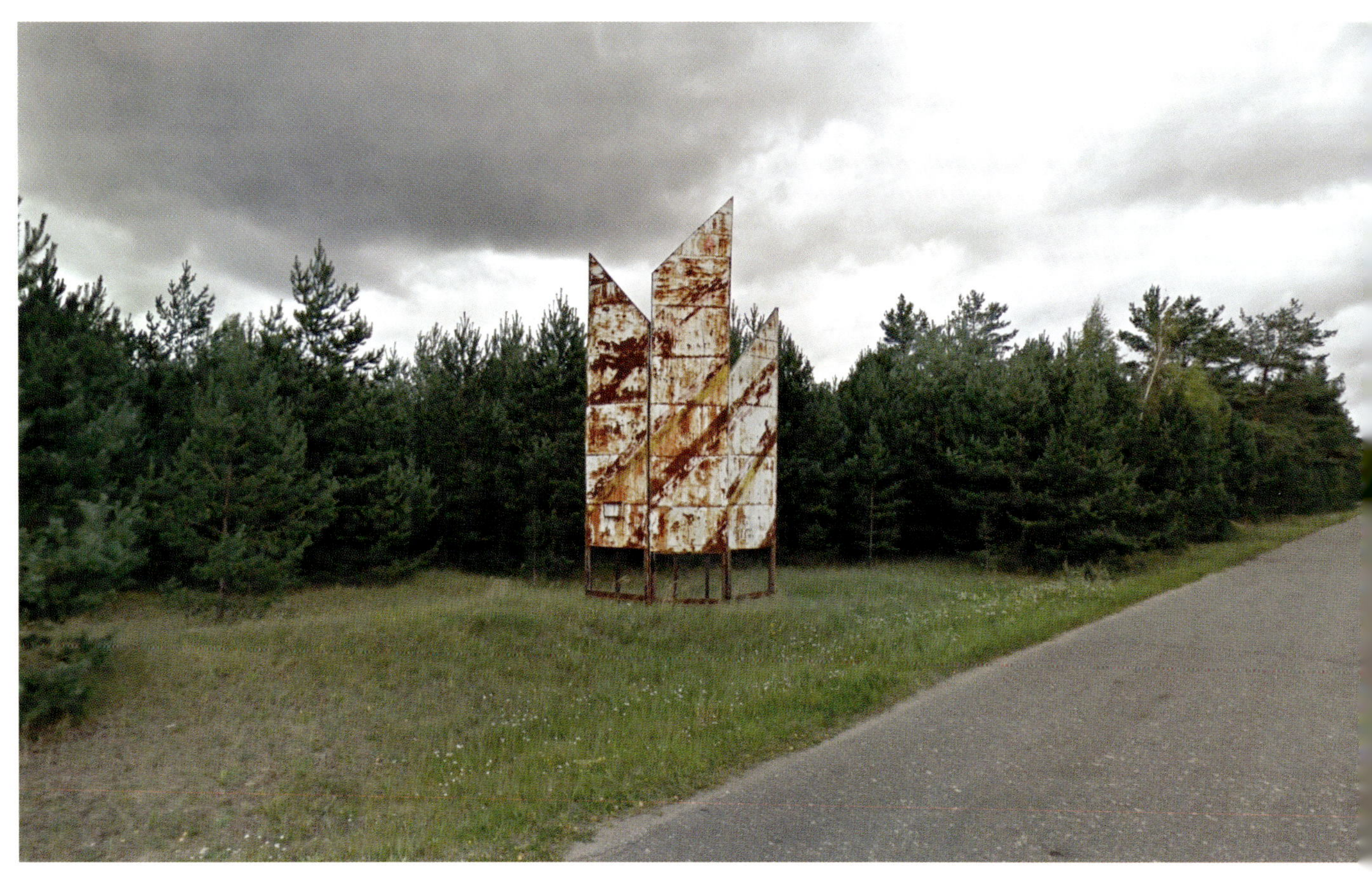

 KADAGA, LATVIA

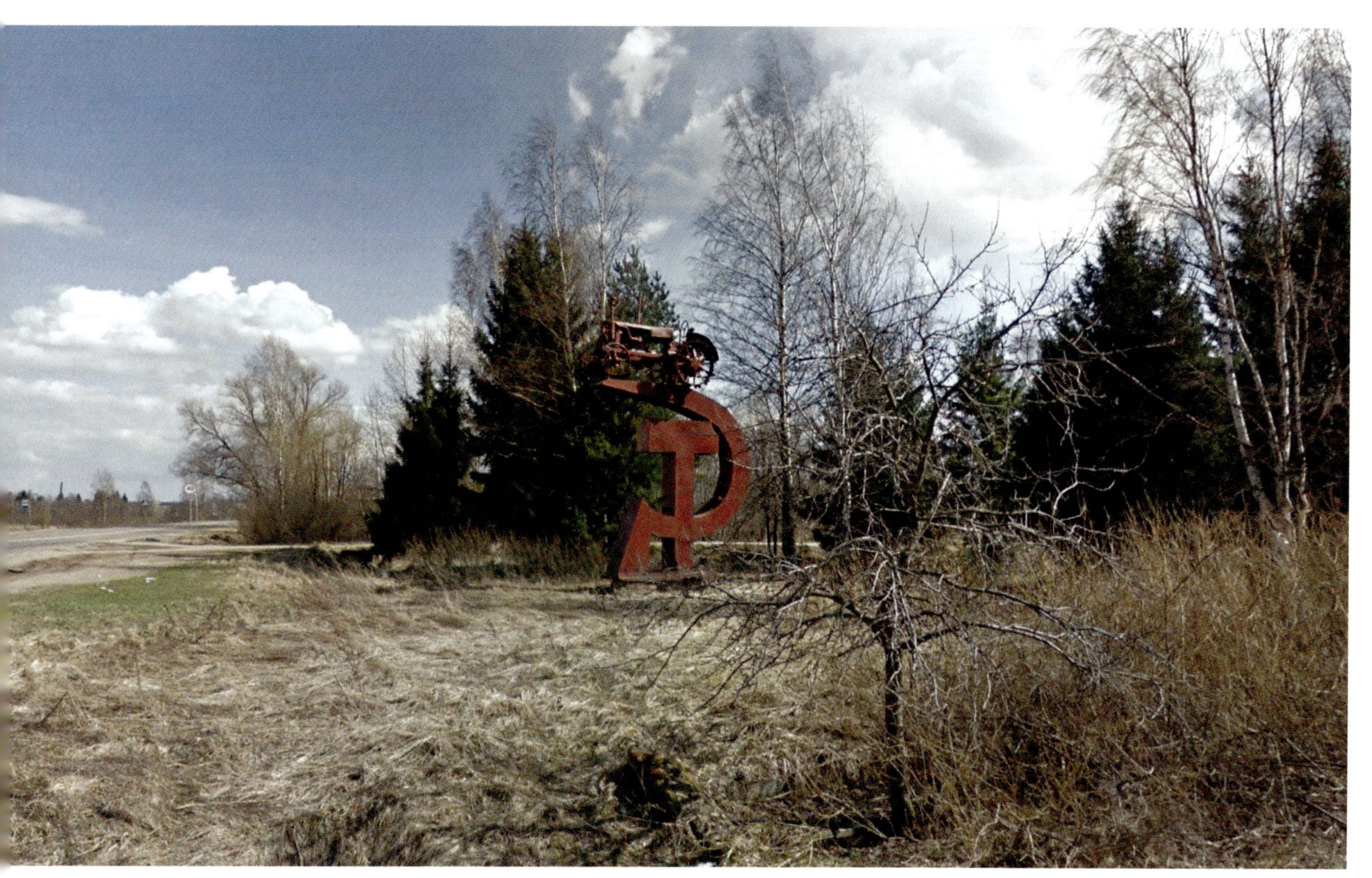

BOROVICHI, RUSSIA

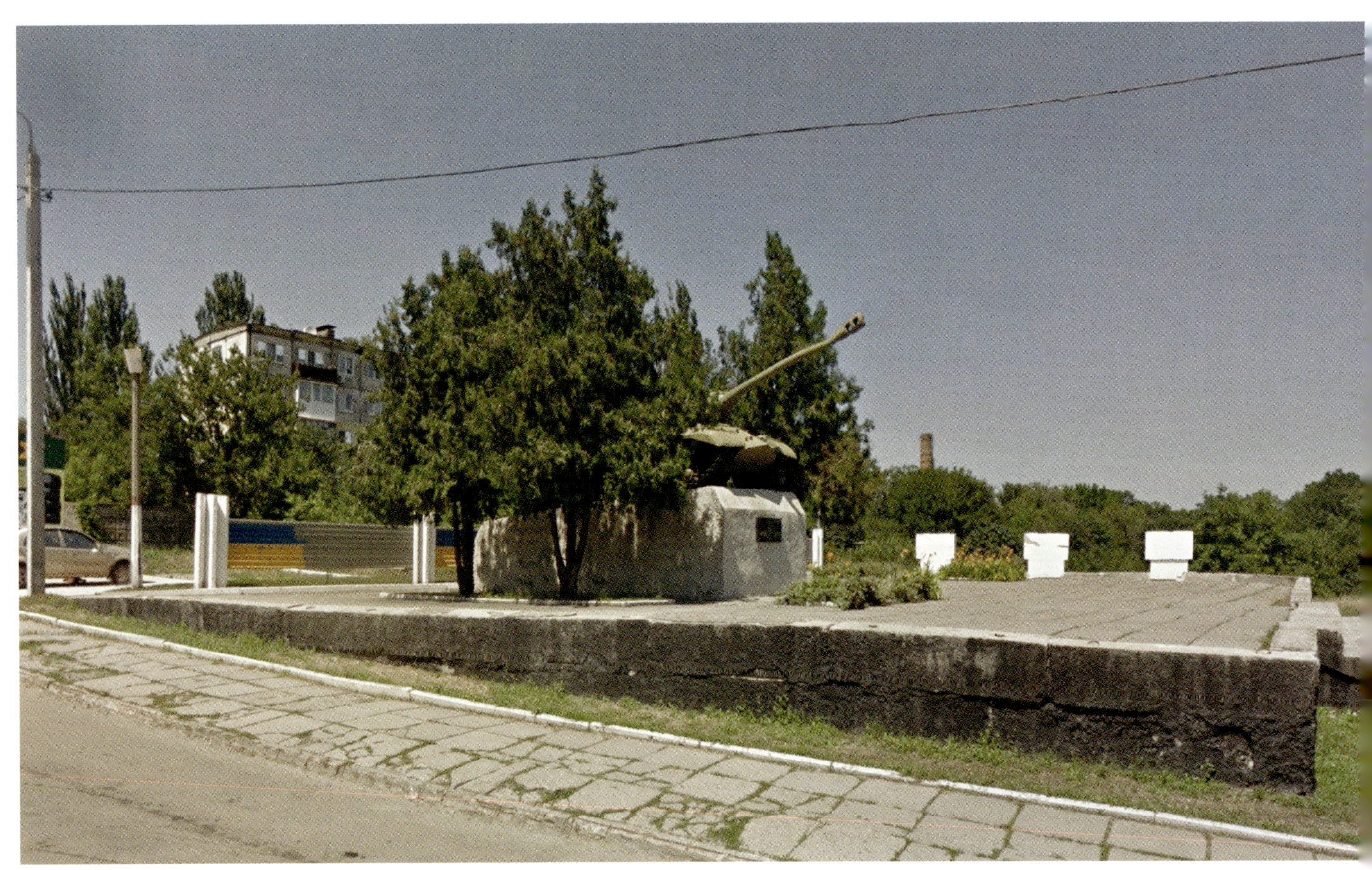

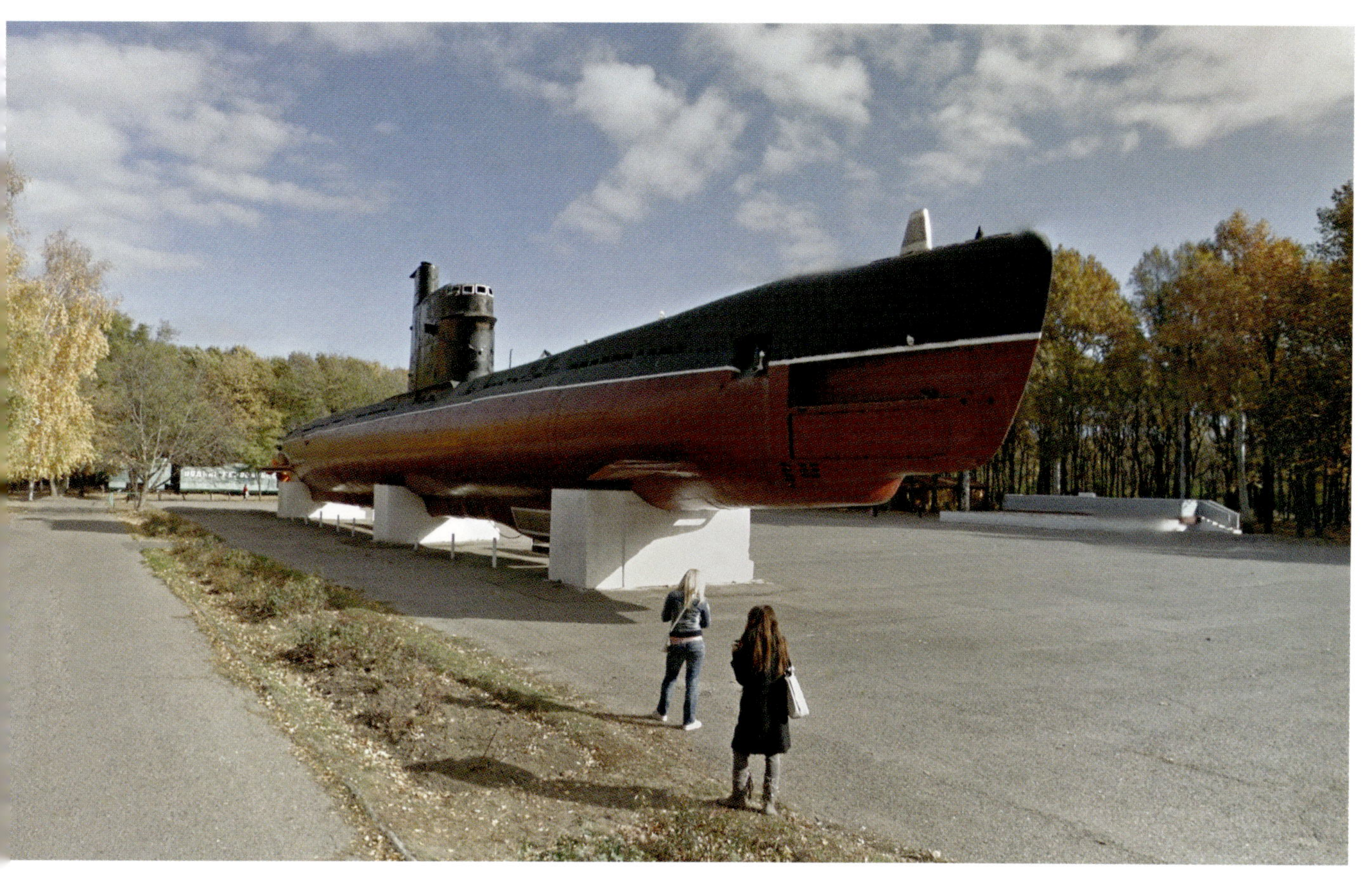

ODESSA, UKRAINE

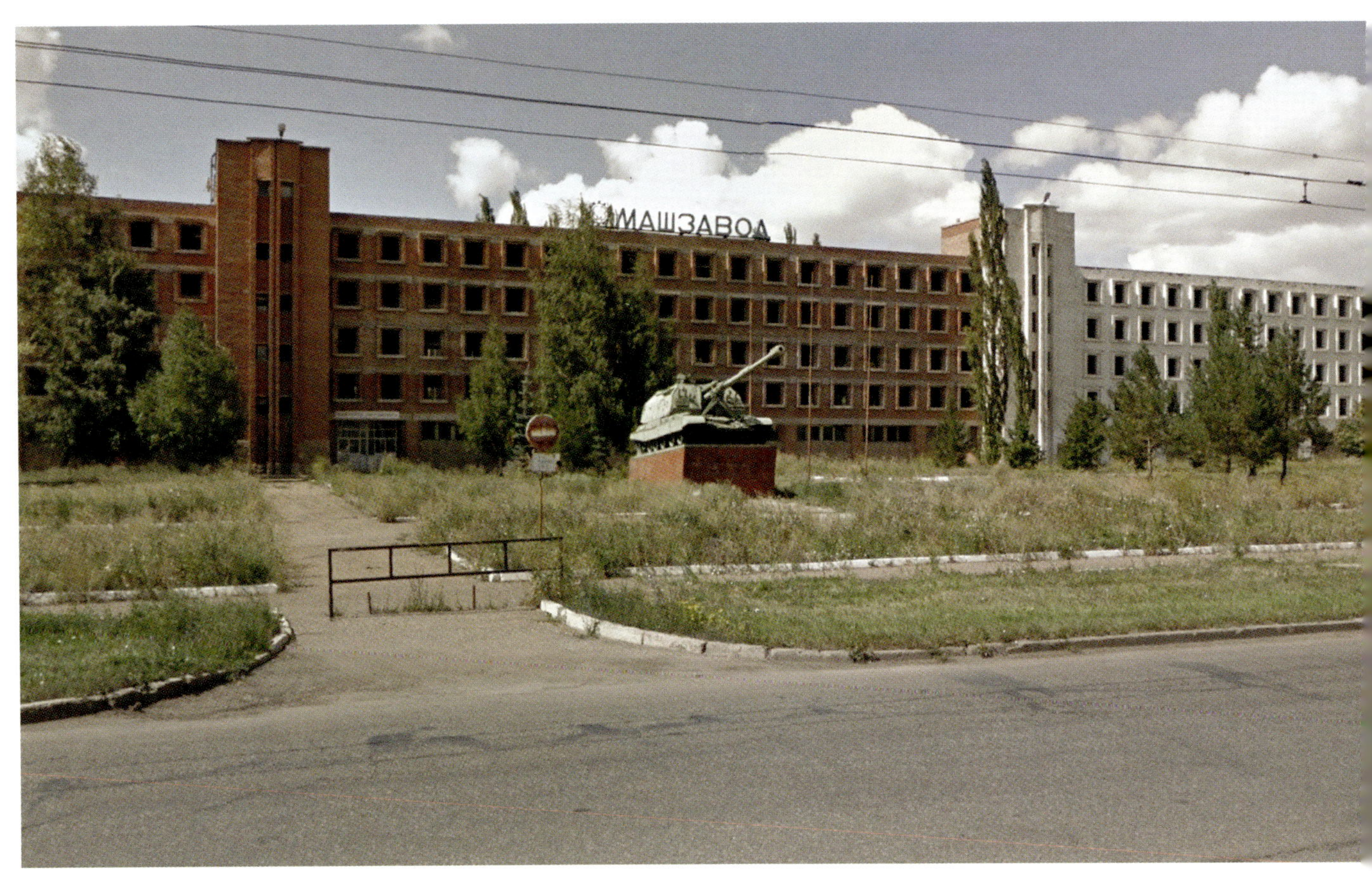

 STERLITAMAK, RUSSIA

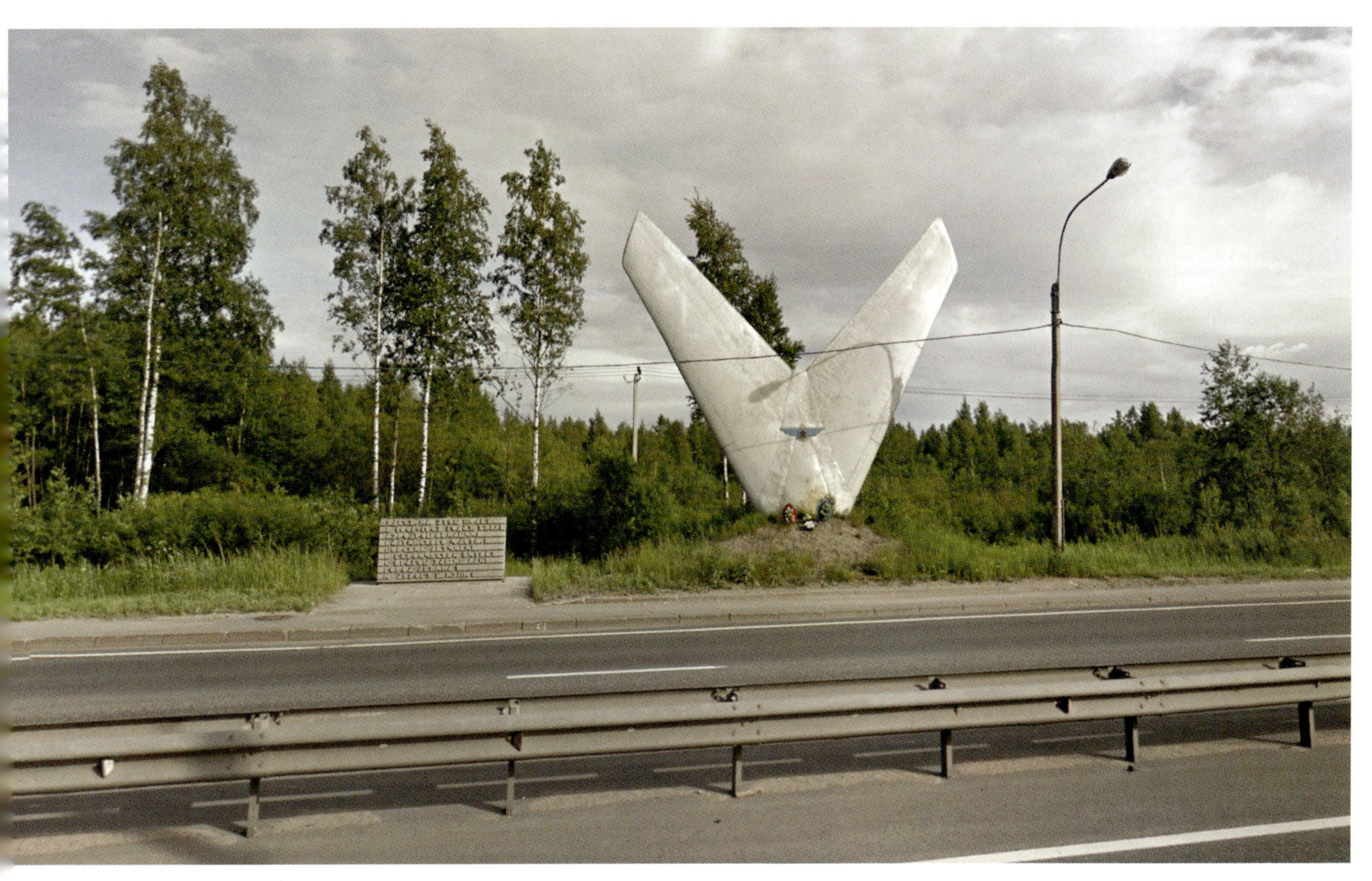

SAINT PETERSBURG, RUSSIA

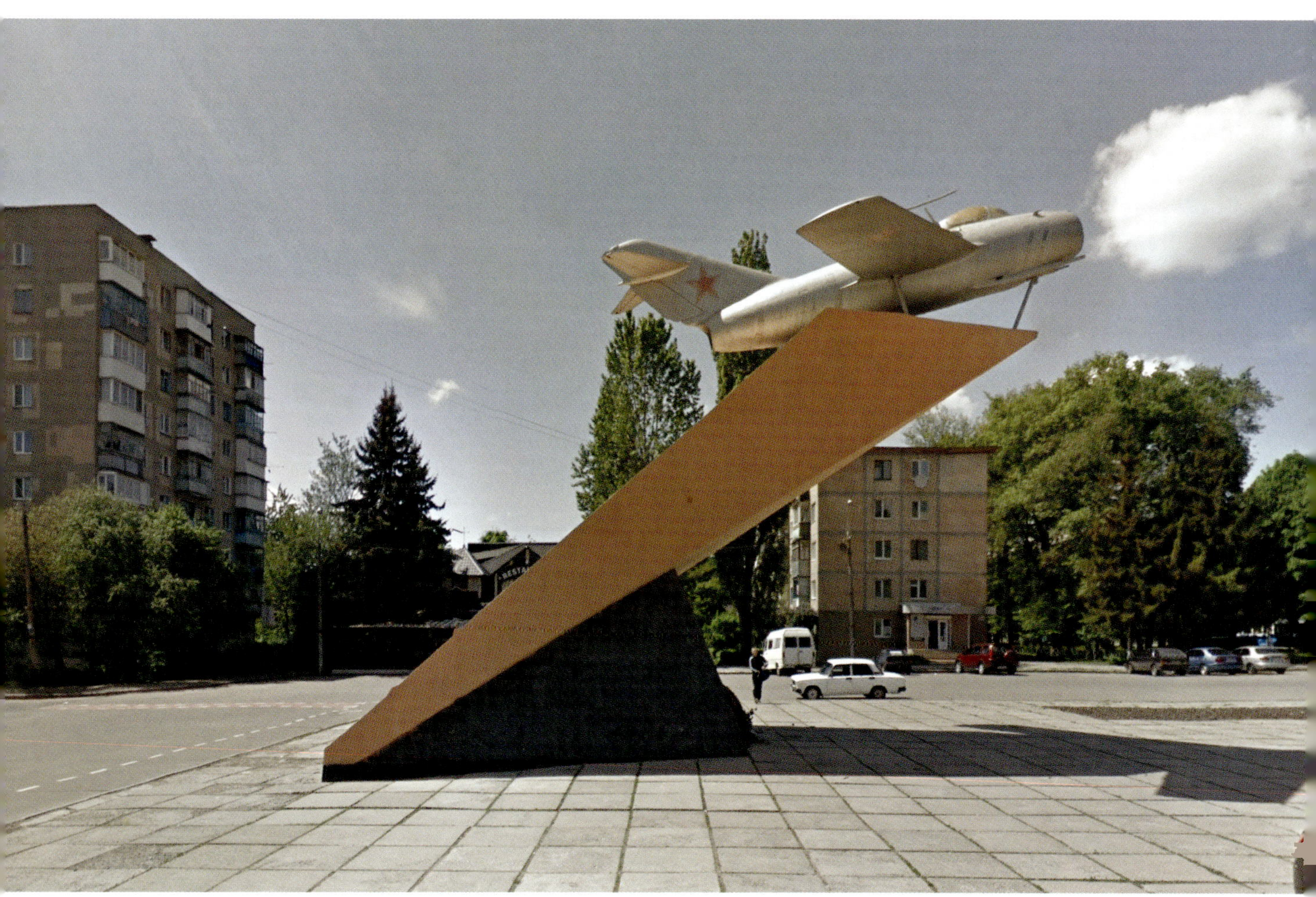

VINNYTSIA, UKRAINE

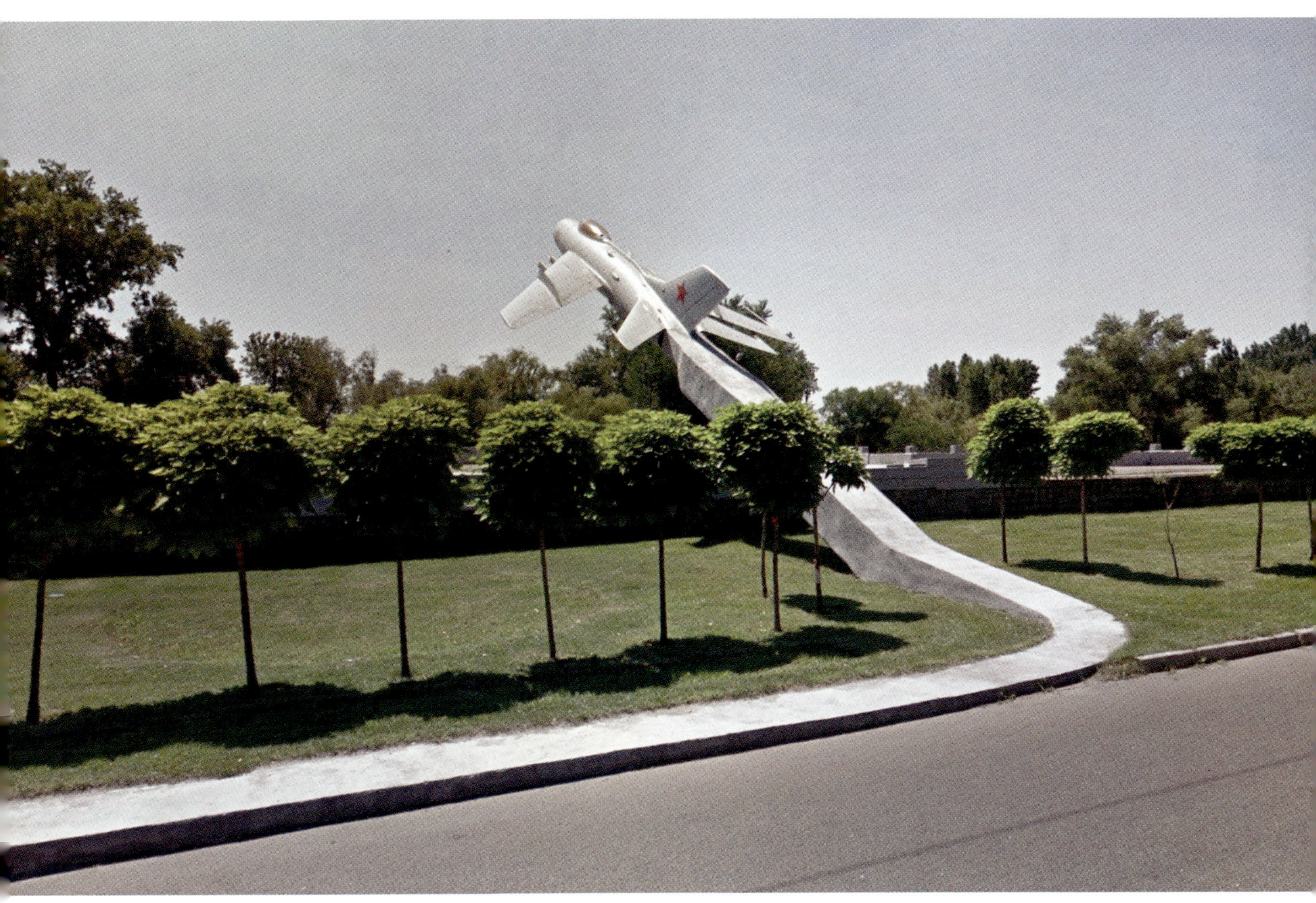

DNIPRO, UKRAINE

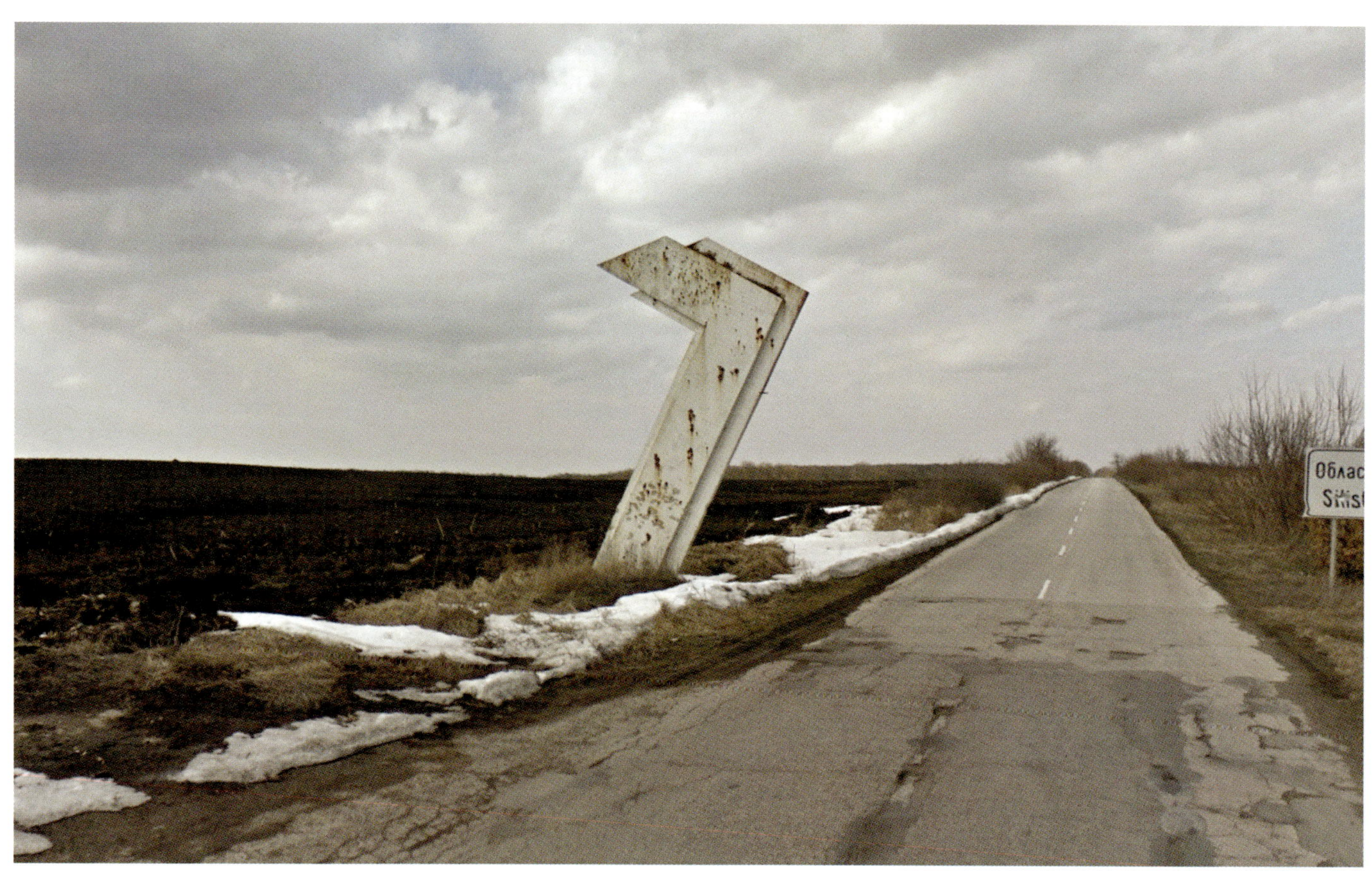

 DOBRICH, BULGARIA

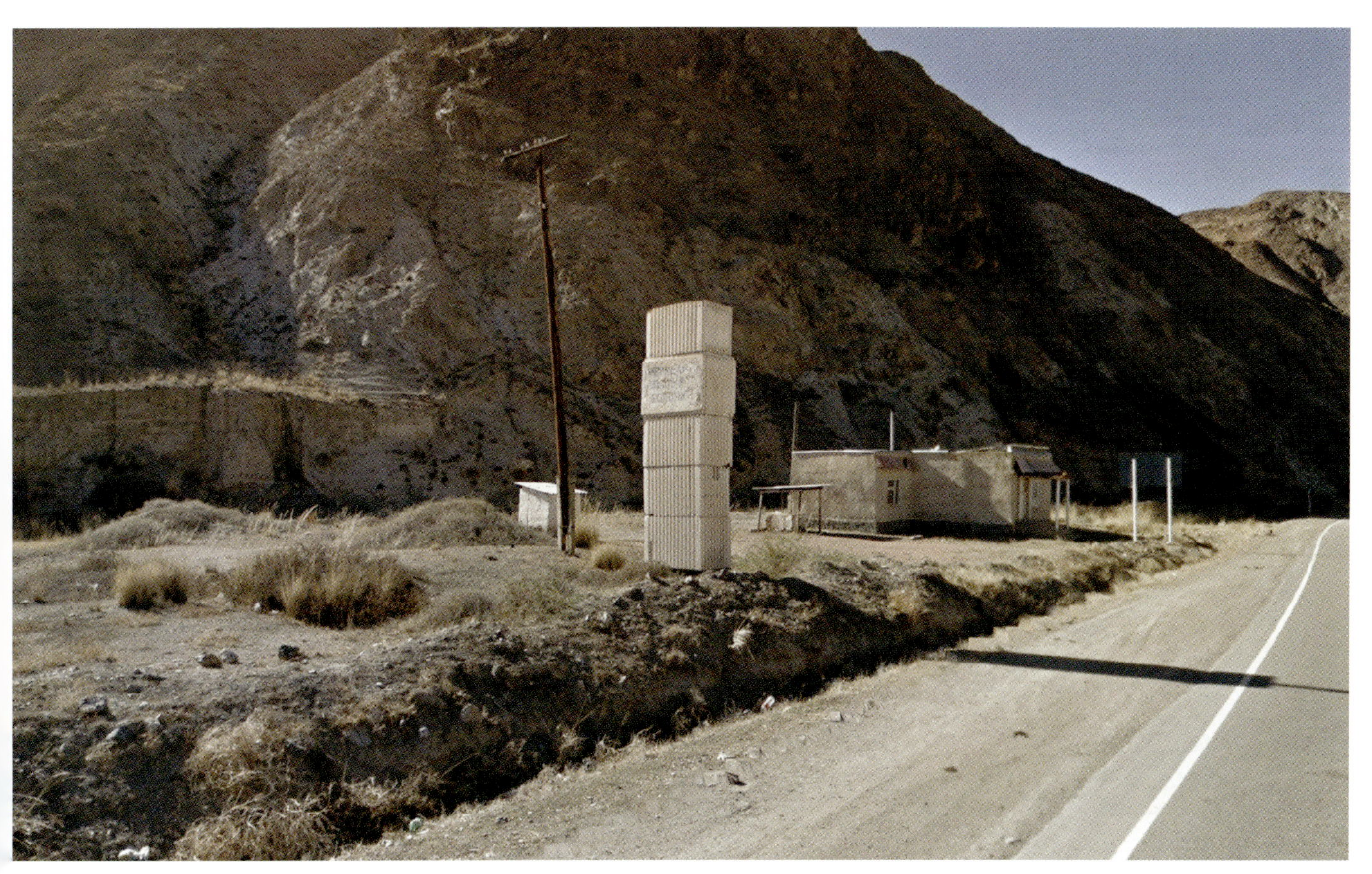

SARYBULAK, KAZAKHSTAN

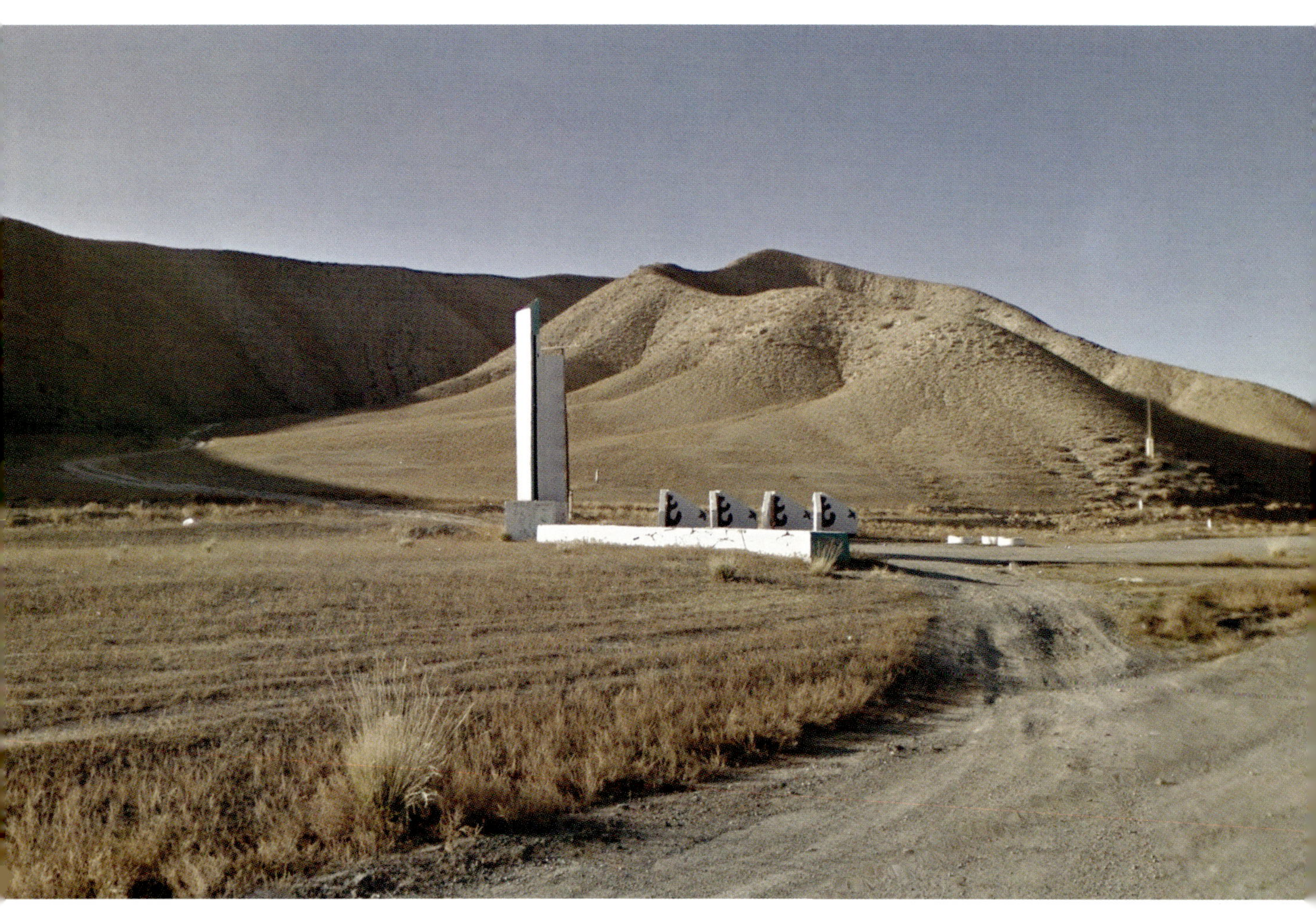

 NARYN PROVINCE, KYRGYZSTAN

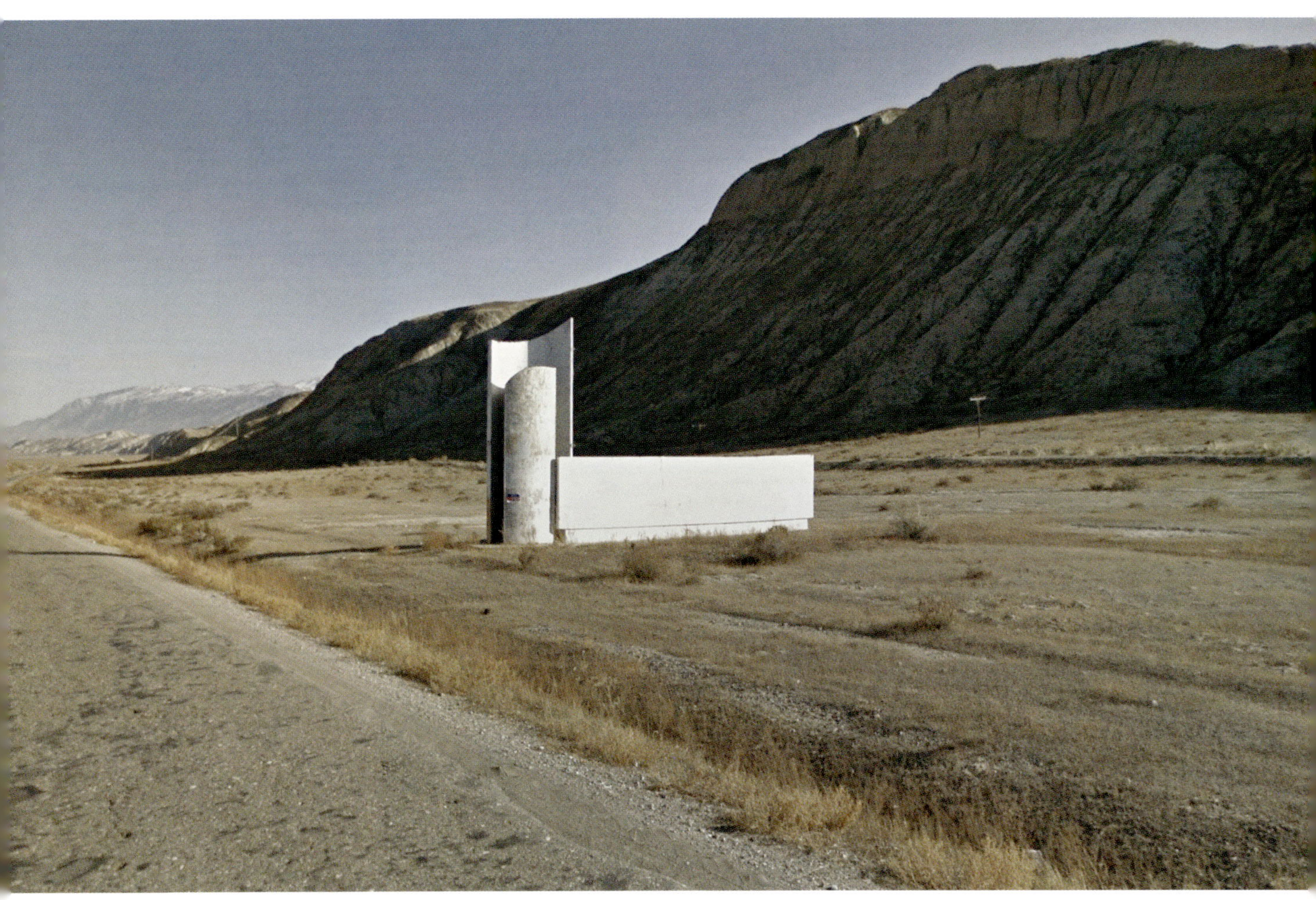

NARYN PROVINCE, KYRGYZSTAN

 SALKYN-TOR, NARYN PROVINCE, KYRGYZSTAN

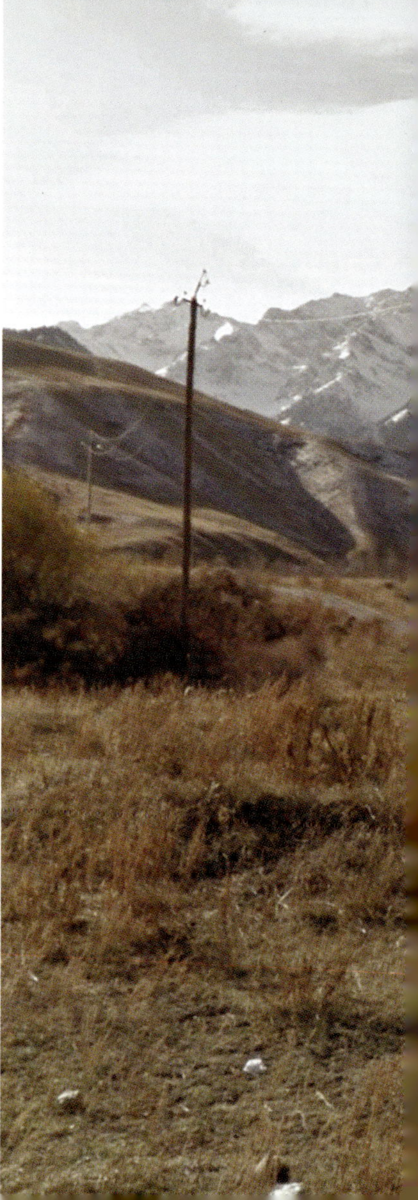

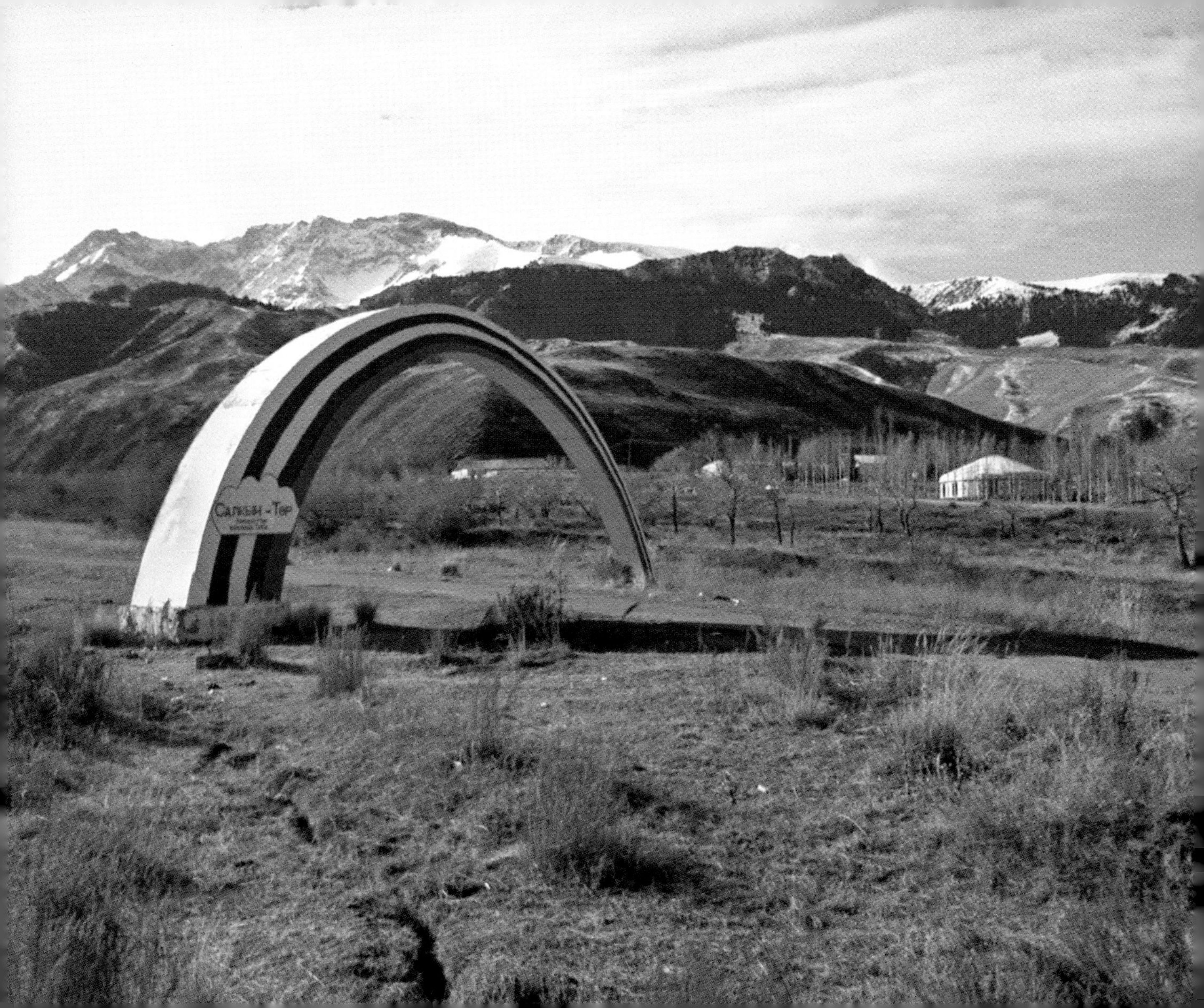
Салкын - Төр

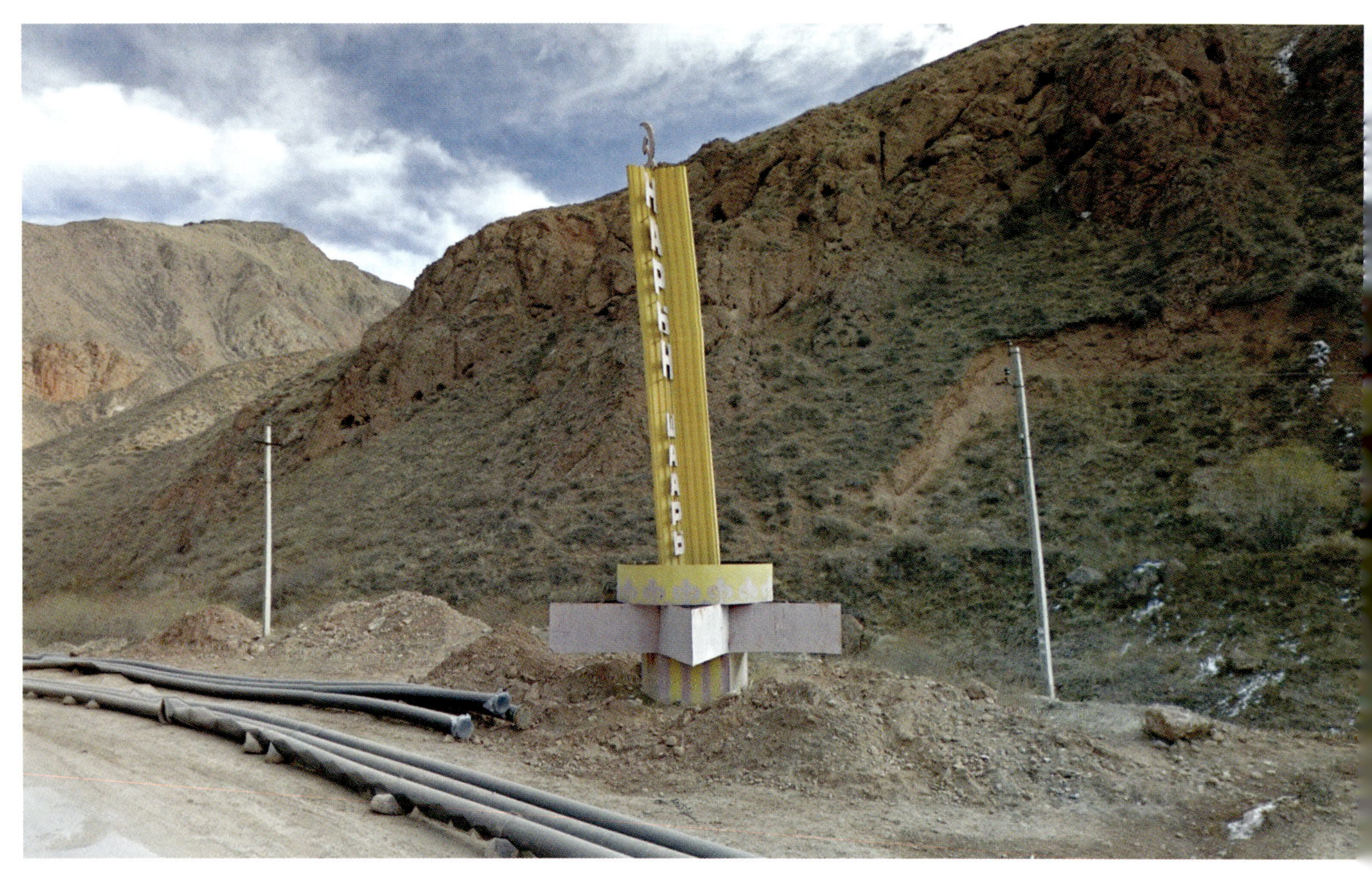

 NARYN SHAAR, KYRGYZSTAN

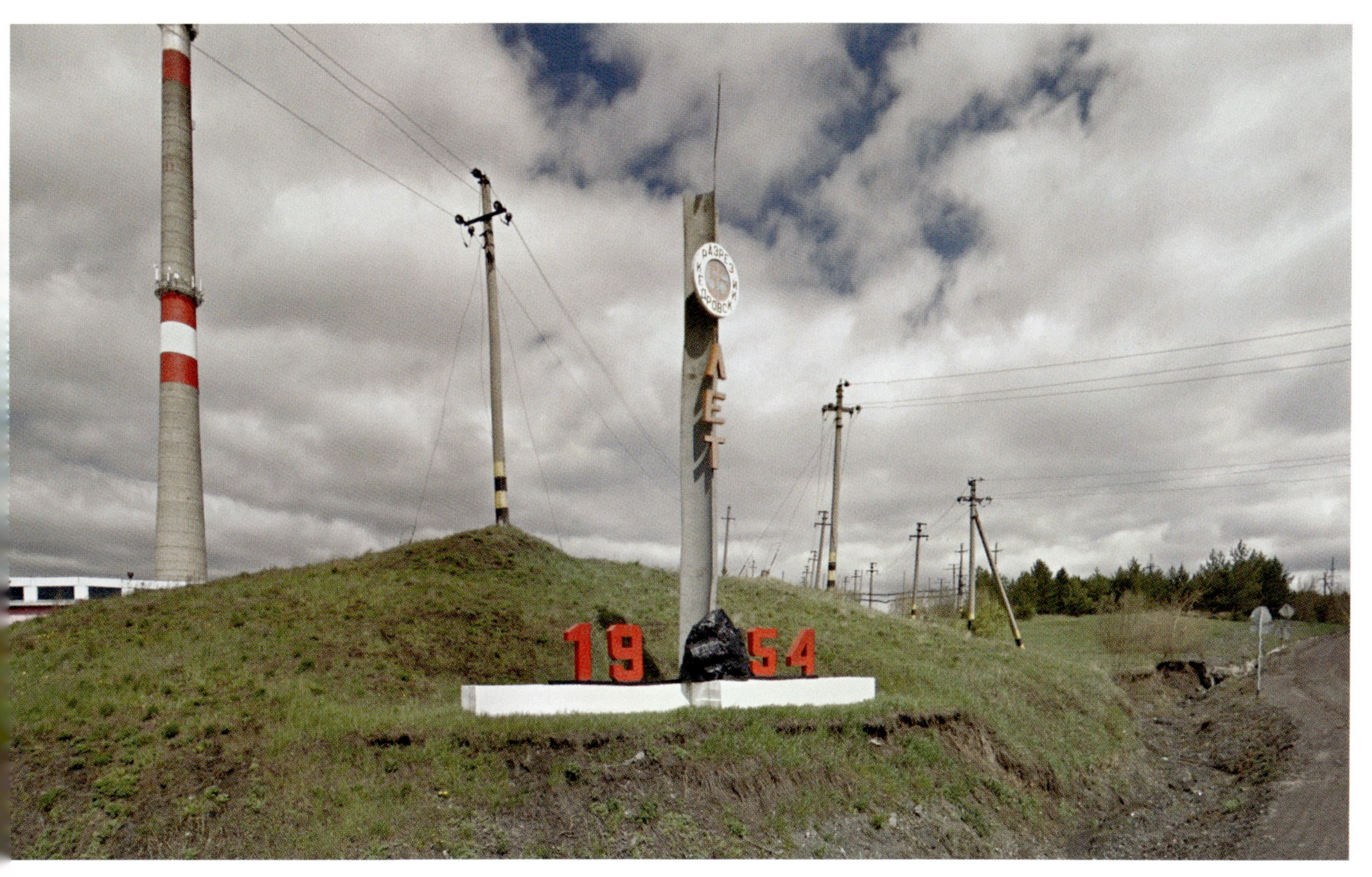

KEMEROVO, RUSSIA

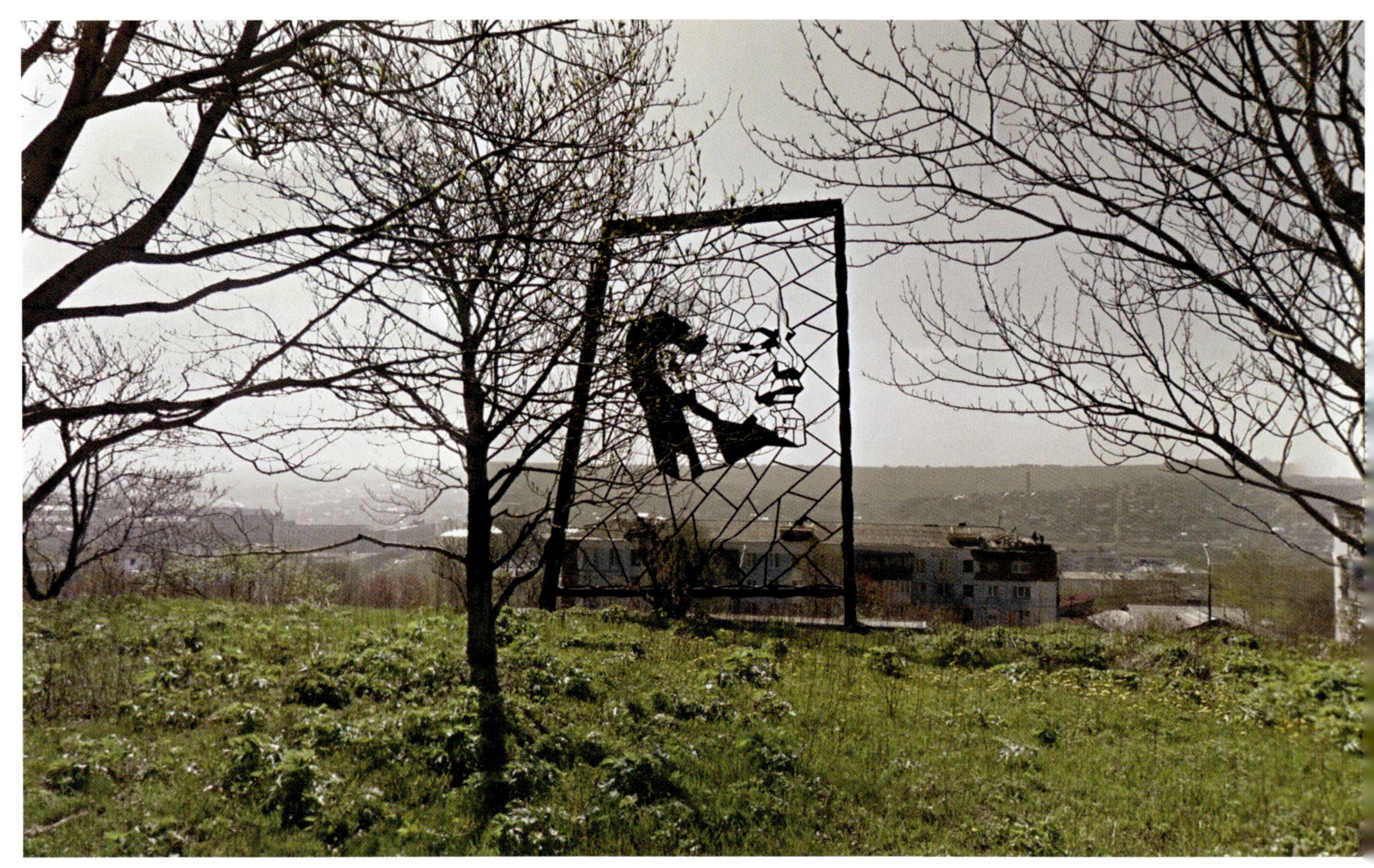

 KORSAKOV, RUSSIA

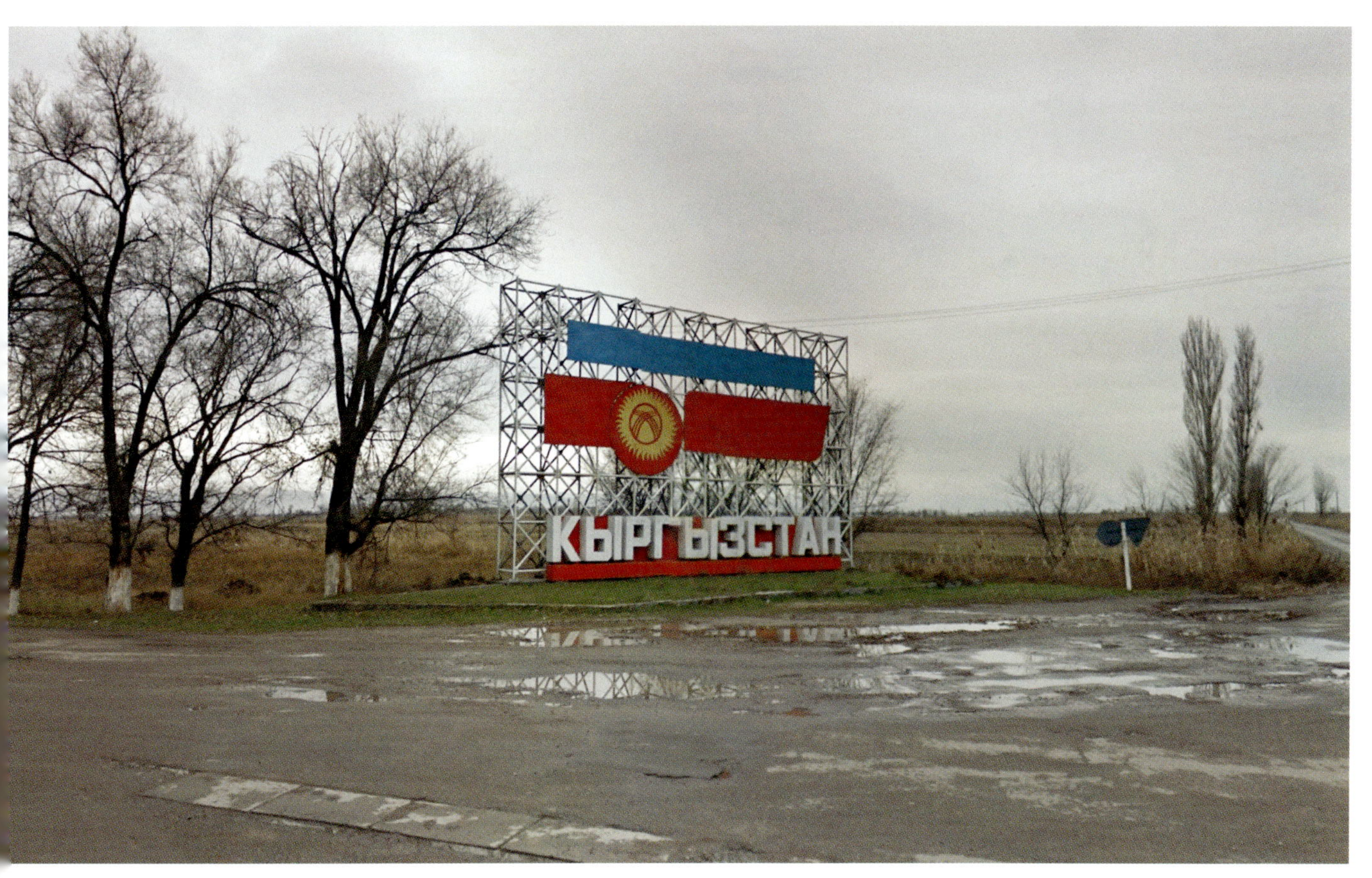

BISHKEK, KYRGYZSTAN

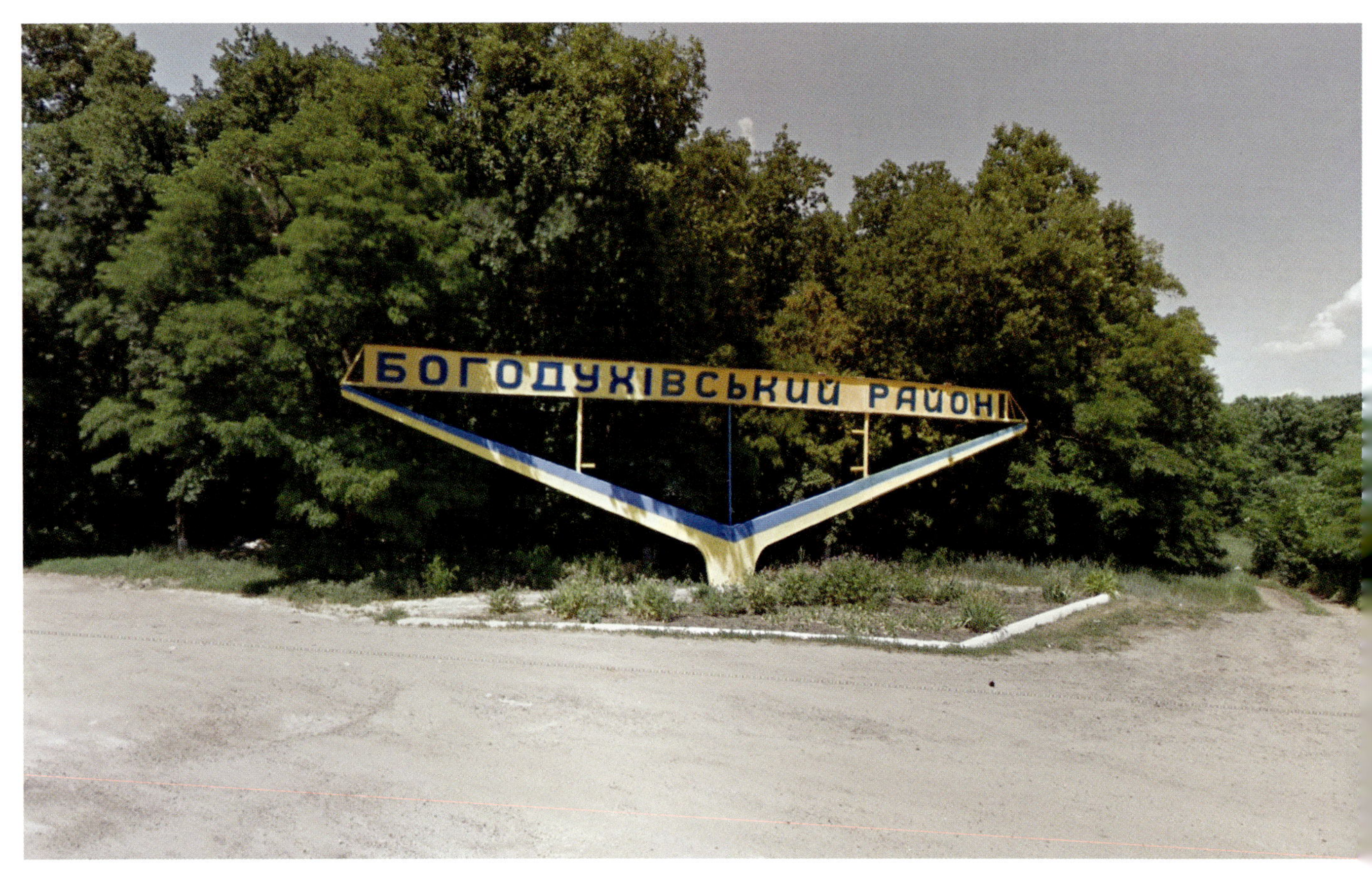

 BOGODUKHOV RAION, UKRAINE

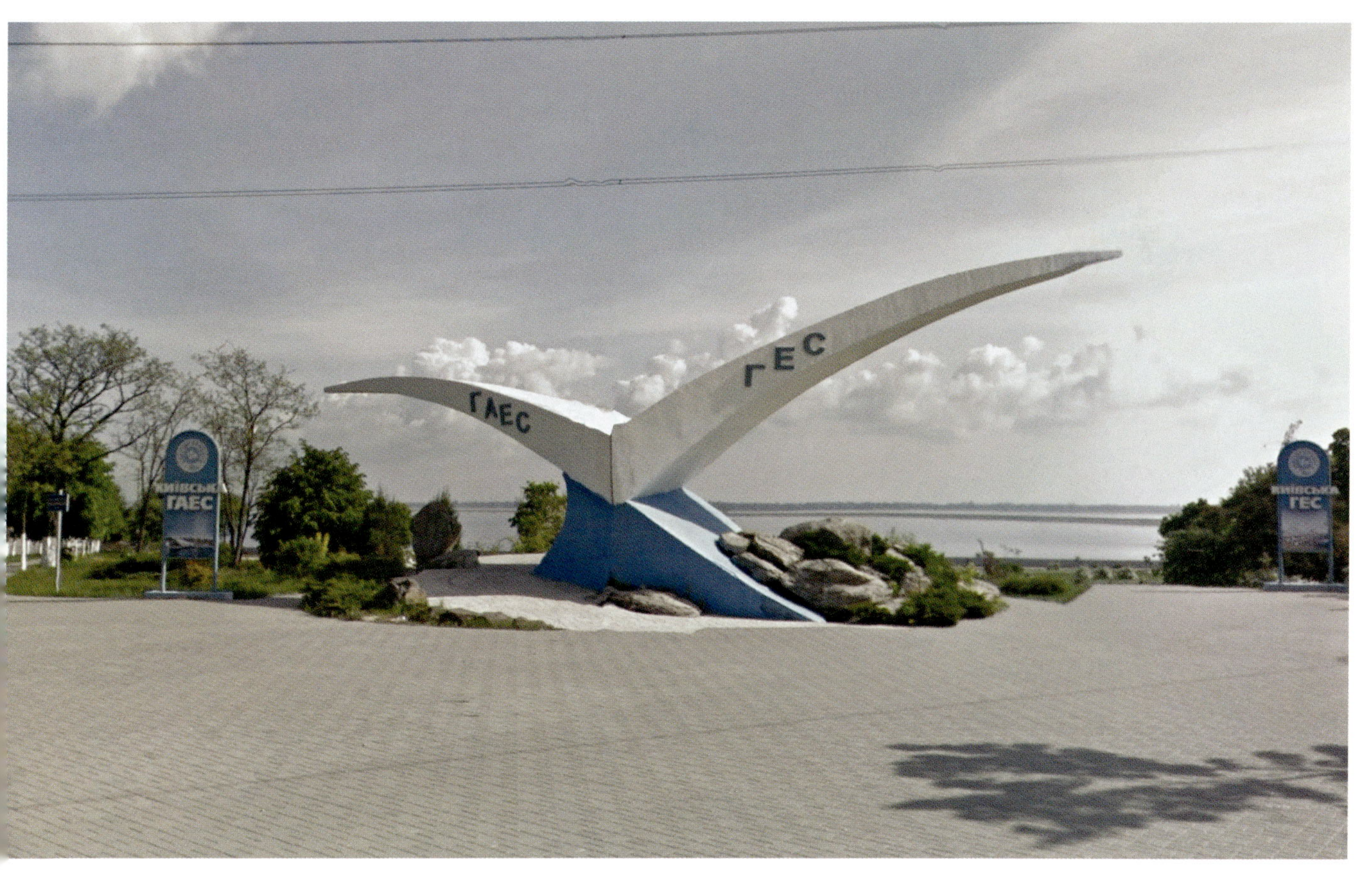
ГАЕС
ГЕС
ГАЕС
ГЕС

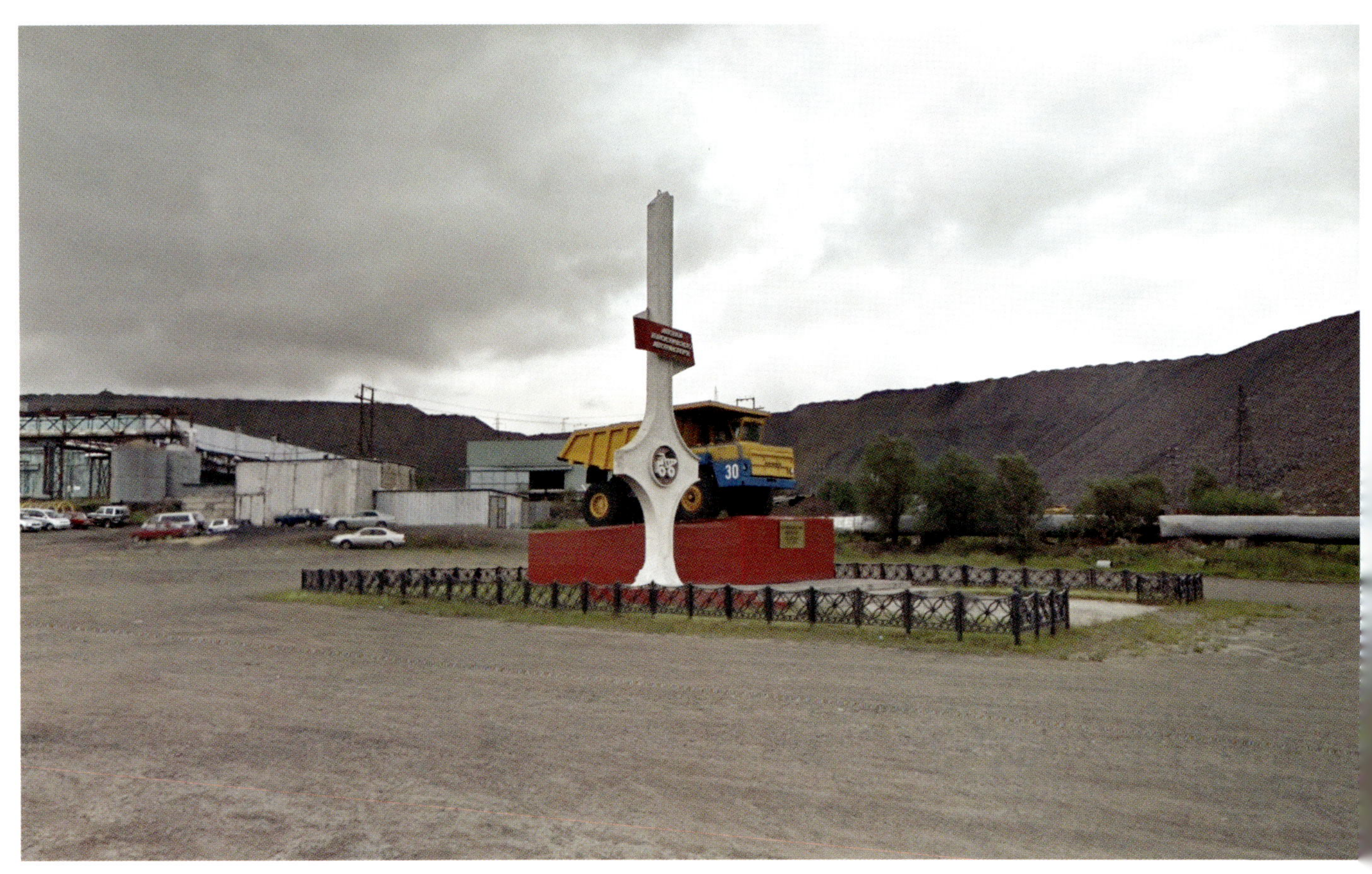

 NERYUNGRI, RUSSIA

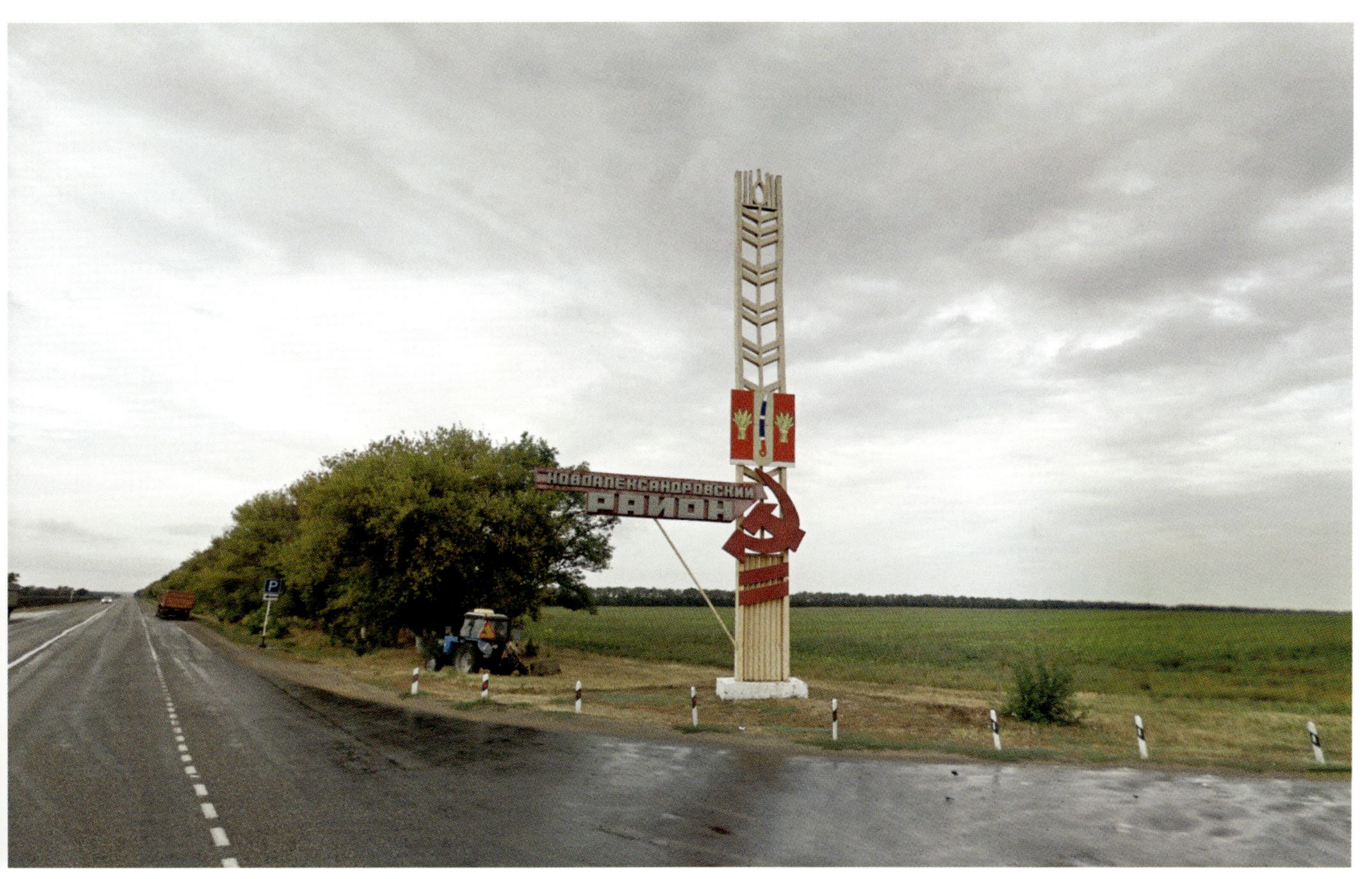

NOVOALEXANDROVSKY RAION, RUSSIA

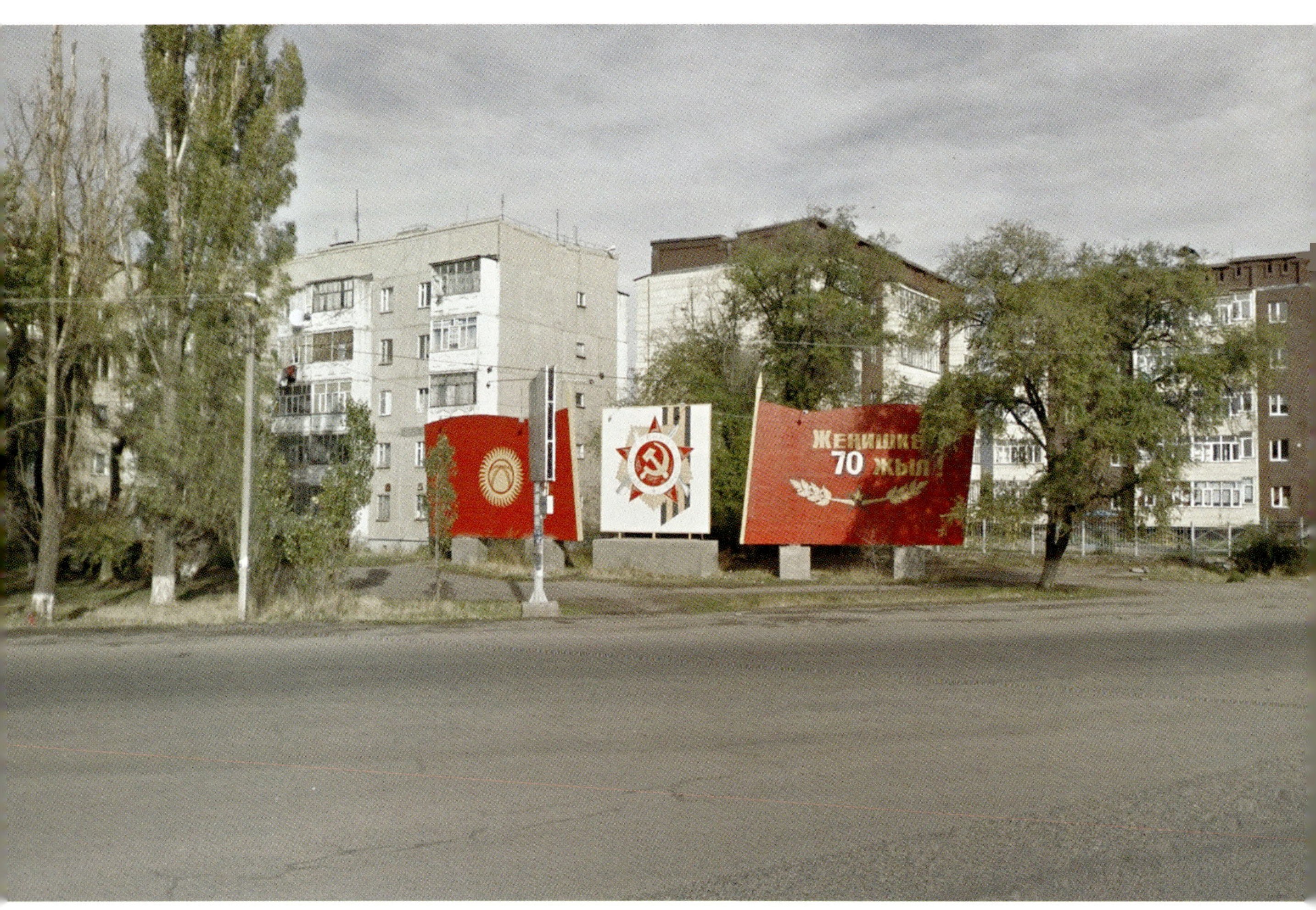

 TOKMOK, KYRGYZSTAN

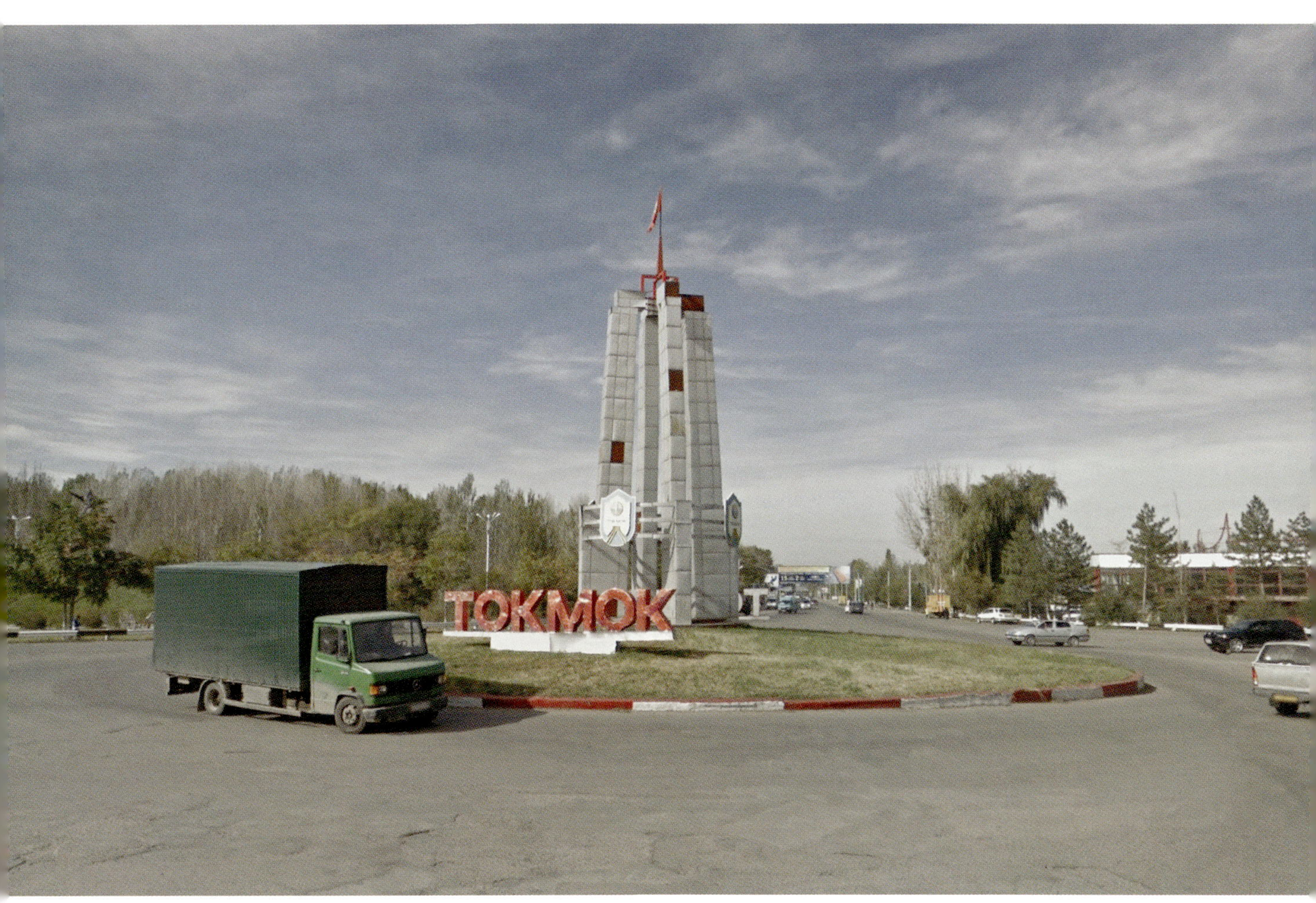

TOKMOK, KYRGYZSTAN

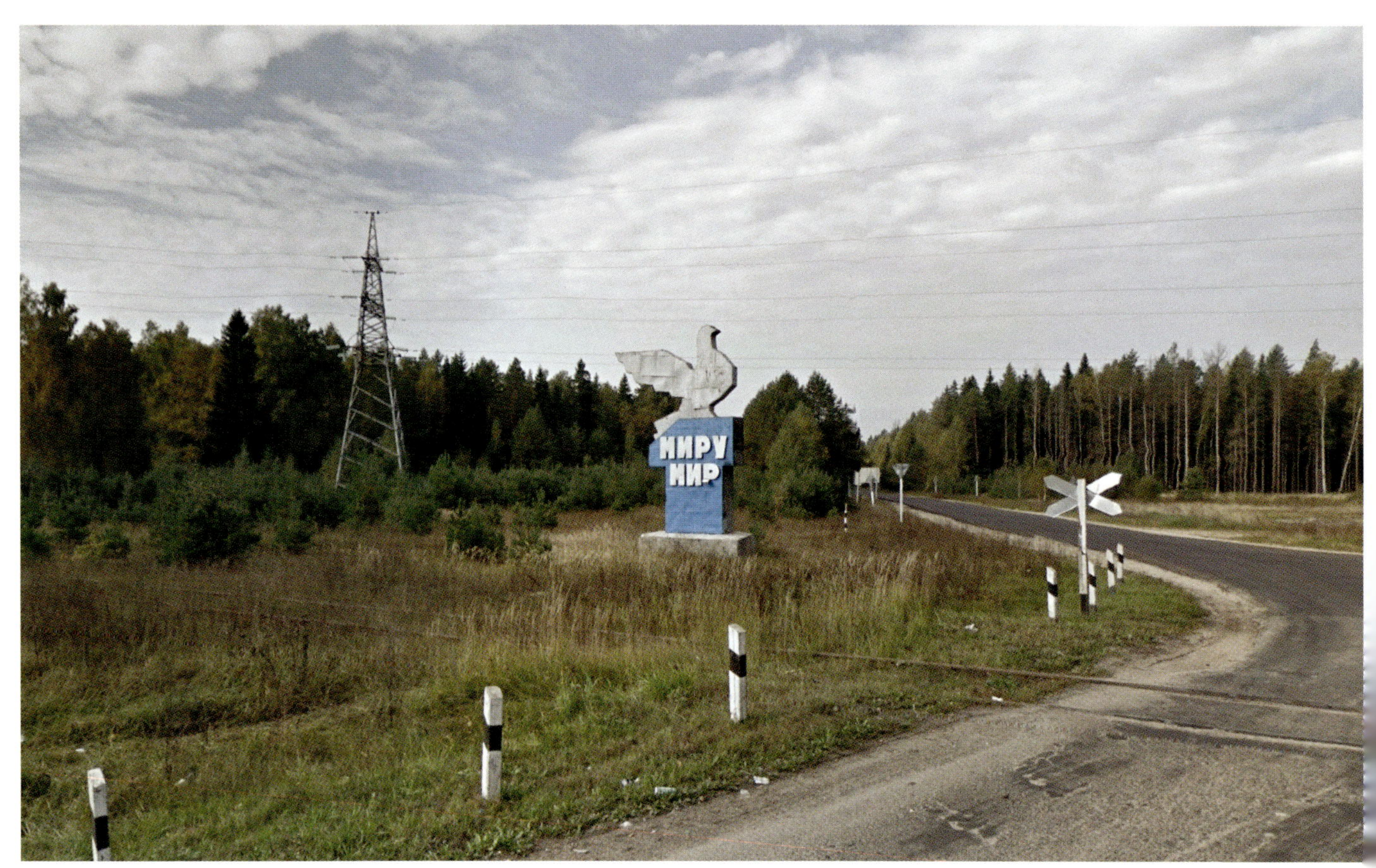

 ‘PEACE TO THE WORLD’, BRYANSK OBLAST, RUSSIA

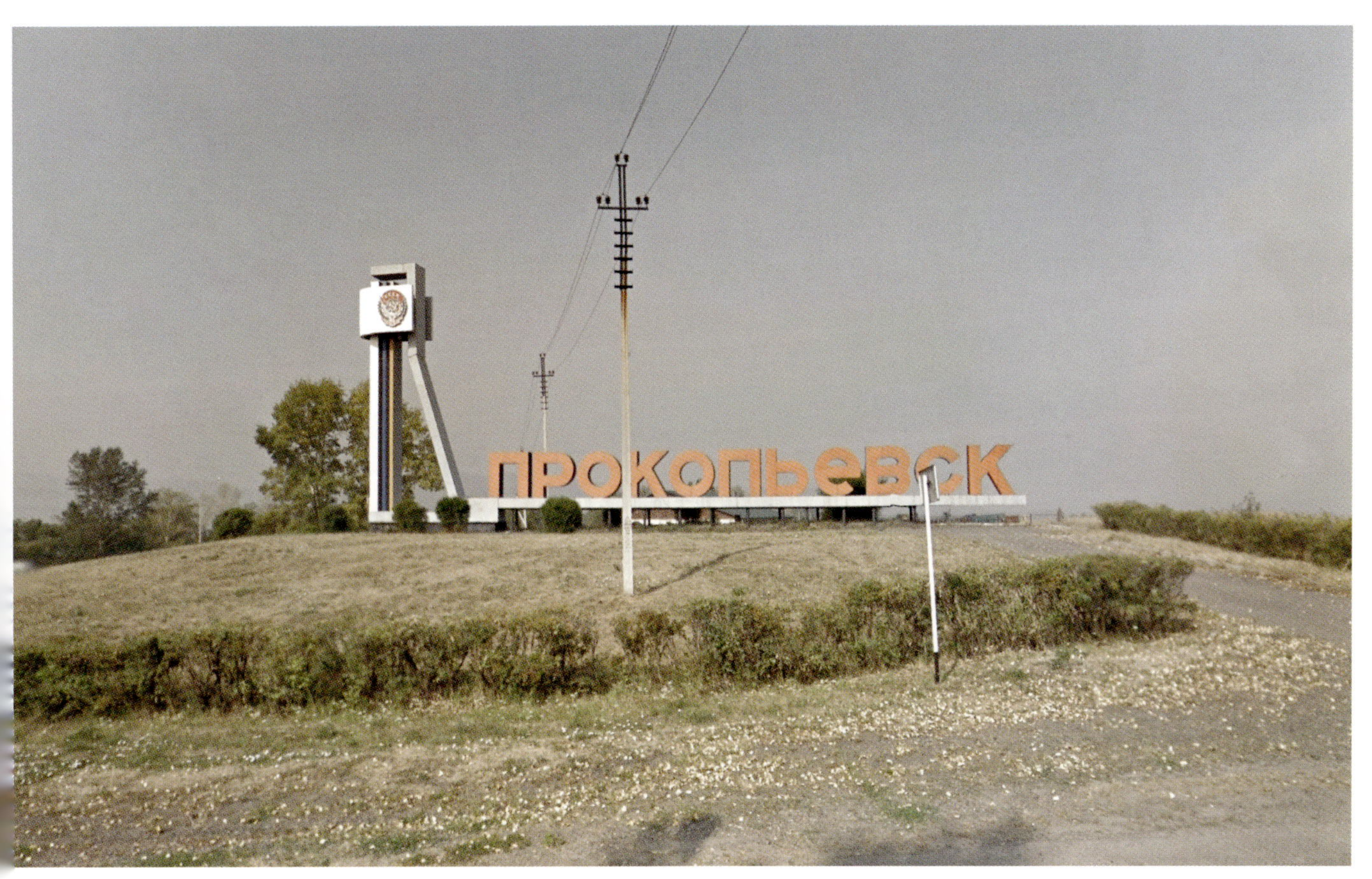

PROKOPYEVSK, RUSSIA

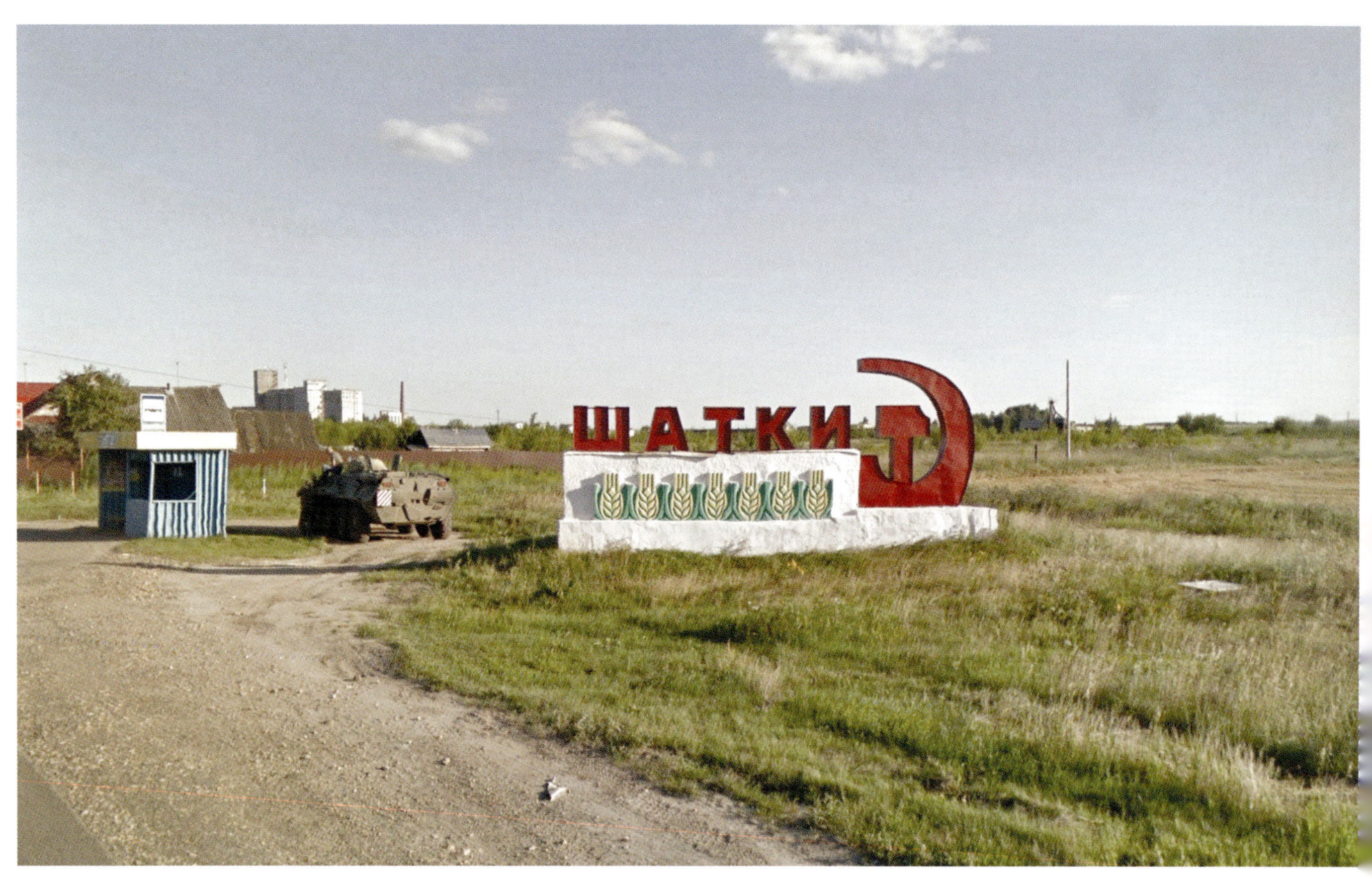

 SHATKI, RUSSIA

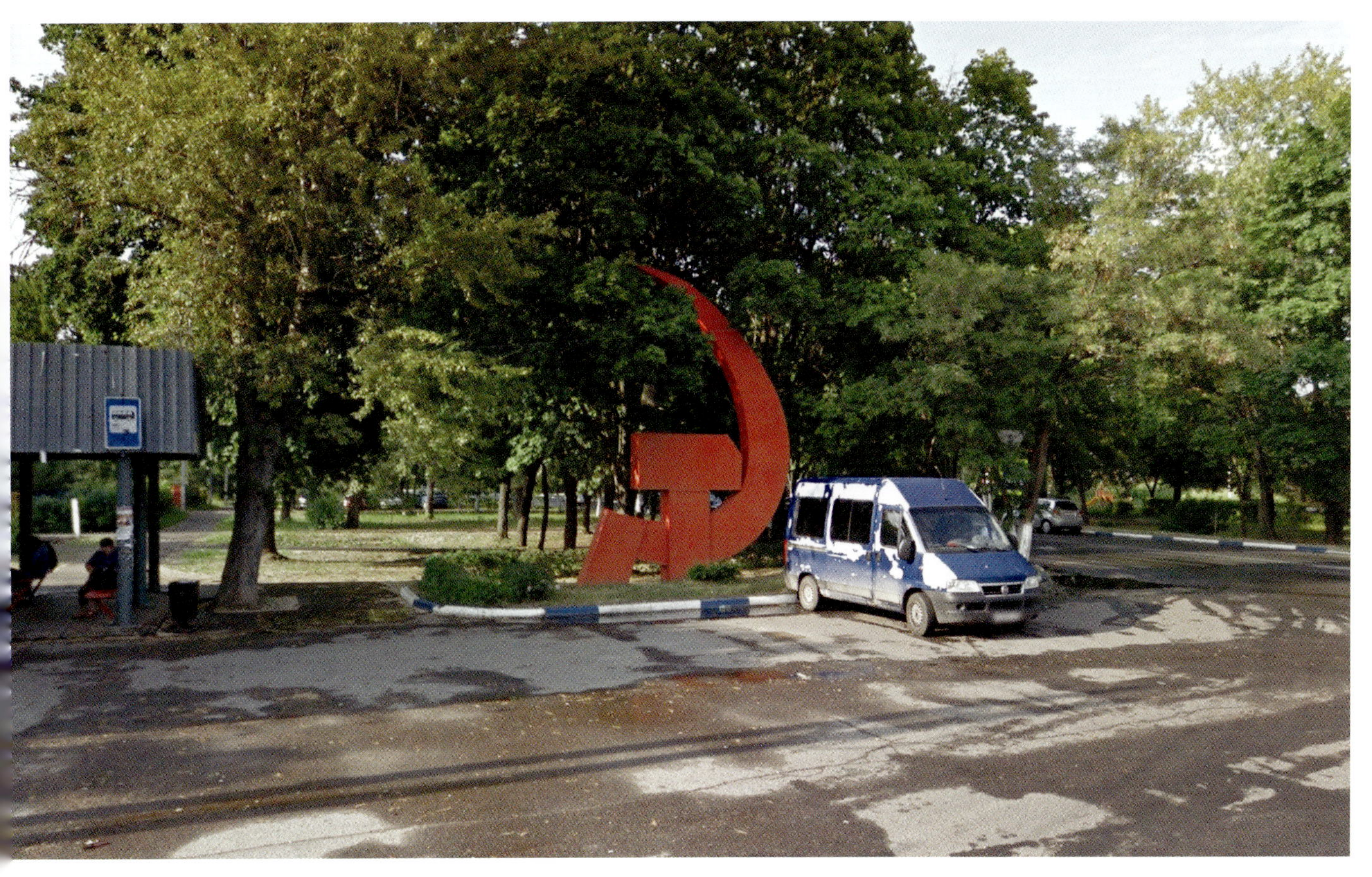

OZHERELYE, RUSSIA

OKTYABRSKY MICRO-DISTRICT, VOLGODONSK, RUSSIA

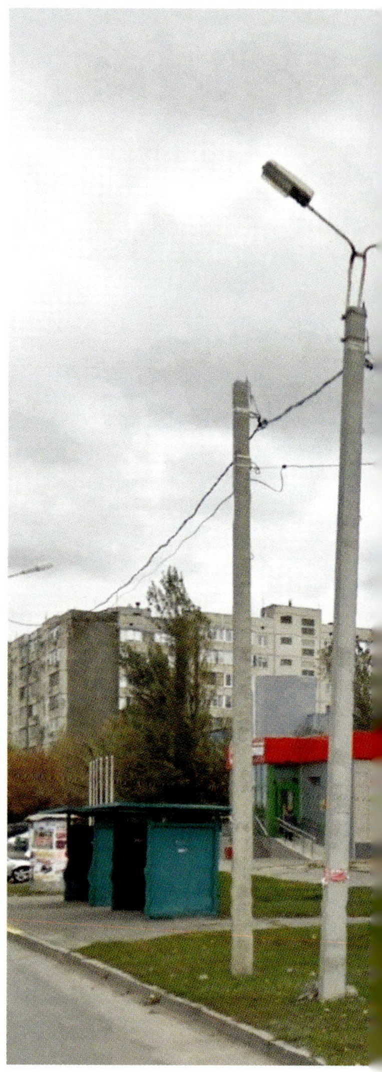

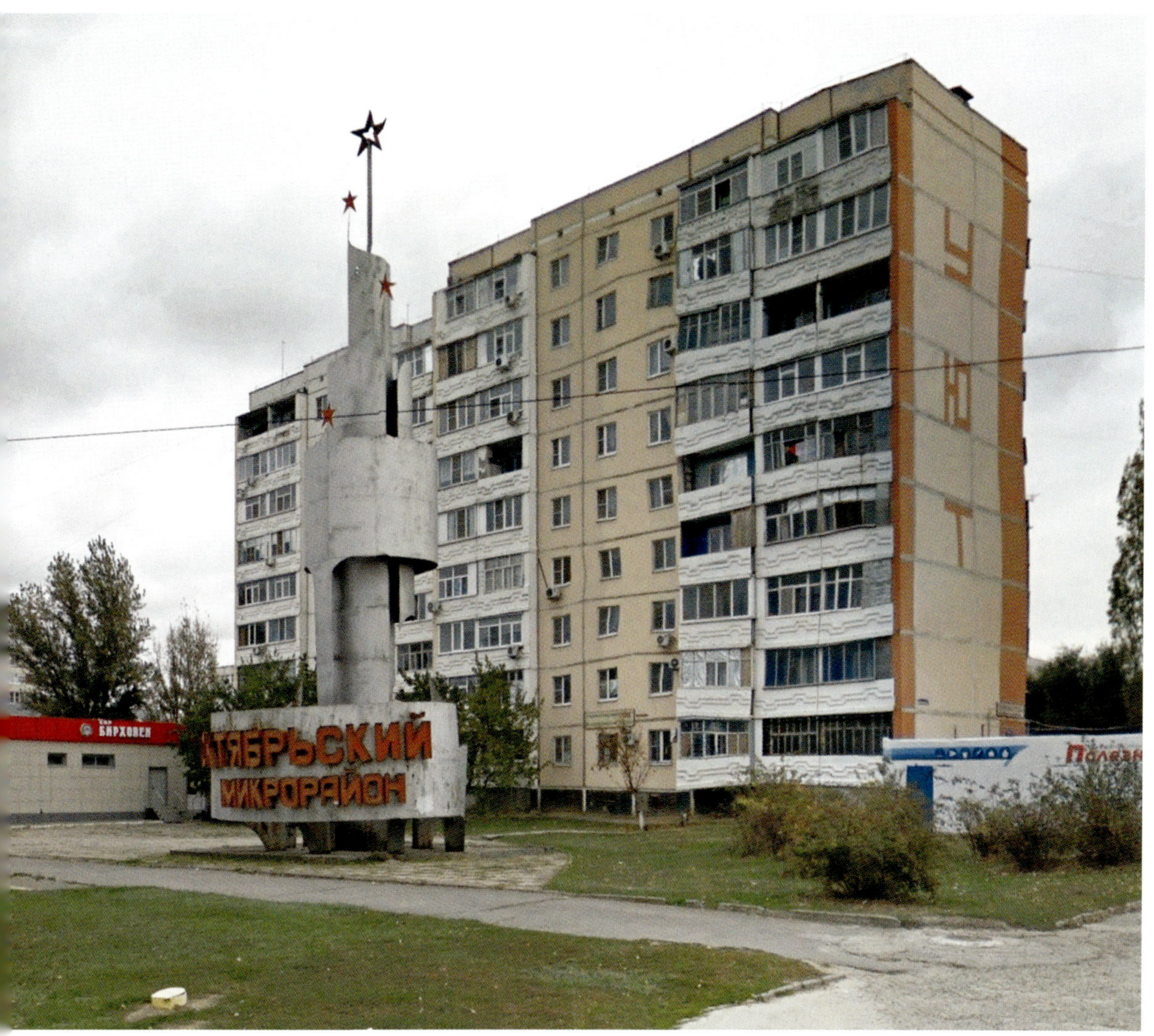
БИРХОВЕН
МИКРОРАЙОН
УЮТ

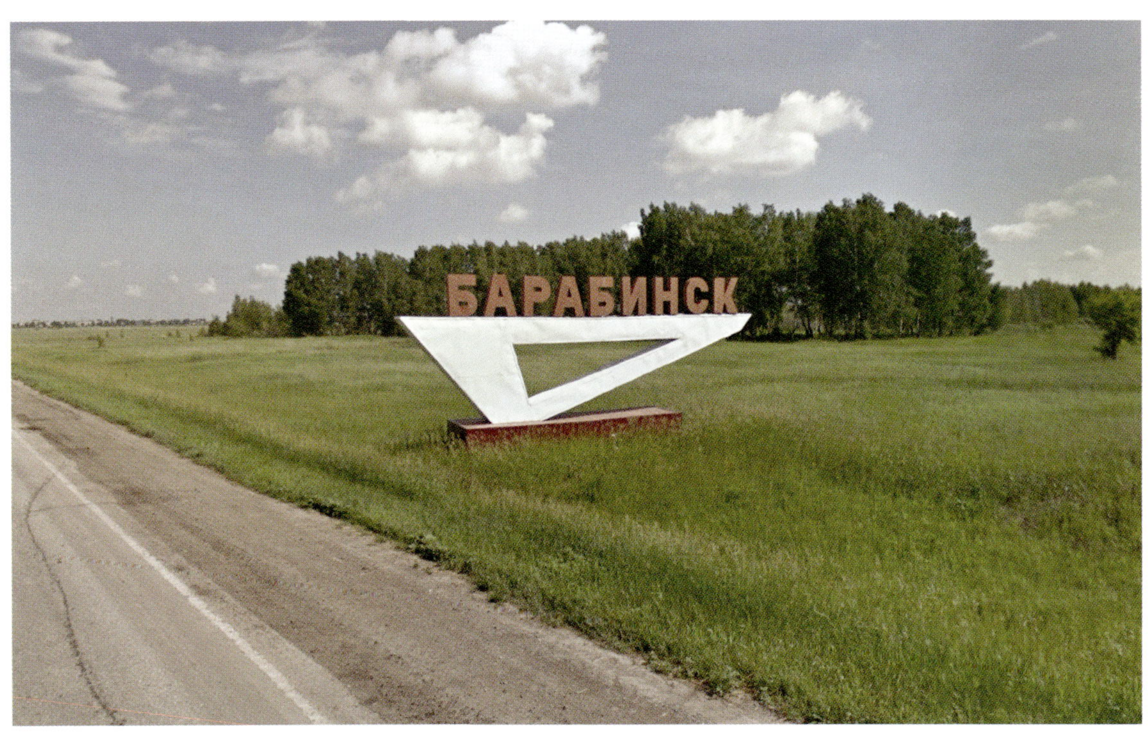

 BARABINSK, RUSSIA

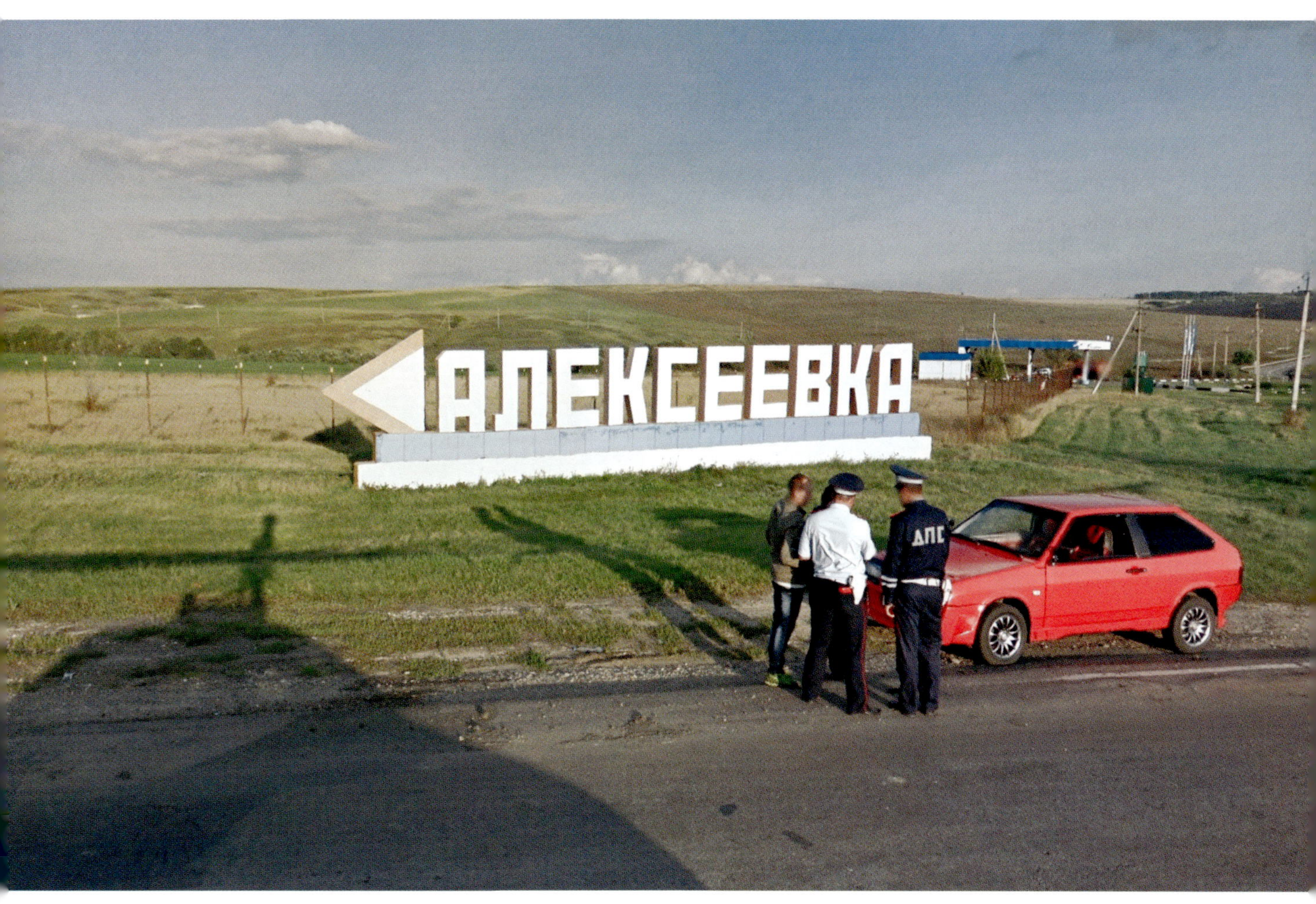

ALEXEYEVKA, RUSSIA

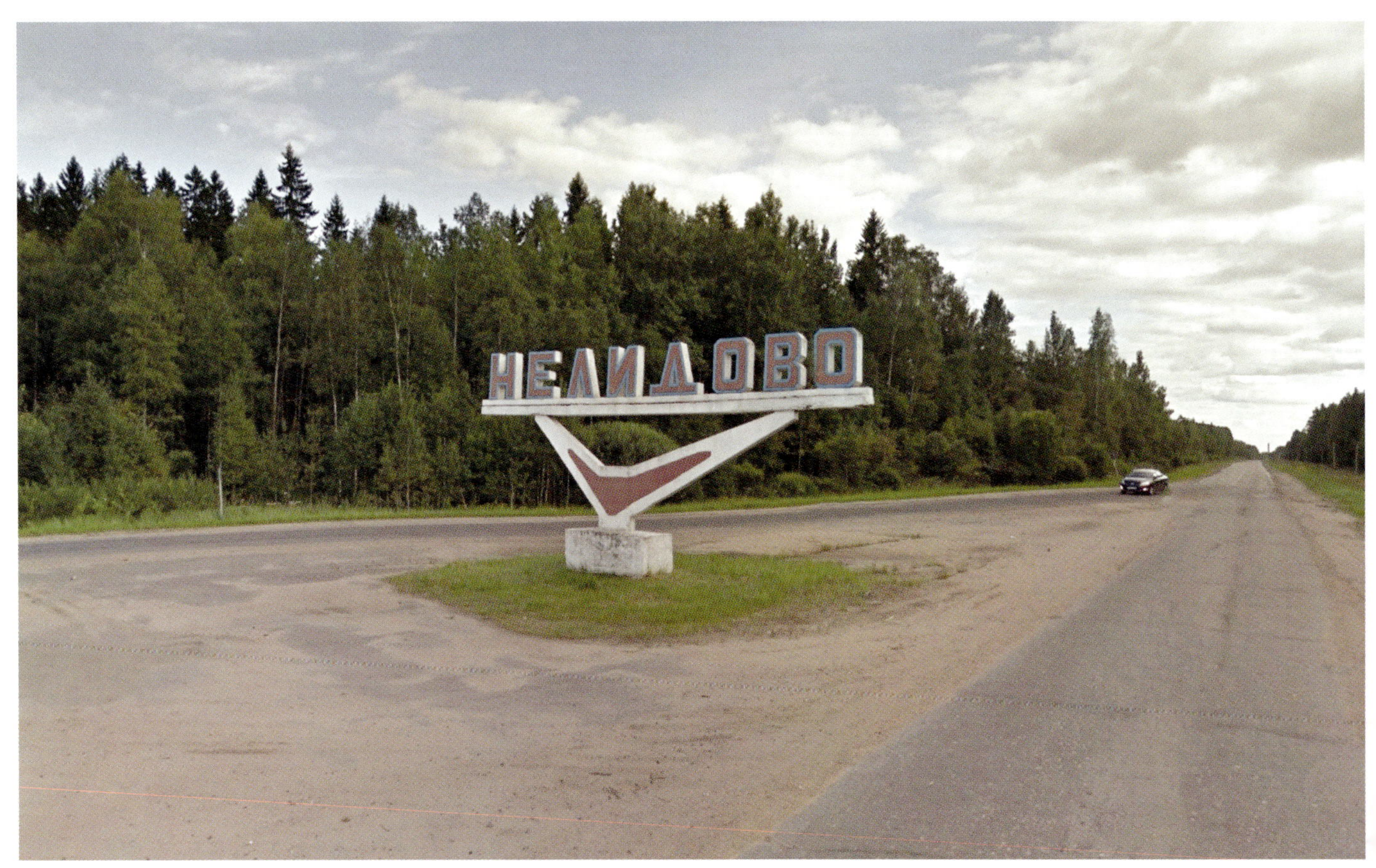

 NELIDOVO, RUSSIA

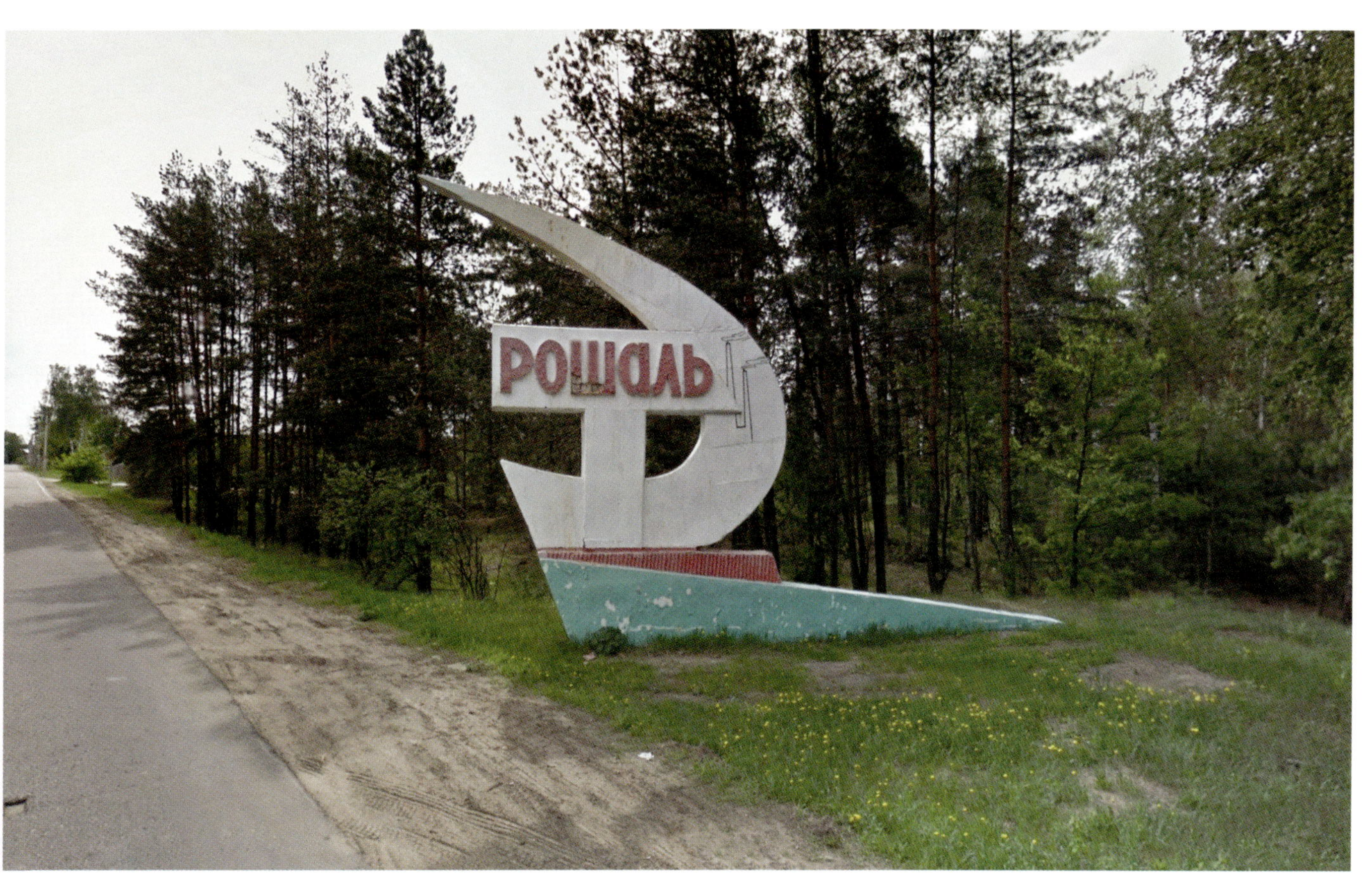
РОШАЛЬ

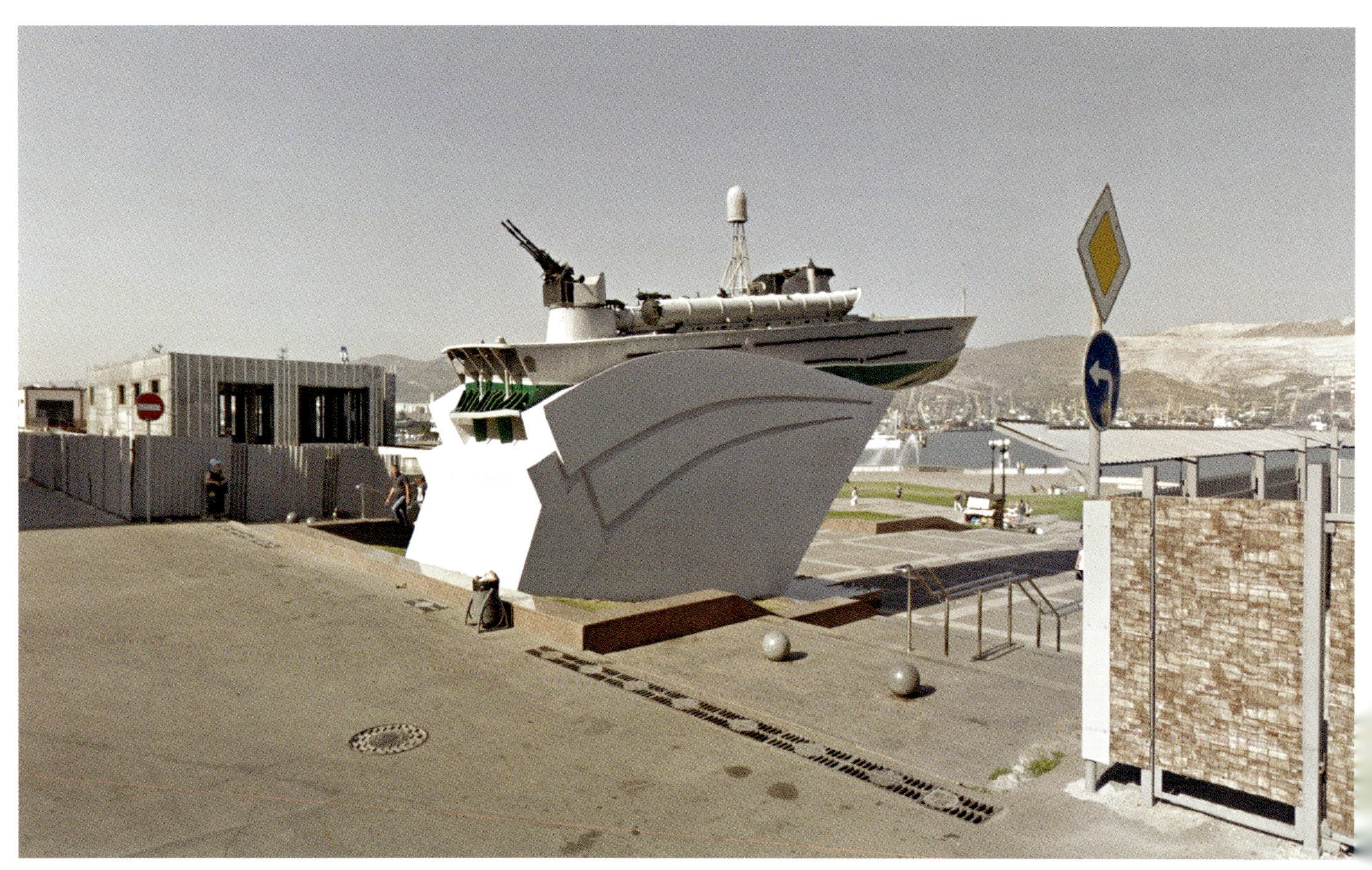

 NOVOROSSIYSK, RUSSIA

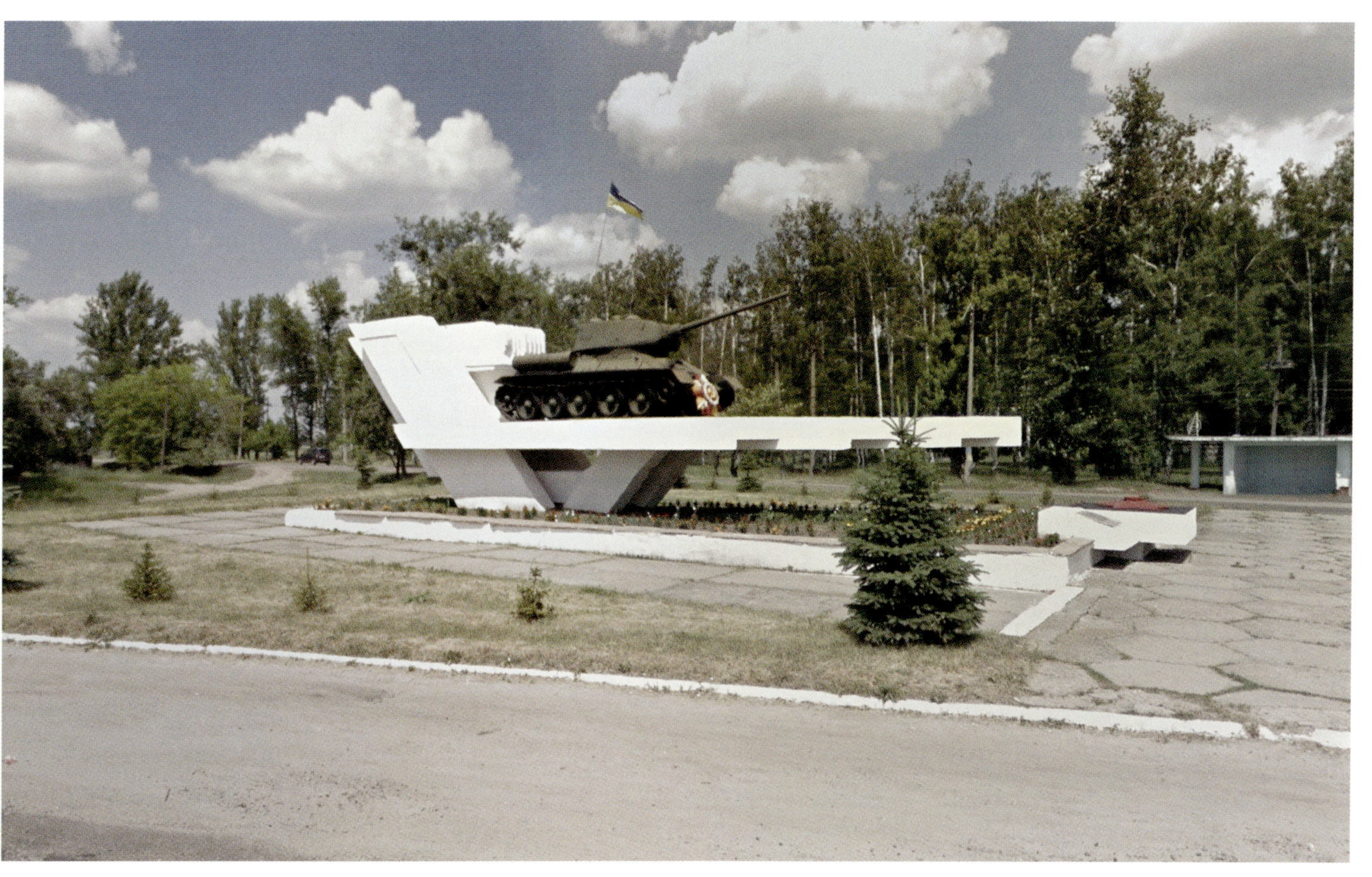

BOHODUKHIV, UKRAINE

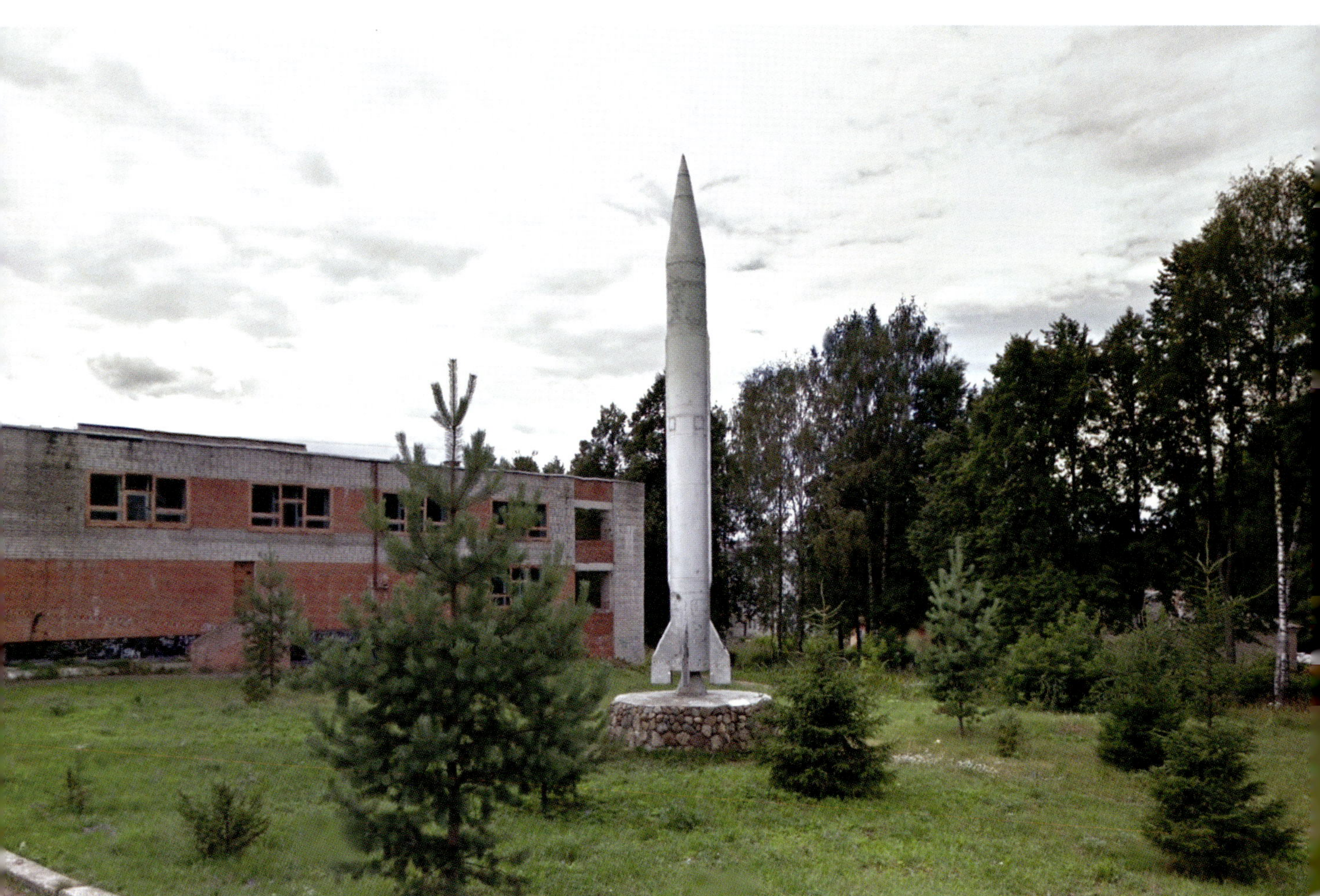

 RYBINSK, RUSSIA

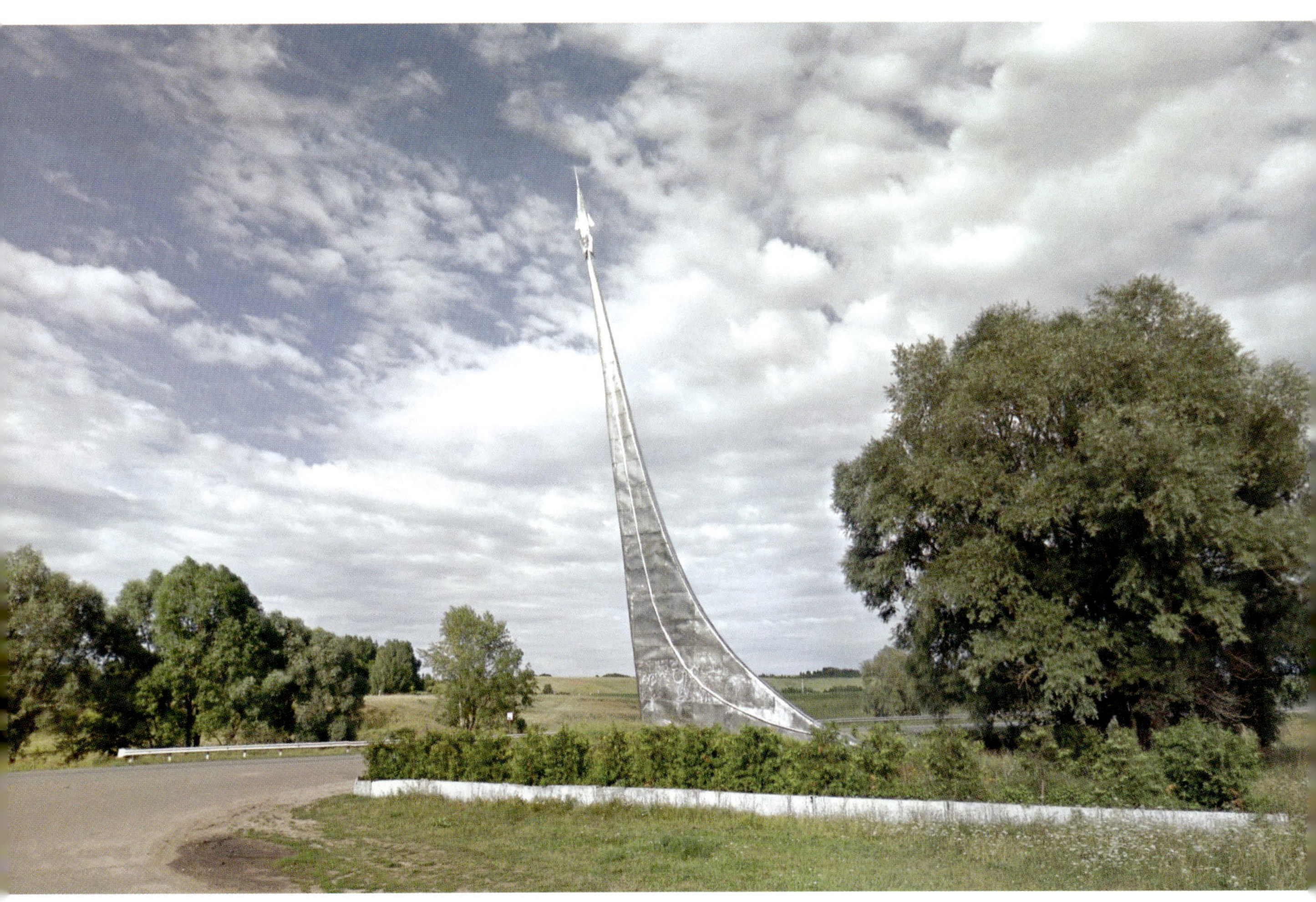

CHUVASHIA, RUSSIA

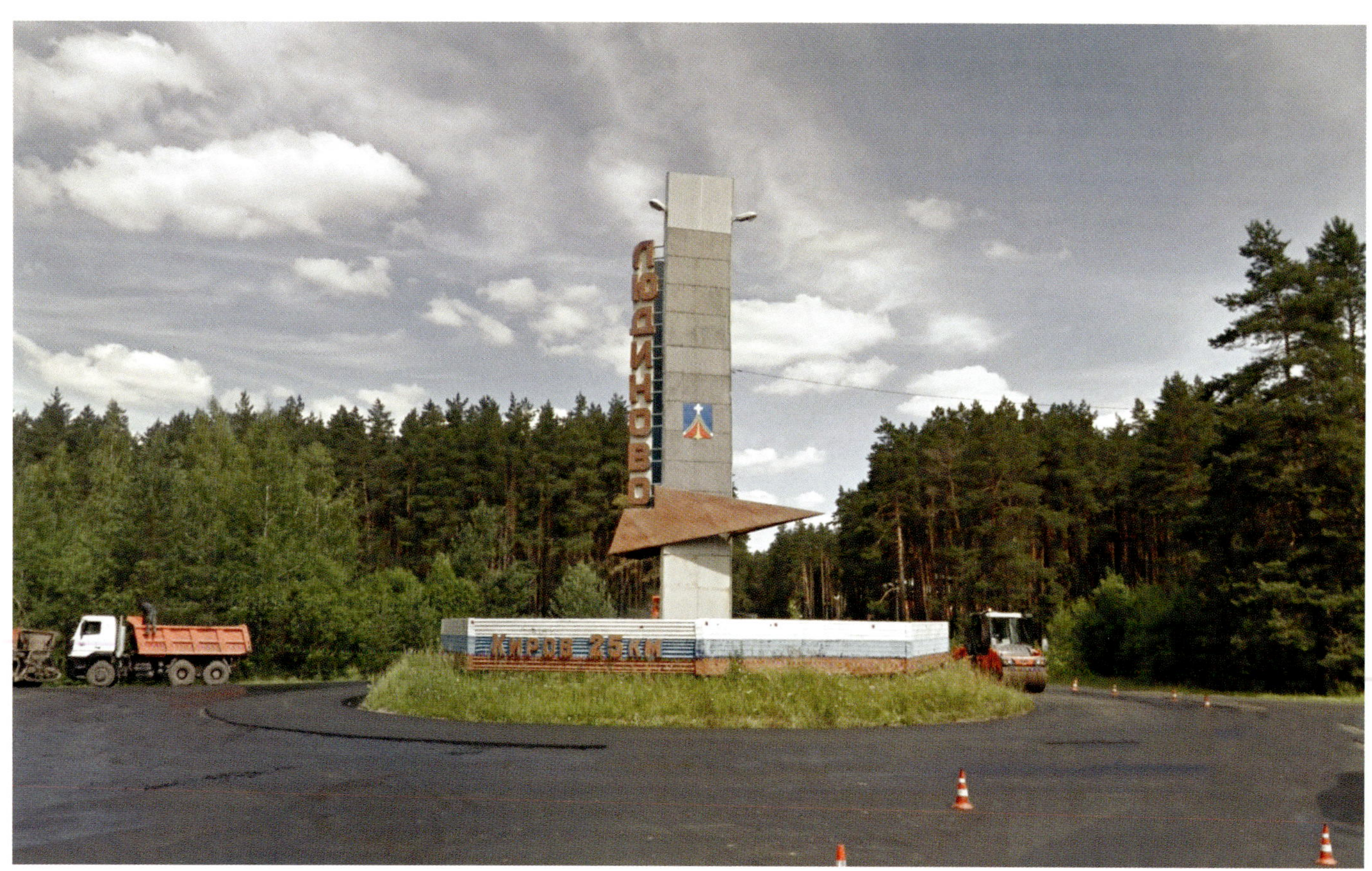
ЛЮДИНОВО
Киров 25 км

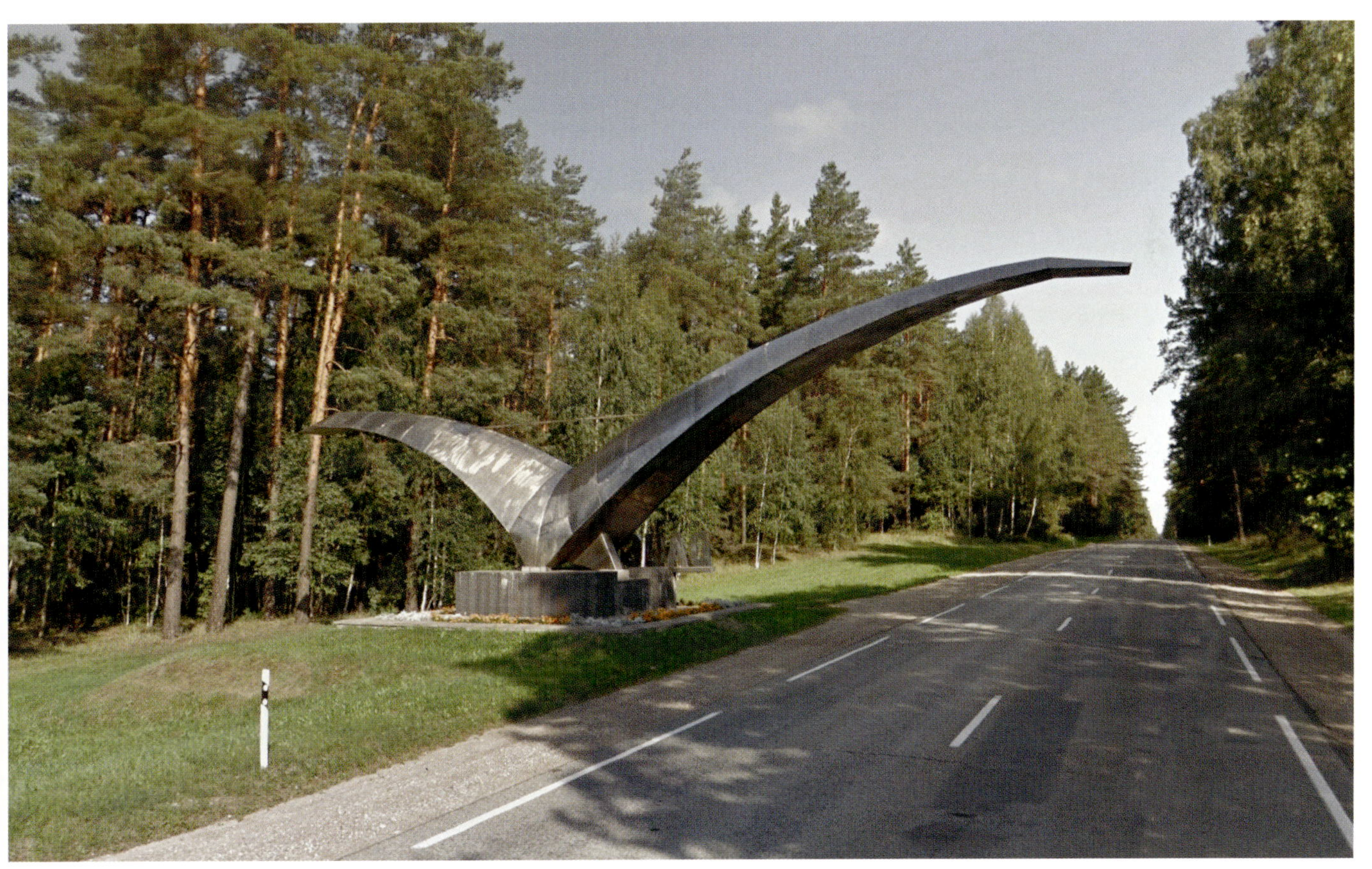

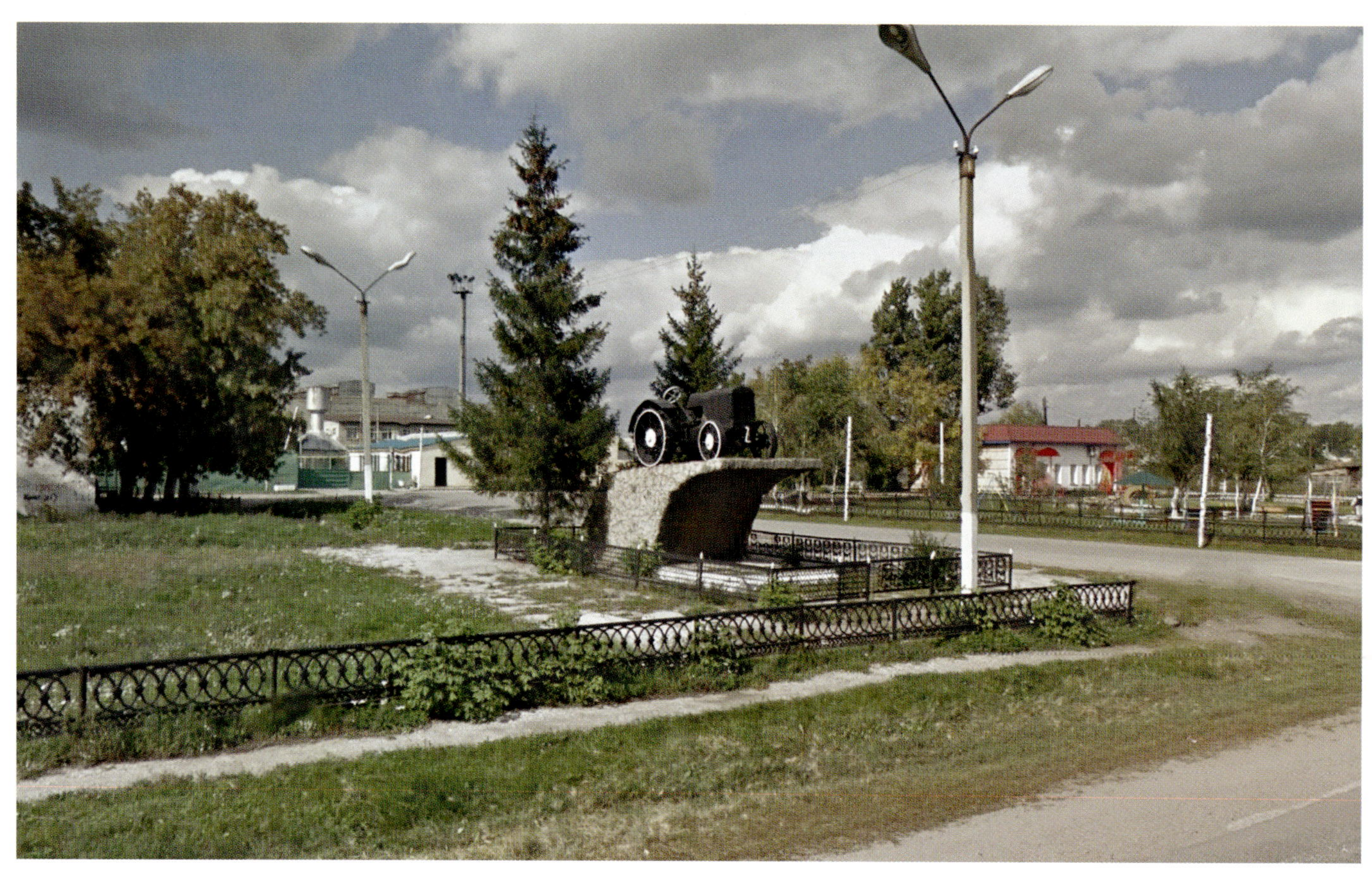

 VARNA, RUSSIA

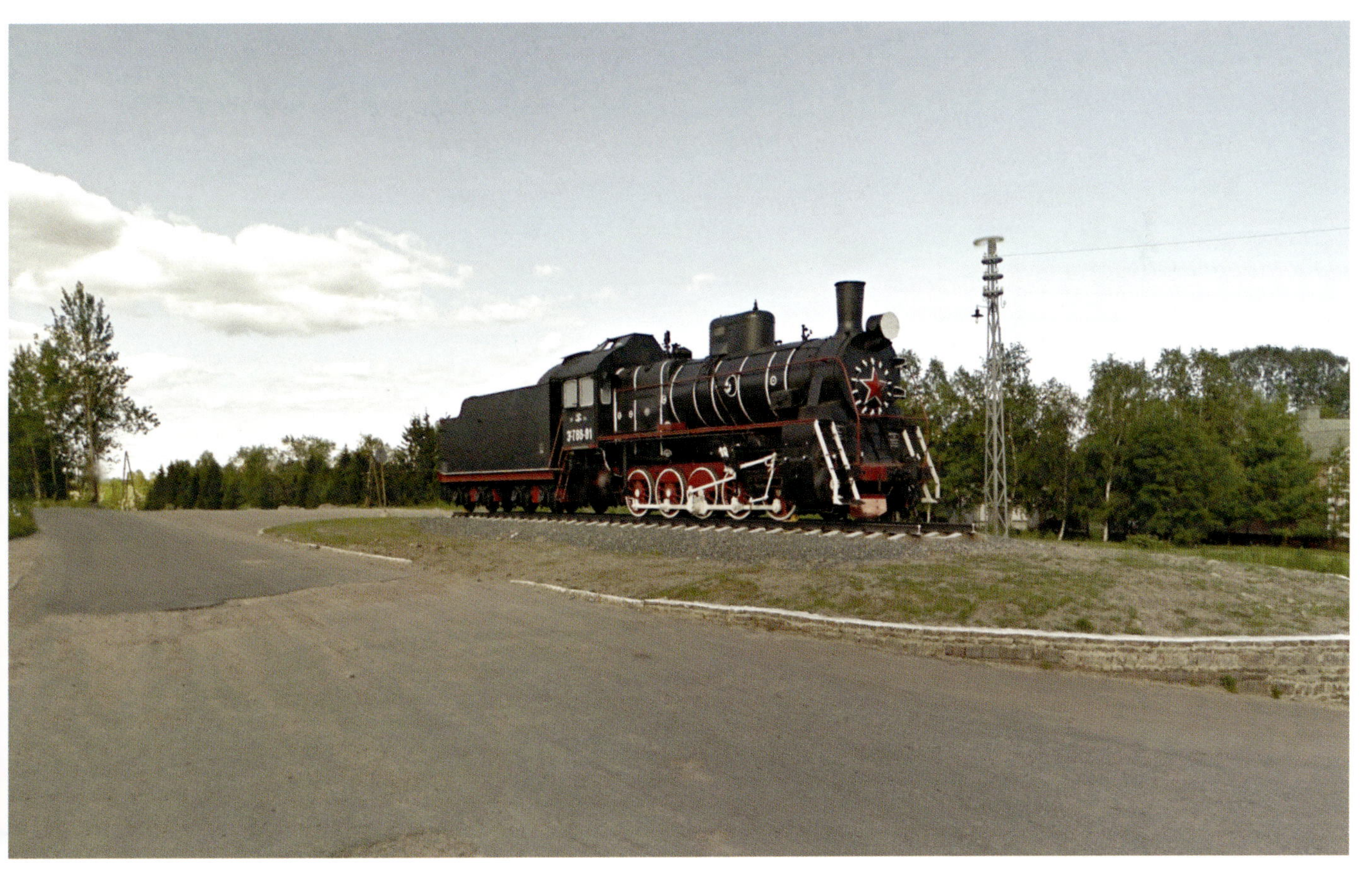

SORTAVALA, RUSSIA

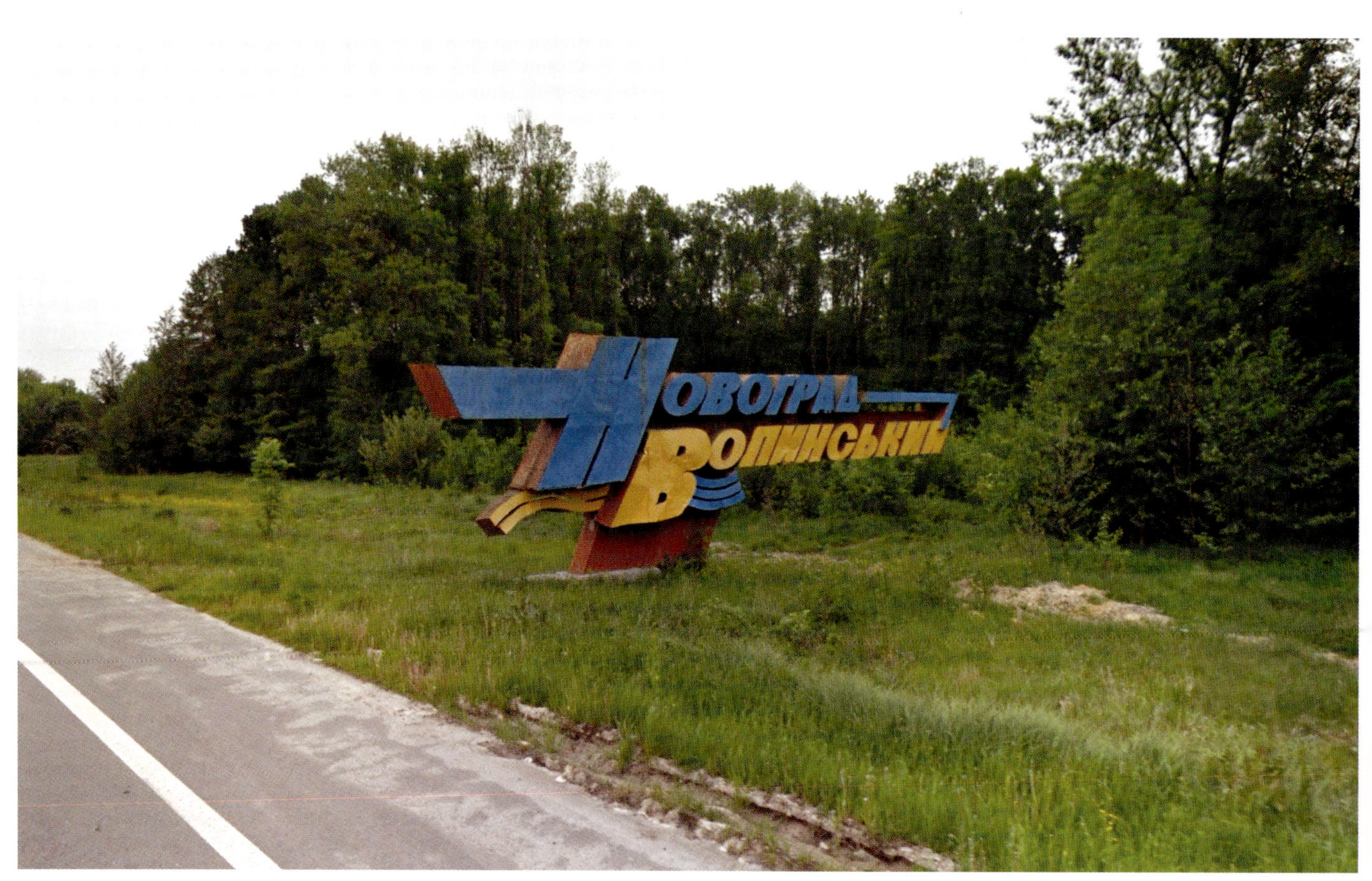

 NOVOHRAD-VOLYNSKYI, UKRAINE

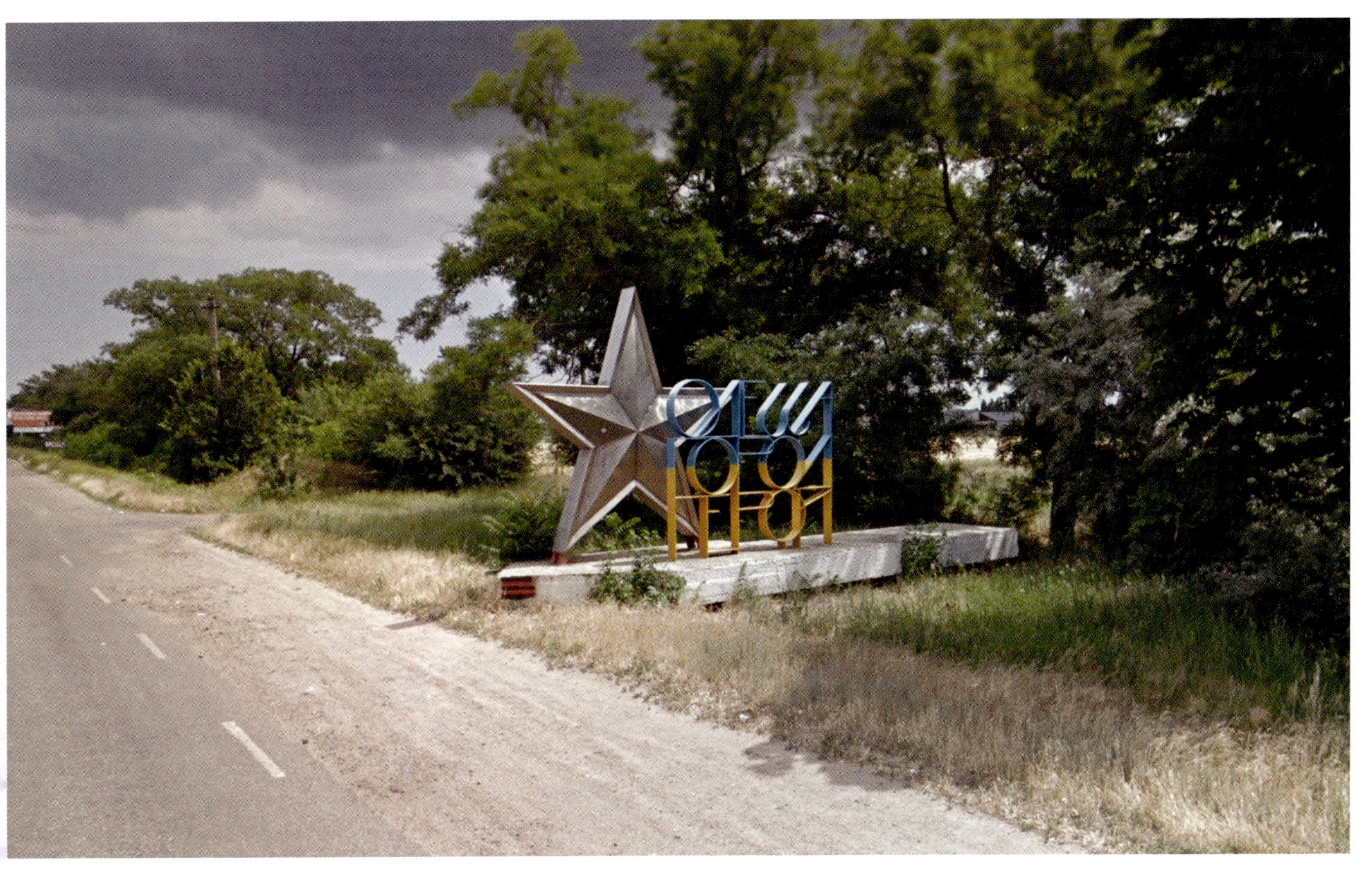

ODESSA, UKRAINE

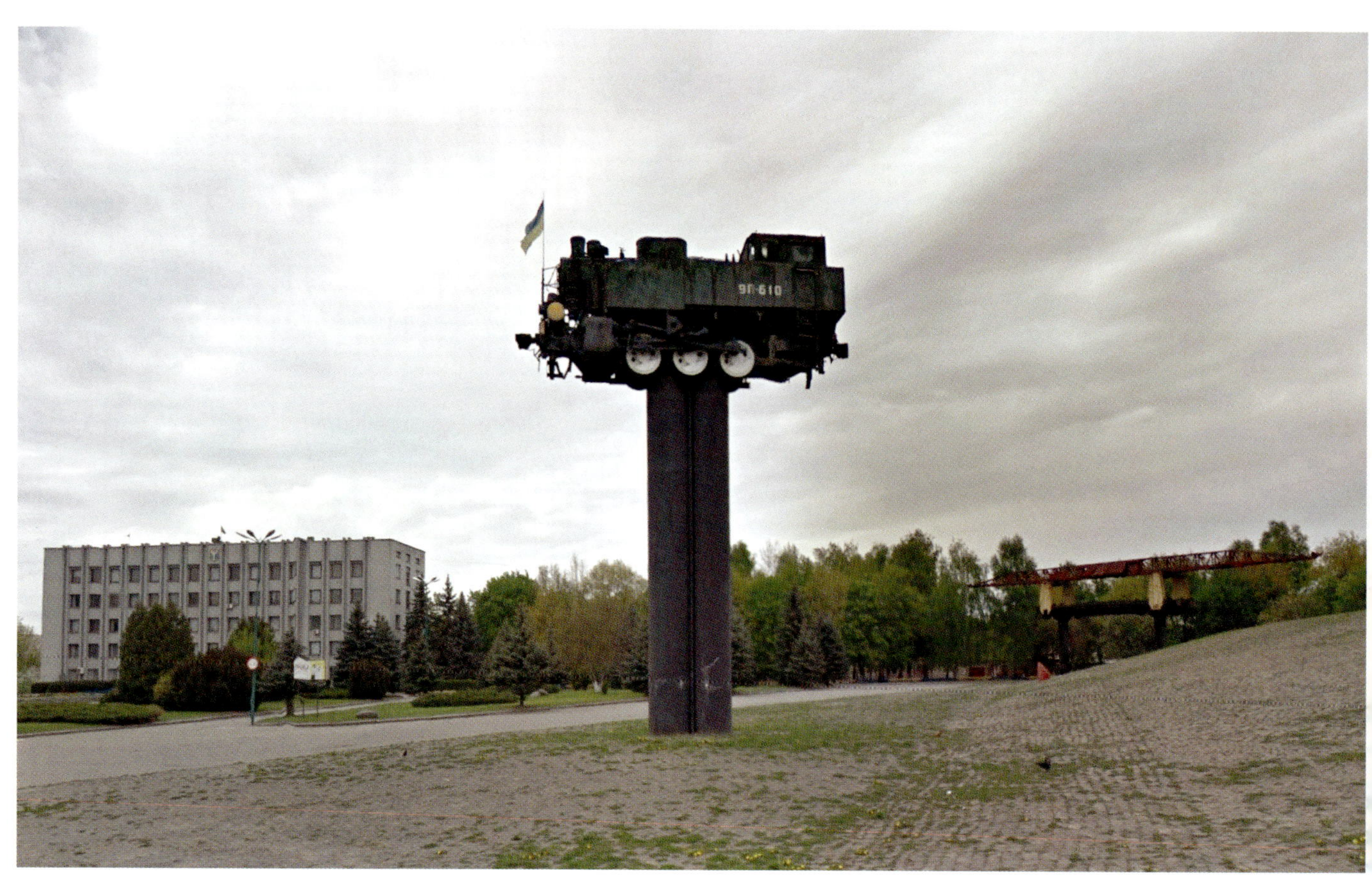

SHEPETIVKA, UKRAINE

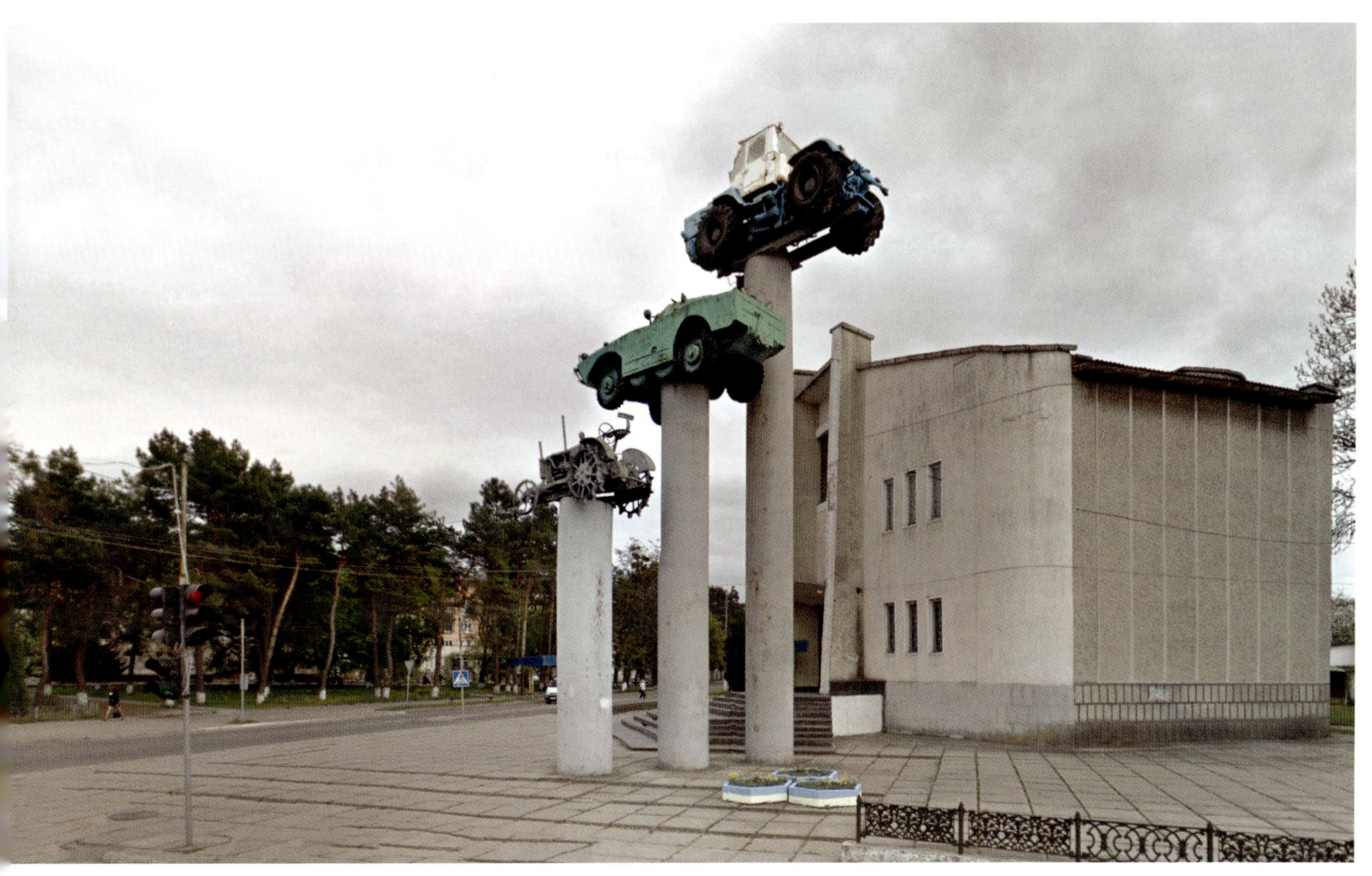

SLAVUTA, UKRAINE

Jason Guilbeau was born in Niort, France, in 1991. He lives and works in Strasbourg. He studied art and architecture at Bordeaux University where he started taking photographs. His work focuses on the landscapes of Switzerland, Germany and eastern Europe and the relationship between form and landscape in architecture.

Jason Guilbeau would like to thank Nathan Guilbeau, Thierry Guilbeau, Sophie Guilbeau and Yohann Gozard.

jasonguilbeau.fr

Published in 2020

FUEL Design & Publishing
33 Fournier Street
London E1 6QE

fuel-design.com

Design and edit by Murray & Sorrell FUEL

Copy edited by FUEL and Fergal Stapleton

Distribution by Thames & Hudson / D. A. P.
ISBN: 978-1-9162184-0-6
Printed in China

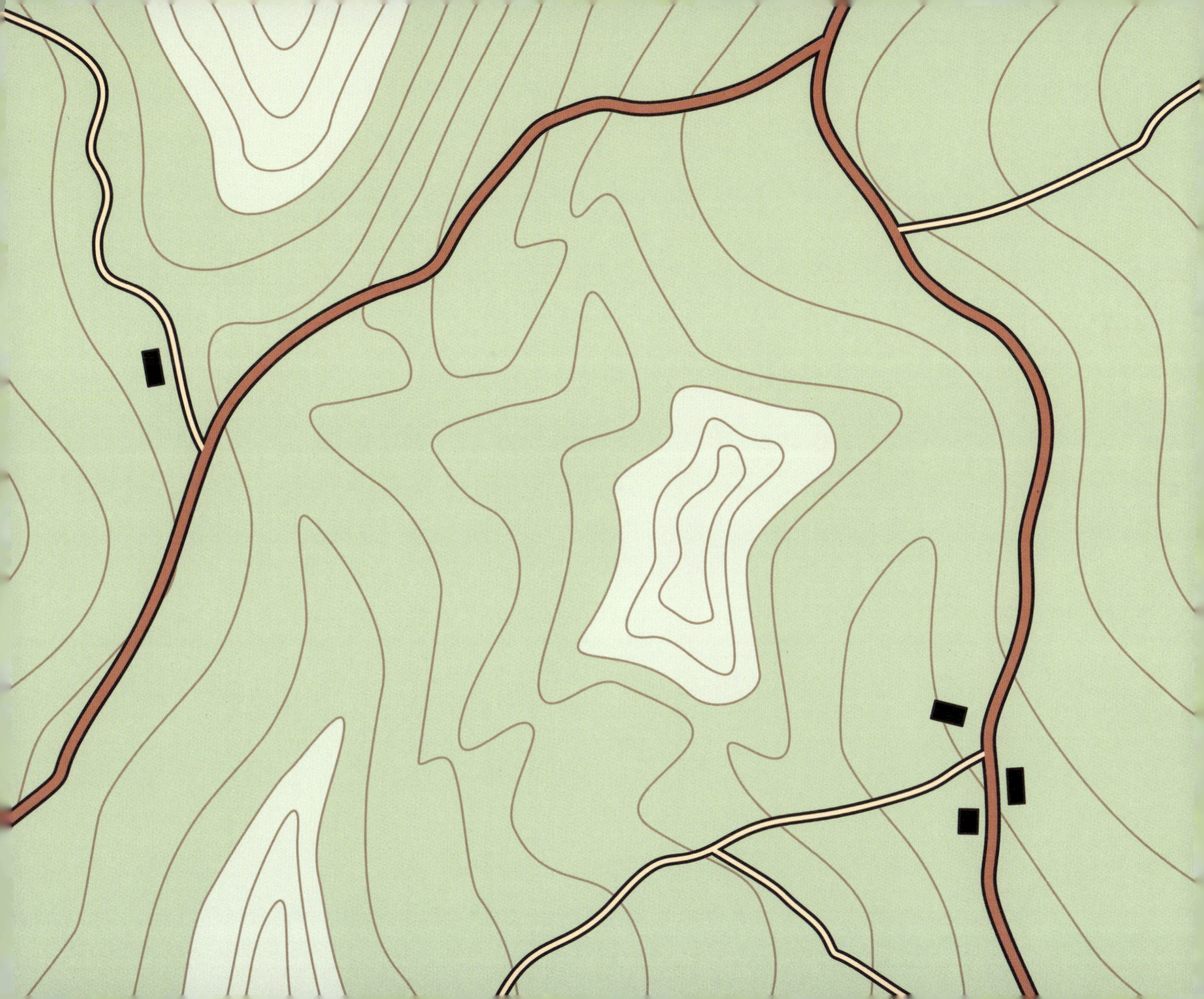

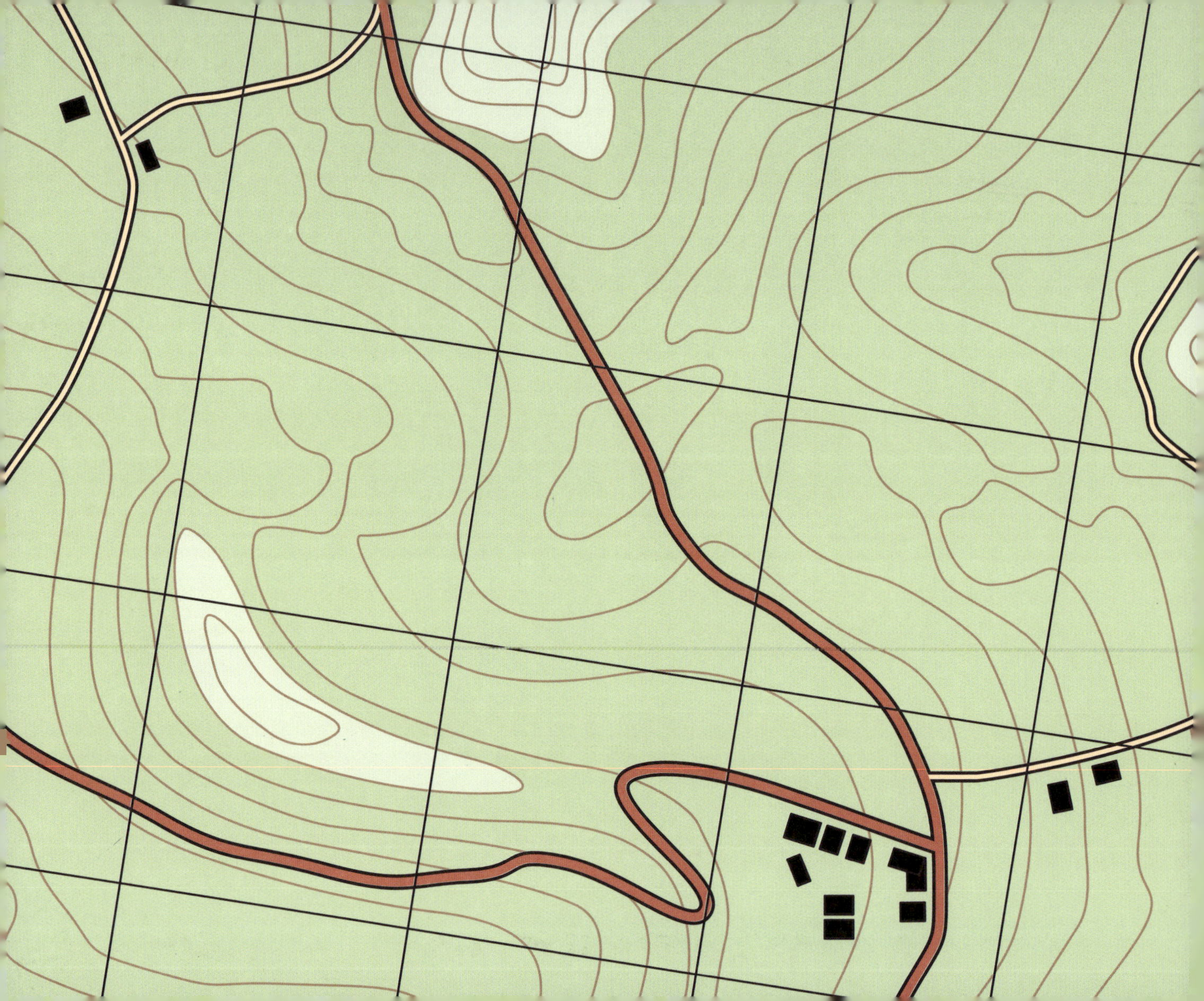